David Bowie

David Bowie

A Biography

Marc Spitz

W F HOWES LTD

This large print edition published in 2011 by
W F Howes Ltd
Unit 4, Rearsby Business Park, Gaddesby Lane,
Rearsby, Leicester LE7 4YH

1 3 5 7 9 10 8 6 4 2

First published in the United Kingdom in 2010
by Aurum Press Ltd

A CIP catalogue record for this book is available
from the British Library

ISBN 978 1 40747 423 6

Typeset by Palimpsest Book Production Limited,
Falkirk, Stirlingshire
Printed and bound in Great Britain
by MPG Books Ltd, Bodmin, Cornwall

For everyone whose heart still jumps with the first beat of 'Five Years.' And for Rob Sheffield, who cares about this stuff as much as I do.

INTRODUCTION

The idea was not even mine. I had just visited with my agent at the famous and now shuttered Cedar Tavern on University Place, where painters and composers and writers once ate and drank. We discussed what my next book should be. I'd lived a rock 'n' roll life and written a lot about rock 'n' roll in my twenties, and by the time I was in my late thirties, I wanted to understand what it all meant a bit better. I needed the next project to really stand for something. It was spring 2006 and I'd just completed a very difficult biography on the Bay Area punk trio Green Day. Spin magazine, where I was a senior writer, fired me that March, after almost nine years following the sale of the publication and an attendant staff bloodbath. I'd never had a career before rock journalism so I'd never stood at a professional crossroad before.

In truth, I was not thinking about the next book as much as leaving New York City, moving up to southern Vermont, or maybe out to New Mexico, and looking for work in an indie record store or a shake shack. I suppose that my agent knew that there was interest in a Bowie book. There's always interest in a Bowie book, which is why there are three or four dozen of them, of varying levels of greatness both in and out of print. Too many, perhaps, which was one reason for my initial reluctance. A few of them are excellent, such as David Buckley's 2001 release **Strange Fascination**. I have had several e-mail conversations with Buckley, who was very gracious and encouraging. There is the stand-alone work **Alias David Bowie,** written by Peter and Leni Gillman. It is the most meticulously researched and fastidiously rendered Bowie book ever written; it is invaluable to any Bowie-ist and certainly anyone hoping to write a book on the subject themselves — even if, unlike Buckley's, it has not been updated since its publication in 1986. Later, I also communicated with the Gillmans, and they too shared advice, empathy and sometimes sympathy. Their book and the vintage oral history **In Other Words . . . David Bowie,** culled from a series of Capital Radio interviews by Kerry Juby, provided invaluable source material when it came to subjects who are now deceased, unwilling to speak or otherwise untraceable. Bowie's autobiography, purportedly entitled **The Return of the Thin White Duke** (after the opening lyric to the 1976 song 'Station to Station') has been rumored for years as well, but either the asking price is too high or it's a bluff; or it's really in the works, and like Bob Dylan's **Chronicles** volume one, it will arrive when it's the right time. Whichever the case may be, it is not here, and short of the text that accompanies Mick Rock's captivating but exclusively glitter-focused **Moonage Daydream** photo book, David Bowie has not written about or authorized anybody else writing about his own life and work. Despite this, they keep coming. There are books about Bowie and bisexuality; books about Bowie and fashion; there is a 33⅓ series book about the 1977 album **Low**; a book strictly about Bowie's brief stay in Berlin with Iggy Pop; there are guitar tablature books; there are encyclopedias like Nicholas Pegg's **The Complete David Bowie**; there is **David Bowie: A Chronology**, which informs those concerned of exactly where Bowie was and what he was doing on November 19,1971, or February 12,1983 (in case you needed to know; in time, I needed to know). At least those were useful in a practical way. Less so were some of the artifacts available on eBay, dog-eared but, with the cruelty of passing time, newly hilarious. Vivian Claire's 1977 publication **David Bowie: The King of Glitter Rock,** for example: 'Bowie is a phenomenon, not only by virtue of what he produces, but how he lives. Take a typical afternoon. Bowie's probably sitting in his 45,000-book library in his Geneva, California mansion where he's knocking out another screenplay (he's done nine already) in a couple of hours; then he'll switch for a break to write two new songs (which will take him less than an hour), sketch, do some painting before he comes downstairs for a two hour interview, all this after twenty hours in the recording studio. He won't have slept for two nights, nor is he the least bit interested in sleep. If someone comes up with a cure for sleep, it will probably be Bowie.' Never once does Ms Claire mention the unholy amount of really good West Coast blow being delivered by open-collared hustlers and nostril-horked around the clock by her prolific and, at the time, very sick and paranoid subject. Bowie actually claims to have forgotten most of this period: the recording of **Station to Station** at Cherokee Studios in Los Angeles; the filming of **The Man Who Fell to Earth** in New Mexico; the White Light world tour, on which he introduced his 'Thin White Duke' persona, reconnected with his pal Iggy Pop and partnered up with Brian Eno with an eye toward inventing New Wave. A lot to slip the mind.

I have not even listed the 'my life with Bowie' tell-alls. It seems like everyone who grew up with, lived with, worked with, slept with, wanted to sleep with, produced, managed or wanted to manage Bowie had cleared some real estate for themselves on those congested 'search results' pages. Ex-wife Angie Bowie has written two excellent books, **Free Spirit** and **Backstage Passes**. The former is much more obscure, and I had to resort to eBay UK to track it down. The latter, first published about fifteen years ago, is a bit more well known, as she promoted it with typical savvy, suggesting to talk show hosts (Joan Rivers and Howard Stern) that she may have caught her ex post-tryst with Mick Jagger. This highly marketable suggestion was also indirectly responsible for one of the best cheap St Mark's Place tourist T-shirts ever, one that I do own and am currently trying to make soft and vintage-looking enough to actually wear: a grainy black and white shot of Bowie, circa 1982 or so, with I FUCKED MICK JAGGER emblazoned on it. Bowie's former manager, Kenneth Pitt, published a book in the early eighties entitled **David Bowie: The Pitt Report,** in which he draws from what could only be his own diaries and logs. As with Angie, I interviewed Mr Pitt for this book, but only via snail mail (at his insistence). He actually sent me typewritten corrections to his spelling and language weeks after our old-school exchange was complete. Very charming man, now in his eighties.

Anthony Zanetta, former vice president of Bowie and his manager Tony Defries's ill-fated entertainment conglomerate MainMan, published **Stardust,** also in the early eighties, when Bowie was enjoying his greatest commercial success. Bowie wasn't a fan of the book. 'David particularly is very, very protective of his image,' Zanetta told me, 'and he was very upset that I did that book even before one word was written.'

Given all these memoirs and biographies, I was concerned that writing my own Bowie book would make me seem a bit like a carpetbagger, or worse, a looky-loo. I will never be able to escape the fact that I was not there or mask my obvious fan-boy awe. The Gillmans informed me via e-mail that they were not fans of Bowie's music before they began their book and at first were able to view him as a subject, nothing more. I, on the other hand, have been e-mailed by Tony Visconti, a man I once, before taking this up, sat adjacent to in the West Village diner Le Bonbonniere and watched eat a pile of toast. Nobody else recognized him. I could only think, 'That man eating wheat toast produced "Heroes," not to mention T. Rex's "Baby Boomerang."' I have had cocktails with people like Danny Fields, who introduced Bowie and Iggy Pop; coffee with Leee Black Childers, the 'advance man,' for Bowie's management company and babysitter for the strung-out Stooges of 1973; and more drinks with Angie Bowie and Jayne County, each of them an icon and crucial figure in the larger Bowie myth. I have also interviewed Lou Reed and Iggy Pop for Uncut and Harp magazines respectively during this period. Lou was far scarier. Iggy, surprisingly punctual. In the collective mind of the myth-aware Bowie-ist, these characters have remained glitter dusted, young, horny alley cat revolutionaries, wearing silver and stomping on some eternal disco floor to a perfect soul soundtrack like 'Band of Gold' by Freda Payne or 'Knock on Wood' by Eddie Floyd. They exist in a perpetual seventies mural. I was apprehensive and sure enough, meeting them all between 2006 and 2009, speaking with them, interviewing them, drinking coffee or liquor with them, e-mailing with them was very strange. They are older now. Some are bitter. Many are simply tired of recounting the same stories. 'When I meet people and it's all "David, David, David," I do overreact and say I don't want to talk about David,' Childers complained to me. 'He is not that much of my life. He was literally, really, two and a half, three years of my life. It was one hundred percent David at that time, and God knows I gained a lot of experience and had a lot of great times, but that's not what I want to be known for.' They are easier to find for a biographer in the info age. Many are on MySpace and Facebook. But they are much harder to establish trust with and crack open and convince that there are new ideas when it comes to a book on Bowie. I've done my best, and I hope mine is worthy of the trust they placed in me.

I suspected it would be a challenge to hold on to my objectivity during the research phase. I, like others who have taken on the Bowie story before, am a massive and lifelong fan. When an interview subject criticized Bowie, as many did, I knew that I would have to check my urge to defend him.

Ultimately, I happened on a device to help maintain a workable harmony between the disciplined journalist that I have become and the fat kid who once dyed his hair orange in hope that it would somehow make him more Bowie-like, svelte and handsome (it did not). I have included at various points in this book that kid's memories. Call them interludes, palate cleansers, whatever you want: they are here, along with the hard reporting. They are a necessity and, I hope, a bit of useful levity.

Finally, the idea of beginning a Bowie book during the largest period of silence in his career seemed strange. As I write this, David Bowie has not released a new album since 2003. He has not toured since undergoing emergency heart surgery the following year. Before this, Bowie had been as prolific as Woody Allen, Tyler Perry, Ryan Adams or Prince – one of those artists who don't let a year pass without offering something to their public. Popular culture is more Bowie informed than ever as it moves from idea to idea in a Twitter age designed for rapid self-re-invention, hype and spin (Bowie once claimed to have 'the attention span of a grasshopper'). Both his scarcity and his importance have been so profound in the second half of this decade that I initially worried that to address a book on Bowie from a pop perspective would be akin to railing at a silent God – one who created everything then split. I actually considered calling this book 'God and Man' (a sort of glib nod to the lyrics of his 1983 hit 'Modern Love'). I certainly fretted to my agent that day over our beers about all of these things and more.

After the meeting at the Cedar Tavern, my agent and I had a smoke, then shook hands and parted. I remained unconvinced that I should take on a Bowie biography but agreed to think about it. Soon I found myself on the southwest corner of Broadway and Tenth Street, waiting for the traffic light to change. Behind me was a Chase branch. On the other side of the street there stood a prewar apart-ment building and the Modern Gourmet market. Kitty-corner was the nail salon that my then-girl-friend frequented for her manicure/pedicures. On the other side of that was the old Grace Church. In the middle of the road, cars, cabs, trucks, bicycles,

Vespas, panhandlers and cops. And immediately to my right, about two feet away, standing in front of a mailbox with his arm raised: David Bowie.

I did what any New Yorker, orthodox Bowie-ist or not, would have done under the circumstances of encountering anyone famous. I said to myself, calmly, almost cavalierly, 'Okay, that guy really looks a lot like David Bowie.' Initial reactions are calm by code especially if there is no alcohol immediately available. We have to forget what these people may or may not have meant to us. We shift mechanically into cool mode and must never, ever let on that we give a damn. We are unflappable New Yorkers after all. The voice in my head was deliberate, like a rabbi's or a math teacher's: 'But it could not possibly be David Bowie. Was I not just talking about David Bowie? It is David Bowie. My, my. David Bowie. How . . . something.'

I'd heard one rumor that he'd grown a long beard and skulked around downtown anonymously since his illness. Some people even said that he donned elaborate disguises like the late Michael Jackson reportedly did. The hunched Asian woman walking the little white dog down Second Avenue? David Bowie. Maybe. The paunchy Hispanic traffic cop writing up your Suburban for an expired meter? Bowie.

My next thought was, 'He looks well.' I had been, like many Bowie-ists, worried about what a post-heart surgery David Bowie would mean, as if detecting something odd in his eternally sharp, vivid and handsome facial features, a sag or a puff, would surely have been a source of internal crisis for us as well. I felt the same way after David Letterman's surgery and eventual return to late-night television.

David Bowie wore a cream-colored sport jacket and a gray shirt. Nobody else on the street seemed to recognize him. Maybe if he was a few blocks up in Chelsea, or down in Soho. But East Tenth Street is pretty neutral, especially during a weekday afternoon.

'What's going on in his head? Right now?' I wondered as I retreated a few paces and allowed myself a shred of fan-boy excitement after realizing I could safely observe him. Nobody was watching me watch David Bowie. 'What is he thinking? That man, who wrote "Quicksand." That person right there who screamed, "I – I will be king! And you – you will be queeeen!" at the climax of "Heroes," which has given me gooseflesh for decades without fail, despite its being used in advertisements and covered by the Wallflowers? Well, I know what he's thinking, don't I? He's thinking, "Cab. I need a cab. Why won't any of these cabs stop for me?"' So unlikely was it that someone as super-famous as David Bowie would be there on the corner of Tenth Street on a Tuesday afternoon, even the taxi drivers were passing him.

I said nothing to David Bowie on that afternoon. I didn't even acknowledge that I knew who he was or that his life and art and music have marked my entire course and that only minutes earlier, I'd been discussing him, considering committing a couple of years of my daily life to rebooting him. I played it supercool like he'd actually taught us Bowie-ists how to be. I was someone else. Adopting a pose.

The light changed, and I crossed Broadway numbly. I walked past the record store on my block, muttering, 'David Bowie . . . records . . . In there . . . "China Girl," "Fashion."' I let myself into the apartment. I called my agent at the office immediately. I told him that I'd thought it over and that I would indeed write the book you are now holding and that I think this is a good time to look for Bowie in the modern world and reopen a discussion about what he means.

'That was fast,' he said. 'Why'd you change your mind?'

'Suddenly feeling much closer to him,' I said.

And I did, but not as close as I do now, and not as close, I hope, as you are about to.

MARC SPITZ

New York City, August 2009

TO BE READ AT MAXIMUM VOLUME

PROLOGUE

It was the second night of the four-day 2005 CMJ music marathon and film festival, known to most simply as 'CMJ.' The Arcade Fire, a Montreal-based collective led by husband and wife Win Butler and Régine Chassagne, were taking what amounts to a victory lap, having created a fast legend for themselves at the previous year's showcase. Their debut, *Funeral*, a meditation on loss that managed to be somehow joyous, earned an almost unheard-of 9.7 from the often praise-stingy music site Pitchfork and propelled them through that blurry, terrifying, find-an-empty-bathroom-at-the-venue-and-lock-the-door-for-a-minute-to-breathe kind of year that only a handful of bands in this decade can understand, the White Stripes, the Strokes, and the Killers among them. It's the kind of run a young band can really only have once, in which they visit and perform in parts of the world that had previously seemed like oranges, yellows and pinkish browns on a map. It's the year in which some of them get to sleep with movie stars, stop worrying about paying the bills with their own checks or not paying the bills at all and *start* worrying about how to write a second album while touring. Lead singers begin to think about things like whether their hair and teeth look as good as they can and if doing something about it (if the choppers do not) means they are compromising their credibility. It's also the year in which you meet your heroes. Anyone who has witnessed such exchanges as I have on a few assignments will note that they are not unlike the president calling the winning team after the Super Bowl or World Series: stilted congratulations and maybe a few bits of advice. Bono and Bruce Springsteen are famous for giving this kind of 'talk' to the reverential and overwhelmed rock star newbie. It's the rare rock legend who takes away something for *himself* from these meetings. And in this week, the Arcade Fire has been in the close company of, perhaps, the rarest rock legend of them all.

'This is a David Bowie song,' Butler, his hair hanging over his high cheekbones, announced to the crowd. Three thousand cell phone cameras were thrust into the air as Butler strummed the opening chords to 'Queen Bitch.' The song is a decade older than he is, an album track off Bowie's 1971 release *Hunky Dory* (Butler was born in the spring of 1980, shortly before Bowie released *Scary Monsters*, if you want a bit more perspective). It's a New York song – an homage to the tough, catty, street-smart songwriting of Lou Reed. At the time of its release, 'Queen Bitch' marked a sharp change for Bowie. A fan would have to go back to his obscure, early-sixties R & B releases (as front man for doomed combos like the King Bees) to hear such a sexed-up snarl. Much of his mid- and late-sixties releases were marked by an earnest voice, at turns folky à la the darker end of Simon & Garfunkel or melodramatic and poppy in the Scott Walker mode.

The Arcade Fire is a big band, a sort of casual collective where a friend visiting from out of town who happens to be carrying a Dobro or a fiddle seems welcome to join in semipermanent fashion. The noise they make is a patchwork wall of sound, one that can easily fill up an arena while retaining a haunted air. It would be easy to imagine a guest vocalist being drowned in this wash of noise (which they play with a passion that occasionally borders on camp, smashing their drum heads madly and the like). But the guy in the white suit who walked to the mic to spit out the opening line – 'I'm up on the eleventh floor and I'm watching the cruisers below' – was, again, no ordinary man. He not only cut clean through the mix (turning the headliners into a backing band before hitting the line 'He's down on the street and he's trying hard to pull sister Flo') but he also cut through the insane roar of excitement and disbelief emanating from the vast field. Not that this was a big secret. The Arcade Fire had clearly charmed Bowie, reminding him, perhaps, of his own bohemian strum sessions in suburban Beckenham at the end of the sixties. These Arts Labs were held every Sunday night and often lasted until sunrise Monday morning; by then big ideas were shared and strengthened and the mettle of new, hopeful, reaching songs was tested. The Arcade Fire's gear, with its scratches and stickers, had the look and feel of such musty, smoke-cured ad hoc 'studios.' Yes, they were genuinely exciting; U2 had recently embraced them as well. Yes, they were new; their songs offered a forceful emotional stir in an era marked by garage-rock swagger. But they were also still liberal arts ragamuffins, with the planet opening up to them rapidly, and this clearly returned Bowie to his creative square one – a place where he needed to be, in light of his own life-changing events of 2004. I will repeat for emphasis, it's the rare rock legend who takes away something for *himself* from a meeting with young up-and-comers.

Bowie had been blogging about the band and had appeared with them on September 8 at Radio City Music Hall in a televised charity event, Fashion Rocks. On that broadcast, only one week earlier, he had still seemed frail. He dressed in a light gray suit and black shirt, and to those familiar with his slim, elegant visage, he appeared a little thicker and older as he performed. Fashion Rocks was his first time onstage since the procedure, and even rock legends are not immune to a case of nerves (one recalls John Lennon throwing up backstage at Madison Square Garden in 1974 before joining Elton John, as if he'd never sold out Shea Stadium or Candlestick Park before). Seven days' exposure to the Arcade Fire, and perhaps the warm night air, had done something good to Bowie. He'd been getting a bad rap as a cultural vampire since the Human League and Devo were considered the next big things, but even if that was accurate, it was all about the rejuvenation of sound. The Central Park show, energized in a way that Fashion Rocks was not, was tantamount to a rejuvenation of spirit, and there, onstage, as he took the lead on the band's best-known song, 'Wake Up' (Butler offering only a burbling echo-drenched vocal), Bowie seemed to be putting his vulnerability, his own impermanence and the immortality of his music, legend and influence into some kind of working order once again. He looked like he'd written the thing himself.

'Something filled up my heart with nothin',' he sang. 'Someone told me not to cry. But now that I'm older, my heart's colder, and I can see that it's a lie.' There, on that stage, he was a god, inspiring awe in both the crowd and the musicians he'd joined. But he was a man too, wary of overexertion, learning the steps again, older than the lead singer and the drummer put together. But brand-new once again.

It is, to date, the last transformative moment in his nearly fifty-year career, and like every previous Bowie incarnation, it keeps us watching for what's coming next and thinking differently about everything that came before.

CHAPTER 1

There's an alien in the window of the house next door to the one where David Bowie was born on Stansfield Road in Brixton, a southern borough of London. It peers out, gray skinned, with black, oval-shaped eyes and a tennis-racket-sized skull, the same kind of inflatable spacemen for sale in the gas station gift shops that one stops at while driving through Roswell, New Mexico. *X-Files*/E.T.-faced aliens. It might not be there now, should you decide to make a new pilgrimage, but it was there when I traveled to Brixton, as if to say, 'Welcome, biographer!'

Whoever lives there certainly knows who was born next door. If the alien had eyelids it'd be winking. Otherwise, this block, like every other block in the area, is as quiet as it must have been six decades ago. The house itself is three stories high, pale brick, with a double-arched doorway painted French white. A chest-high brick wall separates it from the adjacent buildings. Another brick wall girds the property, sectioning off a very tiny lawn and a spindled tree that extends just past the chimney. It's a handsome if compact residence. Unlike the demographics of Brixton, which was predominantly a white, middle-class enclave in the years just after World War II, this home is static. In another fifty-two years, while jet packs and flying cars travel overhead, one can imagine it looking exactly the same. There's no brass plaque here marking David Bowie's birth, but it is, nonetheless, a landmark, one pristinely preserved whether by design, accident, simple lack of means or inclination. That David Robert Jones came into the world here at 9 AM on January 8, 1947, is hardly unique; many children in the late forties were born at home and not in a hospital. Midwives were summoned once the water broke, as one would call a plumber or policeman. The house's real significance has less to do with David's and more to do with his mother and father's story anyhow. This was a second-chance home, the place where they hoped to build a strong family unit after their dark and complicated childhoods and some false starting on either side with regard to romance and parenthood. Brixton was still in wreckage thanks to the Nazi buzz bombs and the depleted nation's inability to quickly rebuild when David's mother, Margaret Mary Burns, from Royal Tunbridge Wells in the county of Kent, met his father, Haywood Stenton Jones, from Doncaster, Yorkshire. She was known as Peggy and he as John. It was not a posh area but it was theirs, a place to create new memories and remain protected from the pain they'd known.

Of the two, Peggy had the most to distance herself from. Several incidents occurred in her teens and early twenties that could cumulatively take on the characteristics of a Burns family curse. Mental illness seemed to be seared deeply into the genetic code (as has been well documented by other biographers and commented on by Bowie himself). David spent much of his early adulthood wondering when, not if, he was going to go legitimately mad. Schizophrenic behavior can lay dormant until triggered by a cataclysmic event. For Peggy, and her four sisters and brother, this event was of course the Second World War. However, Victoria Burns, the second child, and Vivienne, the fifth, began exhibiting signs of mental illness early on. The constant explosions of the Luftwaffe's missiles and the nightmarish prospect of the Nazis occupying the United Kingdom coupled with the heartbreak of falling in love with a series of noncommittal soldiers would push their tendencies into full-blown afflictions during the war years. The disease manifested itself mostly as irrational behavior – nonsensical comments, unkempt appearance, chain-smoking, promiscuity, extreme passivity – so it can be argued, given the seemingly domino-like effect it had on the Burns girls, that schizophrenia itself was another, if quieter, cataclysmic event. Peggy's father, Jimmy, was a professional soldier of modest means, and the home they shared on Meadow Lane was close-quartered enough to amplify any breach in acceptable social behavior. Certain studies do indicate that those with schizophrenic brothers and sisters are more likely to exhibit schizophrenic tendencies themselves. Someone with one schizophrenic parent is even more likely to develop the disease. Peggy, the oldest child, ultimately exhibited behavior that might be considered borderline. She could be loud, theatrical, and act out. She was basically spared the full effects of the illness, possibly because it was not actually something that was inherited but rather a very, very sad coincidence within this one English family. Still, it was certainly a specter, and so, at age twenty-two, Peggy became the first Burns sibling to leave the house. She found work as a resident nanny for guests of a nearby hotel, the Culverden Park Arms. It was during this period that she had a well-documented but exceedingly brief dalliance with the Blackshirts, a faction of nationalists headed by a Parliament member named Oswald Mosley ('Mister Oswald with the swastika tattoo,' in Elvis Costello's debut single 'Less Than Zero'). Much has been made of this in other Bowie biographies, given David Bowie's also well-covered fascination with fascism four decades later in the mid-1970s. One need not be an apologist (or superfan) to see how Bowie's publicly stated and since recanted endorsement of Hitler's charisma and the merits of a fascist leader overtaking Britain, while speaking with Cameron Crowe in a notorious

1976 *Playboy* interview, was the product of cocaine psychosis rather than any real fidelity to notions of racial purity or governmental insurrection. Peggy's attraction (leading to a fleeting attendance of one rally) was, it's been said, even less substantial in its motivation. It was the actual black shirts, those sleek and slimming namesakes, that attracted her rather than loudly spat polemics against immigration and integration.

Relationships started during wartime are often more passionate than those begun during peace and prosperity. Peggy, with her high forehead, elegant nose, pale skin and dark, humorous eyes, possessed a certain unconventional, very English beauty. Although willful and independent, she was not immune to the rush of untethered emotion that seemed to wash over her generation with the declaration of war. While working at the hotel, she began a relationship with an employee, a handsome Jewish Frenchman named Wolf Rosemberg (who called himself Jack). He worked as a porter in the bar. His father was a well-off fur dealer in Paris. Their affair began in secret in the spring of 1937. She believed that she had met the love of her life. Soon afterward, she learned that she was pregnant. Rosemberg proposed. Their first and only child, Terence Guy Adair Burns, was born in the local Pembury Hospital on November 5, Guy Fawkes Day (hence his middle name). Adair was a family name. Everyone called the baby Terry.

Jack and Peggy would never marry, and Terry

would never really know his biological father. Early in 1938, the Nazis began annexing Eastern Europe and eventually invaded France. Jack returned to his family and joined up with the Resistance. He reappeared in London shortly before bombs began falling on Great Britain in '39. Jack attempted to claim the baby but was rebuffed by Peggy's mother, Margaret, as Peggy wasn't at home at the time. Rather than waiting, Rosemberg disappeared, his impatience and urgency surely affected by the pervasive feelings of doom fast engulfing all of free Europe.

Distraught, Peggy, like many young British and American women, went to work in a munitions factory. She raised Terry with Margaret's help. Peggy then entered into a rebound affair with a factory coworker. This led to another pregnancy, this time a daughter. Unable to care for both children on her own, she gave the child over to foster care when she was three months old and continued to make bombs and nurse her broken heart. In some ways, Peggy never got over Jack Rosemberg. He was 'the one that got away,' and this sentiment would foment a resentment that would compromise the peace and optimism of Peggy and John's second-chance home on Stansfield Road (especially after Terry grew into a ringer for his estranged biological father).

Compared with the Burns family, David's father was from relatively stolid genetic stock. John's influence surely had a calming, even a saving effect, on Peggy and David in both the postwar years as well as the increasingly chaotic 1960s, when David rebelled against his class and station and struggled to find success as a singer and song-writer. John's father, Robert Haywood Jones, the source of David's middle name, was a boot maker, and his mother, Zillah Hannah Jones, worked in an industrial wool mill. She died when he was very young. John was sent away to private school and like many British children of his age, he was subjected to a brutally strict rearing full of emotional suppression and harsh punishment for dissent. As a young man, he lost his crippling shyness in the dark of the local cinema. Jones, whose features in photos seem much more pinched than those of Peggy, as if he's constantly straining to avoid saying something troubling or rebellious, became a great fan of escapist films, English music halls, American jazz – anything that temporarily relieved him of his painful diffidence. When his father passed away John inherited a trust of three thousand pounds, to be paid out on the day of his twenty-first birthday in the fall of 1933 (about eighty thousand dollars by today's rates). Jones decided to parlay the funds into a career in the entertainment business and some kind of permanent relief from his painfully quiet life. He left Yorkshire for London and fell under the wing of a fast-talking Irish would-be music hall impresario named James Sullivan.

Sullivan was married to a mysterious Italian

circus performer who was said to have perished before a live audience during a stunt gone wrong. His blond daughter Hilda was confident and socially engaging, a showbiz kid with a head full of yellow curls. She played the piano, sang, danced and seemed to be naturally bred for the stage. John Jones, new to the capital and to 'the business,' quickly became smitten. 'He asked me to go and have a cup of tea with him,' Hilda Sullivan said, 'and he fell madly in love with me. He was very taciturn; nothing made him laugh. You never saw his lips move and you never saw him smile.'

Shortly after their wedding, John happily and excitedly invested two-thirds of his inheritance money in a revue centered on Hilda's estimable talent and charm. The production was booked into various burlesque stages throughout the region and met with utter failure. Despite her gifts, without a canny marketing plan, there was no interest in Hilda's act among jaded music hall fans, who by that point had already heard and seen everything on the burlesque stages that glutted London: animal acts, pantomime and striptease. Unbroken, John decided to invest the remainder of his funds in a piano bar on well-populated Charlotte Street in the city's Westminster section. He believed that there Hilda would build a following. The audience would soon come to her. They christened the club, perhaps unwisely, the Boop a Doop. Chastened by failure, John tabled his show business aspirations and took a job as a porter in a local hotel, the Russell. Hilda became a movie house usherette. Soon the couple began to argue about money and other relatively dreary domestic concerns. This tension reportedly led John Jones briefly to become a heavy drinker, but fortunately, it soon became apparent that he lacked the constitution. One night, after a prolonged pub visit, he became very ill and was taken by Hilda to the doctor and ordered to put down his tipple for good.

Although he abided, the discontentment with his offstage relationship with Hilda remained. John entered into a fleeting affair that produced a baby girl named Annette. John and Hilda stayed together despite this infidelity and Hilda even agreed to raise the child as her own. The drama of it all seemed to ground John. It was as though he realized that his own life could be as turbulent as any film or kitchen-sink play. In the autumn of 1935, he took a job at Dr Barnrado's, a highly respected British children's charity firm, and would remain there the next three and a half decades until his death in 1969, only leaving to serve in North Africa and Italy during the Second World War.

Hilda and Annette were living in Brixton during the war. John moved back in with them upon his return, and for a time, the marriage seemed to have survived. It was during this period, however, that John would meet Peggy and fall in love again. John initially came to Tunbridge Wells on business for Dr Barnardo's, but after spying Peggy serving tea, he began frequenting the Ritz quite a bit. You can almost imagine his intense stare. If he wasn't quite her physical ideal, he impressed her with his manners and gentle way. Although he was still married to Hilda, the two began an affair that was more or less out in the open. For a short time, Peggy even stayed with John and Hilda. Hilda finally told him to leave and agreed to grant him a divorce.

John found the house at 40 Stansfield Road in early '46. Once his legal papers came through, he and Peggy were married the following September. She was thirty-three and he was thirty-four. Both had found a relationship they could remain in, after searching for many years. Terry, a few months shy of his tenth birthday, would stay in Margaret Mary Burns's care for a short time as he was enrolled in school. David was likely conceived that April.

In the October 1995 issue of British *Esquire*, journalist Ian Penman introduced to the world the concept of 'Bowie Face.' 'You think of Bowie and you think primarily of that Bowie Face through time,' Penman writes. Angie Bowie, in her memoir *Backstage Passes*, describes the adult Bowie's features this way: 'Perfectly structured to classical proportions – forehead to nose and nose to chin measurements being equal – with high, wide cheekbones pulled tightly down into a mischievously chiseled chin.' When considering the baby David

Bowie in photos and in concept, it's difficult to avoid pondering the exact moment this face became the unique Bowie Face and ceased to be merely a baby face. According to Peggy, the nurse who aided his delivery into this world, on that frigid Wednesday morning, found him instantly remarkable.

'The midwife said to me, "This child has been on this earth before,"' David's late mother told an interviewer. 'I thought that was rather an odd thing to say, but the midwife seemed quite adamant.' The comment was the kind of sweetly witchy thing one might offer more than once if one were an itinerant midwife, moving from house to house once an alarm is sounded and the dilations begin. She notices five fingers on each hand, five toes on each tiny foot. She possibly regards the relieved and exhausted mother, who has been through this twice before. She makes note of the nervous father, who has been through this twice before himself. Even if it wasn't their first time, it was the first child of this particular union, one of relief and stability after chaos. It would have been almost impolite not to indicate that there was something special about the boy.

'He was a lovely looking baby,' Peggy's younger sister Patricia Burns (later Antoniou) said, 'always smiling and very placid. He never got into a temper.'

Music seemed to conjure this uniqueness very early on, which is also distinguishing. 'If there was anything that caught his ear, he would fling himself about to the music,' Peggy recalled. 'We thought he might be a ballet dancer.'

Life inside 40 Stansfield Road was comfortable but not exactly musical. A careful lack of demonstration now seemed the rule for John and Peggy. Fresh pots of tea were brewed in the afternoon and meals were frequently heated from cans of tuna fish and spaghetti; HP sauce was the only condiment in the cabinet, cod liver oil the only vitamin enhancement. Evenings were often spent listening to the wireless radio or quietly reading the newspapers.

Terry was invited to live with them once he'd completed his 'eleven-plus' school requirements. By all accounts, he became the greatest supplier of unchecked emotion within these walls. David was lavished with hugs and kisses by all as an infant, but as he grew, outward displays of love came only from Terry. Terry himself was not shown much affection. He was fed, cared for and enrolled in Henry Thornton School in Clapham Common, a mile away. But the older child was treated by his mother and stepfather with a form of cold kindness. Much was left unsaid inside 40 Stansfield Road.

As late as 1949, rubble from the Nazi air strikes could still be seen on city blocks of Brixton. Even those untouched by tragedy in any direct way were made to suffer well beyond the war's end thanks to the inflated cost of living and scarcity of essential supplies like gasoline, food and material goods. The phones seldom worked and electrical power was unreliable. Following the Nazis' formal surrender on May 8, 1945, and the bombings of Hiroshima and Nagasaki on August 6 and 9 of 1945, the United States became the world's sole atomic superpower and overtook British culture as a spoil of war. American pop – jazz, Hollywood films, pulp novels – lacked the class of dance, theater and Romantic poetry, but soon the spoils of U.S. power would see them elevated and, inside of a decade, all but render the classic forms quaint and dusty. In one way or another, the global youth of the first postwar generation would be annexed by the booming pop nation that America had become.

The atomic age changed the language and culture in a profound and enduring way. Russia grew vast and wealthy in the postwar years, and by August of 1949, it too was a nuclear superpower. No longer a necessary ally of the Americans, Russia, under the paranoid and xenophobic Joseph Stalin, disengaged. Stalin was no fan of Frank Sinatra, Mickey Mouse or Coca-Cola, which were considered corruptive. Victory and quieted munitions only seemed to illuminate the differences between America and Russia. The arms race between these rivals would, for all their cooperative war efforts, now end in mutually assured destruction if one or both giants pushed the conflict to the brink. Nearly a quarter of a million people were killed in the Hiroshima and Nagasaki bombings. The stalemate between the former allies promised to vaporize millions more in the same amount of time. The uncertainty of any future at all coupled with tales of horror and cruelty brought back by surviving soldiers elevated pop pleasures to a greater level of importance than they'd ever been. Cheap, fast pleasures became, for many, especially the young, the only pleasures that made sense during the Cold War years. This was the atmosphere that every child of David Jones's age in England and America would grow up in. Sensory overload seemed newly practical. For his generation, pop was a powerful salve. Pop was everything.

CHAPTER 2

The High Street in the southern London suburb of Bromley is full of cell-phone shops, Subway sandwich outlets and Starbucks coffee bars that renders it indistinguishable from those of Illinois or of New Jersey: a retail center, narrow, bright and full of pedestrians in casual uniform. A double-decker bus passes, carrying more of them home or to work. And yet there is a pair of favorite Bromley-ite sons who have done much to widen the gap between such humdrum environments and the progression of humankind into a wildly exciting future. In addition to being the town where David Jones came of age, Bromley is also the birth-place of Herbert George Wells, better known as H. G. Wells. Wells, the father of science fiction, often referred to as 'the man who invented tomorrow,' was a progressive as well as a futurist. *The Island of Dr Moreau* and *The War of the Worlds* upstage his essays and less imaginative works of fiction, but his novels *Ann Veronica* and *The Passionate Friends* championed the kind of liberated sexuality that David Bowie and his wife Angie would come to embrace over a half century later. Like the Bowies', the Wellses' marriage was open (and he and his wife Isabel also grew apart and divorced after only a few years). Wells enjoyed dozens of affairs (frequently with much younger women) well into his old age. Like David Bowie, the writer didn't come from money. His mother and father operated a china shop. Herbert lived in the basement. He lost himself in books and the stars (gazing through a borrowed telescope at the country estate where his mother became a caretaker). Like Bowie, Wells used his discipline and intelligence to lift himself above his working-class station. Like Bowie, he showed discipline and aptitude early; he wrote his first novel, *The Desert Daisy*, at age ten (Bowie was taking lessons with acclaimed jazz saxophonist Ronnie Ross at twelve). Most important, like Bowie, Wells had one aim over all: to eventually find a way out of here.

'It wasn't a place of much distinction,' Hanif Kureishi, author of the Bromley-set novel *The Buddha of Suburbia* and another famous son, told me in his clipped, vaguely tough (for a novelist anyway) accent. 'And H. G. Wells was a big source of pride. He was a very hip writer.' To be middle-class in England, I'm also told, is akin to being, say, upper-working-class in America. It essentially means that there is enough money for food and bills but few amenities or luxuries. It means that you can own a small house, as opposed to a tiny flat. Your family might also boast a small tree in the yard, enabling those inside to look out your window and see something green, and ostensibly preventing neighbors from peering in completely.

In the fifties, Brixton became a place where many West Indian immigrants settled and sought work repairing the war-damaged infrastructure. As Britain's economy slowly began strengthening in the new postwar decade, many white families like the Joneses drew on their small savings and left the city for the fast-developing suburbs. The same thing happened in America, only the houses were much larger; so were the dreams of leafy safety and modernized comfort, something to which more people felt entitled. Few upwardly mobile American families would settle for a home as boxlike as the one the Joneses moved into at 106 Canon Drive in south Bromley in the winter of 1953, with no driveway in which to park a new Cadillac or Buick. But for the Blitz-scarred English of a certain age, this was a huge step up. The following year the Joneses moved to a slightly larger house, set slightly back among the rows at 23 Clarence Road. Here they enjoyed an even more effective illusion of privacy. Still, one gets the sense, walking past these homes today (like the Brixton homes, they are largely unchanged), that everyone remained very aware of everyone else's business. Perhaps this is because none of these buildings extend beyond two or three stories and few are farther than fifteen feet apart. For those given to mild claustrophobia, the feeling produced while inside must be akin to quietly choking: inhaling the very same air that your parents and siblings breathe, but also that which your neighbors, tolerated or reviled, breathe. If there's a message implicit in the energy there, it's this: there better not be anything funny going on; if there is, we will know about it.

'In England, the suburbs are a place where people have conservative values,' punk icon Siouxsie Sioux, who grew up in nearby Chislehurst, says. 'Keep a stiff upper lip and mind your own business, but they're also secretly very nosey about everybody else.'

The Jones family's third and final residence in Bromley, at 4 Plaistow Grove, sits at the dead end of a curved road, just behind the local Tudor-style pub, known as the Crown. It overlooks a chain-link fence tangled with vegetation and a dark wood railway station. At night, the preadolescent David could hear the pub chatter emanate from the back room, which was directly under his bedroom window, only about fifteen yards or so away beyond a thin plywood fence. The Crown is still there today, offering 'good food, and fine ale.' Perhaps the pub chatter was lulling, akin to falling asleep with the television or radio on today. Or maybe it was distracting. People do tend to say things after a few pints that a young boy might not want to know about. Did he hear soldiers and merchants talk about travel? Did this, coupled with the trains pulling in and out, also impossible to avoid from his bed, pique David's interest in a world beyond this modest, white two-story house, with its stone walk and little square of lawn, now full of dandelions? The closeness to the pub's back room and the station really do beg such questions. And if all of this did affect him, there were only two ways to escape such taunting: via one's imagination and, eventually, by stepping onto a train at that railway station. This spot may very well be where the confluence of David Bowie's need for intellectual stimulation and unmoored searching might have been formed in the young David Jones's personality. Walk across the elevated concrete bridge and stare down at the tracks, and it's hard not to wonder how strange it must have been for the adult David to return there from the city after a night performing at the Marquee Club in Soho. He lived here, after all, well into his career as a professional musician. I imagine that he could hear Peggy and John snore in their bedroom. On a Bowie-ist side note – and this probably means little to anyone living in Bromley – directly across from the Crown pub and facing the back fence of David's house and the window of his room is a black storefront with a giant glass window full of mannequins attired in Renaissance costume or Victorian formal-wear. Its name: Larger Than Life Stagewear: Theatrical Costumes for Hire. While the store is obviously one of the newer developments on this slowly modernizing block, its wares are symbolic, as

24

theatrical costume would essentially provide David with his H. G. Wells-ian ticket out of Bromley for good.

In keeping with their new stature, the Joneses took pains to make sure that their child was exceedingly presentable. The class photo from his primary school, Burnt Ash in Bromley, dated 1958, shows David with a starched shirt and neatly parted hair, looking more like a miniature man than a tousle-haired kid. Every one of his classmates appears exactly the same.

'David was always clean and tidy and spotless,' his aunt Pat Antoniou has said. 'My sister made a thing of that. Every five minutes she would say, "Pull your sock up," "Have you washed your face?"'

For all of his childhood and much of his adult life, the private David Bowie has been painfully shy. It's naturally difficult to believe that any celebrity is shy, as the very prism through which we view them is public, loud and larger than life. Lots of performers claim to be shy offstage and freely acknowledge the paradoxical elements of their public and private selves. They invent personas who can speak and sing and be generally extroverted (Eminem's 'Slim Shady' and Beyoncé's 'Sasha Fierce' being the latest in a long line that most famously includes Ziggy Stardust), while their true shy selves lie buried and protected somewhere deep inside. Once he'd achieved a kind of perma-fame previously enjoyed only by movie legends, David began to reveal much about his own shyness. In a 1975 interview with Dinah Shore, for example, he admits, 'The one thing I didn't like was being terribly shy. An incredibly shy person. And so I over-compensated. I thought that if I gave myself an alarming kind of reputation then I would have to learn to defend myself and therefore come out of myself.' Henry Winkler, by the way, is one of Dinah Shore's other guests on that show (Nancy Walker of the famous Bounty paper towel ads rounds the panel out). Dinah introduced Winkler as 'the David Bowie of *Happy Days*.' (Eternally polite, Bowie says, 'I'm a great fan of Fonzie.') In the clip, while Bowie and Walker puff away on their cigarettes, Winkler blathers on about art ('The chemicals come together and there's fire!'). It's a telling clip nonetheless.

Rather than being a form of self-denial, many believe that shyness is actually a form of heightened self-regard. This is crucial to understanding how David Bowie, rock star, grew out of David Jones, potential suburban drone. Unchecked, the self-preoccupation manifests as social awkwardness or phobia, but examined and harnessed (as Bowie claims to have done quite literally, explaining in interviews that he would literally itemize things that he disliked about himself, then take pains to remove the useless inventory) one can, with luck and timing in the mix, go supernova. On another interesting side note, I've come across reports that suggest that those possessing the physical characteristics of blue eyes, blond hair and pale skin, which Bowie does, can be more shy than those without. Experts believe it has something to do with melatonin. Shyness can be detected in infants as early as two months.

By the time the Joneses moved from Brixton to Bromley and David enrolled in school, he was exhibiting these tendencies. Famously, during his first day at Raglan Infant school, he was so overcome, he reportedly wet himself.

Those afflicted by self-regard in the extreme frequently require the attention of others either to confirm an observation or suspicion about themselves or justify the fixation altogether. And so, although it would seem antithetical, it's often the most painfully shy people who eventually do become the most flamboyant public figures. Behind the closed doors of his new suburban home, with its neatly arranged knickknacks and chintz and plastic sheets covering every chair as well as the sofa, the preadolescent David Jones was already exhibiting unusual, 'look at me' tendencies, most of which were quickly discouraged.

'When he was about three years old, he put on makeup for the first time,' Peggy recalled. 'We had tenants in the house and one day he went missing upstairs and found a bag of lipstick, eyeliner and face powder, and decided it would be a good idea to plaster his face with it. When I finally found him, he looked for all the world like a clown. I told him that he shouldn't use makeup, but he said, "You do, Mummy." I agreed but pointed out that it wasn't for little boys.'

As with most British youth of the era, David was taught strict manners, and these seem to have stuck. In interviews with most rock stars it's rare to see an abundance of pleases and thank-yous. Grunts and sulking is much more common. Not so with Bowie. Bound by this rigidity, David initially fell neatly in line at school and became popular with his teachers. He participated in school activities like choir and the local scouting troop the Wolf Cubs. His half brother Terry may have been the one who provided, although probably not intentionally, an insight into how this polite and uniform veneer was something of an illusion.

David sensed that Terry – who had grown into a darkly handsome man, not unlike Dustin Hoffman circa *Straw Dogs* in photos – was in a steadily increasing amount of pain. He began to have fainting spells. His reportedly chilly relationship with John Jones only got worse, and as a teen, Terry started to rebel. He stayed in school until age fifteen. Despite what Angie Bowie and others have insisted to me was a fierce intellect, Terry Burns did not go on to college. Instead, as many of his generation did naturally, he joined the workforce, taking odd jobs and finding modest lodgings in the Bromley vicinity. The usual domestic politicking that marks any family, especially one with stepchildren and parents involved, went on in the privacy of the Plaistow Grove house. The only child Peggy and John had together, of the three that they had in total, David was doted on, while Terry, when present, was often ignored. And it could not have been easy for David to accept this without feeling some measure of guilt. David worshipped Terry, by all accounts, and the older child doted on the boy. When friction arose between John and Terry, Peggy was pressured to side with her spouse. While such details are not uncommon, especially in the postwar West, they provide a key to understanding what soon pulled the preteen David out of his inner world and forced him to reckon with the darker, more volatile elements of social engagement and essentially invent himself as an emotionally armored teenage rebel, a sort of proto-Ziggy Stardust; essentially, what led him to music. 'I think he felt very responsible, as children do, for the fact that he was the favorite child,' his cousin Kristina has said, 'and he was given attention by his father, and Terry wasn't.'

It was around this period of domestic volatility when David first heard what would become one of his touchstone songs: 'The Inchworm.'

In 1952 the Brooklyn-born actor Danny Kaye (real name David Daniel Kaminsky) starred in *Hans Christian Andersen*, a musical version of the life and work of the beloved Danish children's fairy tale writer. The songs were composed by the

29

great Frank Loesser, who also wrote the songs for the Broadway musical *Guys and Dolls* and the sexy holiday standard 'Baby, It's Cold Outside.' Although 'Thumbelina' is probably the best-known song on the film's soundtrack, the 'deep Loesser cut' is 'Inchworm,' or 'The Inchworm,' depending on how it's listed.

In the film, there's an unintentionally creepy scene in which Kaye (whose sexual preference was, like Andersen's and David Bowie's, the subject of much ambiguity and debate) walks past a classroom and peers into the open door at the children as they sit in their rows, counting in song: 'Two and two are four. Four and four are eight . . .' The justifiably concerned professor slams the door on him. Hardly chastened, he finds a patch of yellow marigolds, and, happily, another small boy, and as the schoolchildren continue to sing the melody, he sings a counter verse: 'Inchworm, inchworm, measuring the marigolds / Seems to me you'd stop and see how beautiful they are.' It's a practical ditty designed to teach young children measurements, but surely it also instructs them on how fleeting serenity will be as they grow older and fussier – the most mournful song about math ever made.

'The Inchworm' has been covered by everyone from John Coltrane to John Lithgow. Tony Bennett does a version that will give you stomach flutters, but Kaye's rendition, with or without Muppets (he reprised it on *The Muppet Show* in the late seventies), is the standard, and the recorded version became five-year-old David Jones's favorite. Simply, it made him feel safe and hopeful when his increasingly discomfiting family life and shyness filled him with guilt and wariness. The record was never far from his gramophone.

'"Inchworm" is my childhood,' Bowie said in 1993 (curiously, in an interview with fashion model Kate Moss). 'It wasn't a happy one. Not that it was brutal but mine were a certain type of British parent: quite cold emotionally and not many hugs. I always craved affection cause of that. "Inchworm" gave me comfort and the person singing it sounded like he'd been hurt too and I'm into that, the artist singing away his pain.'

When David first began learning guitar and saxophone in his adolescence, the chords for 'The Inchworm' would be the first he would seek out. If you listen to the structure and melody, you can hear the template for many of David Bowie's best and saddest songs. It's there in 'Life on Mars?' and 'Aladdin Sane.' Even his cover of Dimitri Tiomkin and Ned Washington's 'Wild Is the Wind' (first recorded by Johnny Mathis for the 1957 film of the same name, but made famous by Nina Simone in '64, Bowie in '76, and much later, in 2000, Chan Marshall on Cat Power's *The Covers Record*) has a little 'Inchworm' in its arrangement and delivery.

'You wouldn't believe the amount of my songs that have sort of spun off that one song,' he has said. 'There's a child's nursery rhyme element in it. It kept bringing me back to the feelings of those pure thoughts of sadness that you have as a child, and how they're so identified even when you're an adult. There's a connection that can be made between being a somewhat lost five-year-old and feeling a little abandoned and having the same feeling when you're in your twenties and it was that song that did it for me.'

David, by age six, had an even more powerful way to forget his immediate circumstances and dial into a life outside of his parents' house, beyond his discomfort over Terry's treatment, beyond Great Britain and even the realms of planet Earth. In keeping with their upwardly mobile determination, the Joneses were among the first families in Bromley to purchase a television set. The black and white tube, with its small screen and a massive cabinet, seemed more than anything else like a reward and a unifier for an uncertain post-wartime nation. TVs sold like mad in the years after the war as the British took to the invention with a verve that even the most ardent American nuclear family would be hard-pressed to match. The British Broadcasting Corporation, a public network founded in 1922, had been testing TV since World War II but suspended advancement until after the war. By 1946, the first London residents began enjoying rudimentary television programming and an unreliable signal. In 1949, the erection of more transmitters made signals outside of London stronger and allowed television to be enjoyed by the rapidly sprawling suburbanites.

On June 2, 1953, the Joneses gathered around the primitive set to view the coronation of Queen Elizabeth II. This was one of the first highly produced affairs, with multiple cameras and much pageantry. Millions watched as the orb and scepter and the rod, ring and crown are bestowed on Elizabeth. The *New York Times* called it 'the first international television event.'

David and other British schoolchildren were granted a full week off. 'It was like Christmas and sort of New Year all rolled into one,' Greg Tesser, a future music publicity officer and habitué of the Marquee Club, would later recount to me. It may have also been the first time that David Jones realized the scope of the world, as proud English subjects who watched the coronation on TV and heard it on the radio bragged about the massive scope of the listening and viewing audience, some twenty-seven million people in total.

Whereas Terry was a war baby, his father torn away by a world in tumult, David Jones was a TV baby, where the world was literally brought to you and the figures inside the glass tube seemed like family after a while. While H. G. Wells had his borrowed library on the summer estate, early English TV is likely responsible for introducing young David Jones to the concept of outer space, a theme he would later use to such great effect throughout his songwriting and acting careers.

Almost exactly one month after the televised coronation of Queen Elizabeth II, the BBC broadcast a serialized science fiction drama entitled *The Quatermass Experiment*. The ratings were massive and this somewhat pulpy production captivated an entire nation. Watching *The Quatermass Experiment* today (I've located a grainy dubbed videocassette copy), it quite obviously belongs, along with that other wildly popular BBC production *The Day of the Triffids*, to the subgenre of alien-possession-as-Cold War-metaphor films (best exemplified in America by the original 1956 version of *Invasion of the Body Snatchers*). *Quatermass* begins with two young lovers wooing each other in a field when they hear a noise and spot an object in the sky. 'That's not a jet!' the man shouts. A rocket crashlands in the country-side, part of a top-secret British space program mission headed up by the gruff but upright Professor Quatermass, a sort of proto-Dr Who figure in British pop culture. Inside the ruined fuselage, only one of the original three astronauts remains, and there's something funky about him. He will eventually turn into a creature resembling an elephant seal covered with Berber carpeting. What's important about *The Quatermass Experiment* is not the plot and the special effects, of course, but rather the ideas it placed in the mind of young viewers.

Quatermass debuted just four weeks past the international, globe-shrinking hubbub that was the coronation, and one can imagine a six-year-old David Jones's head swelling with possibility and excitement, out there, 'on the other side of the air,' as Quatermass promises. 'There's a whole new world out there.' Young boys made heroes of astronauts in part because of the brewing desire to conquer. But at the risk of putting too fine a point on it, a somewhat emotionally repressed young boy, with occasionally wounding energy in the family living room, could certainly imagine space exploration, and by extension the hard facts of science itself, as a clean antidote to messy human emotion he could not fully understand or protect himself from.

Around this time, Terry decided that he would go off and see the world beyond Bromley for real. In the early fifties, thanks to increasing tensions with the Soviet Union and a last-ditch, doomed effort to preserve what was left of the 'empire,' Britain still had mandatory military service, unless one was ill or otherwise disqualified. Terry's joining up was required but it was most likely reactionary as well. As was John Jones's response to this development. Terry and David shared a room in Plaistow Grove when Terry stayed over, but after he announced that he had enlisted in the Royal Air Force, John began making plans to convert the room into a larger bedroom for his son.

The RAF service certainly took Terry Burns far away from suburban England. It has been suggested that some of the things he saw, while stationed near Yemen, as the British fought one of their final colonial wars against largely uncontrollable tribal insurgents, deeply disturbed him. The Aden conflict, which carried on into 1963, has real parallels with America's twenty-first-century occupations in the Middle East in that it consisted of well-trained soldiers who often found themselves defenseless against guerillas in a sweltering desert theater.

Aden had been crucial to Britain since the early 1800s as a passage to India and a port for the importing of spices and oil. In July of 1956 Egypt's Gamal Abdel Nasser attempted to block this passage and nationalize the European-financed Suez Canal. He also tried to unite Arab nations as a republic but only succeeded in fomenting a fierce anticolonial sentiment. In essence, the British troops found themselves the object of an unexpectedly virulent hatred and violence as they attempted to take back the canal. As with World War II and his mother's generation, once again, the reverberation of armed conflict would take its toll on a fragile Burns psyche.

'Something had happened to Terry while he was serving in the Royal Air Force in Aden,' Angie writes in *Backstage Passes*, 'and whatever it was, it had disturbed him profoundly.' Upon his return, he became disheveled, often irrationally angry or upset. This was, as with any bit of effusive emotion, frequently ignored with the kind of cold

English denial that the Joneses seem to have perfected as a matter of course. The profoundly shaken had no place in Bromley where conformity was quietly but rigidly enforced.

I was born on October 2, 1969 – the same day David Bowie performed 'Space Oddity' on England's weekly Top of the Pops *countdown show. A spot on* Top of the Pops *guaranteed sales and exposure. It was a career milestone for any artist; it meant you had arrived. That night, both of us arrived. 'Space Oddity' was the first David Bowie song that I ever heard and, along with 'Stairway to Heaven' by Led Zeppelin and 'Saturday in the Park' by Chicago, one of the first rock 'n' roll songs I remember from very early childhood. A few years after the song was reissued as part of* ChangesOneBowie, *his 1976 best-of, and enjoyed a new popularity, its lyrics became some of the first to really haunt me. It was around '78, and the older brother of a grade school friend had learned it on guitar. He was sixteen and a high school student. I was nine and still wet the bed. My friend's brother strummed a six-string acoustic guitar with butterfly appliqués along the body like Peter Frampton's had. It was a Saturday afternoon and he was attempting an English accent, poorly: 'Go-round cant-rowl to Moy-ja Tum . . .'*

When he was finished with 'Space Oddity,' he began 'Werewolves of London' by Warren Zevon, also sung in an English accent. I later found out that Warren Zevon was born in Chicago and was widely associated with the Los Angeles singer-songwriter movement of the early to mid-seventies, but by then, I was already a rock journalist. 'Werewolves of London' was sick humor, like the Mad, Cracked *and* National Lampoon *magazines I read with great excitement every few weeks. The lines 'You better stay away from him / He'll rip your lungs out, Jim / I'd like to meet his tailor' fit my rapidly blackening sense of humor. 'Space Oddity' was not as witty ('And the papers want to know whose shirts you wear' is actually a nod to British football team loyalty and not a sly critique of sartorial trends à la the Kinks' 'Dedicated Follower of Fashion') but it stuck with me longer. At night, I would look up at the sky and wonder what it would be like to be Major Tom, trapped way up there in outer space, floating in a tin can forever. Was it technically living? Do you age? Do you have money and hair? Do you see pictures of Jap girls in synthesis? Bowie made me consider existentialism before I even knew what it meant to be alive (and before I ever really thought about my death). It was much easier to reckon with the* Grease *soundtrack and put off the inevitable, but I already knew even then that Bowie's music had permanently changed me.*

CHAPTER 3

David seemed to evolve quickly during the advent of rock 'n' roll, as if his very form was slowly adapting itself for the cultural upheavals ahead. Class photos from the late fifties and very early sixties show David slowly beginning to appear different than his schoolmates do. He was skinnier and paler and blonder than the other boys, but he was not yet equipped, or even inclined, of course, to use these delicate and unique qualities. However, by the end of the 1950s, as he entered his teens, David would amass a series of key influences, many handed down to him by his older brother upon his return from RAF service, which would help ease him into a powerful other-ness.

In 1955, when David was eight, the film *East of Eden* was released in England and was, along with Disney's *Lady and the Tramp*, one of the big hits, both critically and commercially, of the year. Adapted from John Steinbeck's 1952 novel, it begins with a swelling overture and the crashing of the Pacific waves on the Salinas, California, shores. *East of Eden* is epic Americana, full of biblical allegory, violence, poverty and desire. In it, James Byron Dean, named for the romantic poet, played Steinbeck's character Cal Trask, the tortured half brother skulking around a small town, seeking love and affection but unable to express his need to fill the void in his guts. Like Marlon Brando, James Dean made psychic pain and social disenfranchisement seem romantic, even desirable. He 'said it all so clean,' as the Eagles noted in their 1974 ode to him. An icon in America, Dean articulated the same sentiments for millions of British youths encouraged to be voiceless, rewarded for a politesse that clashed with every roiling impulse they were feeling. If possible, he was bigger in England than in America because of such institutionalized repression.

'Dean's impact among British youth was huge,' writer William Bast says. Now in his late seventies, Bast was Dean's friend and roommate in the early 1950s. After the actor's death in 1955, his Dean-inspired play *The Myth Makers* would be broadcast on the UK's Granada TV network, and he would observe the intense English James Dean cult firsthand. 'He was a huge movie star there,' he continues. 'There were large fan clubs. People could relate to his farm boy origins. They have farms, first of all. But with regard to American culture and teenage culture, the feeling of being displaced is not just an American thing.'

Dean's father was a Quaker with a lineage that could be traced to the Pilgrims. He had Native

American blood on his mother's side. She died when he was eight, and he never really recovered from the loss. Fast, sexed-up, palpably sad and searching, Dean was American rock 'n' roll before there was such a thing as rock 'n' roll. What is irresistible about rock, the stylish, slippery, hot freakiness, is irresistible about him. David could not have looked at Dean's androgynous features, prettier than most girls', and not see a kindred soul. Subsequently, Dean remained not just a hero but also a model for the rest of David's life, as great a template for Bowie as any rock or jazz pioneer would become. To be a Bowie-ist, by extension, is to be a student of James Dean. Bowie's celebrated self-conception and/or self-invention (or reinvention) really begins here upon David Jones's discovery of the Hollywood rebel. Dean transformed himself after moving from rural Indiana to California and later, in '51, to New York City.

'The mystery of James Dean lies not in his abrupt end, but in his origins,' David Dalton writes in the classic Dean biography *James Dean: The Mutant King*, which Bowie is busy reading while spending time with journalist Cameron Crowe during their classic '76 *Playboy* interview. 'Dean was probably very much like me,' Bowie tells Crowe in the interview. 'Elizabeth Taylor told me that once. Dean was calculating. He wasn't careless. He was not the rebel he portrayed so successfully. He didn't want to die. But he did believe in the premise of

41

taking yourself to extremes, just to add a deeper cut to one's personality.'

'He was an actor,' Bast told me. 'An actor prepares by watching. Seeing. Trying to live the part. Studying other people. [Russian acting innovator Constantin] Stanislavski wrote that. [Dean] was very much aware of all that and took the opportunity to avail himself of things like that. The end result . . . to become an actor. You can live other roles. He's not going to go around talking like an Indiana farm boy unless there was a certain charm. Then he'd turn it on.'

Dean's death made him an even more perfect model. As he sat in the cinema, watching Dean, brooding about the Griffith Park Observatory in *Rebel Without a Cause* or covered in black gold in the following year's *Giant* (his final film), David knew that this was someone who no longer existed in any terrestrial way. He was somewhere else, 'beyond the air,' as Quatermass would say.

Equally out-there, and next in the crucial succession of formative Bowie heroes, was Richard Wayne Penniman, a.k.a. 'Little Richard.' In the autumn of 1956, several weeks short of his tenth birthday, John gave David a copy of Little Richard's Specialty Records single 'Tutti Frutti.'

'My father brought home a plastic American record with no center,' Bowie recalled. 'An American GI had sent a bunch of singles to Dr Barnardo's and he brought me half a dozen home to listen to. Our record player only played at seventy-eight so I used to put the needle on it and try to turn it at the right speed using my finger. So I got this very weird perception of what rock 'n' roll sounded like at a very early age. That could explain a lot.'

This was no Danny Kaye.

'A wop bop a loo bop a wop bam boom,' the gritty caterwaul declared – words that meant everything and nothing at once. The band fell in with the piano, sax, bass and drums and David Jones felt his entire body rise and shake. It was an electrifying moment. 'My heart nearly burst with excitement,' he said. 'It filled the room with energy and color and outrageous defiance.'

Rooted in gospel and gruff like a blues singer, but also pliant, flexible and light like an opera singer, with the winking, naughty wit of a cabaret star, Richard's voice is still unique in its twisted, somewhat insane timbre and phrasing. He sang like a man who could never sing any other way. It possesses urgency, confidence, bravado and deep, almost biblical need. 'I tried to take voice lessons but I found I couldn't because the way I sing, a voice teacher can't deal with it,' Richard has said of his phrasing. 'I'm out of control.'

As epochal as it was, Richard's 'Tutti Frutti' was *not* a number one hit in America. A watered-down cover version by Pat Boone had topped the charts instead. Richard was an African American and androgynous. He was a double threat to many parents at the time.

'I had heard God. Now I wanted to see him,' David recalled. And he finally did, in hit films like *Don't Knock the Rock* and *The Girl Can't Help It*, both from 1956. In *Don't Knock the Rock*, featuring seminal and soon to be scandalized Cleveland disc jockey Alan Freed (who has a great face for radio), Richard is all cheekbones and sex, flipping a sharkskin leg up on the piano lid and thrusting it into the keys and rolling his eyeballs with extreme camp as his band runs through 'Long Tall Sally.' 'Rock and roll is for morons!', one of the disapproving local officials declares later in the film, 'It's outrageous! Depraved.' In *The Girl Can't Help It*, the better film of the two thanks to genuinely funny dialogue ('Rome wasn't built in a day.' 'She ain't Rome and she's already built!') and a prescient plotline (Tom Ewell's agent attempts to turn Jayne Mansfield's sexpot into a star inside of six weeks at the behest of a gangster) that will reflect David's own rise to super-stardom in the early seventies. In *Girl*, Richard performs the title track, 'Reddy Teddy,' and 'She's Got It,' in a nightclub before an all-white crowd. The film begins in dull black and white as Ewell boasts about the 'gorgeous lifelike color by Deluxe.' Suddenly (with further comic prompting by Ewell, a master of the deadpan delivery) the widescreen transforms into a vivid, burning color scape. A better metaphor for Richard's impact on the young David Jones and by extension, polite, white popular culture, does not exist. To David, Richard was the pinnacle, a consummate weirdo but no outcast; rather an artist with killer power over all who gazed upon him. Even at ten the boy wanted to be . . . *this*, whatever this was.

John Jones, with his music hall background, brief as it was, also understood the appeal of Little Richard and rock 'n' roll. Given his own unexpressed lust for color and noise in his own adolescence, John was likely touched by David's interest in music and was evidently more than happy to supply the boy with 45s.

'Hound Dog' by Elvis Presley, who shared David's birthday – twelve years his senior – was next. David played the 45 one day for his cousin Kristina and couldn't help but observe the effect Presley's voice had on her. The little girl began to sweat as she shook her hips to the mutant hill-billy beat. Puberty had not fully set in but even at age ten, it was clear that this music had a kind of power that his mom and dad's 78s did not. Rock 'n' roll meant sex, something never spoken of in society but always present, hanging in the air like a primal mist. And now, uncontained, an entire generation of English kids seemed to go mad at once.

With rock 'n' roll and pop culture, America liberated Western Europe a second time. Only this time it focused only on the teenagers. David, in many ways, was no longer an English kid and would never be one again. His heart like most English teens, was on the other side of the Atlantic.

'We started to get into various things I have to call "American,"' music publicist Greg Tesser recalls. 'Until about 1954 or-five, it was all a bit bleak and very dark and very austere. My father was in the printing business and he printed posters for Davy Crockett, and that had a huge boom in England. England in the early fifties was just like it'd been in the thirties and the forties because of the war and subsequent deprivation.'

For a short time, David had even forsaken British soccer for 'Yank football,' which he found he could pick up on John's shortwave radio. He would sit and listen to the simulcasts on American Armed Forces Radio out of Germany. Transfixed, he wrote a letter to the American embassy in London requesting information on scores and players and received a uniform, helmet and pad in return, not to mention his first bit of press ink: LIMEY KID LOVES YANK FOOTBALL, in the *Bromley and Kentish Times*. The photo shows an elated David kitted out in his new pads and a tightly pulled necktie. 'It is a safe bet that the people of Bromley may soon be scratching their heads, too, when David introduces "sandlot football" to the youngsters in one of the parks,' the article stated.

Along with these new, American-style freedoms and indulgent desires came an unavoidable generation gap. Those who had fought for king and country in World War I and II were outraged by the apparently ungrateful nature of these kids, who only seemed to want to dance and fornicate.

There's a famous scene in *A Hard Day's Night* where John Lennon takes the piss out of an older train commuter in a bowler hat. 'I fought a war for your sort.' he sneers at Lennon with disgust. 'I bet you're sorry you won,' Lennon snipes back. There's another in *Saturday Night and Sunday Morning*, in which Albert Finney takes a break from pulling factory machine levers, lights up a smoke and scans a row of hardworking industrialized drones, ten years his elder and still there. 'They got ground down before the war and never got over it.' he sneers. 'I'd like to see someone grind me down.' Postwork, Finney dons a sharp suit and heads to a nightclub to listen to American jazz.

Even some British youth quietly puzzled at the Americanization of their country and embodied a sense of inferiority as though they were being shown how to live. This was best articulated by Jimmy Porter, the angry young chain-smoking hero of John Osborne's classic stage play *Look Back in Anger*. Inert and impotent, with nothing he could point to and say, 'That is me,' Jimmy rages from his chair. 'I must be getting sentimental . . . But I must say it's pretty dreary living in the American Age – unless you're an American of course. Perhaps all our children will be Americans. That's a thought isn't it?'

Unfortunately the one organic British subculture of this period, the Teddy Boys, were tied up in sensationalized violence. Teddy Boys, or Teds, were dandies, 'Ted' being a shortening of 'Edwardian.' A precursor to the more famous mods in that one had to be sharply dressed, Ted culture was an odd hybrid of English tailoring and American small-town style. Teds wore thick-soled creepers or pointy 'winklepicker' shoes, loose collars, tight dark trousers, bright Lurex socks and large waistcoats but coiffed and greased their hair like American rock 'n' rollers. The Teddy Girls wore hoop skirts, drape jackets and ponytails. In an effort, it seems, to prove you can look sharp and still be a badass, the Teds roamed London in gangs, vandalizing and tormenting straights but mostly fighting each other like the American juvenile delinquent gangs who were rapidly becoming a cottage industry, both in terms of selling to them and selling cautionary tales about them. The best among these cautionary tales was the film *Blackboard Jungle*.

Released in 1955, *Blackboard Jungle* purports to be a cautionary tale but is really the godfather of all exploitation 'teachers vs. students' movies, from *Rock 'n' Roll High School* to *Heathers* to *Dangerous Minds*. Glenn Ford plays an open-minded English teacher. Sidney Poitier is the smartest of the troubled teens. They form an unlikely bond that helps them both deal with the surly, hopeless, chain-smoking teens around them. The language is pulpy ('You ever try to fight thirty-five guys at once, teach?'). Librarians are sexually ravaged, jazz records are violently critiqued and the generation gap between World War II veterans and their increasingly existentially hopeless offspring has its first black and white document.

Blackboard Jungle, most importantly, blasts wide open with 'Rock Around the Clock' by Bill Haley and the Comets. The song, already a few years old, quickly became a Teddy Boy anthem and the first rock 'n' roll single to sell one million copies on both sides of the Atlantic. *Blackboard Jungle* and its soundtrack caused a few incidents of violence in and around the actual cinemas where it screened, and soon the British newspapers got in on the act, realizing that outrage sold papers. (Haley, also appears in *Don't Knock the Rock* but can't stand up next to Little Richard.)

David Jones was too young to be a Teddy Boy, but he began styling his hair in a rock 'n' roll fashion and adding pointy winklepickers to his school uniform. And he continued to collect rock 'n' roll 45s, which his parents happily provided, by the likes of Chuck Berry, Buddy Holly and the Crickets, Eddie Cochran, Jerry Lee Lewis, the Everly Brothers, Fats Domino, and Gene Vincent and His Blue Caps.

The cultural sea change is most famously lamented in the book *Absolute Beginners* by Colin MacInnes. David Bowie would star in the 1984 film adaptation, an ill-fated musical directed by Julien Temple. *Absolute Beginners* is about, if nothing else, the power of the teenage dollar. Once teens were seen as a target audience, largely because of rock 'n' roll, they had both buying and spending power. With that power came a sense of entitlement, and eventually the social changes that took place, from the repealing of mandatory military service to kids attending art college as opposed to going right into the workforce, would lead to the culture revolution of the following decade.

'*Absolute Beginners* was a posey literary book for adults and literati,' says pop manager and author Simon Napier-Bell. 'Nobody gave a toss what anyone else read. Books were for adults or eggheads. People were far too busy fucking and dancing and fighting.' Oral contraception, approved in '57, helped with all the 'fucking.' Rock 'n' roll (stereos could now be purchased on credit for the first time) assisted with the rest.

England was lacking in stars and, with the exception of the Teds, lacking in style, but a new era was emerging. The 1950s were over and in the 1960s England's role as trend follower and America's role as trendesetter would be reversed almost completely.

David Jones became an official teenager himself on January 8, 1960. In England children take a precursory version of America's SATs at age eleven called the eleven-plus. These standardized exams were designed to determine what line of education a student will be best suited for upon graduation at sixteen: the idea was to keep an eye on career making and focus on the preservation of the strength of the workforce. David was, of course, extremely focused. The only problem was that the objects of his focus – girls and rock 'n' roll – were not part of the eleven-plus. When he didn't ace it, it became clear to his parents that action was needed. They knew he was an extremely bright and clever child. He simply needed the right environment. David interviewed at and was accepted as a student of Bromley Technical High School, or 'Brom Tech.'

A Bromley boy with a strong chin and a strong rugby player's physique, George Underwood, soon to become David's very best mate, knew the boy from their Cub Scouts troop. The most ardent rock 'n' roll enthusiasts at Brom Tech, at one time George and David were so close that they would often try to test out their assumed ESP. One would think of a word and then inquire with the other. Occasionally they succeeded in reading each other's minds.

'I first met David Robert Jones at St Mary's church hall in 1956,' Underwood, a successful painter and illustrator, says today. 'We were both about to enroll into the eighteenth Bromley Cub Scouts group. We started talking about music almost immediately, about skiffle and rock 'n' roll, and that was it. I had found someone who was passionate about the same things I was. David was in and out of things so fast – one week it was Little Richard, then it was the Kingston Trio, the Everly Brothers, Lonnie Donegan. He was difficult to pin down. But I was the same – Charlie Gracie, Tommy Steele, Gene Vincent and Buddy Holly. In fact I went to see Buddy Holly and the Crickets when I was eleven. Twice! I remember David being quite jealous of the fact that I managed to get Buddy Holly's signature. Fame was what fascinated him. All we were into besides music was pussy. We became best friends, walking up and down Bromley High Street, dressed identically, pulling birds – talking all sorts of shit to them, pretending to be American and sometimes scoring.'

While art was studied in practice, it was not a bohemian-style art school where theory and philosophy were celebrated as well. Good jobs in design advertising and technology were the goal, not fame or creative expression.

'The dream was to be employed and to own a house,' Hanif Kureishi, who also attended Bromley Tech in the late sixties, would later confirm to me. 'My parents had lived through the war. The war was really recent. But we were different [from our parents] because of pop basically. For most kids, yeah, you want a good job. But then you got caught up in pop.'

'The notion of making a living as a musician was far-fetched,' Peter Frampton, who grew up in Bromley and attended Bromley Tech (where his father, Owen Frampton, was the art professor), tells me. 'What you're talking about is the difference between the outlook in people in general coming from America with the American dream: "You can do anything, my son." To us in England it was "Don't think you're ever gonna make anything of yourself, because this is your lot." We were just after the war. Just off rationing. In England they were still in shock, I think, and the kids, the baby boomers, had not a clue of what their parents had just been through. My parents and my next-door neighbor's parents were just so glad to be alive. We were the first generation that didn't have to serve. Didn't have to do anything. Seeing rock 'n' roll on TV, what was powerful in addition to the music was the implicit ambition. That was the common ground between David, George and myself at school. I wanted to learn Buddy Holly numbers and they knew them.'

Jones and Underwood would spend entire weekends in the aisles at Furlong's, the local record shop, where David first took a part-time job. 'He was always a bit of a dreamer in that I'd give him a job to do, come back in about an hour and he was still chatting, the job unfinished, so that he had to go,' the shop's owner Vic Furlong said.

Jones and Underwood soon formed a group, George and the Dragons, with a small, revolving gang of like-minded classmates, allowing David a chance to test his musical ability and begin to learn rudimentary guitar strumming on an inexpensive guitar that John had purchased for him along with a tape recorder. 'David and I were pretty good at Everly Brothers-style harmonies and he definitely had a gift or a talent which at that time was difficult to put your finger on. We would sit for hours working out numbers and recording them on his little Grundig [tape recorder].' As with the sax lessons he would soon begin with horn player Ronnie Ross, these sessions inform his later approach to songwriting – natural, born of conversation and improvisation as opposed to any formal training; call it personal discipline.

'We'd all bring our guitars to school and slip them in my dad's office before assembly,' says Frampton, who formed his own group, the Little Ravens, at the time. 'And then at lunchtime he'd leave the door unlocked so we could go get the guitars and sit on the art block concrete stairs, which for guitar sound and vocal echo was perfect. George, myself and David would sit there and play all afternoon. They were the rebels with thin ties and rocker haircuts. I was twelve . . . I had the bowl cut.'

Turned away by John Jones and his mother, and rejoining the workforce himself at a printing company, Terry found solace in frequent trips into London and David would frequently accompany his brother on weekends. During this period, Terry seemed especially enthusiastic about ideas, whether they were found in books, in political treatises or on record. Ironically, like his stepfather, John, Terry was overjoyed that his little brother was becoming a rock 'n' roller, telling all who might listen, 'My brother's got a guitar!'

Alarmingly, Terry could not de-enthuse at the time. A harbinger of his incipient mental illness, Terry's energy seemed boundless and he'd rave about records or French philosophical texts by Sartre and Camus, which his impressionable little brother would dutifully attempt to absorb.

It was through Terry that David would discover London, which was slowly becoming an exciting city for the young again. Terry and David would take the forty-five-minute train ride into Victoria Station, disembark through that widemouth exit and emerge into the instant urban bustle.

'While I was still at school, I would go up to town every Saturday evening to listen to jazz at different clubs, and this was all happening to him when I was at a very impressionable age,' David recalled. 'He was growing his hair long and rebelling in his own way while I was still dressed up in school uniform every day. It all had a big impact on me.'

David had an instinctive feel and appreciation for jazz. It was a language that he could share with his brother. They engaged in rapid-fire discussion on the styles of Jimmy Smith, Zoot Sims, Wes Montgomery, John Coltrane. It was likely the American baritone sax player Gerry Mulligan, who arranged for Miles Davis in the late forties and formed an iconic combo with trumpeter Chet Baker in the fifties, that led David to actually want to pick up a horn himself. Mulligan was a progenitor of 'cool jazz.' He wore his hair close cropped, wore tight, expensive suits and generally cut a high-style figure.

'David was influenced by what his half brother, Terry, was listening to,' Underwood confirms. 'He introduced him to certain jazz records like Gerry Mulligan, who David modeled himself on for a couple of weeks. I am sure when the careers officer came to our school and asked us all what we wanted to do when we left that David was thinking of Gerry Mulligan when he said he wanted to be a saxophonist in a modern jazz quartet.'

John Jones next purchased a white, plastic baritone sax for his son from Furlong's after a typically small amount of persistence. Once equipped with an instrument, David decided, also typically, to fast-track his path toward jazz mastery. Poring over the classified ads in the local paper, he found an address for Ross, a renowned baritone player who performed with a combo known as the Jazzmakers. Ross, who passed away in 1991, had slicked-back hair and wore sharp suits just like Mulligan. He was the next best thing. Ross didn't give many lessons but the teenage enthusiast convinced him to take him on as a pupil.

'I didn't mind teaching if the pupil was really interested,' Ross said. 'I was teaching him about music in general – how scales were formed, about harmony, how to blow and breathe and a little about how to read music . . . I told him that playing the sax was like trying to get the sounds you hear in your head out through a horn and into a room. It wasn't just reproducing notes you saw on paper. It was creating a new language. Communicating your visions without speaking them.'

Ross found his young study to have an odd combination of shyness and hyperenthusiasm on a level that could never really last. Sure enough, after about four months, David decided that he'd learned enough and ended his sessions with Ross. Ross would resurface in the early seventies, when he was hired to perform the now iconic sax solo at the close of the Bowie and Mick Ronson-produced 'Walk on the Wild Side,' Lou Reed's biggest hit.

Terry was picking up his most explicit and exciting cues on how to really live from the new wave of literature by the Beats. He devoured William S. Burroughs, the poems of Gregory Corso and Allen Ginsberg, and Jack Kerouac and distilled their messages of freedom for David.

'My writing is a teaching,' Kerouac once noted in his journal. Terry Burns and, by extension, David Jones were avid students.

Through the Beats, David was also opened up to the concept of Buddhism and was soon reading up on meditation. He wrote a paper for his history class on Tibet and, around this time, saw a film on television about Chairman Mao Tse-tung's invasion of the country in 1951 and the subsequent oppression of Buddhist monks in an attempt to erase their culture and ancient practices. 'That made me interested in Tibet as a country and I started studying its history and its religion,' David has said, 'and while I was still at school, I wrote a thesis on it.' He saw a line from James Dean to Kerouac to Elvis Presley to the Tibetan monks in resistance to the Chinese: they were all rebels. None of the other students at Bromley spent the weekend at London jazz clubs or researching Buddhist monasteries in Scotland. While others were preparing for their inevitable induction into the nation's cramped and airless offices, David Jones was becoming another species entirely: a genuine rebel himself.

This spirit soon found another mentor in the form of Peter Frampton's father, Bromley Tech's unorthodox but august art instructor. Owen Frampton had been a successful graphic designer before he was hired at Bromley and knew both sides of the culture, the liberating and the confining energies that went along with the technical arts. By the time he met David, he had long since made the choice as far as what energy he wanted to pursue and impart. Frampton took David and his group of would-be artists and musicians under his wing. Like Terry Burns, the senior Frampton was a 'mad one,' as Kerouac wrote in *On the Road*. 'Mad to live, mad to talk, mad to be saved, desirous of everything at the same time.' He would not be limited by any curriculum or dress code, and his overjoyed young pupils followed suit.

'He became our mentor,' says Underwood. 'Owen was the best thing about Bromley Tech for me. He encouraged me and we were more like friends than teacher and pupil. If a pet student of Owen Frampton's got into trouble with one of Bromley Tech's other faculty members, Frampton would run interference.'

'He was the only teacher there who spoke to you as a human being,' says Kureishi. 'It was pretty crude, the teaching. It was pretty rough. In those days they still used to hit you with sticks.'

'He was always his own man,' Peter Frampton says. 'He didn't toe the line at all and it got him into trouble occasionally. Basically he had an idea of what he wanted to do and he did it. He made his own syllabus. If you were up for it, he'd take you all the way. You'd do a year and a half of what you were normally doing in college. He was a great artist himself but his joy was teaching. What he got back from what he was giving. I think his enthusiasm was something that people like David just latched on to. They saw a good thing. They couldn't believe that this guy was actually for them.' Owen Frampton was vociferous where John Jones was taciturn, and there was none of the Terry-related domestic drama in the art room. It was a safe space in which to create and scheme and feel strong and valuable.

'I believe he had an estranged father,' says Peter Frampton. 'Remote. For David being not only talented on the musical side but also very arty, he

59

loved my dad and saw this man would push him and was open. He became some sort of a father figure, yes.'

Under Owen Frampton, David learned to be both disciplined and an insurgent at the same time. He was and remains unusually professional in his approach to his rule breaking. If his classmates were wearing pointy-toed shoes, David would wear round-toed creepers. If their ties were tight, his tie would be loose. Peggy would taper his trousers and jackets to his specific details. He had an image in his mind of how he wanted to look, derived, mainly, from films and the album sleeves that lined the bins at Furlong's, and scrounged whatever he could from the local department store and, whenever possible, the shops in London.

'Clothes were a really big deal,' Kureishi says, alluding to some communal Bromley-ite mind-set. 'In the suburbs it was about originality and not being like other people. Being slightly different, sophisticated. You could get good clothes in Bromley but it helped if you wanted to be ahead of the other kids to get something amazing in London.'

Owen Frampton also encouraged Jones and Underwood to take their campus band as far as they could. He allowed them to keep their instruments in his classroom and even encouraged his young son to fraternize with them. Young Frampton was already an accomplished guitarist and was soon a friend of both boys. Twenty years later, he'd come alive, of course, but at the time, he was simply Professor Frampton's child. His group the Little Ravens performed alongside George and the Dragons at campus fetes and once at a school-wide talent competition.

Although Peter Frampton and David would remain friends and move in and out of each other's lives as both became pop stars (Frampton, ironically, would beat David Bowie to stardom as a guitarist with the Herd and Humble Pie in the late sixties), Frampton would not stay long at Bromley Tech. Owen Frampton's charisma and approach to education cast a long shadow for his son.

'I was only there a year because I found it difficult being at the same school as my father,' Frampton has said. 'A few kids, shall we say the one half percent who didn't get on too well with my father, made my life rather like a living hell.' Frampton would soon transfer out of Bromley.

The newly Beat David Jones was a magnet for the young girls from local Bromley High School and Bromley Grammar, and even some fellow students at the all-boys Bromley Tech. It was around this time, he claimed to have lost both his hetero and homosexual virginity.

'When I was fourteen, sex suddenly became all-important to me,' he told Cameron Crowe in their *Playboy* interview in '76. 'It didn't really matter who or what it was with, as long as it was a sexual experience. So it was some very pretty boy in class in some school or other that I took home and neatly fucked on my bed upstairs. And that was it.'

Both boys and girls were attracted to him because of his newly enhanced charisma and experience, and he did not differentiate between those who wished to pay a little physical tribute to it. Given the outrageousness of the Crowe interview it remains unclear just how extensively David explored his sexuality at the time. Surely the Beats, who he admired and took cues from, were frank about such experimentations, but both his best friend George Underwood and future wife Angie maintain that David's motivation was 'pussy,' or 'the p word,' as they described it respectively. If his claim to Crowe is true, fastidious Peggy could not have possibly approved of any same-sex screwing under her own roof; perhaps she would have taken solace in the fact that he did it 'neatly.'

David's sexual fervour could, on occasion, get him into trouble. 'We did have a falling-out over one girl,' Underwood recalls. 'Carol Goldsmith.' This event, which took place in the spring of 1961, has become a legendary part of the Bowie creation myth, and its result has been attributed to a Brixton street fight and even named as evidence of his extra-terrestrial origins, as surely nobody born on planet Earth has mismatched eyes like that. The reality is that he cock-blocked his best friend and schoolmate and got slugged for it.

'When I was fourteen I fell in love with a girl,' David said in 1973. 'I can't even remember her name now – but at the time I was crazy about her. Only trouble was, my best mate had a bit of a soft spot for her, too. I was the winner. Quicker off the mark, I suppose! I moved in before he'd even made up his mind how to approach her. Anyway – next day I was at school boasting to my mate about what a Casanova I was and he became terribly annoyed. In fact he threw a punch at me!'

In actuality, David didn't seduce her as much as make it impossible for Underwood to have a chance. 'David would probably say that he can't remember the actual story,' Underwood has said, 'but he can remember things clearly if he chooses to. He knew damn well why I did it. We both wanted to go out with her and I was lucky enough to get a date. On the day [of the date] David rang me up and said that she had to cancel. So I didn't go, but he'd made up the whole story. The girl stood around for over an hour, waiting for me, as I discovered later. It was a bastard thing to do and I was furious with him, so it developed into a fight between us. And during the punch-up, I caught his eye with a fingernail.'

'It caught me in the eye, and I stumbled against a wall and onto my knees,' David recalled. 'At first he thought I was kidding – it wasn't a very hard punch. But it had obviously caught me at rather an odd angle.'

Underwood accompanied David to the school

63

secretary's office, where the injured eye was treated with cold compresses. The nurse arrived and soon it became clear that the damage was a bit more serious. David was taken to nearby Farnsborough Hospital. There, doctors noticed that the sphincter muscles of his left eye were badly torn, preventing the pupil from dilating or contracting. David's parents rushed to their son's bedside to comfort him.

'At first they thought I'd lose my eye,' he recalled. 'I was scared stiff.' Doctors managed to save David's eye and his sight was not seriously affected, but the cosmetic aspects of the condition would be permanent.

'For quite a while I was very embarrassed about it,' David said in the early seventies. 'Although I could see very well out of the eye, it made me self-conscious.' David grew to relish the attention. He had already started to use his distinctive qualities, his pale, thin androgynous physique to attract it. Now he had something that nobody else had: a screwed-up eye. Rock 'n' roll has a long tradition of stars using their physical flaws in ways that make them unique and sexy. Pete Townshend did little to hide his outsized nose and in fact he held it high and regal. Prince's stature, Meatloaf's girth, Joey Ramone's gangly frame, Dolly Parton's cup size – each of them probably found their unique feature to be a liability during their awkward teenage years but surely felt grateful for the distinction it provided once they were in their twenties.

'We didn't have the Web back then, had no way of knowing the details of why he had that bad eye,' Professor Camille Paglia, a Bowie fan since the early 1970s, told me. 'Now we have much more info about what happened, but at the time, it gave him an abstract look. It made him look like a mannequin. Like Nefertiti. He really does. His face during the *Aladdin Sane* period has a strangled Nefertiti look. Mysterious. The idea of having one eye that sees and one eye that has been touched or blighted in some way, in myth and legend, it implies mystic powers. The bad eye sees within. Sees invisible things. It's uncanny. It's eerie that Bowie has the regular eye and this strange eye that's always permanently dilated . . . always looking but not really seeing. He has a dual vision, really. To me that's symbolic of major artists anyway. They see the physical world and they see the spiritual world. To me they are oracular. Often in legends the artists have a handicap. Homer was blind, so and so was lame. You are physically incapacitated in some way but it gives you this special gift. That blighted eye is the sign of Bowie's special gift, the hallucinatory part of his imagination.'

CHAPTER 4

David left Bromley in the summer of 1963, when he was sixteen. Those who weren't going on to college at that age were expected to get an entry-level job in an office, shop, food service establishment or factory. Despite his intelligence and creativity, David's was a less than sterling academic record. He passed only two 'O-levels,' or final exams. 'I would have got three but they don't award them for imagination,' he would later quip.

Bromley Tech's careers officer responded to David's declaration that he wanted to find work as a professional musician by pointing him toward an open position in a nearby factory that produced harps, but David politely ignored this suggestion. John Jones found him temporary work as an electrician's assistant but he only helped with minimal wiring before politely declining to show up for work ever again. Finally, Owen Frampton pulled some strings and found him work as a designer at the London branch of the famous ad agency J. Walter Thompson.

J. Walter Thompson, or JWT as it's commonly

known today, was and is an industry giant, the first-ever global firm (founded in 1864), responsible for some of the best-known branding images in English and American pop history (from Prudential Life Insurance to Cadbury chocolates). Even a walk-in position at a prestigious corporation like this might have led to a long career in the field. The notion of a finely-tailored young David Bowie as modish *Mad Man* is certainly intriguing. However, David was only a bit more enthusiastic about this than he was about his part-time electrician gig and only because the position would enable him to spend his days in London.

Sometimes he would stay in the city and walk around, browsing the cafés, record shops and boutiques that were springing up daily in light of the continuing economic boom that Britain was then enjoying. There was, however, always the specter of that last train back to Bromley at eleven thirty. If he'd meet a girl or a fellow rock 'n' roller he found interesting, he knew he'd have to extricate himself from whatever experience in order to make it home.

'The last train was a huge part of our lives,' says Hanif Kureishi. 'The last train was a big deal for people from Bromley. If you got the last train you were lucky. Otherwise you had to sit at the station till morning. You know. You had to get the last train or you stayed up all night in London. You had to make this decision whether you're going to pull this chick or whether you're going to make the last train. It was a nightmare.'

'He only took the job for his father's sake, because his father thought that all this business with groups and music could well be a passing fad and that at least if he spent a year or so at work, it would give him some stable grounding to fall back on,' Peggy said. 'So David did go to work there, though not without protest. I can remember him coming home and moaning about his "blooming job" and traveling up and down on the train.'

David's job title, 'junior visualizer,' was appropriately vague. The firm represented various clients, pasting up ads for raincoats and even a dietary cookie with the unfortunate brand name 'Ayds' (which has since been discontinued for obvious reasons).

In all his meanderings outside the office, Dobell's, one of the city's best record shops at the time, located nearby on Charing Cross Road, was where he could be found on most days.

'My immediate boss, Ian, a groovy modernist with a Gerry Mulligan-style short-crop haircut and Chelsea boots, was very encouraging about my passion for music, something he and I both shared,' Bowie recalled in 1993. 'He used to send me on errands to Dobell's, knowing I'd be there for most of the morning till well after lunch break. It was there, in the bins, that I found Bob Dylan's first album. Ian had sent me there to get him a John Lee Hooker release and advised me to pick up a copy for myself, as it was so wonderful.'

'Dobell's was *the* record shop,' George Underwood says. 'David played me some fuckin' great music he picked up there. Mingus, Kirk, Dr John, John Lee Hooker – loads of wicked blues records.'

By 1960, the blues had replaced the first wave of rock 'n' roll as the fave rave music for hip young Londoners. With Little Richard a born-again Christian, Elvis enlisted in the army in Germany, Chuck Berry in jail for violating the Mann Act, Buddy Holly dead in a plane crash and Jerry Lee Lewis plagued by a scandal after bringing his thirteen-year-old cousin and child bride overseas on a 1958 British tour, it seemed like the initial excitement and danger of rock had faded. In the place of the revolutionary first wave came a crop of pleasant pop crooners, like Matt Monro, or clueless teen idols who were in no hurry to change the culture. Many of these were discovered and managed by a figure named Larry Parnes, who would not have been out of place on our current *American Idol* panel. Parnes, clean-cut and handsome himself, was happy to prefabricate stars, package them with a Tin Pan Alley-penned 'hit' and foist them condescendingly on the hungry teenage market. With ethnically vague names like Johnny Gentle, Vince Eager, Marty Wilde, Tommy Steele and Dickie Pride, many of these pop singers borrowed their look from an American icon like Presley or Sinatra but held none of their raw charisma or even adult sexuality. Only the Shadows, featuring Cliff Richard, were an English chart act that wrote their own songs, played their own instruments and seemed relatively authentic. They too were derivative of American acts like the Ventures, but they were a point of pride nonetheless for young rockers like David, George Underwood and Peter Frampton.

'The Shadows were our wildly loved band,' Frampton says. 'They influenced everybody.' While barely known in America outside of a pocket of Anglophiles, the Shadows had a very strong effect on the early leather-clad Beatles who would soon adopt a similar look, if only because of their presentation (smart suits, long hair).

'[Shadows front man] Cliff Richard was a poor copy of Elvis Presley,' says music publicist Greg Tesser. 'In everything he did, even the curled lip. They were boring. The wild men were gone and in their place, you had this real sort of cosmetic, this very sort of sanitized stuff, and it was very boring indeed.'

'Some of the guys who were part of the original rock scene were quite edgy initially but it all softened down,' Dick Taylor, of British R & B legends the Pretty Things, says today. 'One year you had Gene Vincent and the next year you had people like Greg Douglas. For anybody who was really into music, rock 'n' roll was losing its thing. We were pissed off with the fact that there wasn't anything there anymore. It just sort of went into pop pap.'

Working up a passionate interest in the blues seemed an antidote to such cynical and self-interested offerings. Blues artists like Little Walter and Sonny Boy Williamson found themselves in great demand for lucrative overseas gigs. Marginalized in their own country, they were greeted like heroes when they flew to London to play to packed crowds in dank, subterranean cafés in Soho. They also found a presence on BBC radio.

'The BBC had a musicians' union ban on it about playing records. They got 'round this a bit by playing classic *R & B* records in programs that were designated either history or education. This built a market for artists of this genre and many started coming to the UK on small tours – often with trad [traditional] jazz bands. The BBC would put a live band behind them and do live broadcasts and the whole R & B genre grew in popularity,' Simon Napier-Bell says.

The rampant popularity of these easy-to-play but emotionally complex and effortlessly cool forms soon inspired bored teens all over England to found their own soul and R & B combos, all with an eye toward gaining a recording contract. Suddenly, every lead singer needed to play the harmonica. The older pop labels like Decca had signed the Rolling Stones from Dartford. EMI had signed the Beatles from, of course, Liverpool.

71

Pye signed the Kinks from North London and the High Numbers, who would soon change their name to the Who. Months before they would explode, each of these bands was working up their act. There were dozens more: the aforementioned Pretty Things (Taylor was an old art school classmate of the Stones' Keith Richards), Downliners Sect, Van Morrison's early band Them, Long John Baldry and the Hoochie Coochie Men, Zoot Money's Big Roll Band (featuring Andy Summers, later of the Police), Georgie Fame and the Blue Flames, Brian Auger and the Trinity, Chris Farlowe and the Thunderbirds, Graham Bond Organization, Alexis Korner's Blues Inc., Cyril Davies All-Stars, John Mayall's Bluesbreakers.

By '63 London's sweaty underground clubs, modeled on the Parisian jazz cellars, could no longer accommodate the blues-crazed teenagers, and one by one these acts came up from the caverns and took over proper jazz venues like the Marquee. To some, playing the blues in a 'trad' jazz venue was tantamount to Dylan going electric a few years later. 'All the bollocks the snobby jazz fan put on the blues,' Taylor says. 'They thought if you're a musician somehow you can't just enjoy playing. You're selling out.'

To David Jones, now sixteen, the blues boom raised his hopes that a suburban outsider could find a thriving scene in the city, make a living, meet girls and mates, and feel, for once in his life, like he was a part of something massive and growing, rather than some marginalized art school pocket. 'You'd have lots of people who'd come around the stage at the end of our shows, from Bromley or Sidcup Art College. Lost souls who, like us, thought they were weird and different and yet, when they were in a place where music was played, suddenly didn't feel such a weirdo,' Phil May, the Pretty Things' lead singer, has said.

'The clubs were all full,' Joe Boyd, the legendary producer (Pink Floyd's 'Arnold Layne,' Nick Drake's *Pink Moon* album) and author (*White Bicycles*), says. At the time, Boyd, an American, brought many of the original blues artists over. 'The kids cheered Muddy Waters when he played. They knew all about him. There was a way bigger catalog of blues and jazz in British record shops than in the U.S. shops.'

While you won't find a more American form than the blues, the new breed, unlike their Teddy Boy subcultural predecessors, did not dress like Americans. Instead, they fully embraced the sharp-edged, fine sartorial traditions of English tailoring. The mod aesthetic was all about slim and sleek lines as opposed to a conglomerate of shapes and materials. The trousers were skinny and the jackets were three-buttoned, with each of them pulled in tight. The ties were narrow. The hair was spiky but neat. Whereas the Teds were hard men, the mod boys were androgynous. It wasn't necessarily a sexual thing. They used eyeliner and pancake makeup to extend the sharp

73

lines of their clothes to their facial bone structure. If the Teds were purists, happy to preserve and protect an idealized 'cats and chicks' version of postwar youth, the mods, true to their nickname (short for 'modern') flipped over anything new and fluid, heading for tomorrow.

'By the time we're buying you, you'll be going off in one of these,' Tom Courtenay's boss tells him in John Schlesinger's 1963 film, *Billy Liar*. Billy Fisher works in a funeral home, and the partially bemused, partially terrified older man is holding up a sleek plastic coffin. 'You see, people don't realize it's all clean lines nowadays. All these frills and fancies are going out. It's all old.'

An organized and disciplined reaction to the staid, gray, sugar- and butter-free England of the immediate postwar years and early fifties, mods made and spent money like no youth movement before it. Anything that smacked of the fast (scooters, speed, jerky dancing) and new (existential French lit, the films of Fellini and Antonioni in Rome or Godard and Truffaut in Paris, the pop art of Warhol and Lichtenstein and the high-style advertising and fashion design coming out of New York and London) was appealing and quickly consumed.

Mod was a movement *made* for David Jones. The speedy drugs and vast consumer ambitions synonymous with mod (not to mention the idealistic thirst for the 'new') hit David right when you want to be hit by such things: at fifteen or sixteen years of age. He took to mod fervidly, and the ethics of the movement also have a lot to do with his lifelong compulsion to be creative and always seek out the new style. In his teens, he began to refer to his type as a 'raver' because of the logorrhea that went hand in hand with the speedy drugs and the excitement of each new discovery. Since his time in Owen Frampton's art room, David maintained an intense interest in painting and would learn as much as he could about the lives of painters and sculptors, and imagine that one day he might live in a garret in a dirty smock. He continued to create his own paintings and was almost never without something to sketch on. But the immediacy of the fast-developing rhythm and blues and Northern Soul scene was hard to resist, and the portability of a horn or guitar seemed to make sorties into London easier and quicker.

The wit and flash of the new wave of British cinema, fully informed by the mod movement by the early sixties, provided an epic, painterly, visual stimulation anyway. David and his friends could now see themselves in the new breed of working-class movie heroes, from Terence Stamp to Richard Harris to Peter O'Toole and Michael Caine. Even Sean Connery, in the very early Bond films *Dr No* and *From Russia with Love*, had a certain mod appeal.

Musically, by trying to copy black soul music, many of the English mod combos invented something entirely new: maximum R & B, with

England's contribution being speed and volume. The mods did not have the chops and the flow of the Americans, so they distorted the amps. Using attitude and style to compensate for limited instrumental and vocal ability, these acts soon discovered that a five-year-old Chuck Berry tune could sound entirely new.

'There was more blues being played in 1963 in Kingston in Surrey in England than there was in Chicago,' says Tesser. The best of these acts avoided simply trying to sound 'black' and tried to use the lyrics and phrasing as a way to articulate their own feelings. Some of the original intent was, of course, lost in translation. 'When a downtrodden black southerner sang "I'm a man" he meant "I'm a human being,"' says Napier-Bell. 'When Mick Jagger or Eric Burdon sang it, they meant "I've got a hard-on."'

The other foundation of the mod sound was the Stax and Tamla Motown hits that were played on 'pirate,' or non-BBC-regulated, radio stations that were broadcast in the early sixties with strong enough frequencies to pick up a clear sound and a beat. English kids would go out of their way to become pen pals with American kids in order to get the latest records to play live at parties. Soul music, unabashedly emotional, hit a chord with the mannered but incredibly frustrated British youth. Soul songs about unrequited love or blues men singing about oppression and a hidden voodoo was the right message at the right time, and the new youth were feverish.

By 1963, George and the Dragons had mutated into a more professional outfit known as the Konrads, augmented by Dave Hadfield on bass, Rocky Shanahan on guitar and Robert Allen on drums. They eventually added background singers Stella and Christine Patton for local gigs. Their new name was derived from one of these performances. The group, used to any pickup work, was backing up a local pop singer named Jesse Conrad. According to legend, he introduced them as 'my Conrads,' as a play on 'comrades,' and the name stuck. The hyphen was added as a pure flourish. One of Bromley's go-to bands for fetes and functions, they worked up a large repertoire on the bar mitzvah circuit, thanks to endless requests for the pop songs of the day, from Cliff Richard's 'The Young Ones' to the Champs' sax instrumental 'Tequila.' They rehearsed on campus and had a small coterie of loyal but local fans, but at the end of the day, they were a hopelessly suburban venture.

Flush with the excitement of mod culture, David, who was then flirting with the stage name 'David Jay' (tellingly, inspired by a similar but much more successful act, the Jaywalkers), felt constrained by the Konrads' gray corduroy suits and rote 'bread gigs.' His ambition once again put him at odds with the others around him.

'The Kon-Rads played the school fairs, or fetes, as we called them,' Frampton says. 'I remember just being awestruck by them, seeing someone I knew like that onstage playing sax. He was good straightaway. He had it. He knew he had it.'

David wanted to be a full-time star and sensed that this combo might not be able to keep pace with him on his way toward making it happen. David was about to inform his mates that he was moving on when the Kon-Rads caught a break. In the late summer of 1963, the band caught the attention of Eric Easton, the Decca records agent who had recently signed the Rolling Stones. Easton had seen the band play a youth club fete and invited them to audition for the label. On August 30, the band carted their gear into the label's studios in West Hampstead for a session. They recorded an original composition entitled 'I Never Dreamed.' David cowrote the track but can only be heard singing harmony on the backing vocals. The band was terribly excited to find themselves in a professional studio, listening to the playback of the track on the highest-tech hardware in the word. It seemed, for a few minutes, anyway, like they'd made it.

Decca turned down the option to record the Kon-rads, as did legendary producer and tragic cult figure Joe Meek, who was highly sought after thanks to his international hit 'Telstar,' and shortly thereafter David left the band for good. Underwood followed soon afterward. The Kon-Rads continued on without him for a while, opening for the Rolling Stones on their 1965 tour and issuing the single 'Baby It's Too Late Now' that same year on CBS Records before vanishing into obscurity.

'I Never Dreamed' lives on, however. It's noteworthy among David Bowie's compulsively bootlegged recording output for its scarcity. '"I Never Dreamed" has become the Bowie fan's holy grail,' Nicholas Pegg writes in *The Complete David Bowie*, an encyclopedic guide to his music, tours, film appearances and videos.

By the time David Jones parted ways with the Kon-Rads in the early fall of '63, the Beatles had performed for the Queen and scored three number one UK singles. They were rapidly demonstrating just how far a rock and soul-reared combo could go with the right chemistry, timing and drive. David would spend the rest of the 1960s trying to master this combination.

Everybody in the British music industry knew that the Beatles began as a rough-and-tumble, leather-jacketed quartet, and that after they were cleaned up by their manager, Brian Epstein, the masses were able to appreciate their good looks, quick wit and talent. They'd become a perfect product and were endlessly marketable. Timing and fate played a role in their breaking America as their first three singles had flopped here in 1963. Beatlemania offered a powerful balm to a nation traumatized by the assassination of President Kennedy in Dallas on November 22, 1963. It was only one bleak holiday season before their storming *Ed Sullivan Show* appearance in

February, of '64. Of course, nearly a half century on, nobody in pop has accomplished anything close to what the Beatles did, but in '63 and '64, who was to say that any cunning manager couldn't have a Beatles of their own? 'Why was Epstein so special?,' they surmised. 'All you needed was the right face, the right angle and bit of good luck.' As Tin Pan Alley understood it, it was all about publicity. Suddenly the song pluggers switched to a Mersey beat and A & R men signed any act with a northern accent and every London band with a mop top, and the publicists attempted to exploit the postwar culture shift. It was into this market-place that David Jones entered, searching for a break that would put him on the same mantel as John, Paul, George and Ringo.

The Soho rhythm and blues clubs like the Flamingo, the Crawdaddy and the Marquee became places where a clever manager or label rep could scout at both midday and evening showcases. The crowd was overwhelmingly teenage and hormonal, amounting in theory to a contained focus group for selecting the next Beatles or Stones.

'Soho was one part of London then that you could go to and you didn't think you were in England anymore,' Greg Tesser says. 'It was because all the smells, every restaurant or café, was either Greek or Italian or French or Indian. It was something; it was like an international zone. The club itself was extremely sweaty. And lots of people had obviously been taking Purple Hearts.' David Jones knew that the Marquee and the neighboring coffee bar, the Café Giaconda, where kids also mingled with industry types, had officially become the center of the universe, and he buzzed around this stretch semipermanently, even sleeping in a van outside the Marquee at one point. To his parents' great concern, he left his 'junior visualizer' post at J. Walter Thompson and committed to pursuing a career in music full-time.

For a matter of weeks, David and Underwood formed a blues combo (with Viv Andrews on drums) called the Hooker Brothers. 'We would try and copy John Lee Hooker,' Underwood told me. 'Of all the blues records, his was the one we had the most success with. So much so that we called ourselves the Hooker Brothers for a short while, did a couple of gigs, then went on to something else.'

For the King Bees, his next outfit (named after the blues track 'I'm a King Bee' by Slim Harpo, later covered by both the Rolling Stones and John Belushi, the latter on *Saturday Night Live* while dressed in a bumblebee suit), David formally gave himself a professional, buccaneer-themed stage name: Davie Jones. With the exception of Underwood (now a student at Ravensboume College, studying art but happily back for a second shot at Beatles-style fame), the King Bees (also featuring Roger Bluck on lead guitar, Dave Howard on bass and Bob Allen on percussion) were all Londoners. They'd met in the capital at a hairstylist's, according to the band's bio. Although band bios are almost never accurate and always exaggerated to suit an image, the band certainly fed far more off the energy of the London scene than the Kon-Rads ever did or could.

The Beatles success and their appeal was apparent even to those of David's parents' generation. On the advice of his father, David sat down one afternoon and he wrote out a persuasive letter to the wealthy and well-connected Jewish washing machine impresario John Bloom. Bloom had become a society columns figure. The Beatles had attended cocktail parties in his Park Lane apartment.

'I had been reading a lot in the papers about John Bloom,' David is quoted as saying in the band's early promotional material. 'So I put pen to paper and wrote him a letter.' David told Bloom that he had a chance to back one of the most talented and up-and-coming groups on the pop scene. All he had to do was advance the several hundred pounds required to outfit a pop group with the best equipment.

Bloom, of course, declined to invest in an unknown act but admired the 'cheeky' quality of the pitch and passed them on to an acquaintance named Leslie Conn who had solid music business credentials. Conn, who was affiliated with Doris Day's publishing company Melcher Music, was a colorful character who once described himself as 'the only guy in the music business who started at the top and worked my way to the bottom.'

He had been a producer at Decca Records, the home of the Rolling Stones, and had worked with Dick James, the Beatles' publisher, but his irreverent nature kept him from advancing too far up the ladder. 'Les was out there,' says Shel Talmy, the great music producer (the Kinks' 'You Really Got Me,' the Who's 'I Can't Explain') who would later produce David's bands the Manish Boys and the Lower Third. By the time Conn met 'Davie Jones' during an impromptu audition at his Marble Arch residence, he was in need of an act to reestablish him as a player. He felt this was it. 'You can always tell talent,' he said, 'like a tailor handles a piece of cloth – the feel, the sensitivity.'

Conn admired Jones's attitude and youthful confidence. He had not made it but was already acting as if he and his combo were as big as the Fab Four or the Stones. 'David had a total belief in his own talent,' Conn has said. 'He was amazingly arrogant. "I'm the greatest and I don't give a fuck who knows it." He was totally dedicated to what he did. He believed with a passion that he was going to be a big star. And I believed in him as much as he believed in himself.'

Conn signed the King Bees. He tried and failed to get them a publishing deal with Dick James at Decca but was resourceful in finding them work playing a wedding anniversary party (for Bloom and his wife) at the Soho venue the Jack of Clubs.

The reception was lukewarm, however, and immediately diminished some of the band's already puffed-up bravado.

'It was all a bit embarrassing,' David later recalled. 'The party was posh with many of the guests in evening dress. And we turned up in our T-shirts and jeans ready to play rhythm and blues. We really worked hard that night but many of them just ignored us and carried on talking as though we weren't there.'

'Liza Jane,' Davie Jones and the King Bees' debut single, issued June 5, 1964, on Decca's Vocalion Pop subsidiary, is the first officially issued David-related product.

The A side, a traditional blues song despite Conn's songwriting credit, sounds as though it was recorded in an airplane lavatory post-flush. It sucks and hisses and churns but has real charm even as the instruments bleed, the background-vocals croak and David's voice, still tentative and thinner than it would soon become, strains and strains to sound big, black and experienced. 'Liza Jane' nonetheless possesses a crucial rock 'n' roll ingredient: swagger. One begins to sing along with the 'Hey . . . Liza' chorus within seconds. The press release issued with the single heralds it as a 'beaty, action packed disc.' Not far off, but, as history would soon bear out, not yet enough.

Possibly much more interesting to Bowie-ists is the B side, 'Louie Louie Go Home,' recorded during the same seven-hour session at Decca's

West Hampstead studios in the spring of 1964. Although it is technically a cover of an *homage to a cover* (the King Bees doing Paul Revere and the Raiders name-checking the Kingsmen's totemic version of 'Louie, Louie'), it's valuable, as you can actually listen to David playing with his voice, experimenting as he goes, hitting weird high notes that will show up a decade later on 'Young Americans' and 'Golden Years.'

For some odd reason all of David's would-be hit singles up until the very late sixties have superior B sides. It's almost as if they were chosen by people who had absolutely no idea what he was truly capable of creating . . . and they probably were. Still, the press releases are priceless. One informs: 'He dislikes Adams apples, and lists as his interests Baseball, American Football and collecting Boots. Davie Jones has all it takes to get to the show business heights, including . . . talent.'

He wouldn't get there right away. 'Liza Jane' was reviewed on the popular *Juke Box Jury* reviews show the day after its release and given a lukewarm reception. The British sex symbol Diana Dors (who would later be immortalized on the cover sleeve of a Smiths singles collection) didn't dig it at all. The single failed. Hearing it played on television for the first time was certainly thrilling and increased the attendance at their club shows, but it ultimately provided the King Bees with a teasing glimpse of what was out there.

David was not going to stay with the King Bees for long. He had too much to lose. Bromley and the quiet life his family was living out was the only other option. College or being content behind an office desk was not for him.

'It's all right for you lot; you're at college,' David said to Underwood at the time. 'I've left the [advertising] agency and I'm in this up to my neck.'

CHAPTER 5

David Jones wasn't the only seventies British rock susperstar to fail to channel the sixties Beat boom into glory. Marc Feld would wait out the decade with nothing but whimsical image experimentation and titanic ambition to go on. Inside of a half decade Jones would be Bowie and Feld would be Marc Bolan, engine of the Bolan boogie and focal point of 'T. Rexstasy.' They would battle for the singular loyalty of pop music fans and serious consideration from the rock press. 'In my school you had to pick a side. One of the reasons I got into Bowie late, some time after the Ziggy *Stardust* album, was due to my allegiance to Marc Bolan,' Gary Numan says. 'To even buy a Bowie a record felt like a betrayal of T. Rex.' And yet, this sense of 'one or the other' began the better part of a full decade earlier, when neither of them were even semi-famous beyond the fading mod scene. When eighteen-year-olds David Jones and Marc Bolan first encountered each other in the offices of Les Conn (who managed both pop aspirants in 1965) a lasting sense of genuinely valuable competition was created, one that helped both survive their initial commercial disappointments. They were British pop's Shelley and Byron, or at least the notion that they could or should be was powerful. Marc Bolan, it is seldom noted nowadays, remains every inch the icon that Bowie is. He is worshipped just as intensely but ultimately not by as many people. His is a perfect pop death cult, which sometimes overshadows all those excellent T. Rex albums and singles. Bowie's career is fluid, Bolan's frozen. He never had a chance to be a futurist, and among those who knew him there are those who insist that he was content to offer up retro pleasures (Chuck Berry riffs, double-tracked crooning about girls and cars) for all time.

'Marc Bolan was a much bigger deal [in the early seventies],' veteran British rock writer Charles Shaar Murray says. 'Bowie seemed to be offering everything T. Rex were offering, but there was a lot going on for grown-ups. Bolan was writing a lot of lyrics that were catchphrases and cute rhymes. They didn't actually make any sense. They were fun to listen to. Ear-candy. Whereas Bowie's songwriting was a lot more coherent. When you scratched the surface of Bolan's lyrics, you know, you were through to fresh air. You scratched the surface of Bowie's lyrics and there seemed to be a lot going on.' Shaar Murray compares Bolan to 'a little jeweled snake,' adding, 'He talked a very good game in terms of substance but he didn't deliver in terms of the work. I think an awful lot of bravado. We have a saying in Britain, 'More front than Harrods.' Marc was pretty much all facade. It was a great facade. As facades go I would give it very high marks but it was a Potemkin village. With Bowie you walked through the front door and you were in this huge cathedral of mirrors. This mirrored maze.'

Although small with kinky hair (adjectives he would use to describe himself in the T. Rex tracks 'Spaceball Richochet' and 'Telegram Sam,' respectively), Bolan certainly appeared as darkly romantic as Lord Byron. His face seemed unique, cherubic in the cheeks but with a chiseled jaw. His speaking voice had a slight lisp but was raspy, wry and given to hipster parlance (each observation punctuated by a winking 'man'). Marc Feld was born in the borough of Hackney in East London on September 30, 1947. His mother and father, Simon and Phyllis Feld, were working-class Jews. Simon drove a transport van. Like David Jones, Marc spent his childhood in front of the movie screen or the TV set. By his tenth birthday, he was mad for American rock 'n' roll and had also decided that he wanted to be a star.

As with David, Marc's parents also supported his interest in music, outfitting him with a guitar and a drum kit, which he taught himself to play. According to Bolan legend, this process was expedited when Marc touched American rock star

Eddie Cochran's guitar after a gig in Hackney. The magic rubbed off, and possibly the curse too, as both Marc Bolan and Cochran, also small in stature, would die young in London car crashes (Cochran died in the spring of 1960 at age twenty-two). Cochran appears in *The Girl Can't Help It* as well, performing the great 'Twenty Flight Rock.'

By thirteen Marc too had his first group: Susie and the Hula Hoops, with lead singer Helen Shapiro on vocals. Shapiro would go on to have several huge pop hits and enjoys cult status today as another beloved British (and Jewish) singing star. Like David Jones, Marc was a teenage rebel and a smart but underperforming and tempestuous student. There are stories of him kicking classmates and others who crossed him. For a brief time he was even purportedly a member of a *West Side Story*-worthy street gang actually known as the Sharks.

'He could see no point in what he was being taught,' biographer Tony Stringfellow writes in his study *The Wizard's Gown – Rewoven*, 'it held no purpose for him.' A school friend is quoted as saying, 'He was only ever interested in music and clothes.'

In his very early teens, Marc was discovered by a London modeling agent and began to earn his boutique money by posing for catalog ads. Unlike David, who has confessed to doing so, Marc was too proud to go crawling through any garbage cans to pick up discarded wardrobe items (a common mod boy practice). This may be a key difference between the two. There was a strong element of David's personality that was and is constantly searching, but Marc Bolan it seems preferred to stay put and have people and things simply come his way, doting and gushing. And they did, including modeling agents, the gay proprietors of the mod boutiques opening up in London's Carnaby Street, and later, of course, obsessed fans. David Jones, and later David Bowie, pursued such things doggedly. Marc puffed out his chest and simply accepted them as tribute to his magical charisma. This isn't to suggest that Marc the musician remained completely sedentary. He was gifted and intuitive in both his writing and guitar playing (both of which remain quite underrated). Like David, he was highly adept at picking and choosing from other artists and arranging a sort of magpie's nest full of style. There are photos of him clutching a guitar and wearing the same type of snap-brim cap that Bob Dylan wore during his Woody Guthrie-influenced phase. Marc called himself 'Toby Tyler' then and for a brief time played the city's folk venues. An early outfit, John's Children, combined Who-style proto-punk with the startling, tremulous baritone borrowed from soul man Billy Eckstine (an effect Bolan would refine throughout his career, developing a tone that would be much imitated in itself). His restrained playing on the pastoral Tyrannosaurus Rex albums ('The Throat of Winter' on 1969's *Unicorn* out-Nick Drakes Nick

Drake for foliage-hued folk splendor) is as gentle as the tough, salivating and hypersexual fifties-style riffs on *Electric Warrior* and *The Slider* by T. Rex. Bolan defenders point out that this indeed amounts to a complex and varied body of early work. Still, even if he hadn't gone spangly and a bit static with the bubblegum once he hit on a working formula, Bolan's versatility and musicianship were certain to be upstaged by his Napoleonic ego and penchant for boasting to the eager rock press. He claimed in 1971, for example, 'I definitely believe in reincarnation. I believe that all my lyrical ability was learned in a past life as a bard.' Whether taken seriously or not, Bolan remains a major figure in both David Jones's and later David Bowie's life and career, *and* in rock 'n' roll.

Shortly before meeting David, Marc Feld had experienced a life-altering encounter with 'the Wizard.' The Wizard was likely just that, a fantasy creature, sprung from Marc's imagination, but he insisted on more than one occasion that shortly before changing his name permanently to Bolan (after a very brief period as Bowland), Marc was whisked off to see the Wizard at his forty-room château near the Bois de Boulogne. He'd encountered the robe-clad mysterio in a London street. There, with only his cosmic tutor and a barn owl for company, he was tutored in the ways of magic, forming a new, heightened persona and writing verses such as 'Golden eagles at his door / Cats and bats played on the floor.'

'He was a magician actually, very powerful man, very learned man,' Bolan told a reporter years later. 'I learnt a lot of very important things off him, just sort of mythology, good things. I read a lot of books. He had amazing books there, books by Aleister Crowley and handwritten books and things like that. Then I came back home again.'

The first thing Bolan did upon returning to London was (perhaps inevitably) suffer a nervous breakdown (suggesting his time with the Wizard may have been a drug-fueled hallucination). One of the next things he did was record an ode to his magic pal as an audition for Decca records, which released it in 1965. It was not a hit but stands as a harbinger of the cosmic dippy-and-horny-poet mysticism that would make Tyrannosaurus Rex (a duo with Steve Peregrine Took on bongos and Bolan on acoustic guitar) so dense and fascinating, and later the electrified (and nominally abbreviated) T. Rex so commercially massive.

By the time he met David Jones, Feld was formally and professionally 'Bolan' and strongly convinced that he was going to be a huge pop star. It's now hard to believe but the meeting of these two rock icons was as humble as it could have possibly been. Les Conn, managing Bolan and Jones, had promised both future icons some much-needed spending money to whitewash his office.

'Both Marc and I were out of work,' Bowie would later recall, 'and we met when we poured into the manager's office to whitewash the walls. So there's me and this mod whitewashing the office and he goes, 'Where'd you get those shoes, man?' And I asked, 'Where'd you get your shirt?' We immediately started talking about clothes and sewing machines. 'Oh, I'm gonna be a singer and I'm gonna be so big you're not gonna believe it, man.' 'Oh right. Well I'll probably write a musical for you one day then 'cause I'm gonna be the greatest writer ever. No no, man, you gotta hear my stuff 'cause I write great things and I knew a wizard in Paris!' It was all this. Just white-washing walls in our manager's office.'

Marc Bolan was slightly younger but much less introverted than David, giving him the influence of an *older* sibling. Until David blazed past him forever, circa 1973, Marc, it can be argued, held the upper hand in the relationship. He would suggest the use of the signature Stylophone on David Bowie's first hit single, 'Space Oddity,' in '69. It would be Bolan who would first flirt with electric volume, glitter and genderbending while David was still a folkie.

'David idolized Marc for a while,' Bowie's future manager Ken Pitt, who for a time considered but ultimately passed on managing Bolan, observed. 'He was going around to his flat night after night, playing songs, listening to songs, talking about music, and then he'd come back here and we'd talk about our own projects and David would say, "Well, Marc says this," or, "Marc says that . . ."

Bolan had a tremendous influence on him at that time, and David considered him an authority.'

In the history of rock 'n' roll, few ascended so high and fell so far in so small a period of time as Bolan did. Like JFK's, Bolan's glory period would last about a thousand days. He appeared on another chat show, *Pop Quest*, in 1975, bloated and uncomfortably shifting in his chair. He looks like Liz Taylor at fifty. He is only twenty-eight. Two years later, he would be dead. A string of failed releases had left him vulnerable. The British music press was referring to him routinely as 'the Porky Pixie.'

'He lost it,' Charles Shaar Murray says. 'He had his shining hour from [1970's] 'Ride a White Swan' up to 'Children of the Revolution' [in 1974]. After a while, it became apparent that he wasn't doing very much more than recycling the riffs of his childhood with hippie nursery rhymes and a lot of echo. Got lazy and got complacent. He got fat literally and metaphorically. He basically believed that he could sing the phone book and kids would adore him and buy it. Then he did start singing the fucking phone book and they didn't buy it. He turned into this sulky rock 'n' roll Norma Desmond figure.'

In the early morning hours of September 16, 1977, just as he was enjoying a comeback of sorts, hosting a show for the Granada TV network and touring with respectable punk acts like the Damned, he and his companion Gloria Jones (the Northern Soul star who released the original version of the Soft Cell electro-pop classic 'Tainted Love') were driving to their home in the Maida Vale section of London when the car hit a tree. Bolan died, according to the report, of 'shock and hemmorhage.' Jones was hospitalized but survived. The death was ruled accidental.

The crash site is commemorated with a black marble marker: IN RESPECTFUL MEMORY OF MARC BOLAN, MUSICIAN, WRITER, POET. There's a message board by the tree and a bronze bust that makes him look a little too much like Jim Morrison. Bolan was, if nothing else, a hero all his own.

By the time David and Marc were assaulting each other with braggadoccio, David's backing band the King Bees had packed it in, a response to the indifference of the failed 'Liza Jane' single. Conn stayed on as David's manager and quickly recommended another act he had begun working with called the Manish Boys, named after the title of a Bo Diddley song (which spelled it with two n's). After his tenure as a bona fide London-based front man, David was not thrilled to learn that they were based in Maidstone, over thirty miles away. Conn convinced him that the Manish Boys (guitarist Jon Edward, bassist John Watson, drummer John Whitehead and keyboardist Bob Solly) were a hot combo, worth the commute. Likewise, the Manish Boys were not thrilled at the prospect of taking on David. They felt like they'd gotten their act down and were not even auditioning for new members. They already had two sax players playing in the outfit (Wolf Byrne on baritone and Paul Rodriquez on tenor) but Conn hustled them, implying that American concert promoters were interested in a tour, but only if they welcomed Davie Jones as a member.

'Without that I don't think we'd have taken him. We were happy enough as we were,' band member Paul Rodriquez said, adding that David's pallor was also bit disconcerting. Still, both parties needed a break and decided to make the best of it. After some hours rehearsing, they acknowledged that they could at least make a good, loud racket together. David's voice impressed them, as did his horn playing.

It was with the Manish Boys that David Jones first started to get 'out there.' The London mod scene was changing. The speedy tempos were slowing down as marijuana and the heady poetry of American singer-song-writers like Simon & Garfunkel, Roger McGuinn of the Byrds, Scott Walker of former teen idols the Walker Brothers, and, of course, Bob Dylan influenced the scene – Dylan toured England in '65, as captured in future Bowie documentarian D. A. Pennebaker's film *Don't Look Back*, and briefly plunged the then impressionable David into a black-clad 'Dylan' phase. The Beatles released *Rubber Soul* late in the year, marking a sea change in their own sound. Even the formerly clean-cut Beach Boys, as big if not bigger in England than they were in America, became gleefully expansive with the lush, symphonic *Pet Sounds* album and the staggeringly inventive, Theremin-tinged 'Good Vibrations' single the following year.

Young London professionals now embraced a louche, jaded pose, exemplified by actor/filmmaker David Hemmings (another future Bowie tour documentarian) in Michelangelo Antonioni's 1966 film *Blow Up*. In that film Hemmings, a photographer based on premier London fashion lensman David Bailey, receives a giant, polished wooden propeller for his loft space, simply, one assumes, because it is something unusual to look at. Anything to remain interested. Sensing this zeitgeist, David knew instinctively that the Manish Boys, who were quite happy playing the blues, gulping speed and cheap wine and chasing girls, were not going to make it as is. David encouraged the band to grow their hair even longer than the by then socially acceptable mop tops of the Beatles and Rolling Stones.

Inspired by his competitive friendship with Bolan, David pursued success with a brand-new sense of ostentation. During the group's live shows at the Marquee and other Soho blues clubs he would often lapse into lengthy and (to his band) somewhat distressingly campy monologues by way of introducing the still tough-edged blues numbers that made up their repertoire.

With Conn's help, the Manish Boys were soon

booked as a support act on a full British tour with the Kinks, who had made it in England and America with a string of hits like 'You Really Got Me' and 'Tired of Waiting for You.' Even better, the Kinks' stellar producer Shel Talmy had agreed to produce the Manish Boys. Talmy had also made hits with the Creation and Manfred Mann and the Easybeats (whose 'Friday on My Mind' David Bowie would cover on his 1973 covers record *Pin Ups*). He knew how to harness the power of a touring rock band by compressing the volume and verve into a pent-up sexiness that would appeal to both boys and the girls they lusted after. Even better, for the Yank-worshipping David, he was an American. Talmy was born in Chicago and found early fame as a child actor in Los Angeles. In the early sixties, he settled in London to work for Decca. When he saw David with the Manish Boys, he knew he'd found another great talent.

According to Talmy, the still-teenage David stood out as the potential star along the lines of the leaders of the Who and the Kinks. 'I can't tell you what it was exactly,' Talmy says. 'If I could, I would have bottled it long ago and made billions. I'm not trying to be facetious, but you can't explain instinct. I instinctively thought David was one of the brightest kids I'd ever met. He was cocky in a nice way and I had no doubt he'd be a star. Unfortunately it didn't happen on my watch.'

Talmy chose Bobby Bland's 1961 R & B smash

'I Pity the Fool' for the Manish Boys' debut single, confident that it fit their sound perfectly. He recorded the band on February 8, 1965, at IBC studios in Portland Place with his usual session musicians helping to achieve the classic Talmy sound. The track is a slow blues song with crunchy horns and a great wiggly solo in the second verse, played by Jimmy Page, who was then a Talmy session man. 'Take My Tip,' the B side, is jazzier and more sax driven, with David doing a solid Roger Daltrey homage. There's a bit of Georgie Fame and the Blue Flames in there as well, a nightclub bounce and some hipster poetry, courtesy of David Jones, the composer: 'You're scared to walk beside her / 'Cause you're playing with a tiger who possesses the sky.' Sonically speaking, derivative as it was, both sides of the single were worlds away from the King Bees' 'Liza Jane.'

The Manish Boys promoted the single with a May 8 appearance on a new television program on BBC2 entitled *Gadzooks! It's All Happening*, an offshoot of a popular teen show called *The Beat Room*. When the producers saw the band's hair, however, they reportedly demanded that the Manish Boys get it trimmed preshow. The band refused and was bumped from the broadcast. What seemed like bad luck turned into a minisensation once Conn and Jones realized that they could exploit the incident. They went to the local papers the *Daily Mirror*, *Daily Telegraph* and *Daily Mail* with the 'BBC discriminates against long-haired combo' angle and succeeded in getting both blurbs and photos in each one. For about a half a day, the Manish Boys were big.

Listening to songs like the Barbarians' 1965 novelty hit 'Are You a Boy or Are You a Girl' ('You're always wearing skintight pants / And boys wear pants . . .') today, you can't help but giggle. When I think of the sixties, I just assume that everybody let their hair grow. Sideburns got bushier. Flares wider. Skin greasier. I think I got this impression when the shows I grew up watching in reruns after school switched from black and white to lurid, orange-hued color. In doing research on the era, I realized that this was just a show business thing. The people making these programs and the bands taking their cues from the Beatles' and the Stones' tonsorial manifest destiny were all entertainers. Even in the mid-sixties, a time associated with lengthening hair, nearly all men of a certain generation still had buzz cuts or even short, oiled and neatly groomed hair. The skinny boys who grew theirs out like a girl remained, in most places, the object of fear and ridicule.

Having too-long tresses amounted to an easy way to cast yourself against modern society, and in the spring of '65 David Jones realized that in the absence of an undeniable single, the kind Ray Davies, Pete Townshend, Jagger and Richards and Lennon and McCartney seemed to whip up between toast and jam breaks, he needed to exploit this outrage while he still could. It would be the first time his self-fabricated sensation got more attention than the actual song it was cooked up to promote, but certainly not the last.

'It's really for the protection of pop musicians and those who wear their hair long,' David explained in a talk show appearance designed to promote his pop society, the International League for the Preservation of Animal Filament. 'Anyone who has the courage to wear hair down to his shoulders has to go through hell. It's time we united and stood up for our curls.' The Manish Boys netted a booking on another big package tour opening up for Gerry and the Pacemakers, along with Marianne Faithfull and Gene Pitney. After the tour, and back in London, they quickly realized that without a radio hit, there was no way to ride the publicity wave very far. This is something David Bowie would later realize; the stunts had to be fabulous but the music needed to be equally remarkable.

The band still had no real money and no luck, and David remained desperate to transcend his suburban smallness and be a star. When he wasn't home in Bromley, he'd spend his days in Soho, idling in the Café Giaconda on busy Denmark Street, reading the classified section of the weekly *Melody Maker* music newspaper and wondering what it took to make the cover . . . or even page two. Even his ex-bandmate and school friend George Underwood had scored a five-year recording contract with the hot producer Mickey Most, the impresario who handled Herman's Hermits and the Yardbirds. 'He was furious,' Underwood says today. 'Music was his life now and he thought that because I could paint, that I wasn't dedicated enough and it all looked too fuckin' easy! He was working his bollocks off every night with the Manish Boys. I really thought our friendship was at an end.'

The sixties, the decade during which London seemed to take over the world, were not half-over and he still seemed to be playing catch-up with it, wondering where his piece of the glory might be. Even little Peter Frampton was better connected among the London pop scenemakers, having been taken under the wing of the Stones' bassist Bill Wyman. He would have three hits with both the Herd and Humble Pie before David would ever have his first. David did not want to go back to Bromley. Surely the hair wasn't the answer, even though it still got him some attention that carried him through doubtful times.

'My first memory of him was meeting him in the Marquee Club; I suppose I was about fifteen maybe,' says singer Dana Gillespie, a longtime friend from the sixties through the mid-seventies, when she was an artist with Bowie's management company MainMan (she would later appear in bed with Art Garfunkel in future Bowie director Nicholas Roeg's 1980 film *Bad Timing*). 'I had waist-length peroxide-blond hair then, and I was brushing my hair outside the dressing room in the long mirror there and somebody came up and took the brush out of my hand and carried on brushing and said, 'Can I take you home?' And that was him. So I smuggled him past my parents' bedroom into the house where I lived, which was about twenty minutes away from the Marquee Club. And then we spent the night together, but I mean, I was still at school. And I introduced him to my parents the next morning. And they hadn't realized it was a boy until I said the word 'David.' Because nobody had sort of Veronica Lake-style hair. You know, primrose-yellow blond.'

Unlike most Marquee habitues, Gillespie had an aristocratic background. She was the well-traveled daughter of a wealthy Austrian baron. Still, with all her cosmopolitan polish, she'd never met anyone like David Jones.

'Even his eye, you know, the eye that's discolored, he always said he'd got it in a crash while playing American football. And that was an unusual thing to be interested in. And he always dressed differently. In knee-length suede trousers with fringe boots and then a white Russian-peasant-type shirt, baggy, with a waistcoat, looking like Robin Hood.'

Gillespie visited the Jones home in Bromley and noted the quaintness of the modest décor, tiny bedrooms and bathroom, and small, neat kitchen. David's quiet, repressed English parents were like little museum pieces in the wild and mid-sixties.

'It was the first time I'd been to a working-class household,' she says. 'It sounds silly but I didn't know what a little tiny house in a row of houses was like because my life was completely the opposite end. You know, I came from a very good family. I'd only known what kind of . . . another sort of luxury style. And that was a bit of a shock. And even then he said, "I wanna get out of this. I want to get out of this." He didn't want to be in a tiny little place where you sit uncomfortably. We sat there eating tuna fish sandwiches with the parents, and they had the television on and not much conversation went on.'

David's parents didn't really know what to make of his career or the people he was occasionally bringing home to meet them. Between concern over Terry's frequently erratic behavior and their natural tendencies toward insularity, the house on Plaistow Grove was not necessarily inviting. The couple harbored doubts about the direction David was taking professionally as well. As much as they loved him and wished happiness for him, there didn't seem to be any money coming in. One vinyl 45 record, like the one the King Bees made, was something to thrill over, but a collection of financially unsuccessful singles was something troubling. Certainly touring was hard work and a source of income, but David would often return from a road trip even more desperate and with less money than he'd left with. The pop stars that John and Peggy Jones saw on television all had broad smiles and seemed healthy, wealthy and well provided for. The day-to-day life of their impatient and wildly ambitious son seemed something altogether different.

Even within this private culture of hope and disappointment, David did not give up. As I said, he could reliably be seen during this period in the Giaconda café, poring over the music weeklies, the *New Musical Express* and *Melody Maker*, and also catching the sets of more successful bands in the nearby clubs. He'd watch each lead singer and take mental notes, studying what worked and why.

'When [lead singer] Phil May and I started the Pretty Things, he came to the gigs quite a lot and that was it really,' says Dick Taylor of the Pretty Things. 'By the time we got to the point where we were well known, he'd latched on a bit. He'd follow us around. You'd look up at the gigs and he'd be there. He liked the rebellious image. We were fellow art students who were doing it.' Although he was not yet twenty, some front men, like Steve Winwood, then of the Spencer Davis Group, were only fifteen and enjoying a career in rapid ascent.

The Lower Third, David's next step on the path to becoming 'somebody,' was, like the Manish Boys, another marriage of convenience formed in the hungry environment of Soho. 'We were going to have a new singer and hold auditions,' the Lower Third's Denis Taylor told Capital Radio. Among those who showed up to join were David

Jones and future Small Faces front man Steve Marriott, who at the time, with his long, blond hair and thin, pale frame, could have been David's doppelgänger. David was nervous. He showed up to the café with a copy of his Manish Boys single as if to remind the band that he was already in the game. He didn't need to, as he impressed all involved with his voice and surpassed even Marriott (who would become one of his musical heroes and later perform with Peter Frampton in the supergroup Humble Pie).

'David was terrific and we all made our decision in the Giaconda,' Taylor said, 'and that's how it all really started. We liked the stuff he was doing and he really started to develop an image for us as well.'

'We like each other's ideas,' David stated in the band's press release, with little effusion. 'We have the same policies and fit rather well together. All of us like to keep to ourselves and we like things rather than people.' The band, guitarist Denis Taylor, bassist Graham Rivens and drummer Phil Lancaster, hailed from the seaside town Margate, where they'd been playing as Oliver Twist and the Lower Third. They'd been in London for several months, soaking up the scene around the Marquee and looking for a way in. Sadly, they were even less original than the previous two bands that David had been in. At least they reflected his catholic taste in everything from West Coast jazz to Detroit soul and Delta blues. The Lower Third focused their emulation on one act and were such Who emulators that even Pete Townshend was taken aback by it. David's time with the Lower Third also marked the beginning of the end for David Jones and Les Conn. Conn explained, 'My biggest problem was that I hadn't the resources to back my judgment. David was too ambitious to hold under the existing conditions. And to my regret, I let him go. There was absolutely no animosity on either side. The way things were, I would have only held him back and harmed his career, and that was the very last thing I wanted to happen. So we shook hands and parted.'

After Les Conn's departure, the Lower Third was managed by a tightly wound, round-faced man in his mid-twenties named Ralph Horton. Horton had been a road manager for the Moody Blues, who had a huge hit with 'Go Now.' His partner Spike Palmer did time as a roadie with the Rolling Stones. The band auditioned for Horton and Palmer, who quickly got them some gigs and a small publishing contract with the firm Sparta Music, providing everyone with some much needed cash.

The group toured England in a modified diesel-powered ambulance, a gift from Rivens's father. The windows were blacked out, and the vehicle still had a working blue gumball siren atop the white plastic roof. It was big enough to stow their gear, even to sleep in, and could easily cut through a metropolitan traffic jam. The band rode in the back, while David was given the privilege of riding in the passenger seat with Horton, whose affection for his new artist was something that he reportedly could not hide.

'He took a liking to David definitely and from that point it was no longer a singer and a group, it had become a singer with a group, which is a different thing altogether,' Denis Taylor said. While the band shivered in the ambulance, David would often sleep in Horton's flat in relative warmth and comfort. 'David used to travel in a Jag to any gigs,' Taylor recalled. 'He never put gear away when we'd done our work. It became obvious that Ralph was looking after him.'

'Ralph Horton was uptight and tense,' says John Hutchinson today. Hutchinson would play with David in the Horton-managed post-Lower Third band the Buzz. 'He was probably in love with David. He fancied David. I guess he believed in him too. Nothing against him personally but he was a bit uptight, and he got more uptight as things got tougher, I suppose.' His doting on the lead singer drew rancor from the other members of the band, but it was a lack of funding that ensured that the Lower Third would be yet another short-lived entity. The band managed to tour beyond England, playing a short residency in Paris during the Christmas and New Year's holiday of 1965 and '66.

With an inability to gain any real traction, soon the band went the way of the King Bees and the

Manish Boys. Horton stuck with David but it was clear that he was in over his head. He did not have the vision to sell his star and began looking for other successful managers to help with the task.

'Ralph called me out of the blue one day and introduced himself,' recalls Simon Napier-Bell, then manager of Marc Bolan's pre-Tyrannosaurus Rex act John's Children. 'He asked if I would come to see him and have a chat about a project. His flat was a basement in Pimlico and the project was sitting in the corner – David Jones. Ralph asked if I would be prepared to help with David's management and as an introductory offer suggested I might like to have sex with him. Although the boy in the corner seemed acquiescent, the overall sleaziness of the idea rather put me off, so I turned it down. Consequently I neither slept with him nor managed him. In retrospect I admit both things might have been worth doing.' Such events were not unheard of at the time. The London-based pop business was full of gay men, and a pretty lead singer knew that even flirting with an insider with the right connections could lead to career advancement.

'Gay was illegal,' says Napier-Bell. As early as 1966, one could technically be thrown in prison Oscar Wilde-style for committing 'sodomy.' 'Gay people who didn't want to live in the closet had to find something to do with their lives . . . Sexual self-interest was the main force behind casting in

Hollywood since the twenties. It didn't grind to a halt. If you're gay and you fancy a boy, you're likely to be making a better choice of artist for teenage girls to fall in love with than a straight man would make. So trusting your instincts worked well. Getting yourself a bit of sex on the way was just natural.'

David's fifth band in less than five years was called the Buzz, which was ironic, as they too had none. 'He was not even a big fish in that little pond,' says Hutchinson, who auditioned for and joined the Buzz after wandering into the Marquee. 'He was just another singer that hadn't done very much. The musicians knew him but the general public hadn't seen much of David in those days. He was quite a small fish really. But I had enough respect for him. I'd seen his advert in the back of the *New Musical Express*. He used to have a weekly advert. 'We're looking for gigs.' With a little photo of him. I realized that somebody who could organize something like rehearsals at the Marquee Club was fairly organized.' Hutchinson had a wife and child and was wary about joining a pop group but was persuaded by David's professionalism and talent.

By the spring of 1966, the Buzz had a residency at the Marquee and Ralph Horton had secured a backing deal of 1,500 pounds against 10 percent of their royalties from a private investor named Raymond Cook. Things looked like they were about to finally come together. Hutchinson brought in a keyboard player named Derek Boyes who added a thrumming Hammond organ to the band's sound for some of David's new compositions.

'He'd written quite a lot,' says Hutchinson. 'None of us had day jobs. Ralph more or less said, you need this to be full-time. By the time we started playing, the set that we'd set off with would be a mixture, about half and half. Mostly his songs.'

An unusual influence could be detected in some of this new material. David had veered away from his blues influence and developed a creative crush on British entertainer Anthony Newley, then in his mid-thirties. A former child star (he played the Artful Dodger in David Lean's 1948 adaptation of Dickens's *Oliver Twist*), Newley had grown into a singer, dancer and actor given to tuxedos. In middle age, he was not only a sort of white, English Sammy Davis Jr. but he would also write the latter's most famous song, 'The Candy Man.' Other international hits included 'What Kind of Fool Am I?' and 'After Today,' from the movie musical *Dr Dolittle*, in which he also appears. He was briefly married to Joan Collins, but who wasn't? Newley, who died in 1996, was not a rocker, but rather the kind of singer/dancer/actor a show business type often referred to as a 'triple threat.' Hipsters appreciated him ironically or dismissed him as a tacky ball of cheese. Newley's patter was vulnerable to cheeky chappy-isms.

There's footage online of him singing 'The Candy Man' while carrying a child's wicker basket of sweets, tossing them out languidly as he croons. It makes Shatner look restrained. There are no real explanations for just why David fell so hard for the Newley act. Years later, even he would shrug his shoulders and wonder if he'd temporarily lost the plot. One sound theory given David's history as high school rebel is that Newley's shtick was so very different from the gruff white blues singer archetype. The theatricality of a Newley or a Sammy Davis Jr. or even the middle-aged Judy Garland (who would soon become another touchstone for her ability to attack and wring every drop of emotion out of a song) was what struck him. There was no subtlety to Newley, and the lyrical innuendo in sexed-up, raunchy blues numbers had gotten David Jones nowhere.

'It was the right time to be doing that kind of music because blues is really happening in England, but I think he just wanted to be a bit more theatrical. And of course Anthony Newley was around, and for some reason he really adored Anthony Newley-type songs,' agrees Dana Gillespie. 'Anthony Newley is kind of corny, but he seemed to think at that time that was kind of the thing to like. But he went through phases, you know; depending who he met he'd absorb their culture or whatever he wanted, then he'd kind of move on. But Anthony Newley was an odd thing. It's like saying I'm crazy about Dick Van Dyke.'

113

David's Newley fixation also made him wonder if being a band-leader was his destiny after all. Maybe he was a triple threat too and a one-man show. By the end of the year, he would gain representation from a man who would support this instinctive decision, his first truly powerful talent manager. He would cease to pursue success via the modernist blues. He would also cease to be David Jones.

CHAPTER 6

Kenneth Pitt was already nearing his forties when he took on the nineteen-year-old David Jones as a personal management client. Although tall, quiet and buttoned-down himself, much like John Jones, Pitt admired the wit and audacity of performers. Given to good tailoring, expensive books and travel, he was no prissy intellectual. He was a war veteran, having landed in France on D-day working within the British army's signals unit. Also unusual for those in his show business circle, Pitt was openly gay (whereas many of his peers remained in the closet long after homosexuality was formally legalized in the U.K. in 1967). Pitt's approach to his own sexuality was that of a liberated arts enthusiast and committed equal-rights seeker, a quiet revolutionary.

While Pitt has published a detailed account of his years with David, entitled *Bowie: The Pitt Report*, he is taken to task in many Bowie books for guiding his charge away from rock 'n' roll and toward a career in old-fashioned show business, essentially holding him back from what is romantically thought of as his destiny. 'Pitt was quite prepared for David to turn into a cabaret lounge singer,' Angie Bowie says today. 'He could have gotten him eight years in Las Vegas in a smoking lounge and he would have thought that he'd made it. It was a very queer gay-mafia type of management system.' Pitt, as is the nature of this process of hindsight, completely dismisses this widely reported and accepted line of thought. Corresponding via letter, he responds to my questions about early management strategy by asking, 'Is this your bid to introduce that old chestnut about me wanting him to do cabaret? I never ever wanted him to do cabaret for which he was unsuitable.'

Many people I've interviewed on the subject of Kenneth Pitt have also suggested that his focus was also clouded by his romantic fixation on David. Some of these accusers, like Calvin Mark Lee, the psychedelic gadfly who helped get David signed to Mercury Records, were romantically fixated themselves. Others, like David's bandmate John Hutchinson, were not. Pitt denies this as well, characteristically avoiding any prurient detail. 'Nothing impeded my ability to work with D [as he refers to David throughout the letter] until the green-eyed goddess of jealousy reared her ugly head. She decided that I stood in the way of her own ambitions. And I had to go,' Pitt says. Regardless of what he did or did not do with regard to the more personal end of personal management, it can hardly be argued that Pitt failed to help develop the David Bowie we know today. He was a key figure and should be reconsidered as such.

In the mid and late sixties, Pitt lived and worked out of a two-floor flat on London's Manchester Street. Warmly lit, comfortably appointed and bordered with tall bookcases and antiques, the study and guest bedroom became David's first solid home away from home, a place he could turn to when the tiny house in Bromley became too stifling, or, as it would during this period, if Terry's behavior became too upsetting. He would pull a book from the shelf, whether recommended by Pitt or fascinating on its own, and forget about his life for a few hours with the help of Wilde, Swinburne, Waugh and Orwell or the poetry of William Butler Yeats.

By the mid-sixties, Kenneth Pitt was already what could be considered a show business veteran as well. In the late 1940s, after his discharge from the military, he worked for the publicity firm of J. Arthur Rank, escorting actresses like Jean Simmons, of *Guys and Dolls* fame, to functions and parties. His work took him overseas to America and Canada in the early fifties, where he signed and represented several major pop, jazz and swing musicians, including Stan Kenton, Les Paul, and Mel Tormé, 'the Velvet Fog.' He entered the sixties with a very confident style of artist representation firmly in place (for some reason I picture him as Sir John Gielgud in *The Loved One* when I imagine his pre-David existence), especially in Los Angeles. Pitt was primarily interested in finding diamonds in the rough, young talent in need of nurturing, encouragement, refinement and motivation.

'A classic management style,' he has said. 'They were taken from scratch, given an opinion of what I felt they should do, they did it and it worked.' Pitt applied this first to a busker named Danny Purches, whom he turned into a crooner. He signed Crispian St Peters, who had an international hit with 'The Pied Piper,' and had been instrumental in Manfred Mann's career as well.

'Ken was very interested in the growing group of young professionals that he was representing,' says William Bast, who worked with Pitt in the late fifties while promoting his James Dean-based play *The Myth Makers* in London. 'His clients were all young and he was therefore being of a young mind,' Bast adds. 'He liked young people. Talented young people. And at the time, those people were all pop singers. For his age he was basically still a teenager. Still into it all. Very much so. Freedom. He was an older man. He wasn't a kid. Sometimes it was amusing for somebody like me to come in and see him jiving like a kid. He was in his thirties. He was no kid.'

At the behest of Ralph Horton, who remained deep in debt and could no longer handle David's career on his own, Pitt agreed to come by the

Marquee on April 17, 1966, to hear David Jones. Pitt was instantly attracted to David Jones. In *Bowie: The Pitt Report* he writes poetically about the nineteen-year-old's attire as if entering details into a catalog: 'biscuit colored hand knitted sweater, round necked and buttoned at one shoulder, its skin tightness accentuating his slim frame.' He also saw someone with a natural talent, one that could transcend the London pop scene and reach as far as Hollywood, Broadway and Las Vegas. Likely pepped by Horton, David did numbers that had never been performed on the Marquee's stage, such as Judy Garland's 'You'll Never Walk Alone.' Pitt was also impressed by David's natural charm and intelligent, cultivated mannerisms. 'The average pop singer fronting the big groups of those years was the sort of person you couldn't even talk to about things like that or indeed, about anything else,' he wrote.

After the audition at the Marquee, Horton took David to Pitt's office. David too sensed that Pitt was different, not the typically thuggish, road-hardened pop manager, rather an aesthete and a gentleman. Even better, Pitt had worked with, lived with and rubbed up against genuine stars, not just English R & B singers and guitarists. 'Let's do a deal with Ken,' David told Horton.

A five-year contract was put forth but Pitt insisted on first meeting John and Peggy Jones. Again, it seemed the proper thing to do. David was no longer a minor, but Pitt had a courtly policy of making sure a potential client of David's age and experience level was truly ready for the task at hand. Pitt found John and Peggy supportive of their son's career choice but unable to fully mask their hidden concerns.

'I first visited David's home in 1965 when I was sure it was a little more impressive than when you saw it,' he writes in response to my question about its size and whether or not he believed that the close quarters fed David's ambition. 'It was typical of the horticultural terraced cottages that sprang up in rural Kent in late Victorian and early Edwardian times. In the fifties when David's father bought the three-bedroom property and modernized it, it would have been considered to be a comfortable home in which to bring up a child, and David was happy there, in spite of his mother's inability to impart affection, which remained with her until the end of her days. David once said to me, "My mother never kissed me."' Like Owen Frampton, David's Bromley Tech arts professor, Kenneth Pitt was an older man who fortified David with substitute tenderness and encouragement.

While in America in early 1966, Pitt had heard of a new television program based on a Beatles-like pop group and costarring a London-based stage star named Davy Jones (who had appeared most famously in Lionel Bart's West End production of the musical *Oliver!*). It was suggested to his new client, who had been flirting with a name change for five years by this point, that it might be a good idea to commit to one. After a few days' deliberation, David informed Pitt, who informed the record company, that David Jones would hereby and forever be referred to as David Bowie.

'There are too many David Joneses,' David Bowie explained in an early record label biography. 'David Jones is my real name and when I first turned professional two years ago my pirate-like character was just right at the time and the name fitted in with the image I wanted to give myself.' In Martin Scorsese's Bob Dylan documentary, *No Direction Home*, Dylan is asked about changing his name from Zimmerman to Dylan, in homage to Dylan Thomas, a heroic poet from the opposite shore of the Atlantic, and spoke of the liberation that comes with such reinvention. 'I don't feel like I had a past,' he says. 'I couldn't relate to anything other than what I was doing at the present time.'

When David took his name from Colonel James Bowie, the nineteenth-century Texas revolutionary who perished in the Battle of the Alamo, he was making the very same statement about a personal house cleaning. James Bowie was risible and aggressive. He was a veteran of the War of 1812 and took part in several treacherous frontier expeditions in the name of personal fortune and American manifest destiny. And then there's the famous short-bladed, upturned knife that bears his name, the one he used to gut his foe Sheriff

Norris Wright in a famous 1827 duel outside of Natchez, Mississippi. Certainly the name change was suggested to him for professional reasons but in the end, he called himself Bowie because he fancied aligning himself with one of America's greater badasses and ultimately, because he wanted to. It was not a name given to him by Pitt or a professional publicity officer as a marketing tool. It was a name that he certainly had to live up to, but not one that he had to grow into, as it was one of his own design.

Bob Dylan, and David Bowie a few years later, laid groundwork for the empowered reinvention that would become a part of what made punk rock so liberating. Almost without exception, one decade after David went from Jones to Bowie, every punk in New York, London, Paris, Los Angeles and any other city or suburb where a given name and place didn't seem to fit would have a self-invented moniker and a clean slate to go with it. You could almost say that when David became a Bowie, he stopped being a follower and officially began his five-year crawl toward becoming a bona fide culture leader as fearsome in his own realm as Jim Bowie was in the saloons of the American South and Southwest.

I should take a moment to point out here that the correct pronunciation of 'Bowie' is absolutely regional. In America, it's 'Bow' as in 'bowtie' and '-ie' as in 'evil.' In England it's 'Bow' as in 'when the bough breaks, the cradle will fall' and 'ie' as in 'evil.' In 'Up for the Downstroke' George Clinton of Parliament Funkadelic calls him 'David Boo-wee' and cannot imagine him in his funk. Every time I've heard him say his own name, David has used the American pronunciation.

David's first recording as David Bowie was made for Pye Records producer Tony Hatch. In 1999, during a taping of the VH1 series *Storytellers,* he described 'Can't Help Thinking About Me,' his debut single as David Bowie, to the audience as a 'beautiful piece of solipsism' but lamented the lyric 'My girl calls my name, "Hi, Dave / Drop in, see you around, come back if you're this way again,"' as 'two of the worst lines I've ever written.'

Ralph Horton knew Tony Hatch, a proven hit maker, through his association with the Moody Blues, and it seemed like a good match, one that would finally result in a much needed major chart topper. Pye executives saw promise in Bowie as well. In a conversation with Hatch, he explained that Pye, 'as a smaller label, had great success, although the general policy was still to throw as much mud at the wall as possible on the basis that some of it would stick.' Several Bowie biographies claim that shortly before the recording Hatch reportedly handed David the tambourine that Petula Clark had played on the Hatch-produced smash 'Downtown' (although Hatch refutes this, admitting, 'I don't recall Petula having a lucky tambourine').

The fate of 'Can't Help Thinking About Me'

would suggest that if it had existed, Clark had clearly removed the magic from the instrument anyway. Despite the inauspicious start, Bowie and Hatch continued to make records for Pye with his backing band the Buzz. Toiling in the studio, they hoped for some kind of rare pop spark, à la Brian Wilson and the Beatles, and drove the long-suffering engineers crazy as sound levels were set and reset. This was, after all, the cusp of the 'studio as instrument' wave, which would result in masterpieces like *Pet Sounds, Sgt. Pepper's Lonely Hearts Club Band*, the Zombies' *Odessey and Oracle*, and *S.F. Sorrow*, by Bowie's old suburban art school cronies the Pretty Things.

'A lot of the inspiration started coming on the day of recording,' Hatch says of the shift in the approach to recording during this period. 'It was frustrating for the balance engineers because they might have to wait a couple of hours before there was anything to record.'

Best among the Hatch-produced early Bowie singles (which are all available on compilations) is the wonderful 'I Dig Everything.' The organ riff and tempo are straight out of a perfect Austin Powers afterworld, calling to mind yellow solar rays on a wet MG bonnet. The lyrics could do with a bit more irony: 'I wave to the policemen but they don't wave back / They don't dig anything,' but David sells it like a dosed snow cone at a summer be-in. It was released in August of '66, and why it wasn't a smash in the vein of

'Daydream' by the Lovin' Spoonful or 'Groovin' by the Young Rascals is hard to say. It was certainly peppy enough. Its failure must have done a number on its author's mind. He was digging everything but the commercial ceiling atop his animal filament, which not only blocked out the sun but also seemed to be made of brick and mortar. No matter how much he tried, there was no breaking through.

'You released a single, hoped for a good reaction from the BBC, but they wouldn't really get behind a record until it either picked up loads of plays or the orders started coming in,' Hatch says. 'I, particularly, recognized something special about Bowie, although I'm not sure if this was shared by everyone in the company. I personally loved his take on London life and was very disappointed when we couldn't make others realize just how original he was. I vividly remember the day my managing director called me into his office and said, 'We've just been going through your recording expenses. You've spent thousands of pounds on David Bowie and we still haven't had any hits. I think we should let him go so you can focus attention on your other signings.' Contracts were usually for one year with options in the favor of the record company. I don't know how Bowie or his management felt about Pye but, very reluctantly, I agreed that we should part company. But, bloody hell, I knew it wouldn't be long before we'd see him at number one.'

Sensing that his client was miserable with his second-tier status at Pye, Pitt worked out an arrangement with a new label, Deram (a start-up offshoot of Decca Records), using extremely strong new material like 'The London Boys,' 'Rubber Band' and 'Please Mr Gravedigger' for leverage. The deal was modest but it would enable Bowie to record an entire album's worth of solo material. Pitt also secured a lucrative publishing contract, only to find, upon the deal's completion, that the fiscally hapless Ralph Horton had already inked one on Bowie's behalf for far less money (Pitt never told Bowie what he was missing out on for fear of crushing his spirit).

On another business trip to New York City in early 1966, Pitt took a meeting with the pop artist Andy Warhol, with an eye toward representing his as yet unknown new group the Velvet Underground. He returned to London with an acetate of the unreleased *The Velvet Underground and Nico* album, the band's debut. 'Not being his particular cup of tea, he gave it to me to see what I made of them,' Bowie wrote in his self-edited issue of *Mojo* in 2002. That acetate, which Pitt casually handed to him as a sort of souvenir, proved to be a life changer.

'Everything I both felt and didn't know about rock music was opened to me on one unreleased disc. The first track ['Sunday Morning'] glided by innocuously enough without really registering. However from that point on, and with the opening throbbing sarcastic bass and guitar of 'I'm Waiting for the Man,' the linchpin, the keystone of my ambition was driven home. The music was savagely indifferent to my feelings. It didn't care if I liked it or not. It could give a fuck. It was completely preoccupied with a world as yet unseen by my suburban eyes. In fact, though only nineteen, I had seen rather a lot but had accepted it all quite enthusiastically as "a bit of a laugh." Apparently, the laughing was now over. This was a degree of cool that I had no idea was humanly sustainable and it was ravishing.'

The Velvet Underground and Nico demonstrated to the nineteen-year-old, as it has to countless bands over the last forty-plus years, where rock music could be taken. The album demonstrated how a rock lyric could be literary and vulnerable without compromising toughness ('Heroin'), how it could be sexy or romantic without using hackneyed bedroom come-ons ('I'll Be Your Mirror,' 'Femme Fatale') and how the avantgarde and the classical could mix to form something exhilarating and sinister without being oblique and alienating ('Venus in Furs'). Plus, the songs were easy to play. They were primal but felt complex. Bowie learned each of them on his twelve-string Gibson acoustic, the guitar he would use during what was amounting to his first serious run as a song-writer. He encouraged his backing band the Buzz and its short-lived new incarnation, the Riot Squad (essentially the Buzz with a flashing red light, onstage) to do the same.

127

While the Velvet Underground would mark the start of Bowie's love affair with New York City, also around this time, he caught a quintessentially English band at the Marquee that would prove equally shattering. These two bands would be as important to his musical development as Elvis and Little Richard had been a decade earlier.

Pink Floyd (then often referred to as *the* Pink Floyd) was a quartet of blues fans from Cambridge Arts College, led by a dark-eyed, black-haired, handsome kid just a few months older than Bowie. His name was Roger Barrett, known professionally and to his friends as 'Syd.' Syd played slide guitar with a Zippo lighter, giving his blues chords a fat, creepy quality. He didn't try to sound typically American when he sang, unlike most blues-based bands. He didn't drawl. He was, rather, distinctly British in his inflection, and his abstract lyrics and intense stage presence were unlike those of any other front man on the scene.

'There are certain artists that are unprecedented in their time,' says photographer Mick Rock, who would shoot iconic portraits of both Barrett and Bowie. 'I don't think the Beatles and the Stones and Bob Dylan come under that description. It has nothing to do with the quality of the art, but you could hear their derivation. Whatever they mutated into, you could hear the roots. They all acknowledge it. With Syd the first time I thought 'Where the hell did this come from?' When I first saw the early Pink Floyd they had yet to make a record and were virtually unknown. It was as if they had just landed! They didn't look or sound like anything I'd ever come across before, fronted by this beautiful being who was bobbing up and down and making the wildest sounds. The rest of the group were virtually invisible. It was all Syd. It was the same the first time I heard the Velvet Underground and Iggy and the Stooges. You couldn't track where it came from musically. Of course I didn't see Iggy or Lou live until 1972 when I shot the *Transformer* and *Raw Power* album covers.' The Floyd's effortless theatricality floored Bowie, and he became an acolyte of Barrett's.

'Barrett became a talisman for Bowie in how to be an *English* singer,' says early Pink Floyd producer Joe Boyd, who recorded their classic debut single 'Arnold Layne' (Bowie and David Gilmour would cover the track, about a suburban cross-dresser, at a tribute concert in 2006, the year Barrett passed away; he would also do the mid-period, Barrett-free Floyd classic 'Comfortably Numb,' with somewhat less passion).

David Bowie's debut album, released in early 1967, shows none of this influence, as many of the songs were already recorded by the end of 1966 in Decca's studio with house producer Mike Vernon (the album's sleeve is still very rooted in the early to mid-sixties, with a full head-shot of a handsome, vaguely defiant-looking David in his mod shag cut and high-collared jacket). With the

129

exception of the collected singles ('Love You Till Tuesday' and 'Rubber Band'), stylistically, the album leans toward the kind of vaguely dark, arcane English story songs ('Please Mr Gravedigger,' 'Uncle Arthur,' 'Maid of Bond Street') that Kenneth Pitt imagined Bowie performing in lounges, each one almost inviting a lengthy introduction.

'D is for December, D is for David, D is for Deram – December 2nd is D-day all round, for that's when Deram launches its exciting new contract star David Bowie singing his own outstanding song "Rubber Band,"' read the press-release copy that heralded Bowie's debut single. With lyrical references to feeling 'chappy' while eating scones and drinking, it's a cutesy and quaint trifle of a single. 'Dear rubber band, you're playing my tune out of tune,' Bowie quips. 'A happening song,' the press release insists.

As usual the non-LP B side is the far superior 'The London Boys,' 'David Bowie's partly auto-biographical cameo of the brave and defiant little mod racing up-hill along Wardour Street to an empty Paradise,' the press release issued shortly before its release claims. 'The London Boys' is Bowie's most sophisticated and autobiographical track up until that point. Musically, it's a hang-over ballad, hindered by his still-developing sense of melody and song structure. It draws its power from the lyrics, which describe David's weariness with the now five-year-old mod scene. 'You think

130

you've had a lot of fun,' Bowie sings, most likely to someone quite like him, 'but you ain't got nothing, you're on the run.' David would also pen a similarly themed but much more cheerful track called 'London Bye Ta Ta' around this time. It was later released as the B side to the 'Prettiest Star' single in 1970 (but could have easily been a hit for Blur or Supergrass circa the '94 Britpop boom). A version appears on disc one of the 1989 box set *Sound and Vision*.

Bowie's second Deram single, 'Love You Till Tuesday,' gave Aimee Mann's first band its name and inspired the Replacements' 'Love You Till Friday' and the Cure's 'Friday I'm in Love'. It's another Newley-indebted number but more confidently executed and genuinely witty, with a zippy arrangement that, like 'I Dig Everything,' seemed destined for the charts. Released April 14, 1967, it flopped as well, as did the full-length album that followed. It seemed a good time to give music a bit of a rest and focus on threat two in that triple-threat equation. In an interview with *Melody Maker* to promote the singles, Bowie is asked about his ambition. 'I want to act,' he answers. 'I'd like to do character parts. I think it takes a lot to become somebody else. It takes some doing.'

Bowie, with Pitt's encouragement, began auditioning for film roles around this time. He tried out for the John Schlesinger film *Sunday Bloody Sunday*, starring Peter Finch (later of *Network* fame) and Glenda Jackson, and lost that part to singer and actor Murray Head (now famous for the excellent and strange New Wave single 'One Night in Bangkok'), and he starred in an avant-garde short by director Michael Armstrong entitled *The Image*. Its plot is, well, vague. An artist, played by Michael Byrne, is painting a portrait on a rainy night. A winding staircase is shot from various angles in shadow. The painting is a portrait of David Bowie, wearing a beige sweater (it would later grace the cover of *Bowie: The Pitt Report*). Suddenly the real-life David Bowie places his face against the window. A painting come to life? Fortunately there is no dialogue. Bowie on film is, of course, a serious presence, and this is the first time it's really utilized. Even as a ghost, Bowie's features swim together beautifully on celluloid. He is, on camera, a great British beauty, more masculine than he seems in still photos. I'm always reminded of a young Michael Caine (circa *Get Carter*), and vice versa, but I may be alone. As anything more than the first indicator of this photogenic superiority, *The Image* is pointless. Even Pitt, who had invested a lot of energy in encouraging his client to act, dismissed the film as 'dreadful.' As he elaborated for Journalist George Tremlett, 'The film was shot on location in a derelict house. To make it more realistic David was told to stand outside hanging on the windowsill for dear life while buckets of water were poured over him to simulate rain. To make it even worse, he wasn't even standing by a downstairs window but hanging from an upstairs sill, so that if he had lost his hold he would have fallen, and possibly hurt himself. David came back that evening looking like a drowned mouse and complaining bitterly.'

The film would be screened in gay porno theaters in the seventies after David Bowie had made it big, but in '67 it was considered a failure, and there was even more rejection in store. The follow-up single to 'Love You Till Tuesday' was a novelty track entitled 'The Laughing Gnome,' which remains so notorious among Bowie fans that in 1990 when he was accepting requests via a call-in line for the hits that he would play on his best-of Sound and Vision arena tour, the *NME* encouraged fans to vote for 'The Laughing Gnome,' which would have forced Bowie to play this most notorious novelty song amid culture-changing epics like 'Ziggy Stardust' and 'Heroes.' Adding to the Newley-ish delivery and the cornball lyrics, Bowie adds a Vari-speed gnome who essentially duets with him in a voice that Ross Bagdasarian, the producer who (under the stage name David Seville) foisted Alvin and the Chipmunks on the world, would dismiss as shrill. Still, it's winning somehow. The chorus is a nod to Chuck Berry's 'You Can't Catch Me' ('Ha ha ha hee hee hee / I'm the laughing gnome and you can't catch me'), and if there's ever a museum for gloriously foul puns ('Rolling Gnomes,' 'Gnome man's land') the master tape should reside on a well-lit pedestal. 'I am one of the gnomes on that record and am responsible for some of the terrible jokes on it as well,' the late Gus Dudgeon, who produced Bowie and, more famously, Elton John, admitted to a radio interviewer as if whispering to a priest in a darkened confessional.

Bowie himself has developed a good-natured affection for the song over the years. 'I really think I should have done more for gnomes,' he has said. 'I always feel a bit guilty that I just put my feet in the water and never sort of dived into the deep end. I really could have produced a new sensibility for the garden gnome in Britain. Gnomes should have been explored more deeply.'

In the nineties there was even talk of a jungle remake of the track with that tedious genre's biggest star, the metal-toothed DJ Goldie, and acid house music icon A Guy Called Gerald producing. It did not happen. We remain grateful.

'The Laughing Gnome,' despite its legend, was yet another failed single (although it was rereleased in the early seventies once Bowie mania had fully taken hold and enjoyed chart success). At worst, it made Bowie seem dated and out of touch. The would-be hit Bowie composition 'Over the Wall We Go' was another novelty effort about a cheerful Cockney's prison break. Bowie farmed this one out to Paul Nicholas, a second-tier pop singer and theater star, then recording under the moniker Oscar. Nicholas, using his given name, would play demented Cousin Kevin in the 1975 film adaptation of the Who's *Tommy* and enjoy one monster disco hit of his own in 1977 with 'Heaven on the 7th Floor,' a precursor of sorts to Aerosmith's smarmy classic 'Love in an Elevator.' There was an escalating war in Vietnam. The Beatles had gone to India to meditate. Acid had replaced liquor and pot as a means to get out of one's head. The pop audience was changing, and novelty seemed like so much thumb twiddling. People were now looking to their rock heroes for leadership – not novelty or escapism.

'Dylan and LSD were a big factor in the evolution from R & B to psychedelic,' says Joe Boyd. The Pretty Things, for instance, went from a Stones-like band to resembling Pink Floyd as a result of tripping. 'The Laughing Gnome' was released on June 1, 1967 . . . the same day as the Beatles' *Sgt. Pepper's Lonely Hearts Club Band* album. In terms of vision and inspiration, the divide between the two pop products could not have been greater. There was a genuine darkness and intensity descending. You could hear it in post-*Pepper* Beatles tracks like 'I Am the Walrus' and the Stones' 'Jumpin' Jack Flash' (which seemed to disavow all of England's psychedelic foray as woefully naïve in just over three and a half minutes). In America, there were bands like the Doors, Love and the aforementioned Velvet Underground. David, a fan of all of these bands, seemed to understand this in theory but lacked the formula to put it to any use. The blithely

Newley-esque Bowie compositions bore no trace of this wisdom, and the more gothic tracks were fanciful but empty.

While it certainly provided no real solace to anyone, Bowie's half brother, Terry Burns, who was fast spiraling into permanent mental illness, was spot on, zeitgeist-wise. Terry frequently stayed with his aunt Pat. During this period, he tended to wander; he'd disappear and return days later, and he would be cleaned up and reassimilated into a fragile domesticity. One day in 1967, however, he returned from wandering to find Pat's home empty. He went to see his mother on Plaistow Grove in Bromley and was informed that Pat and her husband had moved to Australia, pursuing a business opportunity. Pat wanted to warn Terry but did not know his whereabouts, which underscores just how erratic he'd become at that point. The information, relayed by Peggy with typical frankness, seemed to snap something in Terry. He left the house on Plaistow Grove and walked alone across the train tracks to the neighboring town of Chislehurst, particularly to a series of caverns known as the Chislehurst Caves.

The Chislehurst Caves have a long and strange history. Man-made caverns of cretaceous chalk, according to legend they were built during the time of the Druids. The chalk had been mined since the 1600s. During World War I they'd been a place to store secret ammunition, and in World War II, they were designated an air-raid shelter.

The caves had become a popular tourist attraction for collectors of fossils and local arcane tales of ancient fauna and magic mushrooms. By 1967, rock acts like Pink Floyd and Jimi Hendrix had performed concerts inside the winding maze. David himself had performed there with the Konrads and the Manish Boys. In 1972, the caves were the set for a *Dr Who* special. In the eighties teens would play Dungeons and Dragons there.

'They were very dangerous,' Siouxsie Sioux, a onetime Chislehurst resident, says, her tone a bit more grave than I'd have suspected. 'They used to cordon off bits you couldn't go down. Kids would sometimes go down there and get caved in. It was very creepy.'

By the time Terry reached the entrance to the caves, he'd begun to hear voices. 'I heard a voice saying to me, "Terry, Terry,"' he reportedly said, 'and I looked up and there was this great light and this beautiful figure of Christ looking down at me, and he said to me, "Terry, I've chosen you to go out in the world and do some work for me."'

For many with his mental affliction, hallucinations often take the form of a religious vision, a special message from either God or the Antichrist. Terry was convinced that Jesus Christ had selected him for a special mission. Christ was supposedly surrounded by a blinding light that forced the troubled man to the ground. When he opened his eyes again, he saw that he was surrounded by a ring of fire. Once the vision disappeared, Terry rose up and kept walking until he passed out. He was missing for eight full days and was finally taken into custody after wandering into a grocery store in a dazed and dirty state and asking for a piece of fruit. The police brought Terry back to Peggy's house but soon he was back in Cane Hill Asylum, where he'd been committed earlier.

Cane Hill, which opened in 1883 and was, for the British, the mental hospital of the popular idiom, as Bellevue is to most Americans, always loomed as a specter in both his life and the life of his family. When he was out, it seemed as though it was only a matter of time before he'd have to return.

Terry had been in and out of institutions and prescribed a variety of drugs, after various incidents of picking fights in bars or wandering off on his own for days, only to turn up disheveled and confused. Sometimes the drugs would work and Terry would enjoy periods of calm and functionality. Then he'd either go off them or they would cease to perform, and he would again be overtaken by demons whispering ideas he could neither communicate to others nor live with himself. During a good period, Terry even wed a fellow inpatient while both of them were confined to the premises. The Joneses hoped that he would one day be able to lead a normal life, but he could not hold a job or stay out of trouble for too long and always ended up back in professional care.

Bowie was devastated to be informed of Terry's

latest misfortune and seemed to internalize his pain. 'Terry came home this morning,' he told Ken Pitt casually one afternoon. Despite having met and conversed at length with both David's mother and father, as well as his new client, Pitt reportedly had no idea that David's brother was mentally ill. 'In my subsequent visits I would sit talking with him in what had become his bedroom cum music workshop,' Pitt writes, 'and it was the noise of his late-night practicing that eventually caused his father some discomfort and eventually resulted in his move to a spare room at Manchester Street.'

Bowie was able to place a little bit of distance between himself and the raw, painful goings-on on Plaistow Grove as Terry's illness built to a head. Terry returned to Cane Hill, where he was formally diagnosed as a paranoid schizophrenic. John Jones, who had warmed up to Terry in light of his illness, would lead family trips to the hospital. They'd bring fresh clothes and fruit and show him kindness and concern. It was all they could do.

Shortly after Terry's institutionalization, Bowie began to seriously consider leaving London and traveling north to a Buddhist monastery in Edinburgh, Scotland, where Zen master Dhardo Rinpoche lived and taught. He spoke frequently of giving up his pop career, shaving his beloved long hair and turning his life over to the abbot. Unlike his peers in the consciousness-expanding summer of '67, to Bowie meditation was not a pop fad but rather a serious means of dealing with a cataclysmic world, his underperforming career and a series of private family traumas, which would build to a climax by year's end. With stardom eluding him, Buddhism served to remind him that there were other goals than fame and material gain, and with its implicit dictums that nobody knows anything – each dizzying, new career strategy offered by London's smug scene makers and record-industry power brokers seemed neutralized by chanting and meditation.

'As far as I'm concerned the whole idea of Western life – that's the life we live now – is wrong,' he'd complained to *Melody Maker* the previous year, adding, 'I want to go to Tibet. It's a fascinating place, y'know. I'd like to take a holiday and have a look inside the monasteries. The Tibetan monks, Lamas, bury themselves inside mountains for weeks and only eat every three days. They're ridiculous – and it's said they live for centuries.'

'It was the lord Buddha that he turned to, temporarily, for guidance and inspiration,' Pitt writes. 'My view is that he heretofore abjured all false finery and pride in his appearance and it was in this dressed-down state that he came to the office to meet a Buddhist dignitary who was to honor us with a visit. Our receptionist ushered in the notable, who to our astonishment was flamboyantly arrayed in voluminous saffron robes, flip-flops held to his bare feet by jewels between his toes and over all the strong perfume of sandalwood.'

In 1967 Tony Visconti, then a twenty-three-year-old Brooklyn, New York-born musician and producer, also wrestling with his attraction to Eastern spirituality and his love of Western rock 'n' roll, was brought to London to work with the flamboyant Irish music impresario and producer Denny Cordell (who'd just had massive hits with the Moody Blues and Procol Harum and would, a decade later, discover Tom Petty and the Heartbreakers). One day Cordell brought Visconti into the offices of Essex Music, the firm where David was signed to his publishing deal. He had, like most people on the planet, not heard Bowie's debut record. Many at Essex believed that Bowie was talented. They just didn't know what to do with him and were hoping that somebody with Visconti's instincts, an outsider with a fresh perspective but also a gifted pro, could help them figure it out. According to Visconti's autobiography, he was told, 'You seem to have a talent for working with weird acts. I'd like to play something for you to consider. This is an album made by a writer I've been working with for some time. We were hoping he'd be right for the musical theater but he's become something quite different since he made this record.'

Listening to the tracks, Visconti was impressed by the maturity of the teenager's voice and the humor in his lyrics. In addition to the collected

141

singles, 'Rubber Band' and 'Love You Till Tuesday,' the album contained lushly romantic ballads like 'When I Live My Dream' (the Bee Gees meet Broadway), 'She's Got Medals' (which is more or less Love's 'Seven and Seven Is' in tempo and melody and indicated that Bowie could rock credibly), the Hammer Films-worthy 'Please Mr Gravedigger,' and the Peter Sellers-influenced 'We Are Hungry Men.'

Visconti did not know that Bowie was there that day, waiting in the office by a piano, eager to give anything that might catch fire a shot. Bowie didn't know much about Visconti, only that he was from New York City, from whence his new heroes the Velvet Underground hailed.

'I realized this casual encounter was a setup,' Visconti recalled. Bowie nervously shook hands with the American. By the end of the day they had warmed up a lot and realized they had a real musical affinity for one another. Visconti was impressed that Bowie was so well versed in rock 'n' roll, R & B and soul, as well as music hall show tunes, West Coast 'cool' jazz and Beat-generation novelty recordings like Ken Nordine's loony *Colors* series of jazz poetry. It may be not be irrelevant to point out the timing of the Bowie/Visconti union in relation to David's reaction to his older brother's misfortune. Visconti was a tough, confident American, three years Bowie's senior. While unable to replace Terry or heal the wounds that Bowie's half brother's illness was then

142

inflicting, Tony Visconti would certainly take on an older-brother role in his life, and to fail to note the significant timing of their partnership and friendship would be silly.

According to Visconti, after leaving Essex, the pair went to a revival screening of *Knife in the Water*, the 1962 art-house hit by Polish director Roman Polanski. Though stark and disquieting, Polanski's film features a jazz score at turns sultry or bebop influenced and manic, composed by the cult Polish jazz artist Krzysztof Komeda, and the two fast friends set about deconstructing the film and especially its soundtrack as the theater let out.

Their first recorded collaborations included the Bowie original 'Karma Man,' recorded on the afternoon of September 1, 1967. The guitar and strings are strange and thrumming. The verses are verbose and Dylanesque, reflecting the songwriter and the producer's shared affinity for Eastern spiritual guidance: enlightened souls, 'clothed in saffron robes.' The song's chorus, 'Slow down, slow down,' among Bowie's catchiest, was more or less directly ripped off by Suede for one of their Britpop-igniting singles 'The Drowners' in 1992.

'Let Me Sleep Beside You' is fairly self-explanatory, with a nifty chorus come-on and a fuzz guitar riff that nearly achieved what Woody Allen's Alvy Singer would have called 'heaviosity.' Visconti was a Beatles obsessive and you can already hear him connecting with his inner George Martin. On the records Bowie sounds

143

stronger, clearer and more alive than he ever did on the Shel Talmy-produced garage rock or the horn-driven Tony Hatch-produced pop kitsch. In the cooling weeks following the summer of love, as everything around him with regard to his family seemed to be violently dislodged, Bowie seemed to finally be settling into his own sound. He still borrowed. He sometimes even stole. But Visconti was now there to help make David Bowie records finally sound like their own statements somehow.

Also in 1967, David Bowie would meet another powerful collaborator, one who would help him connect with his *physical* vision. 'I taught David to free his body,' Lindsay Kemp boasted to *Crawdaddy!* magazine in 1974, and he was telling the truth. Kemp was a controversial dancer, choreographer and movement instructor. By 1968, he was already getting a reputation as a master provocateur, having set classical dance techniques on their ear with his touring company.

His father was a British naval officer who was killed in action. Kemp, openly gay like Pitt, was a misfit driven toward the performing arts at a young age. 'Of course, I've always been very fond of the service, but actually joining it was out of the question. I wanted to dance and sing and swing through circus hoops even more than I wanted to sail the seven seas. Now, by being a mime, I can be a sailor whenever I choose to be – and I can be the sea too.'

Kemp didn't fare well at school and had to rely on his wicked wit to get by. 'It was a very rough school and I wasn't a very rough person, so I found that the only way I could survive was to make the other boys laugh. I was like Scheherazade, telling them the most amazing stories night after night to ensure my survival. I amazed and dazzled them – like a bright light trained in wild dogs' eyes.'

After attending the Bradford School of Arts and Media (then already over a century old, it also produced David Hockney), Kemp tried his luck as an actor in the West End but found difficulty standing out. He was balding and pixie-ish, and his features without makeup, feathers and wigs seemed small. Kemp really found his voice when it came to mime. In his twenties, he moved to Edinburgh, Scotland, and studied with the famous French mime Marcel Marceau. Marceau bolstered his confidence and showed him how to use his body effectively. When he returned to London, Kemp founded his own performance troupe. He saw staid and joyless productions and decided that they were ready for a little camping up. He'd see the dancers chain-smoking and cussing offstage, but when they were onstage, they'd pretend to be sculpted and angelic and sincere.

'Camp sees everything in quotation marks,' Susan Sontag wrote in 'Notes on Camp' in 1964. 'It's not a lamp but a "lamp," not a woman but a "woman." To perceive camp in objects and persons is to understand Being as Playing – a role. It is the farthest extension in sensibility of the metaphor of life as theater.' Using this sensibility and combining it with real diligence as far as the body and utter commitment to the performance, Kemp and his collaborator Birkett torpedoed the highbrow dance recitals with bawdy humor and pieces based on edgy literature like Jean Genet's homoerotic Parisian novel *Our Lady of the Flowers*. By the time he encountered Bowie, he was already equally reviled and renowned for his work and his accelerated and archly bohemian approach to life and art.

'Most people think my life is very theatrical anyway because it's played to the hilt,' he has said. 'I like to do everything fully. I drink until I'm drunk. I eat until I'm full, frequently until I'm sick. I don't fancy people; I fall in love with them. Leave out hate – it doesn't come into my work at all. I'm terribly into intoxication – that's the only thing that counts . . .'

Kemp first heard Bowie's music while at NEMS, the British booking agency that was finding him employment as an opening act for various rock 'n' roll shows. 'They were getting me occasional gigs during what was then my mime act, billed as *Lindsay Kemp's a Man Who Mimes His Own Business*,' he says. Kemp is now in his seventies but his speech is still marked with dramatic rolling 'R's and fits of wicked laughter like John Lovitz as 'Master Thespian,' on *Saturday Night Live*.

146

'I'd be put in those kind of university gigs and things with rock 'n' roll singers and skiffle players and so on. And it was one day that I was in the office just checking that there was any work and the girls in the office said, 'Oh my God, Lindsay, you have to meet and listen to David Bowie,' who they had just met. Bowie had been in the office also trying to get work through NEMS even though he was with Ken Pitt at the time.' Kemp says, 'They gave me his record and I took it away and that was the Deram record [entitled *David Bowie*]. And I just fell for him, I mean the songs, the music, the whole thing.' Kemp saw himself in those songs, and he also saw himself moving and performing to them. They affected his body as well as his emotions. He focused on one track, the meandering love song 'When I Live My Dream.'

'It was so perfect for this little piece,' Kemp recalls. 'I liked that kind of plaintive voice you see. So he, the voice and the songs he was singing about, appealed to me immensely. On that first occasion I wasn't actually dancing to his music, I was just playing it as a kind of preset before the curtain went up, you see.'

The song became the soundtrack to his next performance at a small West End theater. Bowie was invited to the show and excitedly attended. This was among the only attention he'd received with regard to his widely neglected debut. The only problem was, nobody seemed to want to give

David Bowie a chance. Dropped by Deram after the failure of his self-titled debut, he was again label-less.

In 1968, Pitt looked to find Bowie a new contract and was meeting with the Beatles' new label Apple, Atlantic Records and Liberty among others. Bowie's family was concerned. The singer was so broke that when it came time for him to pay his taxes, Pitt received a letter from John Jones saying, 'It would be ironical if he was called upon to pay anything in view of the fact that his earnings from show business do not give him sufficient income to pay for his social security stamp.' He was about to gain something more important than immediate financial stability, however. Bowie was about to receive a philosophy. 'He came backstage afterward and it was love at first sight,' Kemp says today. 'Well, most attractions are physical to start with. A blond angel, he was like one of the Ganymedes standing there. I mean, oh.' Bowie was flattered that Kemp had chosen his song and they got to talking. Bowie came the following day to Kemp's small Soho flat, where they had breakfast together. 'We immediately began to put our heads together and create something,' Kemp says. Bowie talked about his fascination with Eastern art and thought, and Kemp told him all about the Japanese Kabuki theater tradition with its outsized costuming and willfully attention-seeking ethic. 'It was a very joyous meeting and a very fruitful one,' Kemp says. 'We began to work immediately on this little show which was called *Pierrot in Turquoise*. Bowie suggested the turquoise, it being the Buddhist symbol for everlastingness.'

The plot of *Pierrot in Turquoise* was basically autobiographical. David played, appropriately, Cloud, a young muse of the titular character Pierrot (portrayed, of course, by Kemp). In a separate sequence, Jack Birkett plays the clown Harlequin. Birkett, a nearly blind dancer who performed under the stage name Orlando, was the star of Kemp's company and another large personality to impress the young David Bowie. Kemp and Birkett seemed lifestyle models, like James Dean, Elvis and Little Richard were, only Bowie had never met Elvis or Little Richard and Dean was long dead. Here was someone who could influence Bowie directly and respond to his multiple queries in person.

'I began to think about costuming music, creating an alternate version of reality onstage. I wasn't quite sure what the balance would be but I was always open to other people's ideas and always so influenced by something I found dramatic,' Bowie has said.

'I really taught him to be audacious, because he was a bit timid.' Kemp recalls. 'Through example. My own example. My example offstage of course, but I mean my example in the theater, on the stage and in the workshop as well.'

Kemp and Bowie enjoyed a brief physical affair as well, with Kemp expressing his desire and having his way with his starstruck new friend, although this act too seemed to be part of a larger curriculum. Bowie plunged into this tutelage with everything he had and there was no longer much talk about shaving his head and fleeing to Edinburgh to become a monk.

'I taught to David the technique of the hypnotist and the lover. One has to hypnotize an audience to enchant them and of course make them love you. The Casanova technique. Not that that I needed to teach him much about the Casanova technique,' Kemp proclaimed.

'Lindsay always gave him hell,' *Pierrot*'s costume designer Natasha Korniloff has said. 'He said he was as stiff as a ramrod and would get nowhere, but he's pretty hard on people anyway. But Lindsay is also a very great teacher.' *Pierrot in Turquoise* quickly became a touring road show, with Kemp, Bowie, Birkett and Korniloff, who was also the van driver, playing theaters throughout Britain. 'We were like a terrible gypsy encampment.' Korniloff recalled.

Reviews were encouraging but critical. 'At the moment it is something of a pot-pourri,' the December 29, 1967, edition of the *Oxford Mail* observed. 'Mr Kemp has devised a fetching pantomime through which Pierrot pursues his love of life, his Columbine, tricked by Harlequin and deceived by the ever-changing Cloud.' Bowie's music, which provided the soundtrack, is singled out as 'haunting,' his voice 'superb' and 'dreamlike.'

Predictably, *Pierrot in Turquoise* was not a commercial success, and both Bowie and Kemp were forced to follow each creative vision with the most threadbare of budgets. This period, marked by Bowie briefly turning his back on his pop gambit, did much for his creative soul but little for his welfare or that of his mentor.

'There were more and more debtors calling at Lindsay's door,' Korniloff recalled. 'All these bills and demands.'

As he struggled, Bowie knew there was always a warm meal and a bed out in Bromley, but it often came at the expense of the great nourishment his creative side was enjoying. Wasn't it much more romantic to starve with these artists? he'd reason. No longer a teenager, he was struggling to find a balance between the world of his childhood and some kind of valuable, productive adult world as an artist. Both realms held darkness and bursts of bright warmth. Meditation only helped balance the two so much. He spent his days and nights stuck in the middle, a bit of a psychic mess. It was certainly no time for first love.

> **Mother:** *Are you going to wear that tie? You might want to dress down.*
> **Ren:** *I like the tie!*
> **Mother:** *In September, when you go to college, you can dress like David Bowie.*
> – *Frances Lee McCain and Kevin Bacon*

151

as *Ethel and Ren McCormack (from Footloose, 1984)*

It was freshman orientation and my mother and step-father had driven me up to Vermont from Long Island. We'd stayed overnight in a bed-and-breakfast and I remember falling asleep to the radio. It was playing a song by Bruce Cockburn entitled 'If I Had a Rocket Launcher.' Next was 'Little Miss S.' by Edie Brickell and the New Bohemians, an elegy for Edie Sedgwick, her namesake (still much better than the Cult's histrionic 'Edie (Ciao Baby).' This was, in Vermont anyway, 'college rock.' I was wearing a black sweater that my grandmother had knitted for me. She complained because I would only wear them in black. Knitters like variety, stripes and checks or squiggles. Cosby sweaters. I was growing a little sick of black myself. I wanted some squiggles in my life and Bennington College offered plenty. The sophomore who led my tour had recently seen the independent film My Life as a Dog *and terrified my mother by answering some of her earnest questions about cafeteria nutrition and curfews with barks and sometimes growls. I thought he was the coolest person I'd ever met. My high school had a dress code and a detention room. Up in the Green Mountains, I could wear whatever I wanted and do whatever I felt like, as long as it was reasonably legal and creative. Such freedom can be dangerous. You can wander too far off the path and just be a far-out individual, creating nothing but trouble for yourself. At night from 'the End of the World,' at the ridge of the*

Commons Lawn, you could see every celestial body. I instinctively felt like I needed a North Star for the next four years, and I chose David Bowie, the Starman, waiting in the sky. Bowie got far out and reinvented himself, I reasoned, and yet never ceased to be creative. This was a discipline, and I would adopt it, both academically and behaviorally. I would major in Bowie-ism. I displayed his compact discs prominently on my bookshelf, returning often to Young Americans – for sex; Station to Station – for drugs; 'Sorrow' off Pin Ups – when crushed out or sad; Ziggy – for when my school was insane and my work was down the drain; and Diamond Dogs – for sex and drugs and being crushed out and sad.

I soon found an accomplice in a student who called herself Flora and later Ufloria. She was from the West Coast, I believe, but mostly she just appeared without much warning, in Manhattan or Boston or Vermont, a vagabond, holding a small, portable boom box and, inevitably, a bag of pot. She later had a loose affiliation with the band the Brian Jonestown Massacre, but it seems like everyone I met at that time did as well. Bennington was the kind of place where you would hear people stomping around the lawn with earphones on, screaming along to the music playing in their heads. There was a Swiss kid named Michael or Michel who shouted Prince lyrics at God. You could hear him from a hundred yards, thanks to the echo in the valley: 'People call me rude! / I wish we all were nude!' Others sang arias from their window. Ufloria sang Bowie, which is why I tracked her down.

153

That and the rumor of her having pot. I was too shy to sing outdoors, or anywhere else, even with the pot, so I just nodded in agreement as she warbled. As it's fairly easy, when sequestered in the mountains, to pretend it's any era you like, we opted for the glittery early 1970s and took to painting silver stars on our faces. The stars were little pledges of allegiance to Bowie ('He's the commander, I'm just a space cadet,' an original star-faced fan memorably says during the live L.A. concert footage in the 1975 BBC film Cracked Actor). *Wearing stars, and outing ourselves as Bowie-ists, made us bolder. When we were hungry or out of pot, we'd stomp into the room of one of our classmates and demand food . . . and pot. Sometimes we'd be sorted. Other times we'd be turned away. Always, we'd bid adieu with 'Bye-bye, we love you' (Bowie's parting words after retiring Ziggy Stardust in '73). Our Bowie union was sexless and innocent and pure. We were both reveling in this new freedom presented to us and the intellectual notion of Bowie, along with the constant soundtrack we maintained in those pre-Playlist days was our key, translating it all and allowing us to make sense and make use of college, and one day get out of the mountains and down into cities better, wiser and more well rounded. The idea of Bowie gave us courage to experiment. I remember driving home for Thanksgiving that November and informing my parents, my sister, her visiting friends and my aunts, uncles and cousins that I'd made out with a boy, just to see what it was like. When nobody asked what it was like, I volunteered. Much the same minus the*

154

stubble. As I recall this two decades on, Ufloria long gone from my life, I of course want to punch myself in the mouth. What a brat! But I am also struck by how brave just saying that out loud truly was, and how doing it in the first place was amazing. It is amazing to me still. I am not that brave anymore. Like losing your virginity, you can really only unleash your inner Bowie once.

CHAPTER 7

'**M**od was finished, then the hippies got going,' Ray Stevenson, the photographer who began shooting Bowie in the late sixties and went on to become one of the most celebrated chroniclers of the London punk scene, would explain to me. 'Very few mods became hippies. Bowie did, Bolan did. I think most of the youth cultures, the people who were part of it stayed with it through to middle age. Why did Bowie and Bolan change? Ambition!' Most Teds remained rockers when the mod movement began in the late fifties and early sixties. Quite a few mods continued to be mod when the hippie era dawned in '67. Very few hippies transitioned into glitter rockers in the early 1970s. And most glitter rockers are still glitter rockers, only somewhat less ravishing to all but their immediate loved ones. The only frizzy-haired glams who ever became punks were very, very young Mott the Hoople fans such as Mick Jones of the Clash. David Bowie and, to a lesser extent, Marc Bolan, was indeed among the few who traveled from cultural shift to cultural shift over the years, pulling the best bits

156

from each and altering their look to suit the times (with Bolan, tragically, being cut off at the dawn of punk) and strengthening their creative and professional hand.

There's a point in most people's lives where they just stop. I dress, for example, the same way I dressed in 1984. That was the moment that I decided that I'd happened on a lasting look à la John Cooper Clarke, the Mancunian punk poet. Bowie did not stop. By late '67 and very early 1968, he'd discarded mod for hippie full-on. Like many in England at the time, he was aware of the American war in Vietnam but was more prone to carrying on with a sort of cultural or social politics as opposed to a street-fighting-man activism. 'We weren't particularly politically concerned, not at that time,' John Hutchinson explains. 'It was more about the personal expansion. Buddhism and, uh, world peace. But I don't think we were connected to the Vietnam War the way we would become in '73 when half of our road crew were Vietnam vets.' The notion that a couple could nest in a hippie love pad, grow and eat their own vegetables, get stoned on hash at the Middle Earth club and change the world via a sing-along or a piece of dance performed on some patch of lawn in Regent's or Hyde Park still held, and for a time, that was exactly the kind of lifestyle Bowie was happy to lead with his first real love.

Hermione Farthingale was not her real name. As far as stage names go, it was fitting, as many who knew her remember her as profoundly old world in her beauty. 'An English rose,' as Lindsay Kemp describes her. Photos suggest her skin was uncommonly pale, almost white. Her chin was strong and her lips were wide and thin as though naturally pursed. She had a dancer's body, compact and muscular. Her hair was a remarkably thick reddish brown, and she wore it in long curls, as was the hippie style of the day. She resembled a more ethereal and soft Vanessa Redgrave.

Bowie was frustrated with Kenneth Pitt's difficulty finding him a new record deal. In an effort to preserve whatever momentum they'd had with the Visconti-produced Deram singles and their commitment to launching David as an all-around entertainer, Pitt figured if one aspect is not working at the moment, best to pursue another. He found David commercial work, selling Lyons Maid ice cream. The ice cream company was intent on cashing in on the hippie culture with their new Luv brand. In the commercial, Bowie, in a shaggy cut, is seen running upstairs while the jingle's 'Luv, Luv, Luv . . .' strains to be youthful and infectious. 'Now with pop cards!' Bowie is heard to say at its end. Whatever 'pop cards' were (tradeable giveaways with Peter Max-style graphics on them, one could assume), they didn't pay the bills. Bowie, as well as Marquee scene pal Dana Gillespie, auditioned for and failed to get a part in the British production of the touring company of the hippie musical *Hair* as well. 'We

158

both got turned down, can you believe it?' Gillespie says. 'Those bastards. But it was only for the touring company to go to Amsterdam, but the whole course of both of our lives might have changed had we been accepted.'

Bowie did manage to find a small role in a BBC production of 'The Pistol Shot,' based on an Alexander Pushkin short story (as part of the network's *Theatre* 625 series). The episode, which aired May 20, 1968, featured Bowie as a dancer in a key scene. It was on the set of 'The Pistol Shot' that he met Hermione, another Kemp student who, like Bowie, also got the job on his recommendation.

'Well, when we were really hard up, and we were always hard up, I got a job dancing. I was asked if I could find other dancers for a television production of this play that had a ballroom sequence,' Kemp says, 'so I took David along and he met Hermione there, who was one of the dancers.'

Unlike Bowie, Hermione was classically trained in ballet and knew ballroom dancing as well. 'Hermione was very nice, and extremely intelligent,' Kemp says, 'and I was very fond of her but I wasn't so fond, so happy to see them, you know, leave the studio together . . .' Kemp was, at the time, in love with Bowie himself and imagined that they were a couple. 'I suppose in one's youth one always hopes that love will last forever,' he says today. 'Yes, I didn't think of it as only lasting for as short a time as it did. We tend not to think about that. [After Hermione] it became extremely agonizing. And there were a lot of other ladies, you see. He never made any commitment to me or anything like that, he didn't slip a ring on my finger. There were no promises, but it was incredibly painful, especially when it was with the ladies [like Hermione] that we were working with at the time.'

The minuet that David and Hermione danced featured both dressed in powdered wigs and eighteenth-century costume. Their courtship, however, would be done while costumed in shawls and beads and other hippie accoutrement. Hermione, whose father was a well-to-do lawyer, lived very comfortably in London in a small Victorian house with a front garden. Before long they were cohabiting, and both David's parents and Ken Pitt saw very little of him. Theirs was a life of hippie bliss for a time. They'd prepare macrobiotic meals and discuss art, Buddhist philosophy and Romantic poetry, while the world outside seemed vulgar and misguided. On weekends, they'd take a trip out to the country and sunbathe in the nude. 'We were naturists for the day,' Visconti, who was also deep into his hippie trip, recalled in his memoir.

It was his first adult relationship, and one that demanded, even in those enlightened, free-loving times, a bit more of a sacrifice or sense of commitment than he was willing to give at his young age and with his often opportunistic but still fearless and enthusiastic attraction to both men and women, something Hermione did not know about and would not likely have approved of. She looked the part, with her natural, flowing hippie hair, but like most hippies, she was actually upper-middle-class, a well-to-do lawyer's daughter with values likely rooted more in her parents' world than in the fast-waning Age of Aquarius. She certainly inspired the twenty-one-year-old Bowie, and in an effort, perhaps, to ground both his personal and professional endeavors, he and Hermione, along with a local rock guitarist named Tony Hill, formed a performance troupe named Turquoise in early 1968.

Hill was in the process of assembling his own band High Tide when his manager informed him that one David Bowie was searching for a guitarist for a strange new kind of act. Hill met Bowie and discovered they had some musical chemistry. He ended up jamming with Bowie and Visconti, and later became a full-time member of Turquoise. Hill found Bowie's 'strange, sort of folky songs' intriguing but didn't know what to make of the delivery at their early folk club gigs.

'David and Hermione did some artistic ballet work along with the music,' Tony Hill says today. 'She was a ballet dancer and he was into Marcel Marceau. It was a little over my head, but I just carried on regardless. I got on with them well, but it was very unusual.'

161

Hill thinks the wigged-out Turquoise was a direct reaction to Bowie's increasing frustration with Pitt's management style, which, as the London pop scene flew headlong into an age of new enlightenment, could have seemed hopelessly outdated. Turquoise felt like the path of least resistance, as well as at least a superficial opportunity to give the middle finger to 'the man.' He wasn't making any money, so why not take loot out of the equation and perform for the 'art' of it all? Although he never recorded Turquoise, Visconti remained within the social fold, while Pitt, the father figure, as well as Bowie's own mother and father, were relegated to the adults' table. Hermione, Tony Visconti and his girlfriend approximated a new kind of family energy, communal and hopeful, genuine and warm.

Predictably, although Pitt thought very highly of Hermione, he was not remotely interested in joining in the crunchy festivities anyway. He was bewildered by David's enthusiastic description of the new 'act.' 'I do not know how much David's brush with cabaret influenced his decision to form a multimedia trio, the soft sound of which was the antithesis of cabaret brashness,' Pitt wrote. 'Perhaps he had been thinking about it before and had been wondering how best he could incorporate Hermione in his activities.'

Bowie encouraged her to sing, but it was clear that the couple's romantic chemistry was much stronger than their creative chemistry. As a singer,

Hermione was . . . a great ballet dancer. 'She had a passable voice,' Pitt observed charitably.

When Hill left to form his own group later in the year, Turquoise mutated slightly into a more musically sound venture with the return of John Hutchinson. Since leaving the Buzz, Hutchinson had spent time in Montreal, working for Air Canada to support his wife and young child, but also absorbing the Canadian folk scene, whose brightest lights included Leonard Cohen and Joni Mitchell. He had no idea that Bowie too had abandoned R & B and the boisterous, brassy pop sound for something quieter.

'I'd become more interested in acoustic songs,' Hutchinson says. 'I'd learned how to fingerpick. When I came back, I'd more or less turned into a more folky kind of player. When I got in touch with David to see what he was doing, I'd found that he'd gone the same way, by a different route. He started to appreciate different kinds of songs. He didn't need a band to pump it out anymore. He was into softer things. So we'd both changed. What he could use from me was my acoustic guitar picking. We also found we could harmonize.'

With Hutchinson replacing Hill, the trio rechristened themselves Feathers. Given the kitsch that goes along with a background in folkmime, a lot is made of Bowie's tenure in both Turquoise and Feathers, but in actuality, there were only about a handful of performances on College campuses like Sussex University and at local art centers in

163

and around London. Club dates were rare. Feathers played the Roundhouse in London on September 14 and the hippie Middle Earth Club on the following day. One of their final shows was at the Marquee in January of '69. During their sets, Hutchinson would play his acoustic. Bowie would play his twelve-string Gibson and the trio would harmonize on Bowie Originals like 'When I'm Five' and covers of Jacques Brel, the Belgian singer and actor whose histrionic and highly romantic numbers were also favored by Scott Walker – a Bowie hero. There were also mime interludes. It did not set the world on fire.

'Ghastly,' says Lindsay Kemp. 'I was there, I was invited and there were just a handful of people there, and I was utterly unimpressed. Unimpressed by David's mime, because at that time he was imitating Marcel Marceau, which is a very different kind of mime than I do, I mean a very different kind of mime; my mime is much more expressive. It's much more of a dance mime as opposed to the French pantomime. Even though I studied with Marceau and I passed on what I learned from Marceau to Bowie. But then David went off into that awful kind of white-faced striped shirt mime routine. He did it because he loved it. He loved to mime and Marcel Marceau and white faces and striped shirts. Whereas I have a great talent as a mime but absolutely no talent as a singer, he has a great talent as a singer-song-writer, but not as a mime.'

Others, like the London-based photographer Ray Stevenson, found Bowie's mime forays to be perfectly in keeping with the sway of the culture. 'The mime stuff. I'm not very big on that but I think he brought something fresher to it,' he says, 'Marcel Marceau that was my idea of mime, but I recall seeing Bowie doing a mime of an old guy walking down the street with a bent back. He stops to pick up a discarded cigarette and it's a joint. Then he stands up straight, has a great time smoking, and as it wears off, he goes back to his bent back. Marcel Marceau wouldn't have done that.'

After the shows, the incense would be lit and hash joints passed around. Maybe a little money would be exchanged for their efforts, but that was not the point.

'In Feathers, he was happy,' Hutchinson says, 'the happiest I'd seen him. The fact that Ken Pitt didn't understand it didn't really bother David. It was the social thing that was the big deal. It was what was happening in London in those days, the Middle Earth, the hippie movement. David was drawn into that and he and Hermione lived in that kind of hessian-and-lace kind of society. I wasn't from that background. I took a job, and that turned out to be a good idea because Feathers made absolutely no money.'

David and Hermione's private life was so hermetic that many in Bowie's social circle claim that they never really got to know her beyond superficial observation. 'We were too close, thought alike and spent all the time in a room sitting on the corner of a bed,' Bowie has said. For Bowie enthusiasts, she remains Sphinx-like. Even the fastidious Peter and Leni Gillman, authors of *Alias David Bowie*, were unable to uncover any information on her whereabouts. 'We tried very hard to find her but failed,' Peter Gillman wrote to me in an e-mail. 'Good luck.'

I was unable to locate Hermione as well despite continued efforts. Some people don't want to be found by David Bowie biographers. Ex-manager Ralph Horton is another who rarely surfaces, if at all. Unlike Horton, the silence suits the myth of Hermione. There is little to remember her by except the music that David began writing after their breakup, songs tinged with heartbreak and regret that seemed authentic and no longer borrowed or imitated. Falling in love and screwing it up gave him some gravitas. His darker forays would never again seem so juvenile.

'Where she was from and what she had done was a bit of a mystery,' Hutchinson says. 'I knew Hermione was not her real name. But reinventing yourself like that was not common in those days. I think she was maybe the daughter of somebody very famous and didn't want it known that his daughter was a hippie. All I knew was that was it. She spoke very well. She was obviously well educated. And she'd been a dancer. So she knew all about show business but not rock 'n' roll business. I don't think she would have joined a rock 'n' roll band. For a while, I think she was okay with the scene. She just leant what she could lend to what David was into.'

David's rock 'n' roll lifestyle would ultimately be the undoing of his relationship with Hermione. He didn't know any other way to live and pursued affairs and kept hours that she eventually could no longer abide, and soon there was tension in hippie heaven. 'I was totally unfaithful and couldn't for the life of me keep it zipped,' he confessed to *Mojo* in 2002. 'I'm sure we would have lasted a good long time if I'd been a good boy.'

'Hermione was in and out of David's life so fast that it is not surprising that biographers have little to write about. Also, unlike most ex-wives and girlfriends of celebrities, she was well bred and had the intelligence to drift away into the obscurity of her own private life,' Pitt writes to me. 'I liked her very much and hoped the romance would blossom and that she would marry David, but it was not to be.'

Among those with whom David may have dallied at this time was an Asian American named Calvin Mark Lee, who seemed happy to be found and to speak about his affair with Bowie when I contacted him. Lee is now seventy-two. He lives alone in Los Angeles in a small apartment near MacArthur Park surrounded by TVs. When I interviewed him for this book in the summer of

2008, he would watch each screen as he spoke and occasionally comment on it. David Bowie himself watched a wall of television sets while portraying the alien Thomas Jerome Newton in his proper film debut, 1976's *The Man Who Fell to Earth*. 'Get out of my mind!' he ended up screaming. Lee is a molecular chemist with over thirty published papers to his credit, and his mind, I think, is porous enough, or large enough, to handle it. A little scary even. Our first interview lasted four hours. We spoke of David Bowie for twenty minutes.

Before he agreed to speak with me, Calvin asked if I would e-mail him a photo of myself – not for any prurient reasons. He is more what I would call a hybrid of super-humanist and aesthetic snob. He loves and has unmatched enthusiasm for all people, as long as they are beautiful, talented and intelligent. 'I believe in beautiful, creative and intelligent people. I believe in them having not just one of those attributes but all three at the same time. That's my criteria . . . beauty, creativity and intelligence. The first thing in taking a photo is the beauty part. If they don't fulfill the first criteria I don't go on any further. If you're a musician you're creative, but I would never take a picture of Elton John. And I've met Elton John.'

Lee came from a family of Chinese American intellectuals from San Francisco. He studied at Yale before accepting a grant to attend Chelsea College in London. He arrived on May 30, 1963 (a Thursday; he made me look it up). 'They were filming a movie around Manresa Road at the time. *The Collector* with Samantha Eggar,' he tells me. Bored with his fellow intellectuals (who embodied only the intelligence part of his three-fold criteria), he began hanging out in the burgeoning pop scene, catching early London sets by the Rolling Stones and the Yardbirds (Lee is in the audience during the famous nightclub scene in *Blow Up*). With his Minox camera, he became something of a collector of his own, taking photos of people as a means to connect with those who met his standards. 'Who are the most beautiful, creative and intelligent people? They were artists and musicians,' Lee would tell me.

Lee has a flair for suspense building in his speech. He will say things like 'There was this one group of four people and they went by the name . . . the Beatles.' Or 'That band was a band with a three-letter name, and that was W-H-O. The Who.'

Lee spent his days in London living on the Mercury Records expense account, taking artists to sumptuous Chinese meals at Mr Chow's in posh Knightsbridge and basking in the glow of their beauty, creativity and intelligence. 'Being paid to wine and dine beautiful, creative and intelligent people – what more of a job could anyone want? I remember taking Jerry Lee Lewis and his companion. I had to explain to him what each item was. What the ingredients were on the menu.'

Others in London at the time might have known the ubiquitous Lee simply as the guy with the third-eye jewel on his forehead. He was locally famous for the plastic prism he affixed there, framed by his long, jet-black hair to great theatrical effect. 'They were what I call a love jewel,' he says. 'That's the love emanating from me to you.' David would incorporate the love jewel into his late-period Ziggy Stardust costume in 1973.

It's possible that Lee met and photographed Bowie before Bowie even started living with Hermione Farthingale. Kenneth Pitt claims to have received a fan letter from Lee addressed to Bowie around the release of the self-titled Deram Records debut. Lee was certainly one of the many affairs that Bowie had once the couple started cohabiting in '68. By then, Lee had parlayed his enthusiasm and intellectual intensity into a position at Mercury. Like Bowie, Lee was open to bisexual experiences. 'I'm basically bi but it's five percent girls and ninety-five percent boys,' he tells me. 'I think it's sort of being greedy; instead of only dealing with fifty percent of the population, I'm open to dealing with one hundred percent of the population.'

He recalls seeing Bowie, Hermione and Hutchinson in Feathers. 'She was a very pretty ballet dancer,' he says. 'I liked her. But I'm sure even if she wasn't English she would not have approved of me and David. You're talking about potential rivals. I'm sure she didn't like Ken Pitt either.'

Pitt despised Lee, whom he referred to as 'the first of the predators' (with Angie, whom Lee would soon bring to Mercury Records as a marketing assistant, being the second). Lee's flat became not only a place for dalliances but somewhere that David could play guitar and complain. Enamored with Bowie's beauty, creativity and intelligence, Lee was happy to lend a sympathetic ear.

'He would get migraines,' Lee says. 'He felt like he was being pulled in all of these different directions.'

Lee told the then label-less Bowie that he belonged on Mercury and even tried to get him a deal but met with resistance from his boss, Lou Reizner. Reizner had recently moved to the London offices to become Mercury's European director and seek out new talent. Among his first coups was signing Rod Stewart, then front man for the Faces, to a solo contract. Despite Lee (who became the assistant European director) and his limitless enthusiasm, Reizner was not interested in Bowie. 'He hated him,' Lee says. 'I think Bowie was too effeminate for him. He wrote a memo . . . I wish I had the letter. It said, "I see no potential for this artist in the U.S."'

Reizner was a singer and producer himself, having released a self-titled album on Mercury that year. 'He was a Tom Jones type,' Lee says. 'A baritone. It's a good album. It's sad that he could not see the potential for David too.'

Although handsome in a tan-and-toothy, Bert Convy-ish fashion, Reizner lacked pop star DNA but took pride in his musicality and ability to discover, nurture and sell new artists. He would later shepherd the prog rockers Van der Graaf Generator and Rick Wakeman of Yes (soon to be a Bowie studio musician). He is also responsible for the film *All This and World War II*, a montage of World War II stock footage scored with Beatles covers. This sounded like a good idea to Lou Reizner. David Bowie did not. Reizner, who eventually permitted Bowie to become a Mercury artist, died of cancer in 1977 at just forty-three.

Hermione might not have known about Calvin Mark Lee explicitly, but she could sense that Bowie's attractiveness was starting to infringe on their idyllic hippie home (in addition to allegedly dealing with Kenneth Pitt's attentions, Bowie was embroiled in a love triangle with Kemp and Natasha Korniloff as well, one that ended with Kemp slashing his wrists in a suicide attempt). Those who knew David well, like Hutchinson, may have worried privately that at heart Bowie was simply too wild for Hermione, his 'English rose.'

'I think they were a really nice match for each other,' Hutchinson says, 'but I guess I would have said that it wouldn't have lasted. David was still very much a rock 'n' roll sort of character. He and myself had gone a bit folksy, but . . . When we were making the *Love You Till Tuesday* film . . . it was when they started to fall out a bit. I never saw it. But I could feel the vibe while we were filming.'

Love You Till Tuesday was a film conceived by Bowie and Ken Pitt as a way to showcase all of David's talents. Pitt raised the money for it himself, and given his good taste, the production value of the finished project is indeed top-notch. Beautifully lit and shot in lush 'Eastman Color,' it is, unfortunately, a throwback to the cheeky-chappy mugging of Bowie's Newley period and is by and large a collection of promotional films for singles like the title track that had already failed to chart.

The strategy behind making *Love You Till Tuesday* was that if people could see David actually performing the songs, along with mime interludes, they would finally connect with what Bowie was all about. It can be argued that much of *Love You Till Tuesday*, which was helmed by a director of little acclaim named Malcolm J. Thomson, was ultimately influenced by the way Pitt viewed Bowie's image: shampooed, smiling, dressed in neat gray suits with comically oversized belt buckles or wild colors. The real Bowie of that period, showcased in the segments featuring Hermione and Hutchinson, was a bit more of a musky street hippie, but the bulk of *Love You Till Tuesday* reduces Bowie to some scrubbed and polished showbiz action figure or doll.

In the segment filmed for the track 'When I'm Five,' Bowie attempts to project the blank-eyed purity of an actual five-year-old as he promises, 'I will chew and spit tobacco like my grandfather Jones.' It's such a sickly-sweet vignette, one is grateful for the unintentional and somewhat cruel hilarity of autobiographical lines like 'I get headaches in the morning,' which clearly reflect his mental turmoil at the time.

'Rubber Band' also resurfaces, with Bowie seemingly on leave from some brainwashed barbershop quartet. 'Let Me Sleep Beside You' is considered again, a rocker in this context, but Bowie's air-guitar strumming handily ruins any edge it might have brought. One can almost smell the polyester sweat and smoke in the studio. During the mime interlude Bowie performs a piece entitled 'The Mask' in full whiteface. 'Ken was very much like [the Lower Third and the Buzz's manager] Ralph Horton,' Hutchinson says. 'His affection for David clouded the whole thing. He didn't understand what David was doing with Feathers. Ken's not rock 'n' roll either. He wanted David to be like Judy Garland. The thing that Ken liked best in *Love You Till Tuesday* was 'The Mask,' because there's no music in it and David had no trousers on. And that says it all.'

Before completion of the film project, Hermione was given an opportunity to audition for a musical entitled *Song of Norway*, starring Florence Henderson of *Brady Bunch* fame. Sensing perhaps that the project she was committed to was a turkey, she informed Bowie that she would not be able to complete the Feathers section of . . . *Tuesday* because of this conflict.

'David seemed businesslike about Hermione leaving for the audition. He was crushed. But it wasn't that long before I walked in and he was in bed with another girl, you know?' Hutchinson says. Many Bowie books talk about his need for loyalty, listing tales of those excommunicated from the Bowie universe after either asking for more money (this would in part break up the Spiders from Mars in 1973) or criticizing his behavior (anyone who told him, 'Perhaps you're abusing the gak a bit, luv,' circa '75 and early '76). The departure of Hermione may have indeed wounded him, even if Bowie did not show it; in the future, whenever anybody's behavior resembled Hermione's they would be rapidly exiled. With the completion of *Love You Till Tuesday*, the Bowie-Farthingale hippie love affair was over, and Bowie, taking a page out of the Lindsay Kemp behavioral guide, dove headlong into flamboyant heartbreak.

'Hey, one's heart gets broken at that kind of age in a different kind of way, you know,' friend Dana Gillespie recalls. 'It was the one then.'

'I was in the depths of despair,' he would recall in 1971. 'It was nearly two years ago but I don't forget it because it was an important period and I'm still living off it.' Bowie channeled his pain into his music and during this period he wrote some of his best material, including the plaintive and literal 'Letter to Hermione' and the more poetic 'An Occasional Dream,' in which he sings of the idyllic 'one hundred days' they'd ostensibly shared ('And we'd talk with our eyes / Of the sweetness in our lives').

Hermione filmed *Song of Norway* but is credited only as 'Dancer.' Her career never took off but she met another dancer on the film's Norwegian set and quickly entered into a new relationship. 'The last time I saw her was about a year ago in the health food shop in Baker Street,' Ken Pitt said in 1974, 'and she told me that she was thinking of giving up ballet because there was no work for her.'

'She quite rightly ran off with a dancer that she had met while filming,' Bowie commented years later. 'Then I heard she married an anthropologist and went to live in Borneo for a while, mapping out unknown rivers.' Hermione reportedly resurfaced years later when Bowie was in the midst of his Ziggy Stardust superfame, and the two briefly reconnected, but it soon became apparent that it was not meant to be. Still, Hermione has never really gone away. 'It was Hermione who got me writing for and on a specific person,' Bowie said. The heartache she gave and the loneliness that he felt in the aftermath of their breakup on the set of *Love You Till Tuesday* would inspire David Bowie's first truly immortal, and some would say signature, song, 'Space Oddity.'

'Like the Deram album the film was intended to be a CV and an audacious innovation at the time,' Pitt tells me. 'It is now a valuable record of what D was actually into and we are left wondering what would have happened if I had not asked him to write what I considered to be an essential requirement of the film. Something new and very special. Would he still have written 'Space Oddity'?'

One of Bowie's favorite albums released during this new darkly poetic wave of '68 was *Bookends*, by Simon & Garfunkel. Songs like 'America' reminded him of his teenage affinity for Kerouac. 'Old Friends' pushed the same wistful buttons that his childhood favorite song, 'The Inchworm' had. 'A Hazy Shade of Winter' was wary and bitter but still somehow glamorous and cinematic. Like the Velvet Underground's debut, and the just-released *White Light, White Heat*, it had New York cool to burn. The record's druggy cred was sealed when Frances McDormand held it up for ridicule in 2000's *Almost Famous* and pointed to the artists' pupils on the cover shot: 'Look at them. They're on pot!' (Bowie would do a stripped down and stirring version of 'America,' at the post-9/11 Concert for New York City in October of 2001.) *Bookends* is one key to this next phase of his song-writing. David, who, according to friends, was only consuming large quantities of hash and drinking wine at the time (despite some reports that he had started using heroin), envisioned a Simon & Garfunkel-style duo taking over where Feathers ended and set about writing songs that would feature two-part harmony rather than three.

'He seemed to think, "Right, Hermione's gone, that's what we're gonna do now,"' Hutchinson says. '*Bookends* had come out. Simon & Garfunkel were big. With them as role models, we did some demos. Bedroom tapes. Two guitars going. He would always just say, "I've got a couple of new ones," and play them for me. There was one called "Lover Till the Dawn." There was another, a song about a spaceman that I thought was a bit more unusual. It had come to him in part because of the current in those days. Space travel just started to happen. But you know that songs write themselves. You get an idea. The song comes to you. He said, 'Silly one, but here it is.' I don't think we thought it was anything special. The title was just a piss-take on the Kubrick film.'

'I remember he came 'round once to that flat that I was in and he said "I've just written this song a half an hour ago,"' says Gillespie. 'And then he got up and strummed the chords and sang: "Ground control to Major Tom. Ground control to Major Tom." And I thought, "What an odd choice of lyric." People weren't writing about things like that.'

If the end of his love affair with Hermione and some form of narcotics-fueled isolation contributed to the vibe of 'Space Oddity,' the tale of an astronaut, Major Tom, who deviates from his mission and winds up helplessly floating in space forever, then the catalyst for bringing it all together was indeed Stanley Kubrick's 1968 film adaptation of science fiction writer Arthur C. Clarke's 2001: *A Space Odyssey*. The film had opened in the West End that spring and attracted all kinds of 'heads' with their stashes to figure out what the nonlinear and often dialogue-free images meant: 'Okay, the tapirs are living among the monkeys until the monolith appears. That's when mankind becomes violent! And the monkeys are no longer vegetarian and . . . whoa! Pass the liquid cannabis tincture, Bud.'

It's most likely the early scene in which an astronaut communicates with his daughter on her birthday that inspired 'Space Oddity' more than the film's iconic opening and paranoid ending. 'Tell mama that I telephoned,' he says before ingesting a 'stress pill.' The notion of space exploration compromising concrete familial affection or unity appealed to the newly single David, someone who had grown up with a short supply of the security and attention any child requires.

Calvin Mark Lee knew that 'Space Oddity' marked his chance to get Bowie signed to Mercury, so undeniable was its hit potential given the strength of the melody and the 'space fever' that had taken over popular culture in the months leading up to the July *Apollo 11* mission.

179

At the start of '69, defying Lou Reizner's anti-Bowie sentiment, he financed the recording of a demo using Mercury equipment and studio time. 'We had to do it all behind Lou's back,' he tells me, his voice swelling with excitement nearly forty years later. 'But it was such a *good* record.'

When Pitt heard the recording he was also excited. He knew that this was something that he could use to secure a new record deal, although he was suspicious about Calvin Lee and Mercury, largely because it was not an English institution but rather partnered with a UK label, Phillips. Its headquarters in Chicago were the object of rumors about mob ties. Pitt even found the money to shoot a promotional clip for the song to add to the *Love You Till Tuesday* film. The result is more like *Barbarella* (the campy, Roger Vadim-directed science fiction film also released that year) than Kubrick. It shows Bowie, looking unnervingly like John Denver in greasy hair and granny glasses, clad in a silver lamé space suit (supplied by Lee) and frolicking with two space babes, played by model Samantha Bond and production assistant Suzanne Mercer. Director Malcolm Thomson reportedly wanted the babes to get it on with Major Tom on camera, but Pitt objected.

The first time 'Bowie and Hutch' performed 'Space Oddity' live at the Marquee they realized that they were able to captivate the crowd with the dramatically sung dialogue. Hutchinson would sing the part of 'ground control.' Bowie would answer as Major Tom. And during the climax, when the 'tin can' floats off into eternity, Bowie would play a small electronic keyboard device known as a Stylophone, given to him by Marc Bolan, who also declared correctly that David had written his first big hit.

'The audiences grew because it was so unusual,' Hutchinson says. 'The small gigs that we did, he would turn up with that Stylophone. He also had an ocarina. You blew into it and it made a funny kind of noise. He didn't care if it was a joke instrument. He was quite happy because it was something that really made an impression on an audience.'

Calvin Lee got his way, and ultimately Bowie signed a very modest deal with Mercury Records (without John Hutchinson, who would once again be called away by family obligation). Pre-'Space Oddity,' Bowie was so marginalized that his deal had to go through the label's New York offices. He was an English singer/songwriter who could not even get a proper deal with the United Kingdom-based parent company of his American label. The first order of business was to record a proper studio version of 'Space Oddity' for release as a single. Bowie assumed that Tony Visconti would be the producer of 'Space Oddity' and was disappointed when his friend passed. Although he has since revised his opinion, Visconti apparently thought the track was a cynical means to cash in on the excitement surrounding the NASA launch, essentially a novelty record. Gus Dudgeon, a sound engineer affiliated with Cordell and Essex, had worked on smashes like the Zombies' 'She's Not There' and quickly realized that a potential new one was within his reach. He jumped at it, dismissing Visconti's wariness. 'Well, he's mad,' Dudgeon said at the time.

'During the session, dear Gus was quaking in his boots. It might have been the first thing he ever produced,' Herbie Flowers, who plays bass on the single, said. 'And I know he only booked me because of my name. Gus and I were from a jazzier background; we were more into Miles Davis and Charlie Parker than Elvis. 'Space Oddity' was this strange hybrid song. With the Stylophone and all the string arrangements, it's like a semiorchestral piece.'

The new version of 'Space Oddity,' recorded in London's Trident Studios (where Bowie would record nearly all of his early seventies music) on June 20, would be an epic. The arrangements were plotted on the studio bulletin board with all the precision of an actual lunar mission. Strings come in here. Herbie Flowers's bass here. Mick Wayne's guitar here. Trident's resident keyboardist Rick Wakeman, who would soon go on to great fame with Yes, was brought in to play the Mellotron, a proto-synthesizer that had been made famous by the Beatles two years earlier on 'Strawberry Fields Forever.'

'Gus and David were looking for a Mellotron

player and Tony Visconti recommended me,' Wakeman says today. He arrived at the studio to find a more hands-on artist/producer collaboration than any he'd seen before. Even in the late sixties, a producer, it was understood, was the didactic voice. The artist was the compliant craftsman.

'Gus was a different class. He worked to get on tape what the artist wanted,' Wakeman says. According to Visconti, much of the arrangement was indeed David's creation. 'David was light years ahead of how the industry thought. Simple as that. I didn't think it was a novelty song at all. I thought it was astonishing.'

Once it was finished, Lee, the technophile, stepped in again to ensure that the single would be truly monumental. 'I wanted a couple things done and got them to do it,' he tells me. 'I wanted the single to be mixed in stereo. That had never been done for a single before. I also wanted to make sure it was as long as possible. Not just three minutes. And I wanted David's picture on the sleeve, which was also hardly ever done [singles were usually issued in plain paper sleeves with the name of the label printed on it]. I wanted to give his first single for Mercury a huge sense of impact.'

His first single for the label has also become, in a way, David Bowie's signature song, traditionally the first track on any of his many best-of compilations. It's as good an introduction as you will get to his peerless period (say, '69–83). Forty years on, it remains one of the half dozen David Bowie songs that are played daily on American classic rock radio, and to hear the watery acoustic guitar intro rise slowly from a segue of, say, a Joe Walsh or Bad Company song provides lasting proof of just how powerful a song it was and remains. It's a mood changer. It's a put-down-what-you're-doing-and-pay-attention-to-this kind of song, a five-minute story song with sonic invention and vocal charisma to burn. In the spring of 1969, shortly before its rush release, it seemed like the only thing that could stop 'Space Oddity' from its destiny of becoming David's first genuine hit single was the failure of NASA and its astronauts themselves. This was in fact something discussed by the Mercury marketing and publicity departments.

'We took a big chance,' Lee says. 'If anything happened to the astronauts, the record would tank. He sings about being lost in space. Nobody would play it. Oh, but it was such a good record.'

CHAPTER 8

The Three Tuns Pub, in the London suburb of Beckenham, is where David Bowie cofounded Growth, an 'Arts Lab' designed to spread consciousness and import the progressive ideas of London and San Francisco to suburbia. The Arts Lab was basically a meeting held every Sunday in the pub's rear (it's now a Zizzi fast food Italian chain restaraunt) and yet the modest venture, drawn from David's romantic and cultural partnership with a recently divorced journalist and mother of two named Mary Finnegan, would provide David with his first permanent base outside of his childhood home in nearby Bromley as well as another quasi-family that would create a pattern for the more flamboyant entourages and professional retinues that would mark his life in the seventies and eighties. More important, Finnegan's modest home on shady Foxgrove Road and the 'Lab' (essentially the pub's back room) would be a place to write and perform his new material. Strumming his Gibson on his tiny bed on Plaistow Grove was fine, but as his songwriting became more ambitious and expansive, he knew he would require more space and equipment, and soon the already tiny area grew crowded with equipment. Finnegan was older, having married and had children in her late teens and early twenties. Taking jobs at various London newspapers and commuting, as Bowie did, via rail, the dark-haired, elegant-looking woman was experiencing a belated sense of abandon when she first encountered Bowie (who had been visiting her neighbor and mutual friend, the local artist Christina Ostrom, and her then boyfriend Barry). 'I didn't have a youth,' she says today. 'So by the time I got to London, I caught up with my youth effectively. I became a hippie. I kept my domestic life going all the time. I was quite responsible about my kids. I made sure that their needs were met.'

Mary Finnegan was charmed upon meeting Bowie and quickly invited him to become a lodger, despite his inability to pay any regular rent. 'I offered him my spare room and he accepted that. Was somewhat taken aback by the mountain of audio equipment he moved in. He was an established name in the music business but he was totally down on his luck then,' Finnegan says. 'Penniless. I supported him for quite a few months. No money at all. Flat broke. But he was living with his parents and he was desperate to get away. I didn't feel sorry for him; he wasn't that sort of person. He had a sort of inherent strength. I just liked him very much. Very exciting.

Played stunningly good music. Charismatic, enormously good fun to be around. Lots of people recognized his talent even then. He just wasn't making it and he was very worried. Profoundly worried.'

At twenty-two, David Bowie was now a veteran in the UK pop world, signed to his third label. He had survived his parents' remoteness and the specter of his brother's illness by finding solace and understanding in music. The advanced self-education process of the previous two and a half years, spent studying Buddhism and devouring the libraries and lectures of both Kenneth Pitt and Lindsay Kemp, had also strengthened his values. But they had also solidified a conflict, one of real art vs. commercial art, that began at Bromley Tech and would last for the rest of David Bowie's career. This conflict was set in cement at the Beckenham Arts Lab.

'The Arts Lab was originally going to be a folk club,' Finnegan says, 'just David having an outlet to perform, but it soon became a place where all sorts of ideas were met with unbridled enthusiasm and intensity. The least likely place you would imagine. It couldn't be more sleepy middle-class suburban. With the Lab, what we wanted to do was reach out to people and broaden their horizons. His means of reaching people psychologically and socially was via music and entertainment. Also street theater. We would walk up and down the Beckenham High Street dressed up in the most outrageous outfits. Engaging with people on a grassroots level. Really quite shocking. Not political in the sense that we would interpret that word today. More social action. Not talking; doing. Taking art into the streets and making it accessible. Taking it out of its ivory tower.'

Bowie found that he could reconnect with his Buddhist spirituality via the Lab as well. 'He was still quite serious about Buddhism. But he'd given up that serious intent by the time I'd met him,' Finnegan recalls. 'I think he realized that if he was going to carry it through he was going to become a monk. Show business and Buddhism didn't really mix and match for him.'

Show business and Buddhism. Art and commerce. These tides seem to be constantly at odds churning inside David Bowie, each a powerful force, bringing with it a strong wave and ultimately a violent collision and temporary abandonment. Sometimes the friction produced brilliant chemistry, other times it led him too far from his better angels, but the rhythm of the waves, art and commerce, vice and verse never stops. Those Bowie fans who care to look into such things can clearly see this pattern. It's a 'one for them, one for me' rhythm that many other great artists with an uncanny knack for commercial appeal but an unceasing need to use their gifts to get at a hard truth have employed (artists like Radiohead and filmmaker Steven Spielberg come to mind). Is there any difference between

Bowie going from his hit 'Plastic Soul' period of '75 and '76 to his highly experimental trio of 'Berlin' records with Eno, and, say, Steven Spielberg's *Jurassic Park*-to-*Schindler's List* trajectory? Every concession to hitmaking and crowd-pleasing is usually followed by one that seeks answers or understanding without fear of getting as far-out as possible. This would accelerate in the eighties and nineties, a reaction to the unforeseen and certainly unprecedented success of *Let's Dance*. He'd follow *Tonight*, the lackluster 1984 follow-up to *Let's Dance*, with his far edgier, proudly English and insular work on the *Absolute Beginners* soundtrack. His lazy duet with Mick Jagger on Martha and the Vandellas' 'Dancing in the Street' (which was recorded for charity, so I won't go into how utterly shit it is) was followed by an '86 reunion with Iggy Pop on the *Blah Blah Blah* record. *Never Let Me Down*, perhaps his most cynical and commercial release, and its Spinal Tap-like Glass Spider Tour in 1987 were immediately followed by his work with the self-consciously noisy, arty and gleefully irritating 'band' Tin Machine. From there we go to the crowd-pleasing and catalog-value-stoking best-of live shows, the Sound and Vision revue. A reunion with Nile Rodgers, the architect of the *Let's Dance* sound, followed with 1993's *Black Tie White Noise*. *The Buddha of Suburbia*, a completely uncommercial soundtrack to a BBC miniseries that was not even released in America and was Bowie's best work of the nineties, succeeded that, and it goes on and on. He protected himself from the dirty business of turning 'Space Oddity' into a hit by immersing himself in the rising Arts Lab-style collective culture that was spreading throughout Britain in the late sixties.

Kenneth Pitt and the staff of Phillips and Mercury Records were struggling to take care of the commerce in the summer of '69. Meanwhile 'Space Oddity' made its unofficial debut before a crowd of thousands during a Rolling Stones concert in London's Hyde Park on July 5, 1969, at their memorial concert for the recently deceased founding member of the band Brian Jones. This was alternative marketing four decades before iPod ads and movie trailer bumpers, but at the time, it was marginalized. It was pop chart success or nothing. Kenneth Pitt, confident that this was the one, reached into his own pockets to try to pay off a 'chart rigger' and get his boy on the almighty *Top of the Pops*, shelling out, according to his memoir, 140 pounds and seeing the single rise to number 48 almost immediately.

'At the top of my head, I kept hearing David's plaintive cry, "I just wish something would break soon,"' Pitt writes in his memoir, 'and constantly it was spurring me on.'

'Chart success *was* success,' says Simon Napier-Bell. 'It wasn't an illusion of success. A top ten record meant *Top of the Pops*. That generated more sales. That meant live performances, *New Musical*

Express interviews, *Melody Maker, Record Mirror.* All this for a hundred and forty quid in a chart fixer's hand. What a bargain! And in all of these things, Britain, all America, it still is. Illusion first, success follows. That's the music business.'

In 2009 if a radio DJ receives a vodka-based cocktail or a pair of basketball sneakers from a major label, the leaked e-mails end up a major news story on corruption in the media. In the sixties, such transactions were frowned upon but rampant to the point of being banal. Still, for all of Pitt's efforts and even with the power of NASA on his side, he could not, in the summer of 1969, turn 'Space Oddity' into a real hit. He didn't lack drive or strategy; it was the record label staff who had no idea how to create a hit. The people with all the money and power did not know how to apply it.

All the while, Bowie was running on a much more organic energy source; he spent his long, sunny afternoons hippie-strumming for a few dozen people atop a simple wooden stool among the block tables and stored casks in the Three Tuns' sunny back room. 'I remember him getting ready for the Arts Lab one Sunday evening, about four of us lying around in his room. He was playing the Gibson twelve-string, a total outpouring of spontaneous music. Just came out of him,' Finnegan says. 'It was just absolutely totally superb. Brilliant off the cuff. Some very wonderful music happening. After the Arts Lab, everybody who had performed used to come back to

Foxgrove Road and stay up until two or three in the morning. Lots of spontaneous jamming.'

As the hit single he'd spent the entire decade pursuing was about to chart, Bowie had convinced himself that the pursuit of authenticity was his 'chief occupation' and boasted to a reporter about the Lab: 'There isn't one pseud involved. All the people are real – like laborers or bank clerks.' It was easy to view Kenneth Pitt with a measure of cynicism as the hippie movement placed his old-fashioned manners and dress in sharper relief. The Arts Lab, like Turquoise and Feathers, baffled the older man, and he kept away.

'To call it an Arts Laboratory was a bit of a misnomer,' Pitt has said. 'It was just a room attached to the Three Tuns Pub.'

Guitarist Keith Christmas, who would play on the *Space Oddity* album and hung out and performed at the Lab that summer, was only a bit more charitable.

'It was just a wee committee of people,' he says. 'It was all sort of quite peace and love in a very middle-class sort of way. Beckenham is a sort of suburb of London which is very middle-class. Terribly, terribly middle-class. It had a big garden out the back. It was sort of terraced and it was stretched back to the car park. So of course in those days when sort of smoking dope was fairly illegal, people could go out in the garden and smoke and chat.'

It's fair to surmise that the infectious, almost

192

pathological focus and drive of the young Angie Bowie, then Mary Angela Barnett (and only a few months out of her teens), was a force that ultimately helped steer David away from the leafy, insular Arts Lab life and its attendant navel-gazing complacency, and toward the earth-shaking rocker he would become in the seventies. Angie had known of David, having been briefly introduced to him by Calvin Mark Lee during a performance of Feathers at the Roundhouse, a converted railway roundhouse, on March 3, 1968.

How Angie materialized is a matter that varies according to different people's recollection. Bowie notoriously informed Cameron Crowe during their September 1976 *Playboy* interview, 'Angela and I knew each other because we were going out with the same man.' While it is not chronologically perfect, the statement is more or less an accurate one. 'I think David was very, very open in that interview,' Calvin Mark Lee says. 'I was having an affair with Angie. And I did introduce her to him at the Roundhouse. So we were going around with the same person.'

'I was absolutely gobsmacked to find out about her,' says Finnegan, who was convinced that she and David were monogamous. 'Shattered. Deeply deeply miffed. I was really hurt. Once we established some common ground it became clear she'd been around pretty well the whole time that he was with me. Although neither Angie or I were aware of it.'

*　　*　　*

I have a Polaroid photo of myself and Angie Bowie sitting in a banquette at a friend's Lower East Side bar. I don't remember posing for it but for some reason I've saved it. It's about seven years old at the time of this writing, so I would be about thirty-one and Angie would be in her early fifties. She is slim and tan, with high cheekbones, plucked eyebrows and a shock of bleached white hair. She wears a spaghetti-strap black dress and in the photo, one of the straps is falling off. I am wearing sunglasses indoors. I have a cigarette dangling out of my mouth. My hair is short. I wear a short-sleeve black shirt and an iridescent green tie. My head is tilted to the left and touches hers as we pose, as thought we've known each other for fifteen years. It was the first time we'd ever met in person. That should tell you something about Angie Bowie's energy. I've asked other people who've known her whether or not they felt the same thing upon meeting her in person: a sense of hyperfamiliarity and comfort, as if she's never stopped being a hostess, coordinator and leader of some kind of ever-flowing outsider scene. I've known people like her. The politically incorrect term for some of them is 'fag hag,' I suppose, and doing theater in New York, I've certainly had my share of association with this type. But there's something different about Angie, and it's entirely possible that her place in the larger Bowie myth is that difference. In a way, she is a great artist in her own right, only her art is socialization. I had never thrown a party for anyone in my life and, as I said, was already over thirty when I threw a party for Angie Bowie. I feted

194

her. Invited friends in the music and publishing industry, took care of the music, the cocktails, took care to make sure she was comfortable, as this type of thing seemed somehow more important than I'd ever thought it could or should be. This photo is a document, in its way, of Angie Bowie's often unsung but no less great talent.

I also wish to mention that Randy Jones, the cowboy from the Village People, attended this party. I just want that on the record, since I have no Polaroid of him.

CHAPTER 9

Mary Angela Barnett was born on the northern coast of the island of Cyprus in 1949 to her mother, Helena, and her U.S. Army colonel father, George Barnett. Her father had relocated to Cyprus after the war.

'My father escaped the Depression by leaving America and becoming a mill operator in Saudi Arabia,' she tells me. 'Then to the Philippines. Unfortunately the second year that he was there, the Japanese bombed Pearl Harbor. He was in the ROTC. He had no choice but to go up into the mountains and fight in a guerilla war against them. All these people who worked for my father went with them. For three years in the American army no one knew who was alive and who was dead but they kept hearing that the guerilla resistance was harassing the Japanese and generally causing havoc. They couldn't send supplies. They sent nothing. But for three years they lived in the mountains of north Lausanne. When he came back they asked him to go to DC and become a general. He went on a recruiting tour of America. He saw what was happening in the South and he told them there is no place in these times for an army. The way this country is now, I have fought with brown men for three years and you want to treat these people so badly?' He wouldn't accept the generalship. He accepted a mining job in Cyprus instead. He went there as a lowly foreman with no degree in mining yet. For three years they argued with him about the GI Bill. Finally the army gave him his allowance to go to college. He went back to America for three years and got his degree. My older brother went to college the same time as him. That was the kind of man he was. He was a bona fide person who did what he said. He did not believe he was a hero. That really affected who I am. I'm very focused. I think it's because of him. My mother encouraged me to learn from him. At that time, women had nothing. They had no choices. No rights. So from when I was born in 1949 to the invention of the Pill in 1962, I had fourteen years of women being broodmares – this is how they were perceived – and women being second-class citizens.'

At age nine, Angie was shipped off to St George's, a small, private Swiss boarding school in the city of Clarens. Although comfortable, Angie was one of the only Americans and her family was relatively one of the poorest; her education was funded by her father's mining firm. It was there that she first discovered her rebellious spirit. 'Like most boarding schools there were many rules and regulations,' she writes in *Free*

Spirit, the first of her two memoirs. 'No gum, no swearing, no playing jacks on hall tables and only two to a piano box during practice.'

She studied all the major subjects as well as art and theater, showing expert aptitude in all areas as a matter of course. 'I was a great student. I was a prefect. I couldn't get into trouble. That wasn't a possibility. My father and mother couldn't afford to send me to that school; our company sent me to that school. I was an extension of my father's dignity. I had to do every single thing correctly, have great grades, be a prefect, be house captain, do everything that had to be done, learn French, learn Spanish, learn Italian. That was my job. The only thing that was of any importance in our house was having a function.'

This isn't to say that Angie avoided trouble. Her natural inquisitiveness and rebellious spirit often put her at odds with the more provincial aspects of her faith. 'Catholic school was a nightmare,' she says. 'I couldn't stand the smell. It smelled of peanut butter and plastic.'

When she was seven she was caught being kissed by a neighbor, incurring the rage of her otherwise good-natured father. 'I got beaten within a fuckin' inch of my life by my father,' she says. 'He came back from work and found me with this boy Billy McDonald. Billy said to me, "Oh, come into the woodshed," and I guess he tried to kiss me. Billy was sent off. My father was just the most wonderfully well-read and pleasant man I had ever come across, but his face had become like a monster and he chased me into the house. The company, Cyprus Mining Corp., used to provide all the furniture. The bed that was in my room had one of those old-fashioned iron bed frames. He got a camel whip and he tried to swat me. He was red in the face and furious.

'To me it was the most natural thing. The little boy tried to kiss me and I'm nearly murdered? The only thing I wanted to know was why nobody would talk about sex. It was interesting to me. I really had a problem with it. You have to understand we're talking about the 1950s. Nobody would say jack. No one would explain jack.'

A lifelong intellectual curiosity that directly led to her and David Bowie becoming bisexual rock 'n' roll liberators a decade and a half later began with the swing of that camel whip. 'It has to do with investigating what the problem was with everybody about sex,' she says. 'Couldn't understand it. Didn't get it. Obviously the motivating feature of the planet. All the major religions were about making cannon fodder so you could recruit more people to your religion, but basically if you're not fucking everything that moves and inseminating people that you conquer then what's the point? The whole thing was about sex. They needed more pussy.' Angie has written a slim book on bisexuality called *Bisexuality* ('I do believe in intellectual sexuality,' she writes. 'That's what makes me bounce out of bed every morning and attack life') and is currently working on a more epic history.

Before studying economics and marketing overseas at Kingston Polytechnic College in London, Angie studied in America at Connecticut College, then a women's school. There she began an affair with a troubled student named Lorraine. It was a union that the faculty and authorities considered scandalous. 'What else was I supposed to do?' she tells me of the affair. 'I promised my father I wouldn't get pregnant.' While at school she began to realize that society was not set up for her to enjoy the kind of options she felt best suited to. 'Being someone's wife was never an option for me.'

Angie's heroes were, tellingly, all male. 'I was big on Gandhi. He was assassinated about the time that I was at school in Switzerland. I read *Nine Hours to Rama*. All about the gentle nature of peace through nonviolence and the whole idea that men and women share all domestic tasks equally. That resonated with me. I was just crazy about Gandhi. Then when I was at college, as everyone does at college, I read Khalil Gibran books, and that finished any idea of organized religion for me. And with that it finished any kind of idea of being a wife and mother. Do you know Khalil Gibran? He was a very brilliant Lebanese man. Being in school and being alone and isolated, Khalil Gibran was like a toss-back to my home. He was a friend, you know what I mean? Between the covers of a book. And the most important line of his that I remember all the time is that "children are the arrows that you shoot from the bow." To me that was totally accepted. I never looked back, never wanted to go back and be a child. Never wanted to live amongst my family. [After school] I was happy to be the arrow. Fly through the air.'

A self-described 'Europhile,' Angie was already familiar with London culture. She had family friends who lived there and spent holidays in the city. 'It was exciting. The magazines. Pirate radio was happening. And the bands. British youth didn't want to accept this whole American rock 'n' roll thing; particularly the Rolling Stones were reminding everyone that rock 'n' roll was based on the tunes of African American artists. The mods-and-rockers thing was fun too. The mods versus rockers riots were the first time anyone young was on TV. They were talking about them like they were criminals; didn't matter, they were on the news. It was giving them power. By the late sixties, we all felt on top of the world. We felt like the idiots who caused wars had gotten out of it by the skin of their teeth, and now the next generation was gonna prove that peace was a better thing.'

In her senior year, in 1966, at age sixteen, she tried to start a career that might enable to her remain in London. 'I tried to do some modeling my last year of college in England. Took the shots. "Sorry, you look far too intelligent to be a model."'

'Did you think you were beautiful?' I asked her, wondering how someone would just decide to launch a career as a professional model.

'No. I thought that I looked intelligent. That was not beautiful. You gotta look dumb and suck a lot! That was considered exciting by anyone in the entertainment business at that time. I don't have that attitude and certainly wasn't prepared to give them an inch.'

The fact that Angie offered herself up to the modeling industry gives you some idea of her force of will and sense of confidence. She wore her dirty-blond hair short, was given to wearing tailored men's suits and used her extreme charisma to make an impression on both men and women of all persuasions, including Calvin Mark Lee and Lou Reizner (whom she also began dating around this time).

'I always dressed as a man, which was probably another reason that Calvin and I got along very well,' she writes in *Backstage Passes*. 'I decided that we were quite sympathetic and we got along quite well – a similar sense of humor and lewd attitude towards women.'

Lee encouraged her to pursue a serious position at the label. 'Calvin was from San Francisco,' she says. 'He understood that you couldn't sweep women under the carpet. Lou Reizner was old school. But [label head] Irving Green loved me; every time they would come to London to see how their operation was going they would insist to Lou, "You have to make sure Mary Angela is there. You should give her a job. She needs to work for Mercury." I was still thinking, "What am

I going to do and how am I gonna stay in England?" I had to get an American company to hire me. Green cards were so hard to get. I would be taking a job from an English kid. So by the second year of college I was already figuring out how I could stay. I thought if I could become indispensable to Calvin and Lou as a marketing agent, I would be able to stay in London. So that's what I got busy doing. David was my first marketing case.' She was essentially his A & R person as well, helping Lee convince Lou Reizner to allow Bowie to be signed to the label in the first place.

'[Reizner] hated me,' David told Cameron Crowe. 'She thought I was great. Ultimately she threatened to leave him if he didn't sign me. So he signed me.'

By the time they got together romantically, David Bowie was a Mercury artist. The story of their union has been told many times in many Bowie biographies, as well as Angie's own memoirs. At Calvin Mark Lee's invitation, she attended a record release fete for another Mercury signing, King Crimson. She was wearing a purple velvet three-piece suit with a matching silk tie and stood out among the hippies, professional and otherwise. David, in T-shirt and simple trousers, could not resist asking her to dance (famously inquiring 'Do you jive?' – a pick-up line that does not work unless you are David Bowie). Angie did indeed jive, and soon . . . they were jiving and then some.

'I came back from being away for a few days; the flat was spic and span,' Finnegan recalls. 'David never ever cleaned up after himself. He was a total slob. Always a sink full of dirty dishes, overflowing ashtrays, clothes everywhere.' Given his fastidious mother ('She was a very strange sort of uncommunicative woman. Very straitlaced, very stiff,' according to Finnegan), David must have relished having his own space to leave in funky disarray. Angie was not, however, going to abide it.

'Suddenly it was all washed up tidy,' Finnegan says. 'David and I were always in and out of each other's room in a perfectly normal, natural way. We'd had a relationship. So I went into his room and there I found a half-written song lying by his bedside. The lyrics were talking about "beautiful Angie." So the penny dropped. The next thing I knew he'd moved her in. Sensing I was miffed, Angie of course launched a formidable charm offensive. She was a very highly strung young woman. Openly bisexual, incredibly creative and formidably energetic and very beautiful. I think he was in love with her.'

Despite the powerful sexual attraction and what must have been a hint of narcissism (they were similarly built physically, had similar hair and skin color), Angela and David really bonded over a shared sense of ambition and drive. 'He studied mime,' she says, impressed still, some four decades on. 'To be with Hermione he learned ballet. I

204

thought if he was that well versed and Ken Pitt had been making sure, as far as acting was concerned, he could do whatever we needed him to do, it made him different and my job was to market him. You start with what you've got and you work on that. He had this ability to pick up a skill. He was extremely talented. Please do not believe any of the bullshit about him. He's very brilliant. He's a multi-instrumentalist. And the focus that it takes to learn those things, I'm sure it was one of the reasons we were good together. You can't have big ambitions and big dreams if you think the person that you're dreaming them with can't handle it. You know what I mean. You would fall flat on your face before you got out of the gate. So my dreams were inspired by him. Those dreams that I thought of putting together were because he had the goods.'

'David was ensnared by his first experience of meeting a female of that American pushy raucous coed bobby-soxer syndrome. He had never seen anything like it, whereas I had become acquainted with the species during my many visits to the U.S.,' Pitt writes me. 'I did regret that she chose not to support me in my work for David but to do all she could to undermine it, all to her own personal advantage of course.'

'I have a very soft spot for Americans,' Ray Stevenson says. 'They just do things where English people go, 'Oh, that would be nice, but . . .' And yet Angie was a bit pushy. A bit loud. What really

205

blew it: we were up watching the moon landing and Angie decided she was going out for a walk. Came back a half hour later telling everyone, "I saw these little green men, they landed at the end of Foxgrove Road!" What you expect from a three-year-old. Preposterous.'

What's indisputable is that she put the Arts Lab in perspective and helped extricate Bowie from what might have been a terminal case of hippie navel-gazing. 'The whole Arts Lab scene. I got so sick of it,' she says. 'It's so political. Just the mention of it flashes me back years and I'm right back in a "meeting" arguing over who had kudos and who didn't . . . it was a nightmare! I had a diploma in marketing and economics. I couldn't do that bullshit. I'd look at them and say, "Look, the movement is just a marketing thing. Everyone who's saying no to us, they're idiots. The [older generation] had a world war. They killed all these people. We've got to reclaim the world." And it was a big deal for me. They shushed me a lot. I was written off as the intellectual.'

If Angie's accelerated approach to empowerment clashed somewhat with the elliptical Arts Lab, her approach to the handling of Bowie ran head-on into Kenneth Pitt's gentlemanly fifties-and-early-sixties-bred style. In July, Pitt had arranged several appearances designed to promote the 'Space Oddity' single, including a 'song festival' on the Italian island of Malta. Pitt was likely happy to be alone with David after the distance put between them thanks to Bowie's less manageable stints in Feathers and at the Arts Lab. Despite the more contemporary, rockier material he'd been working on for the *Space Oddity* album sessions with Visconti (who was back on board after declining to produce the title track), Pitt suggested that David sing 'When I Live My Dream' from the two-year-old Deram debut.

Angie flew home to visit her parents in Cyprus to tell them all about her new boyfriend. David sent her postcards from Italy while traveling with Pitt. Either put off by Pitt or in emotional need, he gave Angie the sense that her presence was missed. She talked her parents into booking an airplane ticket and soon, to Pitt's chagrin, she was joining Bowie in Italy. Angie agreed with him about the relative dustiness of the old cabaret material. She even criticized the outfit Pitt had picked out for Bowie and loudly insisted that he start dressing in more modern gear.

'David was thrilled; Ken wasn't,' she writes in *Backstage Passes*. 'He had to find another room and I don't think it was the inconvenience that really bothered him. Talk about a snit. And there's nothing, thank God, like the ire of a queen whose affection has been spurned.'

Ken Pitt says he initially figured Angie was Jewish because she was so forward. I asked him about this and he answered, 'I knew a number of people named Barnett and without exception they were Jewish. I suppose that when Angela appeared on the scene I might have asked D if she was Jewish. And he would then have said to her, "Ken thinks you are Jewish." I didn't think she was Jewish, I only wondered. To this day I don't know and quite honestly I couldn't care less. But then again perhaps I didn't ask D that question at all and this is just A's troublemaking.' As I indicated earlier, Pitt would later identify her as the second (to Lee's first) of the predators who would help remove David from his care. At the time, he thought she was more or less amusing. He simply did not know who he was dealing with.

There were several incidents around this period that also helped prime Bowie to pursue rock 'n' roll as opposed to pop or cabaret. Marc Bolan was busy transforming Tyrannosaurus Rex, his bongos-and-acoustic-folk act, into a lean, sexy electric rock band called simply T. Rex. He was reinventing himself as a Les Paul-wielding rock god with tight satin trousers and muscle tees with his own visage emblazoned across the chest. Bolan invited Bowie to open for him during a short tour in the late winter of 1969. Bowie opted to do a mime performance designed to publicize the plight of the oppressed Tibetan people, as well as his standby 'The Mask,' and was often heckled. Also that year, he spent time on the road with Peter Frampton's new act Humble Pie, which was managed by the Stones' ex-manger Andrew Loog Oldham and featured former Small Faces vocalist Steve Marriott, an early Bowie hero, on vocals.

They were enjoying huge success in both England and America. This time he played material that would end up on the *Space Oddity* record and saw a veritable fork in the road professionally. The older, folkier songs left him jeered at and pelted. The more energetic songs were cheered and hooted over. He witnessed how Humble Pie were treated: like rock royalty with rock royalties. It was tempting.

'He was our special guest,' Frampton says. 'David just played a twelve-string acoustic. He had no road manager, no tech; when he broke a string, he literally changed the string onstage.'

While Bowie was in Italy making his much contended appearance, his father took seriously ill. Angie had recently flown back to visit with her own parents in Cyprus. David returned to England proudly carrying a trophy he'd been awarded at the festival. John Jones had collapsed in the street with a fever days before and rather than take him to the hospital, Peggy kept him confined to bed in hopes that he would recover. Without professional care, his fever turned into pneumonia.

'David arrived home carrying the statuette that he had won at the contest that he'd been to with Ken Pitt and dashed straight up to see his father, who hadn't been well for a number of days,' Peggy recalled. 'David handed the statuette to his father, telling him that he'd won the contest, and his father told him that he knew he would succeed in the end. He died not long afterward.'

Bowie called Angie to tell her the news, and she quickly made arrangements to come to his aid once again, a pattern that would emerge in their relationship both before and after his superstardom. He was naturally overwhelmed emotionally. He did not know how to deal with his bereaved mother, the funeral and John Jones's affairs on his own, and soon Angie was applying to this tragedy the same forceful sense of getting it done that she had to Mary Finnegan's kitchen, the Three Tuns Arts Lab and David's career. 'It wasn't easy,' Angie recalled. 'There were only two bedrooms and I had to share a bedroom with David's mother, a living arrangement that I just wasn't used to. I felt David's mother didn't really like me, and having to share a bed with her really drove me nuts.'

John Jones kept his papers neatly arranged. Aside from sad details such as how to dispose of his false teeth, the real challenge was dealing with the survivors. John had controlled the bill paying and general organization of things, leaving, like many of his generation, the housework and homemaking to Peggy. Now both Peggy and Terry Burns would need care.

To say that David Bowie changed as a person when his father died is to state the obvious. The death of a parent in any context is cataclysmic, but when it hits unexpectedly during a rush of professional commitments, it's especially jarring. It should be noted that his work changed as well.

At John Jones's funeral in the first week of August 1969, he didn't cry but rather seemed to be internalizing everything. The cast of his music would suggest this as well. *Space Oddity* and its follow-up, 1970's *The Man Who Sold the World*, are among his darkest albums. Both depict a man coming of age in a world that is increasingly depraved and barren. 'He was in an absolutely foul mood,' Finnegan says, recalling one of the Arts Lab events that followed John's demise. 'Black as thunder, rude and nasty to everybody.' These new songs wonder, both abstractly and directly, who or what to turn to for spiritual and parental guidance. By 1971 *Hunky Dory* would reflect the romance with Angie and the birth of their child, but it would take some time to arrive at that warmer and happier place. David was a boy, cared for by managers and those who found him attractive and charming.

This shift was observed by others who knew him then. 'I remember when David's father died he was very solemn, as anybody would be when their father dies, and he took the responsibility of looking after his mother very seriously,' Visconti has said. 'David automatically assumed the role of his father in matters of domestic finance. He appeared to grow up instantly . . .' Within a year, he would be a husband. Within two, a father. And in three, the biggest rock star in England. Angie had been right on. Things were changing fast.

CHAPTER 10

The greatest concentration of 'space fever' was, of course, in America, and Bowie's new single seemed a perfect way to finally introduce him to the biggest pop music market in the world. Shortly after the final recording and mixing of 'Space Oddity,' and in the midst of preparation for Bowie's full-length debut, Mercury Records' American publicist Ron Oberman, a former college music journalist, was brought to London to meet Bowie. While Mercury's UK partner Phillips would release *Man of Words/Man of Music* in England, Bowie remained a Mercury artist, his career, at that time, handled by people an ocean away. Oberman, who worked out of the label's spacious Chicago offices, was surprised to find how inconsequential Mercury's London headquarters were.

'It was almost like an apartment,' he says. 'I came out and said hello to David. He was sitting there cross-legged, like Indian style, on this big over-stuffed chair. And we hit it off right away. We had a great conversation. We spoke about publicity and getting some materials together, press materials, bio and photos. So I went back to Chicago; I was very excited about David Bowie and really tried to talk him up among all the executives there. I've always had great ears for singles, and to my mind there was no question that "Space Oddity" should have been a number one single. I was Bowie's biggest supporter at the company. And other people in the promotion department seemed to like the record. At that time back in the sixties, if you really wanted to get a record on the air there were certainly ways to do it. But Mercury never really pushed it that hard. It wasn't a hit initially because Mercury really didn't get behind it the way they should have gotten behind it.'

The Phillips and Mercury marriage was a relatively new one and there was still infighting going on between people who were reluctant to cede any power to one side or another. Bowie's fate seemed to rest on the possibility of a tenuous harmony being achieved. Rather than reaping the huge publicity benefits of the *Apollo 11* landing, 'Space Oddity' languished in the outer reaches of the British Top 40 for most of the summer and barely registered in America. If NASA couldn't help get him a hit, what hope did he have? Bowie would see his first stroke of real professional luck with the arrival of Olav Wyper at Phillips.

Wyper was a former journalist who had happened into a career as a copywriter in the ad department of the massive EMI Corporation, which distributed the Beatles and the Beach Boys' records. He had managed to move laterally into a different department (a feat still difficult today in the eternally compartmentalized record business) and by the late sixties he was the marketing manager at CBS Records. Wyper increased the marketing staff at CBS from three people to seventy-six people and transformed the entire department, gaining the attention of every other troubled label at the time.

'I was headhunted to go and take over the Phillips company,' he remembers. 'And before I left I was aware that Phillips had released this extraordinarily brilliant single, 'Space Oddity' by David Bowie. I heard it because it was played on the radio. It was reviewed in the papers but we didn't have a hit. At the time, Phillips was a very run-down, depressed, dreary place.'

Despite its early sixties success with its Fontane imprint, which had enjoyed major hits, including the Troggs' immortal 'Wild Thing,' by the end of the decade, Phillips was in the midst of a dry period. Wyper found Bowie in person to be charismatic and the song to have limitless potential for Phillips. He made selling David Bowie the label's first and only priority. The sole order of business under his new rule: make 'Space Oddity' go.

'I didn't know a hell of a lot about David at that time but he was clearly an interesting young man who had a completely different take on things, and he had a unique sound and it was a unique record,' Wyper recalls. 'And it may have been that the record would in the normal course of events not have been a hit and then not been taken out and dusted off and tried all over again. But it was because we as a company had nothing else in the immediate future and in the immediate past that was worth working on. It was already a hit in my view, it just hadn't been a hit.'

'Space Oddity' enjoyed a second ride up the charts, eventually reaching number 5 and landing Bowie his first *Top of the Pops* appearance in October. He spent the waning months of 1969 finishing up his Phillips/Mercury debut with Tony Visconti. The new songs were complicated, reflections of the twenty-two-year-old's darkening vision. While not iconic, as his seventies albums would become, *Space Oddity* is first-rate as trippy rock records go. After some R & B singles and pop kitsch forays, this was David Bowie's first 'heavy' offering.

The album opens, of course, with 'Space Oddity' but shifts quickly into the extensive hard-rock jam 'Unwashed and Somewhat Slightly Dazed.' 'I'm a phallus in pigtails / And there's blood on my nose,' Bowie declares, and the deciphering begins. 'This is a rather weird little song I wrote because one day when I was very scruffy I got a lot of funny stares from people in the street,' Bowie said at the time. 'The lyrics are what you hear – about a boy whose girlfriend thinks he is socially inferior. I thought it was rather funny really.'

'Don't Sit Down' is more or less an interlude,

something Bowie would continue to employ during this period. 'Eight Line Poem' on *Hunky Dory* is another of this kind. The verse of 'Don't Sit down' is 'Yeah yeah baby yeah.' It's repeated several times. The chorus is the title. It is an excellent song.

'Letter to Hermione,' based on a lovesick letter never sent, is next; it's an acoustic lament with a literal title that is rare as far as Bowie songs go. At nine minutes and thirty seconds, 'Cygnet Committee' returns us to the expansive realm of the post-psychedelic freak-out. 'Well it is a bit long I suppose,' Bowie said. 'It's basically three separate points of view about the more militant section of the hippy movement. The movement was a great idea but something's gone wrong with it now. I'm not really attacking it but pointing out that the militants have still got to be helped as people – human beings – even if they are going about things all the wrong way.'

'Cygnet Committee' meanders in typical late-sixties fashion, but certain changes are interesting to a trainspotting Bowie-ist, as quotes from it will later show up in tracks like 'Time,' on 1973's *Aladdin Sane*, and 'Rock and Roll with Me,' on '74's *Diamond Dogs*. The lyrical shout-out to the MC5 'Kick out the jams / Kick out your mother' is also, someone should formally point out, very cool.

Occasionally the pressure would get to Bowie and Visconti. They knew, in light of the 'Space

Oddity' single's success, that the album needed to soar as well. While recording the relatively simple acoustic track 'God Knows I'm Good' ('Surely God won't look the other way,' he sings), Bowie, in a rare show of vulnerability, lost control of his emotions.

'He broke down during that,' recalls guitarist Keith Christmas, who plays on the record. 'I mean I think if he hadn't had "Space Oddity" on that album it would have just died the same as the first one died. They all came out, got a few nice reviews, and then just disappeared back into the sort of wash of albums that were around then. But that one single sort of pulled it up by its bootstraps.'

In their fervor to be big and attention grabbing, Bowie and Visconti made use of the facilities and recording budget by punching up some of the more cinematic songs, like 'Space Oddity''s B side, 'Wild Eyed Boy from Freecloud,' with full orchestration. 'Freecloud' recounts the last moments of a condemned man. As far as 'about to be executed' songs, it's no Nick Cave's 'The Mercy Seat' or Johnny Cash's 'Joe Bean,' or even Led Zeppelin's 'Gallows Pole,' but it is arresting, as Bowie, for the first time, manages to wed a sprawling rock number with his die-hard penchant for Anthony Newley/Richard Harris-style melodrama.

'I remember inside they had this great big studio which would have been used for thirty-piece string orchestras,' Keith Christmas says. 'This was obviously one of the things it was used for was orchestral recordings. You had to go up some stairs to the control room, which had a sort of window looking down on this space. And then you had to go up some more to where the tapes were running. They were on a different floor. And it wasn't that long before I was reading that the engineers used to wear white coats. They were considered like engineers, lab technicians almost. And as I recall they had an intercom and they had to call up to get a rewind on the tape. Laughable when you think of making thirty-two, sixty-four tracks on a computer now.'

Angie functioned as the cheerleader and de facto caterer, running errands, making lunch and generally coordinating the vibes. The excitement surrounding the record, which was indeed David's finest music to date, carried over into the planned promotional events, but the bad luck that had dogged him through the 1960s initially seemed difficult to shake off.

A record release party dubbed 'An Evening with David Bowie' was scheduled for November 30, 1969, at London's Purcell Room, a small venue in the basement of the larger Queen Elizabeth Hall, on the south bank of the Thames river. David would be backed by a local band named Copus as he debuted the strong new tracks from the album as well as the hit single 'Space Oddity.'

According to Kenneth Pitt, Calvin Mark Lee was put in charge of coordinating the press for 'An Evening with David Bowie.' On the night of the show, however, attendance was good but the industry and media presence was almost nonexistent. Bowie and Copus, unaware, turned in a high-energy, sweaty set. Afterward, Bowie excitedly ran backstage to inquire about the VIPs in attendance, who, he assumed, had just witnessed one of the best shows he'd ever done. Lee sheepishly told him that there was nobody there. Bowie was furious and, in an act that would also emerge as a pattern, banished Lee, placing him well outside the inner circle. Their friendship did not survive the Purcell Room debacle. 'His name was never again mentioned,' according to a secretly relieved Pitt.

Speaking of the incident today, Lee plays down the outrage and insists that he did, in fact, coordinate an important review. 'The *Observer* gave it a good review,' he tells me. 'That's a *Sunday* paper. Sundays are high-class papers. That irritated me. But what could I say?'

Angie, meanwhile, was now 'vagabonding' between London and Mary Finnegan's house in Beckenham or David's mother's home in Bromley, with her clean and dirty clothes in the same bag. She was in the process of locating, securing and establishing a home in which Bowie would feel not only like a rock star but also, crucially, like someone with a family and an infrastructure to cushion some of these ego blows in the future as he made yet another attempt to break out. 'Angie was determined to find someplace where they could live together, and she was quite right,' says Mary Finnegan. 'They couldn't stay holed up in the single bed in the small room in my flat. I didn't want it to go on either. I wanted my life back basically.'

They found the perfect location in Haddon Hall. Haddon Hall is important to the Bowie myth. In essence, this suburban mansion was the hive or nest where so many of his indelible early songs were first written and demoed. It was a salon where key allies and collaborators would exchange ideas, create costumes and fine tune concepts that would define the new decade. David and Angela spent Christmas 1969 together and early in the new year moved their belongings into the once grand, now dilapidated three-story, red brick Victorian building, a former candle manufacturing factory, nestled at 42 Southend Road, Beckenham, amid a vast English garden and a clutch of looming, barren trees. Behind it lay an eighteen-hole golf course.

The downstairs neighbors, a couple named Sue and Tony Frost, were young and accustomed to taking advantage of the abandoned space by blasting reggae at top volume. They did not object to a young would-be rocker moving in.

Bowie was impressed by the sheer size of Haddon Hall. The long, circular driveway that led up to the residence seemed palatial, especially when their new purchase, a used Jaguar, was parked out in the shade. The living room was massive, as was the hallway, which led to the staircase and a stained glass window that was some forty feet wide. With its many rooms, great winding staircase that led to nowhere (the top floor was boarded off and rented out to another tenant) and ornate stained glass window, Haddon Hall possessed a regal feel.

'Unfortunately, prior to our moving in, twenty-seven cats had lived there with a professor of history and his wife, who were a little eccentric,' Angie recalled. 'There were a lot of plants and the cats felt they were in a jungle of their own in the hall. You can imagine the smell.'

They painted the walls and ceilings hunter green in the living room and a light blue in the bedroom and scrubbed the tiles in the fireplace. Bowie began a series of collages on the bathroom walls by pasting up magazine and book clippings. Angie also insisted that they install a telephone so that they could stay on top of business affairs. She soon regretted the decision, as many of the calls were not from Kenneth Pitt reporting increasing sales and bookings, but rather from Bowie's mother, who made no secret of the fact that she felt abandoned as soon as her son officially moved out of Plaistow Grove. Angie would take Peggy shopping and lend an ear to her self-pitying declarations that her life had lost meaning – this while taking care of the extensive maintenance of Haddon Hall, as well as helping roadie the small gigs Bowie managed to get in local cabarets and workingman clubs. Seeing this end of his career firsthand, and how he went over, Angie fully realized the extent to which her boyfriend was being, in her opinion, mismanaged. Soon she was loudly complaining about Pitt, and Bowie felt even more supported and understood. It was a problem.

'I think David was beginning to turn to me in place of his father,' she writes in *Backstage Passes*. 'John Jones had always been the supportive, accepting person in his life and a strong force standing between his son and Peggy's disapproval. Now that he was gone, David needed someone else in that role.'

Famously, before they moved in together, Bowie asked Angie if she could 'deal' with the fact that he did not love her. There are at least three ways of looking at this disclaimer. One, perhaps he closed that door after Hermione and did not open it up again until he encountered the supermodel Iman (his second wife) in the early nineties; two, perhaps his mother and father's lack of demonstration toward one another made him wary of any effusion or confirmation of emotions; or three, maybe he actually did love her but it simply wasn't hip to say so. 'The truth of the matter is that later it became obvious that he may have said what he thought sounded cool, but that may not have been what he felt, because he acted like a jilted lover [years later] when I left him,' says Angie. According to her, she took to saying 'In your ear' instead of 'I love you' as a term of endearment. While she wanted some form of exclusivity, and was very nearly having it, she was aware that times were changing, as were the notions of cohabitation and monogamy. 'While I was in love with David and ready to share him with anyone he nominated, I still wanted to hold that privileged and treasured place as his wife,' she writes in *Free Spirit*. 'I was prepared to bow to convention that much. I wish now I had subscribed to convention more because it would take its natural revenge.'

In order for Angie to remain in England at length, and, in the long run, for Bowie to be able to stay in America, it was decided that they would have a civil ceremony and marry as a matter of course. 'If it hadn't been for that we probably wouldn't have gotten married,' Bowie told journalist George Tremlett. 'To use the legal ceremonies of marriage are just a formality that don't mean very much if a couple cease to be in love with each other afterwards. Although we were in love with each other, we don't feel the need to get married to prove it. The actual ceremony didn't mean that much to us.'

They would eventually marry on March 19, 1970. Angie, dressed in a pink and purple dress, and Bowie, in a shearling-trimmed long coat, exchanged vows and four silver wedding bracelets at Bromley's register offices. Peggy Jones was a witness, as was Tony Visconti's girlfriend Liz Hartley and drummer John Cambridge. Ken Pitt was not present. The couple 'honeymooned' at their new home in Haddon Hall, relatively as exotic in its comfort and expanse as anywhere else they might have considered.

Bowie's devotion to Angie, although technically without 'love,' can be detected quite plainly in his first composition of the 1970s, 'The Prettiest Star.' The track, which would later appear on *Aladdin Sane*, was recorded at Trident Studios on January 8, 1970, Bowie's twenty-third birthday. Phillips/Mercury issued it as a single, hoping that the poppy and romantic tune might become a proper follow-up to 'Space Oddity' and demonstrate Bowie's range as a songwriter. It did not sell, however. Worse, Marc Bolan, who laid down his guest guitar work, according to legend, in just one hour, would, within a year, become the biggest pop star in all of England.

Meanwhile, Pitt was still trying to get his distracted client to organize his schedule, increasingly from a distance, as he did not feel completely welcome in Beckenham. 'Haddon Hall started with the best intentions but it soon became a pseudo-hippie commune with A [Angie] as earth mother,' he says via letter. 'Even Tony Visconti, who has said that HH [Haddon Hall] was a lot of fun, finally fell out with A and quit, but not before he had caused mayhem with D's recording sessions. He could never understand my role in David's career and daily affairs and that recording sessions had to be arranged with me. He always seemed to be unaware of the fact that it was I who gave him the job of producing D's recordings. He would arrange dates with A and D only to find that they clashed with D's live engagements. It was finally agreed that a list of D's engagements should be displayed at HH for all to see, but A, who had attended a business studies course at Kingston, proved to be incapable of maintaining such a list. If only she stuck to costumery, for which she had flair.'

While Bolan was lustily celebrating 'hot love,' Bowie was either dispassionately scrawling a song list for Pitt – 'Can't Get Used to Losing You' (a number made famous by Andy Williams and later covered by the English Beat), 'Sunny' and the now perilously dated 'I Dig Everything' among them – or spending the remainder of his 'Space Oddity' royalties on antiques. 'I think he just got some royalty money and he showed off his new coal scuttle,' Ray Stevenson, who frequented Haddon Hall at this time, says. 'He was really proud of it. It's an English thing. In the old days, we had a fireplace and a pile of coal out in the yard. You'd leave the bucket and scuttle next to the fire. David's was an art deco one. Beautiful shapes and lines to the thing. It was the beginning of him collecting whole loads of art nouveau and art deco for years.'

Kenneth Pitt was ahead of the curve in one respect, as he encouraged David to give an interview to a local gay magazine, *Jeremy*, around this time. Pitt hoped to turn Bowie into a gay icon à la Judy Garland, who'd recently died while performing in London. Twenty thousand fans, most of them gay men, attended her funeral in New York City that summer. 'Having worked with Judy Garland, I had seen how gay men adored her,' Pitt told journalist George Tremlett, 'thronged to her concerts, filled her dressing room with flowers and mobbed her at the stage door. Men who loved men, those women held strange platonic attraction for them.'

Published on May 10, 1970, the interview is not especially intriguing. Bowie talks plainly about painting, Buddhism, the Arts Lab puppeteers ('I'm trying to get them a TV show at the moment'), his older brother, Terry, and his most embarrassing moment ('When I was singing with a group called the Buzz four or five years ago. I forgot the words to three songs in a row. That was dreadful'). Yawn. While a champion of sexual liberation, Angie Bowie was having none of what she considered Pitt's flummoxed machinations.

'People who wanted to watch Judy Garland should just stay home and rent *The Wizard of Oz*,' Angie wrote of the cultural shift that eluded Pitt. 'This was 1970 for God's sake. Anyone illuminated by even the dimmest of bulbs knew whatever flavor you came in, you just had to rock.'

Detecting the flow of the zeitgeist and boldly challenging accepted notions of sexuality were integral to Bowie's crucial transition from sixties also-ran to seventies visionary, but in rock 'n' roll

226

vision needs sound, and it's fairly safe to surmise that even with Visconti on board, none of what they were all about to achieve would have happened without the addition of Mick Ronson. If Visconti provided focus and sonic clarity, Ronson made David Bowie's new music bigger, tougher and sexier. He was the muscle in the mix.

'Mick came from a place called Hull,' Dana Gillespie says, 'where they speak in an accent that is pretty ugly on the ear. Unpronounceable and difficult. He was quite a simple lad from up north. He didn't have the kind of crawl-your-way-to-the-top attitude. He was just a working musician. All he ever wanted to do was work.'

Michael Ronson was born on May 26, 1946, at his parents' modest home on Beverley Road in the northern city of Hull. His parents, Mini and George Ronson, were strict Mormons, and young Michael was schooled in the faith. 'I have no idea how they came to be Mormons,' says his widow Suzi Ronson (formerly Bowie's Ziggy Stardust-period hairdresser Suzi Fussey). 'Probably someone knocking on her door and talking her into it. Mick wasn't a devout Mormon by any means but that's the way he was raised.'

His father was also a musician and encouraged his boy, a shy and unassuming child, to play. 'Mick,' as he was called early on, took to the piano initially, and there was talk of formal, classical study. He also expressed interest in string instruments and for a while studied violin and

227

cello. This forced the quiet child to toughen up, as it prompted puerile taunts from some of his classmates. 'He used to carry his violin case around, so [if he was] put in a corner he could fight,' Suzi says.

As with Bowie, the advent of rock 'n' roll, however, dovetailed with Mick Ronson's adolescence and soon he was asking his parents for a guitar. His father purchased an acoustic guitar with trade stamps, and Mick soon began playing along to rockabilly and blues on the radio. By his teens Ronson had grown into a lean, handsome man with a strong chin, aquiline profile and thick, shoulder-length hair who played in several local bands, like the Crestas and the Mariners. By 1965, Ronson was obsessed with the Yardbirds' guitarist Jeff Beck and went down to London himself in an effort to emulate him. He would hang around local cafés like the Giaconda and may have very well crossed paths with Bowie without knowing it. Both men were hungry and searching at the time.

'I never had any money and I used to sit there with one cup for five or six hours,' Ronson, who died in 1993, once said. 'I'd just sit there and sort of bump into someone by accident and say, 'What do you do?' I was terrified. I used to get really depressed.' There he joined an up-and-coming band called the Voice, which was affiliated with the Process Church of the Final Judgement cult (which worshipped both Jesus *and* the Devil).

Clearly this wasn't his thing, and it wasn't long before he was toiling in another obscure act, the soul combo the Wanted, whose name can only be considered ironic.

'He tried so hard,' Suzi says. 'He starved in London a couple of times. Can-of-beans-a-week kind of thing. One night the band got pulled over by the police and everyone else ran out of the van, leaving Mick and all the equipment. He had no license, no insurance. He got into so much trouble. He kind of quit after that. He decided to be something else. A school gardener is what he became. Took a lot of persuading to get back down and do it again.'

Back in Hull, Ronson – a naturally gifted musician who wrote the dazzling string arrangements for both Bowie's 'Life on Mars?' and Lou Reed's 'Perfect Day,' just to name a pair of immortal tracks, simply by ear – spent his days working as a gardener. He figured he was done with rock for good. 'There was something about it, cutting grass, pruning roses. I had sheep to look after too. I really enjoyed it,' he said years later. 'I thought maybe this is what I'd end up doing.'

'He had no idea how good he was really,' Suzi says. 'Never had any idea. When you are good at something naturally you kind of assume everybody else is like that. So easy. Mick was a bit like that. He thought he was okay.'

Eventually he was persuaded to audition to fill a vacancy in the Rats, one of Hull's biggest bands (this, of course, being a highly relative distinction). The Rats toured and filled clubs and halls with their loud party blues rock. Ronson made enough money on the road to quit his gardening job. He figured he had it made but soon recognized the Rats' creative limitations. Bolstered by Ronson's talent and scope, the band were soon laying down an acid rock number called 'The Rise and Fall of Bernie Gripplestone.' By the end of the sixties, Cambridge had left the band and was in London recording with Bowie and Visconti on the *Space Oddity* album. He was replaced by another Hull musician named Mick. To avoid confusion, everyone called Mick Woodmansey 'Woody.' The band continued to tour and record commercially inconsequential tracks.

Soon Ronson was gardening once again, and he might have continued on that way if John Cambridge hadn't returned to Hull in spring of 1970 with the express purpose of drafting Ronson to be David Bowie's new player. According to legend, he found him one afternoon grooming a rugby pitch for the Hull City Parks Department. Ronson met Cambridge with skepticism. He'd been to London once already and failed to generate anything at all. 'I thought, "Wait a minute. Is it going to take me another two or three yeas to pay this lot off?"' Ronson said. 'I told him, 'I'm not sure about this, John.' Then I decided I had to go.'

Ronson packed up his guitar and a small suitcase

and headed south to Beckenham. He met Bowie and Angie in Haddon Hall. Bowie was sitting in the living room, playing his twelve-string. 'He was sitting playing the guitar and I picked up a guitar and started playing with him,' Ronson has said. Bowie began singing and Ronson found himself impressed by just how sophisticated and different Bowie's original tracks were. He had a great voice. 'I thought, "Well, here we go." I really liked David and his songs. It was real classy. It was different. I was in London. I was all set.'

When the session was over, they piled into the Bowies' Jaguar and drove to a local fish and chips shop to hash out the details, such as where Ronson would live and how much he would earn. One of the first practical tasks, once Ronson was fully moved in to Haddon Hall, was converting the space under the vast stairway into a rehearsal and recording studio. Ronson, unlike Bowie, was strapping and handy, and with the assistance of Angie and Tony Visconti, they soon began renovating the tiny, six-foot-by-ten-foot space.

'I've never seen so much joy centered on a Black and Decker in many years,' Angie writes in *Backstage Passes*. 'In seemingly no time, they had soundproofed and brightly lit a natural little bunker for us kids to play in.'

That spring Alice Cooper, and his Detroit-based garage combo known for their onstage theatrics, played England, and Bowie and Ronson caught the show. Bowie had seen this schtick before in cheeky British 'horror rockers' like Screaming Lord Sutch (whose 'Jack the Ripper' is a gothabilly classic). Fellow Beckenham resident Arthur Brown's 1968 single 'Fire' reached number one in the UK largely due to his flamboyant promotional appearances, which found the typically hippie-ish beardo screaming, 'I am the God of hellfire and I bring you . . . ,' while wearing flame-spurting headgear. Alice's songs were loud, fun and trashy, and his sense of shock theater was not unlike that of Lindsay Kemp, only much more accessible to a mass audience. But like Sutch and Brown, he offered little beyond the macabre. It seemed like theatricality and serious song-writing, not to mention real sex appeal, were not an easy match. Nobody had pulled it off yet.

Back in Haddon Hall ideas were brewing and the living room, kitchen and tiny rehearsal bunker were hopping with energy and feedback around the clock as Bowie, Ronson, Visconti and Cambridge wrote and played. 'Memory of a Free Festival,' the second single from *Man of Words*, was issued in June of 1970, split into two parts, on the A and B sides. An ode to the Arts Lab, it failed to capitalize on 'Space Oddity''s success. David was starting to worry that he was going to be remembered as a one-hit wonder.

As they plotted their next moves, Angie presided over the salon, typically as hostess and muse, feeding and advising her mates. 'Angie was real cool,' says Dana Gillespie, who attended many meals at the Haddon Hall salon during this period. 'You could literally give her a potato, an onion and a carrot and she'd feed four musicians and three friends. I used to go down there and hang out with them. Angie was always supportive of David. She always listened to his songs as they came off the production line and she'd always say, "That's fabulous."'

Angie says, 'I would do my best plotting during what other people would think was my down-time – when I was washing dishes or ironing shirts. Because there's something about menial tasks that makes one very creative. And in those times, I would have all kinds of brilliant ideas and more schemes and more plots . . .'

When she wasn't cooking and critiquing, Angie was costuming. 'Determined to make David's band the smartest in the land, I would preach to the boys about their day-to-day appearances,' she recalled. 'It's just as essential to look handsome off stage as it is on.'

'It was theater that I was interested in,' she tells me. 'I wanted the band to be big, huge and musical. I wanted it to look as great as theater looked. Be as brilliantly lit as theater. It was to be an experi-ence. I'd spent seven years going to classical concerts every week at school. Just the venues were magnificent. They raised your spirits, and raised your heart. So when I got involved with David's career, all I could really add to the mix, because the music was great, was the theater. I thought if

I could mix serious theater and the music, no one's doing that.'

Ray Stevenson, who became a member of the informal salon that was being conducted inside Haddon Hall, insists that that idea to create a highly theatrical and colorful rock experience was his.

'I had this philosophy: observe the trend and do the opposite,' he says. 'I mentioned this to David. Who said it before? Possibly the surrealists. Duchamp. Or maybe back to da Vinci. The trend was denim, singer-songwriter stuff. These people in denim pretending to be just like the audience and they really weren't. And then doing the opposite would be rebelling against that. "We are superheroes." It was one of those evening conversations that kind of finished. We moved on to, I don't know, cooking after that. Just the next time I went back to Haddon Hall, Angie was sewing all the costumes. Ever since there has never been any acknowledgment of that conversation. It all comes back to ambition. I didn't realize how ambitious he was. There'd be a bunch of people including myself sitting around smoking dope and he wouldn't. He just wanted to absorb and use whatever was said.'

Angie purchased a sewing machine and began making stage costumes for this as yet unnamed new group. With Alice Cooper-mania on his mind, Bowie was chatting over the Haddon Hall phone line to Kenneth Pitt one day when he happened to quip, 'It's all hype, isn't it?' Something clicked and he realized that he'd stumbled on the perfect name for this new, attention-hungry crew. They wanted to generate some hype, so they would *literally* generate Hype.

By the spring of 1970 it was official. The Hype, referred to sometimes simply as Hype, were born, outfitted in Angie's costumes and with newly christened, sensationalist stage personas. Bowie was Rainbow Man, his costume a prism of rainbow colors; Visconti was Hype Man, a sort of crime-fighting, bass-playing superhero; Cambridge was Cowboy Man, with a hat and fringe; and Ronson, his blond hair newly dyed jet black, was the pinstripe-suited Gangster Man.

In an interview with *Melody Maker* that month, Bowie explained the group's creation: 'I deliberately chose the name in favor of something that sounded perhaps heavy because now no one can say they're being conned. Especially nowadays there's a lot of narrow mindedness among groups or at least behind the organizers who claim to be presenting free music for free people but I don't see how they can because they're so hypocritical in everything else. I suppose you could say I chose Hype deliberately with tongue in cheek.'

Live, the Hype's set consisted of covers and material off *Space Oddity* and the upcoming *The Man Who Sold the World*. Critical reaction was mixed. They made their debut opening for the denim-clad and long-haired hippie clan Country

Joe and the Fish at the Roundhouse in late February of 1970. 'Musically it was a great gig,' Visconti writes in his autobiography. 'Although we were heckled initially, and called a variety of homosexual epithets.'

Disc and Music Echo magazine observed of a later gig, 'David had much more confidence and stage presence with this backing group, and as his songs are suitable for grooving to as well as just listening to, the brightest hope could well change categories,' but dismissed the show as a 'disaster' in terms of technical execution. Still, it was clear that Bowie was beginning to come into something with the Hype. It was a baby step in platform shoes.

'It should have been a complete rethink,' Stevenson says. 'They got the costumes right but they were still doing old songs. Those little ditties. They required new songs. The kind he later went on to write. "Fame" would have been fantastic in those costumes. The audience were just milling around waiting for the main act.'

'For me this will always be the very first night of Glam Rock,' Visconti recalled in his memoir. 'Marc Bolan was visible resting his head on his arms on the edge of the stage, taking it all in. Bolan never admitted he even went to the gig.'

In the spring of 1970, T. Rex released the magnificent, Tony Visconti-produced 'Ride a White Swan' single. It was that rare track that manages to be both trivial and a model for how to conduct the rest of your life ('Ride it on out like you were a bird,' Bolan instructs). It was the first in a series of chart-topping hits that would make him the focal point of a Beatlemania-like pandemonium dubbed T. Rextasy. By the time Bowie set about rehearsing the music for his next album, *The Man Who Sold the World*, his old friend from the mod days seemed to have done just that. At one point, T. Rex sold one hundred thousand records in a single day. Bowie had not managed to come anywhere near that in nearly six years of trying.

Always on the verge of egomania, Bolan took to wearing top hats and T-shirts emblazoned with his own corkscrew-haired visage. In concert his duck walks, comic shouts of 'Yeah!' and double entendres ('I'm gonna suck ya . . .') were outsized.

'Boley struck it big and we were all green with envy,' Bowie recalled later. 'It was terrible – we fell out for about six months. It was [sulky mutter] "He's doing much better than I am." And he got all sniffy about us who were still down in the basement.'

Eventually, as it had done in the sixties, the competitive spirit between Bolan and Bowie manifested itself as a positive energy force. They would continue to try to one-up each other, and as a result, they produced some of the greatest English pop music ever recorded. Bowie was far too busy with family and business concerns to wallow in envy as Bolan's star went supernova. Angie was pregnant with their first child, and the pair were about to pursue a radical change in management.

Pitt took much of the blame for the success of peers like T. Rex and the relative obscurity of David and his ventures, only never directly. '[David's] habit was to whine a lot and resist passive aggressively, never really speaking up for himself or taking charge of a situation,' Angie writes in *Backstage Passes*. According to Angie, Pitt would use his parental-figure status in Bowie's life to quell any potential uprising, assuring David that things would right themselves if he would only trust in Pitt, behave himself and carry on. 'Ken's profile of the ideal son/client/sex object, on the other hand, was a young man eager for direction, convinced that Daddy knows best. And so the relationship staggered along under all that baggage,' she writes.

Angie decided that the time had come for her to act on this and again help her man out of a troubling and sinking arrangement. She decided to go to the Phillips offices for advice and turn to an acquaintance, A & R man Ralph Mace. She asked Mace if there was any way to break the management contract with Pitt, as all the inquiries she'd made were met with dismissal. In the British music business you did not break contracts. It wasn't gentlemanly. It was anathema to the process.

'We had to hire someone to get rid of Ken Pitt,' Angie says today. 'I had to go and find someone. I asked Ralph, "Look, does anyone know where I can get my hands on an attorney? Because all

238

these British attorneys are scared shitless to break this contract.'''

Mace turned to his boss Olav Wyper, who remained sympathetic to Bowie despite the lack of record sales for the *Space Oddity* album. 'I was a friendly shoulder to cry on,' says Olav Wyper. 'David had come to me before that and said that he felt totally frustrated. He felt he was "drowning," which was one of the words that he often used. He said he was drowning in the relationship. And he didn't feel that Ken really understood what he was doing creatively. The personal relationship, because Ken was clearly deeply in love with David, was completely skewing the commercial relationship. And he had this wonderful chance that he'd been given back the hit that he thought he should have had. And clearly I was at the center of that. He'd say, "You've gotta help me. You've gotta help me."'

Wyper recommended an associate named Tony Defries to the Bowies. Defries, then only twenty-seven, with his great nose, neat gray suits and lacquered head of curly hair, carried himself like a man ten years older. Defries was not technically a lawyer.

Defries reportedly went out of his way to color his background so that it resembled more of a rags-to-riches story. The Defries family was of Dutch origin and had been living in Britain for three generations. His father, Edward, had been an engineer and had lost his fortune during the

Great Depression, but by the time Tony came of age, he'd rebounded and had begun a thriving antiques dealership in the marketplace in Shepherd's Bush. Defries tells of his father sending him through the markets of London to find the prices of competitors' wares and report back so that his father could mark his own wares down. Whether this was a temporary chore or a way of life, however, remains part of his greater mystery.

The youngest of three and a sickly child with life-threatening asthma, Defries spent much of his childhood cot-bound in the family's Croydon home. He attended a respected school, Heath, but resisted formal education. Like Bowie, he educated himself by devouring books and essentially teaching himself the ins and outs of the legal profession without actually becoming a lawyer. By his early twenties he was working at various law offices in London as a clerk. By the time he met the Bowies, he had already revolutionized one industry single-handedly.

'He had a very good legal mind but he was not a qualified solicitor,' says Wyper. 'And he'd never claimed to be, which is why he always identified himself as a lawyer. One who practices the law. But he wasn't actually qualified. And I knew this because he told me. He was a solicitor's clerk who was looking for opportunity. He did eventually become very involved in intellectual property. One of the first things he did that got his name known in British showbiz circles happened when he was representing photographers. At the time, they basically didn't control their own work. And he set up the first association of fashion photographers and models. That's the organization that most major photographers in the world now belong to.'

'He was always somewhat of a visionary,' says Laurence Myers, who would become Tony Defries's business partner in the early years of his relationship with David Bowie. Then an accountant for South African pop music impresario Mickey Most, and now a theatrical producer, Myers was the entrance into show business that Defries was looking for, and soon the men were sharing an office and had formed a management company named GEM. 'He was a visionary. I remember him telling me many, many, many years ago that one day everyone at home will have a laptop computer in their home,' he says today. 'At that time, he was sort of eccentric. He had a very strange suit, I seem to remember. A sort of Doctor Seuss checked frock coat and this huge mass of hair. One day he said to me, "You know, models really get treated very badly. They're stars, they don't get paid, agencies never pay them, they exploit them. I think they should be stars."'

The Bowies were often without money, cold and fretful, during the recording of the new album. '*The Man Who Sold the World* was conceived during a period when we were really having a rough time,' Angie writes. 'We were really poor. We didn't have any money. Our band were really frightened.'

Defries met David and Angie and patiently listened as they told their tale of woe. Bowie played him the material for the upcoming *The Man Who Sold the World* album, and Defries decided that he was in the presence of a major talent. Breaking a contract in the British music business was considered ungentlemanly and vile, but Defries insisted to David that he felt it had to be done and that he would ensure that it would be handled swiftly and cleanly. In Defries's eyes it was Pitt, not Bowie, who had broken the arrangement by failing to make him the star he so clearly deserved to be.

Sure enough, within days, Kenneth Pitt, who had never heard of Defries before, was shocked to receive a legal notice in his morning mail. 'All the plans for David's imminent success had been made,' he writes, 'but on April 27, they collapsed like a house of cards.'

Defries and Bowie requested confirmation that Pitt would cease to be Bowie's personal manager from that point on. Pitt was a wreck. 'I felt only sadness and, sadly, I put the letter aside.' Days later, Pitt responded to the letter, suggesting that they meet and discuss a civil way to dissolve their professional relationship. He also suggested an alternative scenario in which he would continue to be involved with Bowie professionally but only as a handler of contracts and other paperwork. Defries shot this down quickly. He wanted a clean and fast break.

'When this was all happening, Ken did come

and see me. We did talk about it two or three times and I did advise him that he was riding a wave that he was in no position to control,' Olav Wyper says today. 'And my advice to him was to do a deal with Defries and Myers if he could and get what he could out of it. He had no chance of riding that wave with David. And he should get off and get the best deal he could.'

Pitt, Bowie and Defries had an awkward meeting on May 7, 1970. While Defries spoke, David stared off into space, silent and frail looking. Pitt instinctively detected that Defries was not just David's legal representation but his next manager as well. Pitt informed Defries that there was compensation due for his losses as well as a percentage of David's future earnings. Defries agreed and promised to come up with an appropriate figure (at the time Pitt was reportedly willing to settle for a mere two thousand pounds). When the meeting was over David shook Pitt's hand and left him with a simple 'Thank you, Ken.' And then it was over. From his window, Pitt watched Bowie and Defries walk up Manchester Street and disappear around the corner.

Pitt retired from professional talent management in 1982, has lived in Australia and Washington DC over the years and now spends much of his time in the countryside. He and Bowie have kept in touch. 'He sends me rare secondhand books that he knows will interest me and I am sure it is true to say that we continue to respect each other,' Pitt writes.

Liberated from Pitt, Bowie tried to pour all of his energy into completing *The Man Who Sold the World*, but he still could not seem to focus. The musical landscape of the album, Bowie's hardest and darkest yet, was largely down to Visconti and Ronson (the latter intent on creating a heavy blues record worthy of Cream). Bowie, as a rule very good about giving credit to collaborators when it was due, admitted as much, telling *Mojo*, 'The sonic landscape was Visconti's. The band contribution – how the drums and bass should work together with the guitar – was something Mick got really involved in.'

Visconti and Ronson bonded in the studio. A sharp student of music since his preadolescence, Mick used this opportunity to learn as many production and arrangement techniques as possible. 'He was with me all the time, even on the mixes,' Visconti told *Mojo*. 'He would ask me tons of questions: "Why am I doing this?" "Is it possible to do this?" I was so glad to have a person that keen on the team because Bowie was really uninterested.'

While producer Visconti and Ronson were forming the album's musical vision, Bowie spent much of his time shopping with Angela. Terry Burns, during one of his intermittent periods outside of the Cane Hill asylum, had come to live with them in Haddon Hall. On many of the lyrics, which were written often moments before the vocals were due to be recorded, David drew some inspiration from this proximity: it was the closest he and his half brother had been been since the 1950s.

'I just tended him and treated him like a special guest and spent time with him and just chatted away,' Angie has said of this period. 'He was a very well-read man and a very interesting man, but with the drugs that were prescribed, he would tend to really not talk too much. I think David attempted to be up-front about the fact that his brother was unwell and it was an excuse for himself later during drug-induced paranoia.'

Much of the lyrical content on *The Man Who Sold the World* seems to be abstracted observations of Terry's life, both inner and outer. The most explicit of these are the title track, the prog rock 'Width of a Circle' (which has no less than three guitar solos!) and 'All the Madmen.' The former marks his first real foray into homoerotic lyricism ('He showed me his leather belt round his hips'). The latter is a terrifying track, beginning slowly, with a humdrum narrative device 'Day after day' and thundering into a terrifying chorus with Ronson slashing out his protometal chords and Bowie promising, 'I can fly, I will scream, I will break my arm, / I will do me harm.' There's black wit ('Give me some good old lobotomy') and a folky outro chant of 'Zane, zane, zane / *Ouvre le chien*,' which would go on to become a hallmark of sorts, appearing on both 1994's *Buddha of Suburbia* soundtrack and as a slogan printed on the backdrop of his 1995 tour in support of *Outside*.

Its literal translation is 'open the dog.'

'Black Country Rock' is a funky T. Rex homage that some interpreted as a piss take on Bowie's ascending rival (à la Simon & Garfunkel's 1966 Dylan parody 'A Simple Desultory Philippic,' Paul McCartney's broadly Lennonesque 'Let Me Roll It' or Weird Al Yankovic's Devo homage 'Dare to Be Stupid'). If nothing else, it's a testament to Bowie's expert style mimicry. Employing his gift for mimicry, he out-Bolans Bolan. His old friend was reportedly upset upon first hearing it but came to see it, as he came to see most everything, as a tribute.

'After All,' with its 'Oh, by jingo' refrain, is another throwback to his late sixties penchant for English macabre. Bowie sounds like Boris Karloff settling down for a pot of cozy-warmed Darjeeling in the hollow of a cold marble crypt. 'Running Gun Blues' takes on arms dealing with irony. 'I'll plug a few civilians,' Bowie threatens. 'She Shook Me Cold' is Zeppelin-style blues. Best of all is 'The Supermen,' a sort of Freidrich-Nietzsche-gets-taken-in-from-the-rain-by-a-family-of-cloaked-Druids psycho-folk workout with an odd Latin tempo. It's Bowie at his most committal as far as facing and voicing the strange is concerned.

With the album completed and due for an April 1971 release, David began considering the artwork. On one of their frequent shopping trips, he and Angela spied a medieval-style tunic draped over a mannequin in the Mr Fish boutique in Savile Row (the boutique's storefront can be seen in a snapshot during the *Love You Till Tuesday* film). The Bowies agreed that this would be an ideal garment to wear on the album's cover, and although it was prohibitively expensive at nearly a thousand pounds in total, they also snapped up three long, slim, Chinese silk velour dresses in pale green, pink and blue. Bowie, his perm now grown out long and straight, posed while reclining on a divan in the great living room in Haddon Hall.

Upon submitting the cover art to Mercury, the Bowies claimed to be shocked when the executives balked at releasing it as it was. Before the cover was restored on subsequent reissues, the American version depicted a George Underwood cartoon of a demented man with a rifle under his arm and a torn-up cowboy hat atop his head. The Cane Hill asylum, where Underwood was once committed himself after a breakdown, looms in the distance, providing a more or less direct reference to Terry and his illness. The 'S' in 'sold' is a dollar sign. Why they deemed this more appropriate than a lithe, befrocked Bowie, who can say?

'Bloody philistines!' Bowie reportedly shouted when he first heard news of the label's reaction to his original cover choice. More likely, however, both Bowie and Angie knew that word of a banned or controversial sleeve would get them lots of ink. It was a throwback to the Manish Boys' Society for the Preservation of Animal Filament gimmick of 1965. This isn't to suggest that the couple didn't find the dress a genuinely pleasing frock. Bowie, according to Stevenson, would even wear it in his downtime. 'I went 'round his place and he was wearing it,' he recalls. 'It was the type of thing a flamboyant Arab would probably wear in the street.'

Bowie's androgynous style was not uncommon at the time. Any photo of Mick Jagger circa 1970 would suggest a growing comfort with blurring gender lines. There is also a long tradition of drag among British performers from Shakespearean productions up to the Rolling Stones gussying themselves up for the cover of their 'Have You Seen Your Mother, Baby, Standing in the Shadow' single sleeve. *Monty Python's Flying Circus*, launched the previous year, featured drag performances in nearly every episode via Terry Jones or Graham Chapman.

'Lots of English comedians dressed up as women,' Hanif Kureishi says. 'It's part of English culture to dress up as a girl. It's all performance and putting on voices. Messing about. It's not the same as being gay. *All* Englishmen dressed as women.'

Bowie debuted the songs from the upcoming record in front of a crowd of just 1,500 that summer during the very first Glastonbury Fayre, which is now the massive and prestigious annual summer gathering the Glastonbury Festival of Contemporary Performing Arts. The event was held on a farm in the southwestern countryside by Glastonbury Tor, a hill where, according to Arthurian legend, the Holy Grail was supposedly buried. Bowie performed with Traffic, the Grateful Dead, Hawkwind and headliners T. Rex, among others. Glastonbury was the latest in a series of concert events (beginning with Monterey Pop in 1968) that seemed to confirm rock 'n' roll's power to unite and its key role not just in culture, but in the political world as well. Shortly before traveling to the event, Bowie completed a new song that reflected both this shift as well as his personal journey. 'I was already a Beatnik, I had to be a Hippie . . . ,' he wrote in a letter to his songwriting publisher that fall. 'Now I am 24 and I am married and I am not at all heavy. And I'm still writing and my wife is pregnant . . .'

These developments are as scary to young people today as they were in 1970. Before 'Changes,' however, they had no anthem to assuage them. 'Turn and face the strange,' he sang, most likely to himself. The bridge, however, is directed to his parents' generation: 'And these children that you spit on / As they try to change their world / They're immune to your consultations / They're quite aware of what they're going through.' A sentiment as old as the Grail itself but so eloquent (even when he swaps 'spit' for 'shit' on 1974's *David Live* album) in delivery and conviction that John Hughes would use them to open 1985's *The Breakfast Club*, all alone on a black title card. It would not be David's last anthem. He has many ('All the Young Dudes,' 'Heroes'), but 'Changes' (which would open his 1971 album *Hunky Dory*) is his most durable. It's a young person's song that manages to follow David through his career with grace and not nostalgia (even when he brought it out during his 2000 headlining set at the now massive Glastonbury festival).

Haddon Hall's gothic splendor was demolished in the mid-seventies and converted into a block of ugly flats that must have felt very modern at the time. Thirty years or so onward, it's now a real eyesore. It resembles a Travelodge off the interstate, with thick, frosted glass windows and drab brown bricks. There's a row of garages, and the great driveway where Bowie's Jaguar was parked has been converted into a parking lot. Haddon Hall's current landscape exudes none of the energy of its legendary days, and the titanic music that was dreamed up inside can no longer be heard. Many of its current residents probably have no idea that they live in the haunted house of the modern age.

CHAPTER 11

When the Irish literary aesthete Oscar Wilde disembarked from the USS *Arizona* on January 3, 1882, in his green coat, seal-trimmed collar, blue necktie, silken turban and patent leather shoes, he was famously asked by customs officers, 'Have you anything to declare?' and answered, cigarette in hand, 'I have nothing to declare except my genius.' The press from every major newspaper, including the *Saturday Evening Post*, the *Herald* and the *World*, was there to cover his first trip to America. When Bowie – at this point intent on being part of the continuum of aesthetes both decadent and profound, and determined to represent a modern-day version of Wilde's fin de siècle philosophy and pose – went through customs at Washington's Dulles International Airport on January 27, 1971, only Mercury publicist Ron Oberman was waiting . . . with his parents.

It was determined that Washington soil, rather than that of Chicago or New York, would be the first that Bowie would step on, and not for any real strategic reason. Oberman was more or less his only companion in and liaison to this new world, and he happened to be staying there with his parents.

Bowie, who would later develop a notorious fear of flying, flew eagerly, having almost no experience to base any rational fear on. While he had no work visa and could not legally perform, Oberman was determined to introduce him to the right people (hip journalists, ambivalent but charmable Mercury employees) at coordinated exhibitions in New York, Chicago, Los Angeles and San Francisco. The *Man Who Sold the World* album, which was released in November of 1970, was not a hit. Mercury *had* managed to break Rod Stewart on a global scale. His single 'Maggie May' was number one on both sides of the Atlantic. Also in 1971, Marc Bolan and T. Rex had an American hit with 'Bang a Gong' (curiously only after altering the song's original UK title 'Get It On'). Elton John, another figure from the Marquee Club rhythm and blues scene, was quickly becoming one of the biggest stars in pop. Even Bowie's old Deram Records labelmate Cat Stevens was becoming a big star in America. His melancholy 'Wild World' was ubiquitous on AM radio. The thinking was that if only Americans could meet Bowie, via the press, and see how charismatic and unique he was, he would surely be next in line. It would not be so easy, of course. Bowie was more authentically arty and different than any of these peers, certainly more so than

Tony Orlando and Dawn, the Osmonds, Bread and other American hit makers of the time. Even getting through customs was a challenge: 'We were waiting outside the plane, fifteen minutes, half an hour, forty-five minutes; there was no sign of him,' Ron Oberman says. When Bowie emerged through the gate an hour and a half later, Oberman was relieved. 'I said, "What happened?" And he answered, "Oh, they held me on the plane. Maybe because I look so strange."'

Once in America, Oscar Wilde was taken to a fete in New York City where he met the great American poet Walt Whitman. David Bowie was taken to Hofberg's kosher deli in Silver Springs, Maryland, for a corned beef on rye. Oberman asked Bowie what he would like to do after dropping off the luggage at the hotel in downtown Washington, DC, he'd booked him into. 'He said, "Oh, I'd really like to meet some American people,"' says Oberman. 'Hofberg's delicatessen had the best corned beef that I've ever had in my life. So we went to the restaurant and had a great dinner there.' His first taste of kosher cuisine was accompanied by a lot of curiosity on the part of the locals. 'He got a lot of stares,' Oberman says. That night, Bowie attended a suburban kegger. Oberman and his brother drove the star to a house party in nearby Garrett Park. 'We walk in and the place is just filled with pot smoke. There are huge bongs being passed around all over this party.'

Bowie had, of course, been fantasizing about

America since his preteens. It did not disappoint. For someone as shy as he was, it seemed an ideal place socially. People came right up to you. There were no painful silences, no repression. Americans were aggressive and inquisitive and Bowie's slim, elegantly androgynous appearance fascinated them. They approached and even touched him without hesitation, as if he were some exotic zoo animal.

'He was wide eyed,' Oberman says. 'He could not believe he was here. I would say he had the mentality of a tourist. He wanted to see things and meet people.' That the nation itself was essentially broke, with a severely devalued dollar and the unpopular Vietnam War drawing hundreds of thousands to protest in Washington and San Francisco, did not seem to matter. This was the land of Evel Knievel and Muhammad Ali. This was the land of Mickey Mouse (Disney World had recently opened in Orlando). Even our boogey men, like Charlie Manson (then on trial for the Tate-LaBianca murders), had outsized style.

(Of the abovementioned people, only Knievel would not be mentioned in a David Bowie song within three years [although Ali is referred to by his pre-Muslim name Cassius Clay in '74's *Diamond Dogs* track 'Candidate']. And this may be due to his rhyming options [discounting 'Evel' itself, or 'evil,' what do you have left besides 'boll weevil'?])

From Washington, DC, Bowie traveled to New

York City, where he was met by Paul Nelson. On the verge of becoming a very influential and respected music writer at *Rolling Stone*, Nelson was then doing freelance work for Mercury Records. 'I hired him because he had great credibility. They got along really well, David and Paul,' Oberman says. 'And Paul had set up a number of interviews with him in the city. The plan was to align Bowie with some of these insightful writers.'

Manhattan was freezing and Bowie amplified his androgynous flamboyance with a giant fuzzy winter coat and beret. Bowie stayed at the Holiday Inn in Times Square, then the world's nucleus of sleaze and decrepitude. The fear and unease contributed to the adrenaline rush that he was already naturally feeling from all the attention. Bowie would spend the rest of the seventies seeking privacy in expensive hotels. This would be his first and only real time spent among the people, inviting them to approach him. As he visited the Metropolitan Museum of Art or browsed the jazz LPs in the Colony record shop, people would point and whisper. One brazen elderly woman asked him what sort of pelt was used to make his coat. 'Teddy bear,' he quipped, and she furrowed her brow and crept off. That night, he caught folksinger Tim Hardin's set in Greenwich Village. As he walked around, he thought of all of his heroes who'd trod over the same pavement: Jack Kerouac, Bob Dylan, Charles Mingus, Lou Reed.

Next Bowie visited Chicago, where he was feted by the Mercury office staff. The office workers, expecting a gender-bending rock 'n' roll wild man, were shocked to discover the shy, polite Englishman eagerly offering his hand. Sensing, perhaps, that it might be best to temper any incendiary conduct while in the Midwest, Bowie remained on good, if restrained, behavior.

'In Chicago, New York, he didn't wear any dresses,' Oberman says. 'But he wore the dress in L.A.' Los Angeles was much more encouraging when it came to such things. They loved a good show. Bowie was met in Los Angeles by then Mercury Records publicity officer Rodney Bingenheimer. Bingenheimer, who would later open the legendary glitter nightclub Rodney's English Disco and become one of our best and most influential disc jockeys (he is still on the air at KROQ in Los Angeles), was known for his flawless rock taste. He'd been an assistant to Sonny Bono and, ironically, a stand-in for Davy Jones, the Monkee who inspired Bowie to change his name. A tireless Hollywood gadfly, in '71 Rodney was already a super-Anglophile, well turned on to Bowie when almost nobody in America knew who he was. Before being hired by Mercury, he was one of the few people in America who actually bought the *Space Oddity* record. Bingenheimer would routinely shop for imports at a record store, just up Hollywood Boulevard from the local Mercury office. 'It was like the only store at that time that actually had import albums,' he tells me. 'I bought the *Space Oddity* album there. By the time I went to Mercury of course I already knew all about him. I loved his music and his style. He seemed like one of a kind. Kind of different for a British artist. It wasn't that jangly pop.'

Rodney was as much a music fan as David was, and they quickly bonded over pop records, movie gossip and girls. The diminutive scenester was excited to take Bowie to local clubs and introduce him to all the right people, including his friend and fellow skirt-chasing pop obsessive songwriter/producer Kim Fowley.

Bingenheimer's enthusiasm for Bowie ('godhead' is the word he uses to describe such artists, as in 'Brian Wilson is godhead. Oasis are godhead.') was greater than his loyalty to his employer. He had contacts at every label in town and was happy to conflict with Mercury's interests by parading Bowie before executives from other companies who might poach him for a bigger and better setup. With two failed Mercury records and his ears full of kibitzing about the kind of rock 'n' roll largesse afforded Los Angeles-plundering acts like Led Zeppelin and the Rolling Stones, Bowie seemed eager to be poached at the time.

'I'd take him over to Liberty Records. We would walk down Orange, walk right past Hollywood High, and the kids would be out there having lunch. And that's how the rumor went out that we were trying to pick up girls at Hollywood High. Actually he wanted to pick up a new record contract. Liberty Records was across from Hollywood High.' Bingenheimer also arranged for Bowie to stay at the well-connected record producer Tom Ayres's house in the Hollywood Hills. Anybody who was anybody stayed at Ayres's place when visiting L.A. There he also met Gene Vincent, the fifties rock icon famous for his echo-drenched hits like 'Be-Bop-a-Lula' and a somewhat jarring stage act in which he led his combo, the Blue Caps, through a rockabilly set while dragging his leg, which was permanently injured in a motorcycle crash, behind him. Vincent with his cavernous bone structure and towering physique, was ill and down on his luck, but like many of the first wave of rock 'n' roll heroes, he remained a star abroad. Bowie was thrilled to meet him and the pair jammed on early versions of 'Hang On to Yourself' and 'Moonage Daydream' (both of which would end up on the *Ziggy Stardust* album two years later). Such specactles didn't seem unusual inside the Ayres palace. Ayres, a former paratrooper, had been a nocturnal Hollywood character since the beatnik era, producing novelty hits like 'Hot Pastrami' by the Dartells and connecting the right people to one another as a sort of self-deputized public service. Ayres's place was just off Sunset Boulevard, high above the old Source health food store (made famous in the last L.A. scene in *Annie*

Hall, where Diane Keaton tells Woody Allen she is not going to return to New York with him). It was a grand 1920s castle patrolled by a massive Great Dane named Blue.

Another taste of Hollywood opulence whetted his appetite for a greater success, the kind he did not achieve with Kenneth Pitt (as well as the kind that Oberman did not have the infrastructure to provide and the kind that Tony Defries, the legal adviser who was fast becoming his full-time manager, saw as well within his reach). In early February, Bingenheimer and Ayres threw a party to introduce Bowie to the in crowd of L.A. Although Los Angeles would five years later be the location for Bowie's darkest period (and, some say, his best recorded work), at the time, he was smitten, and, according to Fowley, cannily sober. 'It was his "I'm new in Hollywood, how does this place work?" phase,' says Fowley. Bowie was studying the lay of the land and making notations. He would sit on the floor, clutching a leather briefcase, which probably contained lyrics and notebooks. He scribbled ideas to himself as people passed around him and Warhol superstar Ultra Violet, also in attendance, did her best to steal much of his attention. 'She looked like a prune version of Paulette Goddard,' Fowley would recall. Bowie was getting hundreds of musical ideas as well. While at the party, Fowley offered Bowie a copy of a record by Wigwam, a new Finnish band that he was producing. Sure enough, Fowley would detect not only some of Wigwam's melody style on Bowie's next album but also the line 'Look at those cavemen go,' in a song called 'Life on Mars?' It's a direct lyrical nod to the Hollywood Argyles' 1960 number one hit 'Alley Oop' (which Fowley produced when he was still in high school) and reveals just how adept Bowie was becoming at refining the sounds and snippets of overheard dialogue swirling around him and turning them into songs that skirt pastiche and seem entirely original. One thinks again of the party chatter in the back room of the pub behind his childhood home in Bromley. He didn't know how to process all the information back then. He was too young, but the notion of such things as raw materials surely got into his head very early on.

Also in attendance was journalist John Mendelsohn. Mendelsohn, another one of the hip writers Oberman had reached out to, was profiling Bowie for his first-ever *Rolling Stone* feature story. Published in April, under the headline 'David Bowie: Pantomime Rock?,' it's hard not to read the interview today without seeing it as a sketch for what Bowie was cooking up. Bowie frets about being dismissed as 'mediocre.' He needn't have worried. Mendelsohn describes Bowie as 'ravishing, almost disconcertingly reminiscent of Lauren Bacall.'

'My performances have got to be theatrical experiences for me as well as for the audience,'

Bowie told Mendelsohn. 'I don't want to climb out of my fantasies in order to go up on stage – I want to take them on stage with me.' In the most oft-quoted point in the interview, Bowie channels Lindsay Kemp, telling Mendelsohn, 'I think [music] should be tarted up, made into a prostitute, a parody of itself.' He signs off with, 'Tell your readers that they can make up their minds about me when I begin getting adverse publicity: when I'm found in bed with Raquel Welch's husband.'

Everywhere Bowie went, people seemed to be pressing records into his hands. At a radio station in San Francisco, Mendelsohn played Bowie a record by an obscure garage band from Ann Arbor, Michigan, who called themselves the Stooges and were fronted by a man named Iggy.

'On the first radio tour he heard Iggy, also the Legendary Stardust Cowboy, Annette Peacock and in Los Angeles a lot of L.A.-based talent: Kim Fowley, Randy Newman and the poet who lived in motels! What's his name? Tom Waits!' Angie told me during an interview we did in 2000. 'He ransacked their ideas! Of course! That's what artists do. Experience life through listening and interacting with people and other artists and then reinterpreting it in their peculiar way. That's why they don't have day jobs! Too much intellectual pillaging and looting!'

The trip was successful in a creative way. Professionally, despite some of the important connections he made, the venture did little to sell records. *The Man Who Sold the World* was not a success, but Bowie was fast picking up what it took to write a hit. England had one official radio station, a few independent stations like Capital Radio and some pirate transmissions that broadcast from boats and barges anchored off-shore and therefore unregulated. America had *hundreds* of stations. Traveling across the country, his brain was bombarded with popular music in a way it had not been before; hooks and more hooks seemed to radiate into his creative cortex, from Three Dog Night's 'Joy to the World' to Jean Knight's 'Mr Big Stuff,' to Bill Withers's 'Ain't No Sunshine,' to Sly and the Family Stones' 'Family Affair,' to the Carpenters' 'Rainy Days and Mondays,' to just about every track on Carole King's megaselling *Tapestry* (the year's biggest hit).

Bowie returned to gray, freezing England from sunny California that winter determined to get his act together. The professional life he'd left behind was, when compared to the lives of his new friends in America, in shambles. Worse, Tony Visconti and Defries did not like each other, not least of all because Defries reportedly approached Visconti like an employee and not an artist. With Bolan's career in gear in both England and America, it wasn't long before Visconti decamped semipermanently (he would return in 1974). 'Defries also wanted to manage me as a producer,' Visconti wrote. 'I wasn't so enamored with the idea and didn't like his style so I was not easily seduced.'

With no support for a tour or any further promotion on the part of Mercury, Bowie's band subsisted on a small deal for a Bowie-free record by the Hype, with new drummer Woody Woodmansey permanently replacing original drummer John Cambridge. It didn't result in any product and soon it became harder and harder for Bowie's backup group to justify remaining in London while David dealt with a change in management and, eventually, a change in record labels. In Hull, Ronson could work and record and play when he felt like it. Down in the capital, he was left waiting for something to happen. He returned north, played occasional gigs under the name Ronno (Ronson's nickname) and did some session work (including an unused guitar part during the recording sessions for Elton John's 'Madman Across the Water').

Meanwhile, Defries suggested to Bowie that he relax, concentrate on his family (Angie was about to deliver) and continue to write and record demos, something he could use to drum up interest in a new record deal. David had tons of inspiration. Upon returning to Haddon Hall, he realized he had enough material for literally dozens of songs. He simply had nobody interested in recording them. Despite the absence of Visconti and Ronson, this was a period of songwriting that was much more fruitful than that of the previous project.

Personally, happier events were unfolding. On

May 30, 1971, David became a father. Angie gave birth to a boy they named Duncan Zowie Haywood Jones (his second middle name a tribute to Bowie's deceased father). A crib was set up in a small room in Haddon Hall with blue stars affixed to the ceiling above it. Much has been made of the couple calling the boy by his second name, Zowie. It rhymes with 'Bowie' but is really just an altered spelling of the Greek Zoe, which means 'life.' (Visconti joked about naming his son Monty Visconti, and Marc Bolan would later *actually* name his son Rolan Bolan.)

'If when he gets old enough to care about his name he doesn't like it, he can always change it, or give himself a nickname, it's okay by me,' Bowie told a fan club journalist in 1973 (he did just that, going simply by Duncan Jones once he'd grown up). It's implicit that naming their boy after the Greek word for 'life' was in part intended as a message to the Bowies' parents' generation. When you have a child, a pact is formed. Mother and father are bound to try to give their offspring a better life than their parents gave them. Naming the boy Zowie was tantamount to tracing a line in the sand in a way, akin to mandating, 'Now this has to be new.' And yet, giving him the very proper, English first name 'Duncan' and the third name 'Haywood,' in addition to the latter being a tribute to Bowie's father, was a characteristic nod to conventionalism from the half-urban/half-suburban Bowie. While Bowie was building his image as a way-out, sexually ambiguous rock curiosity, they raised their baby with an eye toward health, accountability, companionship (neighbors would nanny when business called) – everything that would seem antithetical to the rock 'n' roll lifestyle. The flair for duality worked to their advantage when it came to parenting.

Again, we must return to art and commerce, straight suburbanization vs. urban hipster progression. Money was still a concern. Bowie was about to be without a record label for the fourth time in his short career, but he wasn't the anxious, migraine-stricken, too-thin figure he'd been just a year or so earlier. Creatively, however, he was moving at an almost unstoppable rate toward a solid vision, and everyone knew it.

Bowie booked time at London's Radio Luxembourg Studios, shortly after his appearance at Glastonbury, and worked like mad. Backed by a local group from nearby Dulwich College named Runk, Bowie laid down nearly three dozen songs, many of which would end up on his next two albums (*Hunky Dory* and *The Rise and Fall of Ziggy Stardust and the Spiders from Mars*), including early versions of 'Hang On to Yourself' and 'Moonage Daydream.' Melodically, these versions are the same as the ones that would appear on the *Ziggy Stardust* album (discounting a slightly altered chorus for 'Moonage Daydream') but the tempo plods like that of many demo tracks do, and Bowie sings somewhat meekly at the high end of his register (Ziggy's voice would, of course, be much more aggressive and sure). Given what was later done with this undeniably sophisticated material, listening to these tracks today can only really feel like an excavation.

He wisely suggested to Runk (guitarist Mark Carr Prichard, bassist Polak De Somogyl and drummer Ralph St Laurent Broadbent) that they change their name, and so the legendary Arnold Corns was born ('Arnold' being an homage to Pink Floyd's debut single 'Arnold Layne'). The Arnold Corns material would become widely bootlegged, and the single 'Moonage Daydream' would be released in a limited run on local label B and C Records. Hearing the demos, which also included 'Life on Mars?' 'Oh! You Pretty Things' and 'Andy Warhol' (written for Dana Gillespie to sing and recorded by both artists), Tony Defries felt they were remarkable and went about scheduling meetings with major labels in New York, intent on wresting a rock star-sized deal. Sensing, perhaps, a turning point, even Mercury Records attempted to extend Bowie's contract, but Defries promptly informed them that his client would 'not record another note' for the label and reportedly paid off all the outstanding debt himself, so as to be complexly free and clear of the past.

Bowie's contract with Essex Music had expired as well and his new publisher, Bob Grace at Chrysalis (soon to be a major industry power-house but then an upstart with just Jethro Tull on its roster), was equally thrilled with the new material, farming out 'Oh! You Pretty Things' to former Herman's Hermits singer Peter Noone, who would take a watered-down version of the bleak and doomy ditty into the English charts that December (famously changing the lyric 'The Earth is a bitch' to 'The Earth is a beast,' which seems even more harsh if you ask me).

Most crucially, David Bowie himself knew he'd made a breakthrough. He was beginning to synthesize all of his influences, from Bob Dylan, to the Velvet Underground, to British music hall, to modern jazz and avant-garde, into something entirely his own. Before going into the studio in July and August of 1971 with engineer Ken Scott producing, Bowie brought Ronson and Woodmansey down to put the band back together (Trevor Bolder was recruited to replace Visconti on bass). Ronson and Woodmansey were shocked by how sharp the new material was and set about helping bring Bowie's vision to light.

In Haddon Hall and during sessions at Trident Studios in London, Ronson began writing string arrangements for new songs like 'Life on Mars.' 'He used to write the strings sitting in the toilet,' Suzi Ronson says. 'In the loo. Without even a keyboard. Only by ear. It was quiet in there.' Yes, one of the grandest, most sweeping pop singles of all time was partially created in the bog.

Meanwhile Bolder and Woodmansey began working up the eccentric but fluid rhythms that would propel tracks like 'Changes' and the Velvet Underground homage 'Queen Bitch.' 'By this time we were all kind of focused,' Woodmansey said. 'David was writing almost on a daily basis as we all lived in Haddon Hall. I'd hear him on the acoustic and he'd just started writing on the piano. He'd say, "Woody, come and listen to this," so there was a lot of material to work on. We were all listening to stuff to get ideas on different approaches to recording etc., from Velvet Underground to Lennon and Neil Young. I remember hearing a Neil Young and Crazy Horse track where the drummer didn't hit the cymbals until halfway through the song, but when he did it really lifted the whole track. I kind of got into the 'less is more' approach from this point. So we were continually working through *Hunky Dory* and then straight on to the Ziggy album. Seemed normal to us by then! Work hard and play hard!'

'I saw it every day. I knew it was happening,' Angie says of this period. 'It was easy. It was a piece of piss. If everyone hadn't been so great and so perfect . . . If Mick Ronson hadn't been so talented . . . If Woody Woodmansey hadn't been such a laugh . . . If Trevor Bolder hadn't been so solid . . . If Ken Scott hadn't been such a great engineer . . . none of this would have happened. It was a convergence of events that caused something amazing to happen and I was just very grateful to be there and the person who may have orchestrated some of it. I'm a good organizer and I can get people moving.'

Lots of artists have their 'it all came together on this one' record: the one that allows them to have a long career and finally says. 'This is who we are and what we are about.' It's rarely the debut. The Rolling Stones had *Beggars Banquet*. Tom Petty and the Heartbreakers had *Damn the Torpedoes*. U2 had *War*. Radiohead had *The Bends*. For David Bowie, it's *Hunky Dory*.

As Bowie finished the music and lyrics there in Haddon Hall that summer, the combined experiences of fatherhood, life changing, going to America and the end of his relationships with his father, John Jones, and father figure Ken Pitt poured out in song. It rang true. It was special. Life was chaotic. The future was uncertain. All that was true was a lack of constancy. The songs that reflected this would be collected under a classically ironic album title: *Hunky Dory*, an English slang term indicating that everything was right in the world. *Hunky Dory* is such a special record to so many people because everyone goes through similar transitions. Anyone who falls in love with a partner or a child or a sense of calm amid chaos that they wish to return to should own a copy. Nesting and fatherhood ('Kooks'). Death, pessimism and depression ('Quicksand'). Dread ('Oh! You Pretty Things'). Survival ('Changes'). Optimism ('Life on Mars?'), madness ('The Bewlay Brothers') and a series of homages paid and cameos that draw sincerely and enthusiastically from Bowie's recent experiences

269

('Andy Warhol,' 'Queen Bitch'). Whether you've heard it or not, you've lived it. If you are going to buy a David Bowie album, this is not a bad place to start. Many of my rock writer friends and peers consider it his first shot.

'The first Bowie album I actually lived with was *Hunky Dory*,' says British rock critic Charles Shaar Murray. 'I was intrigued by the amount of sheer imagination involved. Bowie was one of the transitional artists on the cusp from hippie to post-hippie. He was the first to evolve a coherent vision of life after hippie. There was enormous range as well. It's a very eclectic record. The unifying factor is Bowie's own fractured sensibility. The tracks are all very different but he is what they have in common.'

'In truth I didn't really register David's early recordings' says Mick Rock. 'I later learned he had a hit with 'Space Oddity' in '69. I'm not sure why it passed me by, because it's a great record. Maybe it didn't sound subversive enough to the hippie student that I then was! The first thing that made me really aware of him was *Hunky Dory* and that album floored me, the way Syd and the Velvets had. I must have played it twenty times the day that a friend gave it to me. Especially "Life on Mars."'

One of the keys to appreciating *Hunky Dory* is to view it as a piano-driven record. Bowie had written all of his previous material on an acoustic guitar. There was no room for a piano in his

Plaistow Grove bedroom. There certainly wasn't room for it while playing clubs or local bus tours with his previous groups. Haddon Hall gave him more of a sense of permanence, a home of his own where he could sit and compose with more comfort and deliberation. This affected the sound of the record (an inviting, plunked percussiveness) as well as the feel (warm, whereas *Space Oddity* and *The Man Who Sold the World* were albums you wanted to throw a blanket around). *Hunky Dory* is, like the best records, a triumph of sequence, a masterful rising and falling of moods that somehow unites as a complete and singular piece.

It opens with 'Changes,' a sort of state of the union demarking the end of the sixties ('Every time I thought I got it made / It seemed the taste was not so sweet') and the call toward achievement, now and not later, that the coming decade demands ('Look out you rock 'n' rollers / Pretty soon now you're gonna get older'). 'Oh! You Pretty Things,' another piano-driven composition, follows seamlessly. It's the rare bit of science fiction that manages to be soulful (truly this is Bowie's gift to the genre). 'All the nightmares came today / And it looks as though they're here to stay,' he sings, drawing from George Orwell, H. G. Wells, Kubrick and even Nietzsche and Ayn Rand ('You gotta make way for the homo superior'). The chorus presages the coming glitter movement ('Don't you know you're driving your mamas and papas insane') while tweaking his own parents' suspicions of his still unproven career (it's also a shout-out to one of his favourite bands, the Pretty Things).

'Eight Line Poem' is just that: a snapshot interlude of some bohemian apartment ('Tactful cactus by your window') that still manages to pull the listener in. (I always wondered about the line 'Clara puts her head between her paws.' Is Clara a dog? A cat? A ferret?)

In the fall of 2007 'Life on Mars?' was named the third-greatest song of all time by the British music magazine Q (between the Beatles' 'Strawberry Fields Forever' and the Rolling Stones' 'Sympathy for the Devil'). Q lists are often a little dubious (Oasis and Radiohead's first three records frequently edge out the Beatles, Stones and Beach Boys on their top-ten lists), but it's no stretch to say that 'Life on Mars?' is one of the best pop songs ever written. Even Barbra Streisand has covered it (surprisingly, her version is fairly faithful). It concerns a suburban girl transcending her 'mousy hair' existence at the local cinema, where she is 'hooked to the silver screen.' The song speaks to the longing for something more exciting that everyone has, the kind of universal theme that, when married to a sweeping melody and executed with style (Ronson's string arrangements manage to be simultaneously epic and disciplined; Rick Wakeman's muted, vaguely cocktail-jazz piano is bawdy and haunting at the same time . . . and played, famously, on the same instrument that Paul McCartney used on 'Hey Jude') will remain the stuff of best-of lists and subpar covers. 'Kooks,' a kind of realistic lullaby to Zowie, warning him, essentially, 'we are weirdoes, and you're gonna get picked on,' captures the spirit of Haddon Hall in the imagination of a Bowie fan. Sonically, it introduces the loudly amplified acoustic strum that is a hallmark of the *Hunky Dory* sound, also heard on 'Andy Warhol,' 'Quicksand' and the record's closing track, 'The Bewlay Brothers.' Sequentially, 'Kooks' is the light to 'Life on Mars?''s pathos. 'Fill Your Heart,' a song made famous by American freak folkie Tiny Tim, and the bemused 'Andy Warhol,' on which Bowie instructs the proper pronunciation ('Warhole, as in holes') of the Pop artist's name, provide the comic relief to 'Quicksand,' a track so bleak ('Can't take my eyes from the great salvation of bullshit faith') that the chorus is actually 'Don't believe in yourself . . .' Somehow 'Quicksand' skirts self-pity. I think it must be the sheer complexity of the lyrics that give it a fleet rather than a wallowing quality (shout-outs to Heinrich Himmler, Aleister Crowley, Greta Garbo and Winston Churchill included). 'Queen Bitch' was Bowie's most convincing rocker to date and, along with the Arnold Corns tracks, points toward not only Ziggy but the kind of English punk rock that would distill New York City street jive for English schoolkid consumption (and has anyone bettered that title?). On 'Song for Bob Dylan,' Bowie expertly imitates Dylan's tough, adenoidal 'awww' (which ups the cosmic nastiness factor of 'The Ballad of a Thin Man' and 'Like a Rolling Stone'). Its title is a clever take on Dylan's Woody Guthrie exhortation 'Song for Woody.' Dylan was still laying low up in Woodstock following his 1966 motorcycle crash when Bowie penned the track, which outlines just how bad the culture needs him to return.

'Now hear this Robert Zimmerman / Though I don't suppose we'll meet,' Bowie sings on the final verse, and it's hard not to laugh when I think about how they did, obviously, meet, and how Dylan was apparently an 'asshole' to Bowie. 'The Bewlay Brothers' has long been interpreted as a song about Terry. Its lyrics presage the kind of cut-and-paste word jumbles that would mark Bowie's mid-seventies albums ('The Factor Max that proved the fact / Is melted down') but like 'Quicksand' its potentially fatal cleverness or poetic pretentiousness is offset by a feeling of genuine lament ('And the solid book we wrote / Cannot be found today') and the touched-by-God genius of some of those phrases he turns ('Kings of oblivion,' 'stalking time for the moon boys'). The record ends with an ellipsis. Over Doors-like Latin percussion, the song fades into Victorian sing-along: '. . . . I'm starving for me gravy / Leave my shoes and door unlocked / I might just slip away . . . just for a day . . . Please come away . . .')

'The only pipe I have ever smoked was a cheap

Bewlay,' Bowie would write years later, explaining the cryptic title in London's Daily Mail in the summer of 2008. 'It was a common item in the late sixties and for this song I used Bewlay as a cognomen – in place of my own. Having said that, I wouldn't know how to interpret the lyric of this song other than suggesting that there are layers of ghosts within it.'

By the time you read this, there will be no Virgin Megastore on Broadway off Union Square, but I was recently browsing in the Virgin Megastore on Broadway off Union Square and happened to see Hunky Dory *stocked along a wall marked 'Lost Classics.' This seemed strange to me, as it's been such an important record in my collection and the collection of just about anyone I've ever known or trusted. Classic, sure, but 'lost'? The fact that* The Rise and Fall of Ziggy Stardust and the Spiders from Mars *followed so closely after the original release of* Hunky Dory *(a minor commercial hit but a solid critical one) might have something to do with it. Or maybe it's that 'Changes,' the album's best-known song, has since appeared on so many singles compilations. Hunky's legacy suffers from timing. I have never seen it included in any of those '458 albums you need to hear before you die' lists that men's magazines sometimes put out in an effort to convince their readers that they need to step up on that resolution to figure out who Vic Chesnutt is and really listen to* Sketches of Spain. Ziggy Stardust *is always on these lists. Deservedly so. But if you don't own* Hunky Dory, *you must, because one day you too will die (or worse, find yourself in a too expensive London hotel with an uncharged iPod, like I did about ten months ago) and not be able to hear it whenever you want to. An album that sends you into a panic attack because you cannot immediately put your ears on it should be upgraded to simply Classic, if you ask me.*

CHAPTER 12

In the summer of 1971, at La Mama, a small theater space off Second Avenue in New York's East Village, *Pork*, a play 'written' by Andy Warhol and culled from two hundred tape-recorded hours of nightly telephone conversations between the artist and his best friend, the socialite Brigid Berlin (all transcribed by Warhol Factory speed freaks), had its world premiere. Originally conceived as the first *twenty-nine-act* play, it had no real plot but was (very) loosely concerned with the druggy downtown adventures of Amanda Pork, a thinly veiled Berlin, who earned the nickname Brigid Polk or 'Poke' after publicly injecting herself and others with syringes full of amphetamine. The character of Pork (pronounced 'Pawk,' as in 'I'm Pawk from New Yawk') was played by actress and Warhol star Cherry Vanilla. Warhol is named B. Marlow and was played by Tony Zanetta in white wig and black turtleneck. Wayne, now Jayne, County played Vulva, a take on another Warhol superstar, Viva.

Adapted for the stage and directed by new theater visionary Anthony J. Ingrassia (an alumnus of

Charles Ludlam's pioneering Theatre of the Ridiculous), *Pork* featured masturbation, full frontal nudity, simulated shit-eating (actually chocolate pudding) and generally perverse gallivanting across sets designed to resemble the Warhol Factory and its habitués' primary hangout, the back room of Max's Kansas City. Each vignette concluded with a fade to black and the amplified sound of a busy signal. *Pork* received a favorable *New York Times* review, but to the great relief of Berlin's mother, the well-connected Upper East Side socialite Honey Berlin, it closed after just two weeks. (Honey Berlin gave Warhol her own review, according to legend. She screamed at him: 'You're nothing but a fucking faggot. Fuck your fucking Factory!')

That might have been the end of *Pork* had it not coincided with Warhol's first career retrospective, which was about to travel from the Whitney Museum in Manhattan to the Tate Museum in London. In an effort to promote the exhibit, enterprising English producers offered *Pork's* director and cast a spot at the Roundhouse, the West End venue where David had supported the Who with Feathers and first met Angie. *Pork* opened on August 2, 1971, and immediately polarized the local media. It was impossible to be a well-connected Londoner without having some knowledge or opinion on the production. It was either a revolutionary piece of art or a blight on the nation, straight from the gutters of Manhattan. To the red-top scandal sheets, the cast of *Pork* was like Christmas in August: priceless copy. 'They fanned the flames,' Zanetta said. Cast member Geri Miller (who can be seen in the Warhol film *Flesh*) exposed her breasts in front of the Queen Mother's residence. 'What's the big deal? The Queen's got 'em,' she quipped, to the delight of the half dozen reporters in attendance.

The cast all stayed in an apartment complex called Langham Mansion in the Earls Court section of London. Reporters from the *News of the World* would come to dub it 'Pig Mansion' and followed these kids wherever they went in hopes of getting a headline.

'To be recognized by Warhol was to be recognized as art yourself,' Cherry Vanilla remembers. 'We were living art for him.' Vanilla had the unlucky task of having to memorize *Pork's* speed-freak logorrhea and act alongside actors who didn't even bother to get off book. 'I'll tell you, every night was an adventure in *Pork*. When you're memorizing a script you can often put some logic to it. You know, A goes to B goes to C. "Would you like a cup of tea?" The next line is "Do you take sugar?" But in *Pork*, the conversations were so disjointed. I was talking about having abortions one minute, and in the middle of the sentence I'd be going into what society ladies my mother was serving tea to, to go to what a bitch my maid was. Tony Zanetta played Andy and he'd be sitting there and all he had to say was "Mmm-hmm. Interesting. Uh-huh."'

David Bowie, already besotted with Warhol's discovery the Velvet Underground for nearly a half decade, was instantly drawn to the cast of *Pork*. He and Angie took in multiple performances, including opening and closing nights. The cast embraced the Bowies as well. They had much in common. Most of the Warhol crew were lapsed Catholics and turned the rituals and strictures of the religion into irreverent parody (best exemplified by 'Pope,' Ondine's sequence in the 1966 film *Chelsea Girls*). Their thick accents were so theatrical and extreme. They weren't troubled by real emotions. They never cried; they only 'cried' to again reference Sontag's 'Notes on "Camp."' They were always on, always performing. This was like catnip to Bowie. They had no trace of 'Don't say what you really mean' English politesse. 'We had a lot more freedom,' Zanetta tells me. 'And we had the freedom to be more self-expressive rather than to fit into a mold. We weren't trying to be investment bankers.' Like Bowie, they were motivated by an almost biological hunger for fame and attention. 'We were also very influenced when growing up by movies and TV and records, and a lot of us had stars in our eyes,' Zanetta says. 'A lot of us were obsessed with this idea of stardom. Something that magical that was beyond our ordinary lives. We were into the magic of what we thought stardom was.'

Angie, the theater student, who had admonished the slovenly members of the Hype to dress for success both on and offstage, found the Pork cast's total commitment to theatricality equally inspiring. 'It wasn't really a policy, just a habit we had, as I said, of always being on,' says Leee Black Childers, who also went over with *Pork* and later worked with Bowie and the Stooges. 'Whether we were onstage or offstage. So David very much clasped onto that idea of creating a personality and surrounding himself with similar outrageous people. He also got the idea of strength in numbers. That if you had a lot of crazy people around you then you'll look crazy too.'

Despite his significant creative leap, visually, Bowie didn't look at all unusual discounting his natural androgyny. He was still in his long-haired folkie mode and did not perform in his 'man's dress,' but rather sat on a stool, Arts Lab-style, and strummed his new songs and old album tracks. This despite early American press like John Mendelsohn's *Rolling Stone* piece (reported during Bowie's visit to California that winter) that described him as wearing a dress. When the cast of *Pork* travelled to a local venue called the Country Club, where Bowie had agreed to a short residency, to take in a Bowie performance, Jayne County says, 'He disappointed us visually because we expected something really bizarre. Because John Mendelsohn had written an article, very little tiny article, that just said he'd gotten in trouble for dressing in dresses. And I think he said 'dresses,' he could have said 'women's clothes.' I

281

thought his music was very folky. When we saw him it was all acoustic and sounded like Joan Baez on downs!'

Cherry Vanilla is a bit more generous. 'He definitely had something going on,' she says. 'He definitely had poetry, he definitely had charisma, he definitely had sex appeal.

'He definitely had musicianship. And that's why we got so excited about him, at least I did, because we recognized, 'Wow, this is something special.' It wasn't just another folkie.'

'Well, we were not very impressed with him but we did like him and we kind of took him under our wing,' County admits. 'And we all decided to help him out. You know, glam him up and make him more outrageous.'

By and large they all found Angie to be much more impressive than her husband.

'Angie was loud, aggressive and sometimes obnoxious but with a charm. We loved her. David was a drip,' County says. 'He would be in his baggy pants and long hair and we would be in painted nails, makeup, glitter, outrageous clothes. We got all the attention and David was so jealous. I overheard Angie telling him that he needed to change his image and start getting some attention too.'

'Angie was very, very smart,' Vanilla says. 'Very observant of the world. I think she both educated him in a lot of ways and she complemented him in a lot of ways. She balanced him. And you know, they were very, very well balanced. I mean he himself had ideas about what he wanted to do and how he wanted to look and she brought him that much more. And I think that's what – the whole success was just a matter of personalities and people coming together at the right time really. I think that the gay glitter scene was budding over there. And yes, us coming probably confirmed for them that they could even go further with their scene. That we were maybe miles beyond them in decadence. And that they were cool and could go further. On the other hand, we did drop a kind of bomb in that, uh, a lot of press hated the play and hated us and we had hecklers every night. And a lot of people thought it was just disgusting and it was like, 'Go home, you filthy New Yorkers,' you know.'

'London was very dull and then we knocked the town off its ass,' County concludes. 'No one was doing what we were doing and the drag queens there were all super-conservative. We were like aliens from another planet. The drag queens there were practically nuns! David and Angie Bowie were there every night and David was practically coming in holding a pen and paper!'

In the interest of fair play, it should be mentioned that Bowie and Angie did have another equally powerful clutch of fashion-forward, outrageous and inspirational characters already in London. This revolving salon was centered around a gay bar known as the Sombrero Club. The

Sombrero had a flashing dance floor like the one made famous by the film *Saturday Night Fever*. The DJ would play loud soul and proto-disco and glitter rock. The downstairs area was dark and discreet. 'There were a lot of drag queens, a lot of people who might have been girls who might have been boys,' Children says. 'And there was a lot of picking up. David and Angie went there very much to party and had been going there before we went.'

Bowie may have been inspired by the cast of *Pork* but later, when it came time to harness their energy into the *Ziggy Stardust* machine, it was the talent pool at the Sombrero, people like Freddi Buretti and Daniella Parmar, who would truly help him realize that vision. Their outsized personalities, dark wit and sincere commitment to a certain splendid kind of superficiality troubled some members of the more idealistic hippie Arts Lab set, like Mary Finnegan. 'They were a very strange couple,' she says. 'I was not happy with the atmosphere. There was a very funny sexual ambiguity going down. This guy Freddi and his girlfriend, they were completely interchangeable. Completely androgynous. It got to be very – I don't know – decadent. It sort of made me not want to be there. I felt out of place. It was getting very showbizzy at that point. The David who became Ziggy Stardust, the one who left Beckenham, was an entirely different personality from the one I just met.' The Bowies, of course, had already moved on culturally, socially and sexually. They found Buretti and Parmar to be fabulous, easily seeing the Wildean soul and creativity behind their flamboyant aesthetic. They were not only happy to be a canvas for Buretti, but they saw him as one as well, one upon which Bowie could experiment with his new palette. Around this time Bowie renamed Buretti 'Rudy Valentino,' an act that can certainly be seen in hindsight as Bowie space-monkeying around with name changes, alter egos and fabricated high-concept pop stars shortly before recasting himself as Ziggy Stardust. Buretti, backed by Arnold Corns, recorded some new, harder-edged Bowie-penned material, including the bluesy single 'Looking for a Friend,' featuring the excellent lyric: 'This semi-acoustic love affair is driving me to the brink.'

Meanwhile, Tony Defries traveled to the RCA offices in New York City with tapes of both David Bowie and Dana Gillespie's new material. He was confident that he would return to England with two major record deals, despite the fact that Gillespie had only a few failed singles to her credit and Bowie was a three-time loser as far as albums were concerned. He was so certain that Bowie would be the biggest new star, not just a Bob Dylan for the seventies but also a Marlon Brando, a James Dean and an Elvis Presley, that he made a grand gesture of securing the rights to Bowie's then worthless Phillips/Mercury material. If most RCA executives did not know who David Bowie was, none of them had any idea who Tony Defries was. They would soon find out.

'They brought me in to bring in the strange and freaky stuff, the underground stuff,' John Cale said of his tenure as an A & R man at Warner. 'So there we were with *Hunky Dory*; the deal was on the table and everyone was trying to figure out how this cabaretish, Brit art rock could work. At Warner's at that time, you had the Doobie Brothers and Alice Cooper and all of that, which they understood. But coming around to the art side of things, they just didn't understand what David was doing. Everyone was scratching their heads, saying, 'How do we do this?' It's a very difficult thing to fight for in a large corporation like that if nobody understands where they're going with it. It really wasn't fair, certainly not to David. There were certain things you knew you weren't going to get your hands on in those days and that was one of them. You were struggling in the trenches most of the time. You'd see the writing on the wall during meetings, when you'd ask a question and people would just turn away from you. But I loved *Hunky Dory*. It was unique and strange and very unorthodox. But if you tried to explain British music hall tradition to the executives, they just wouldn't get it. I was really disappointed I couldn't do anything at Warner's with him. I think later on in the seventies when I saw the thing build with Bowie, it all started to make sense to people.'

Defries was undeterred by this rejection and remained confident that this material would result in a superstar deal. 'David was an almost totally unknown name but Tony had grand ideas,' Gillespie says today. 'Defries was good; he created this mystique, you know. He talked big and people became – they got hooked in on what he was talking about. They liked how he was talking.'

Defries made good on half his claim. RCA's Dennis Katz passed on Gillespie but could not deny the power of David Bowie's new material. RCA at the time had Elvis Presley, but their rock division was lackluster as far as new young stars were concerned. Katz could see how Bowie would be perfect for the label and as a result found Defrie's bluster charming as opposed to off-putting. Still, even by record industry standards, this was an aggressive character.

Upon his return to London, Defries informed David that he was on the same label as Elvis Presley. The RCA contract was modest. Two years, three albums, at just over thirty-seven thousand dollars each. The royalty rate was standard for the time. It hardly lived up to the rumor of a million-dollar deal that Rodney Bingenheimer was spreading throughout L.A. music circles, but RCA had major power, and Defries had created a wedge into the music business and, even better, the American market. A devotee of Elvis's audacious former carny turned manager, Colonel Tom Parker, Defries had gotten an artist signed to Elvi's label. As far as he was concerned, the gilded doors were unlocked, and all he and Bowie had to do was storm through.

His next order of business was dismantling and restructuring the publishing deal that Pitt had set up, which he attacked with the same lack of regard for English propriety. When it was done, he showed Bowie a piece of paper that indicated that he was already technically a millionaire. Forget that he hadn't sold any hits or made the money yet. It was there. On paper. Again, all they had to do was go through the formality of actually doing it. And while they were carrying this out, Defries said, it would be good if David would *act* like a millionaire rock star. David and Angie were impressed that the success he'd been pursuing since his early teens was now just a matter of following instructions, like heating up a can of Heinz beans.

Any suspicions were allayed when the Bowies placed Zowie in the temporary care of their neighbors in Haddon Hall and flew to New York to formally sign the RCA paperwork in the fall of 1971. RCA had gone out of their way to make the Bowies feel special. Mercury had put him up in a Holiday Inn. This time, RCA booked him into the Warwick Hotel on Fifty-fourth street, the William Randolph Hearst-built palace where Elvis, the King himself, stayed. Waiting for them in their suite was Presley's full vinyl catalog, as if to say, 'This is the good company you will be in.'

'This is it, isn't it?' Bowie reportedly said to Angie as they looked down on Central Park from their window. After nearly a full decade of chasing fame and power, this was it.

He and Angie never did get to meet Elvis on that trip. The King was in Vegas, but Bowie did meet several figures who had been, in his eyes, just as important as Elvis Presley. The first of these was Andy Warhol. With his associates from the cast of *Pork* as ambassadors, David was brought to the Factory for an awkward tête à tête with the pop art king on the afternoon of September 14. After surviving an assassination attempt in June of 1968, Warhol had tightened security at the Factory and Bowie had to prove that he was who he claimed to be before gaining admittance to the Factory.

Wearing a floppy black hat and baggy trousers, his hair long in the blond, Veronica Lake glamour girl style (he had posed as such on the cover of *Hunky Dory*), he sniffed and shrugged. Bowie played Warhol the song he'd written for him. Warhol was polite but later took offense at the lyric 'Andy Warhol looks a scream.' Bowie told Warhol he was a great admirer of his art. Warhol told David that he was a great admirer of his yellow leather shoes.

'I met this man who was the living dead,' Bowie would later remark in a *Rolling Stone* interview. 'Yellow in complexion, a wig on that was the wrong color, little glasses. I extended my hand

and the guy retired, so I thought, 'The guy doesn't like flesh, obviously he's reptilian.' He produced a camera and took a picture of me. And I tried to make small talk with him, and it wasn't getting anywhere. But then he saw my yellow shoes. He then started a whole rap about shoe design and that broke the ice.' Twenty-five years later, Bowie would re-create Warhol's oddball appearance and all of his ticks quite expertly in Julian Schnabel's film *Basquiat*.

More fruitful was Bowie's meeting with Lou Reed. Reed was himself an RCA artist, albeit one whose bloom was not nearly as full as Bowie's. Reed's self-titled first post-Velvet Underground solo release, despite strong material like 'Wild Child' (which rhymes 'piece of sweet cheese' with 'our lives and our dreams'), had been a flop. The failure of the self-titled effort and the then-marginalized legacy of the Velvets had put him in jeopardy.

'Lou was going through an incredibly bad patch around the time that I first met him, and he was being left on the side in terms of what his influence had been,' Bowie has said. 'And none of us knew what his influence was going to be – the direction of the Velvet Underground's reputation.'

Reed was polite but quiet and a bit sullen as they dined at the Chinese eatery the Ginger Man. The coolness was shrugged off as Lou being typically 'New Yawk' as far as Bowie was concerned. Defries's eyes lit up as he watched Reed sneer and roll his eyes. Reed clearly had the potential to be marketed to high heaven. Bowie was merely starstruck. They went on to Max's Kansas City, the Warhol hub on Park Avenue. Reed begged off but Bowie was not finished meeting heroes. 'I hope we see each other again; this has been such a thrill for me,' he told Reed.

At Max's, Lisa Robinson placed a call to Danny Fields, the downtown habitué who had first signed the Stooges to Elektra Records. At the time, the Stooges had been dropped by the label, and although Pop's solo contract had been retained they were largely considered a spent force. Iggy was deeply addicted to heroin and essentially babysat by Fields. Fields was at the end of his rope. A student of pop culture, he knew exactly why Bowie would be attracted to Iggy. 'Any touch of Iggy made you cool,' he says today. 'There was a kind of indefinable poetic brilliance that he saw in Lou and Iggy that there's no word for. And I think David thought that he was more practical and that they were loonier artists in the real sense of artists as madmen. I think he liked that about them. Because David was never a madman. I think he felt guilty about not being a madman, because how could you really be a good artist without being a madman? And now he had two of the maddest madmen in the world, one on each arm, Iggy and Lou, both of whom I had managed and so both of whom I was glad to be rid of. For me, it was just a load off my back, off my mind, off of everything. I felt so guilty about the Stooges. I signed them to Elektra and they didn't sell any records. I thought their music was brilliant and I still do. But I couldn't get them arrested and they were back in Ann Arbor getting in trouble and holding up gas stations to pay the rent. The house was getting torn down. Iggy was getting deeper and deeper into drugs.'

Iggy Pop, in his opiate fog, had less of an understanding about just why he should be attracted to David Bowie sight unseen. He was in Fields's apartment, only a few blocks away on West Twentieth Street in Chelsea, absorbed by a movie that was playing on television. He couldn't be bothered to tear himself away, and in his state, the commitment of traveling a few blocks was already massive. Fields knew who Bowie was and insisted that this was worth it.

'I heard about him from the British press,' Fields says. 'Iggy knew nothing about him. No one knew anything about him at the time. In *Melody Maker* I think there was a poll of artists who were trendy or important in the UK at the time and they asked David Bowie who his favorite new male vocalist was and he said Iggy Pop, and that blew my mind. I told Iggy this over the phone and he said, "Oh, that's nice. How does he know who I am?" And I said, "You know, they pay attention in England to what we're doing here in America more than we do." I poked him and I prodded and I put a splash of water on him. Iggy's laying there with a lot of clothes on, passed out. Max's was only two or three blocks from where I lived. So I said, "That guy David Bowie who said that nice thing in *Melody Maker*, remember?" Iggy says, "Yeah? What about him?" "Well, he's here now and he's with Lisa and Richard Robinson and he's at Max's and he wants to meet you." And Iggy groans, "Oh, God. I'm so tired." And I said, "Come on, come on. We have to do this. It's good for your career because he's now more famous than you are." So we went over to Max's and Lisa and Richard were sitting at the round table in the back room. I introduce them. They start talking about music or something I hate and I just backed off and let them talk about it. And that was it. They were musicians talking about music or records. Thank God they had something to talk about and I don't have to participate. I did my job. Iggy thanked David for saying those nice things about him. And their relationship was made that night. They became friends. David at that time immediately took Iggy under his wing and said, "Let's work together," and I was up to here with Iggy. I couldn't take it anymore. Iggy wasn't in a good place and they were costing me a fortune and I wasn't making a penny from them.' 'He was doing real well in the business,' Pop has recalled. 'And I wasn't exactly ripping up the entertainment world.'

Todd Haynes's 1998 quasi-Bowie biopic *Velvet Goldmine* re-creates this moment, and by most accounts, it's accurate. Brian Slade, the David

Bowie figure (played by Jonathan Rhys Myers) asks Curt Wild, the Iggy Pop figure (played by Ewan McGregor), 'How can we help you, you must tell us. What do you need?' Wild replies, 'Everything,' explaining, 'See, heroin was my main man. But now I'm on the methadone and I'm getting my act together. You come here and you say you wanna help and I say, "Hey, far out." You could be my main man.' Slade stares at Wild and we see hearts in his eyes. Slade's manager, Jerry Devine, the Tony Defries figure (played by Eddie Izzard), stares at Wild and we see dollar signs in his eyes. 'I liked what I saw,' Pop said of the meeting with Bowie and Defries. 'I started hanging about with him, and he approached me with the idea of a management contract. Steve Paul [manager of Edgar and Johnny Winter] also approached me and others who wanted to make me into David Cassidy. I think Tony had this idea at first. I had the idea I could talk him round to doing my music instead of something churned out by specified musicans.' Only Defries had his eye on more than just Pop. He wanted the entire back room at Max's on his mission.

'Bowie's manager was fishing,' Fields says. 'It was a large fishing expedition and he was collecting back-room people and he wanted to create a world of his own, a management organization that was well connected, able to tap into the resources of brilliant people who really had nothing specific to do.'

The Max's Kansas City network was the early-seventies equivalent of viral marketing. Although marginalized in a way that hipsters of today are not, their reach as far as spreading the word about an exciting new performer like Bowie was vast. Everyone knew someone who knew someone who simply had to hear all about him . . . and tell all of their friends. Because he was even vaguely associated with Warhol, those with a vested interest in staying up on such things started dropping the name 'Bowie' at the right parties. The fact that these were essentially kids and not professional record industry personnel didn't matter to Bowie and Defries. They had street smarts and personality, and that was more than enough to qualify them for executive roles in this new management office (which would be named, perhaps in honor of Iggy's comments, MainMan).

'Tony Defries was very calculating,' Childers says, 'but he had a very dry but very good sense of humor about it all. He kept things in perspective very nicely. But he would say – because we would say, "We don't know anything about business, we don't know what we're doing." And he would say, "That's exactly why you're here. You're doing exactly what you should be doing. You're just acting crazy, breaking all the rules and causing a sensation, which makes David look like he's breaking all the rules when he doesn't have to because you're doing it." Make no mistake, we were thrilled. What would have happened to us? We would have just gone down in flames possibly. We weren't making any money. We were making negative money. Those of us who could read and write had jobs. Others just lived the best way they could. I worked for David Bowie for over two years before my mother ever told anyone in the family what I was doing. I told her that I was teaching school up north.'

Zanetta was made MainMan's 'president.' Childers was vice president. Vanilla was press secretary.

'We had a sense of show business,' Childers says. 'You know, we knew how to mount a show very well. And we knew how to sucker a sucker. That's the same thing, the record companies were the suckers and we were the pickpockets. We knew how to do that.'

'You're spreading goodwill for David Bowie,' the late Cyrinda Foxe (who would star in Bowie's 'The Jean Genie' video two years later) writes in her Danny Fields-coauthored autobiography *Dream On*. '"Fine. I'll have a magnum of Veuve Clicquot. I promise to think very highly and often of David." It was unbelievable. People who couldn't pay the rent on their squalid flats a few months before were now spending thousands a week on frivolities.'

'Everybody we knew, this guy is the next biggest thing. You're gonna die, you're gonna freak out, he's so sexy, he's so hot, he's so talented,' Cherry Vanilla recalls. 'And a few writers we did let get to him began to make a little buzz and then the

296

press started calling us. And when they would call us, for most of them we would say he wasn't going to do any interviews. But I would talk to them because I had had these things published. And I would even send out pitch letters to radio stations and things saying, "I'm Cherry Vanilla." And I'd send copies of my poetry that had been published in things and say, "If you want I'm available to do interviews on your radio station." So I was the one now doing the interviews for him. Because I naturally like to talk about him and like to talk in general. I hardly knew that much about him, to tell you the truth. I made up stuff. I didn't push the bisexuality, I pushed the sexuality. He was creative. Theatrical. Innovative. Fashionable. He was breaking ground. He was new and different and all of that kind of stuff. I pushed mostly that he was really sexy. I mean, that's what I was selling was sex appeal. Because that's what I felt. I personally found him very sexy. I've always found sort of delicate boys sexy.'

Rumors began to circulate among the gossipy Warhol set about the source of Defries's cash. The manager must have been tickled pink about the whispered chitchat.

'I don't mean to say anything bad about him but there were rumors about him dealing Krugerrands and unpleasant international activities,' Fields says. 'There are only rumors and I don't know first-hand, and they could've been put out there by people who just didn't like him. I had no idea.'

297

Max's Kansas City is now the Green Deli, adjacent to the W hotel on Union Square. There's nothing about it that suggests the counterculture vanguard or the crucial old New York art elite. It's a place for cold mashed potatoes, cheap sushi, coffee and the papers. It's hard to imagine just how excited David Bowie must have felt being ushered inside by genuine Warholians, how it must have seemed like all of New York City was unfolding for him. It must have felt a little like that party at Tom Ayres's house in the Hollywood Hills, only a million times more inspirational, as this was not L.A. This was New York in the fall, almost obliging him to unveil his next and most lasting creation. Ziggy was ready.

CHAPTER 13

The old-style phone box in which David Bowie stood on a cold, rainy night in Soho in January of 1972 is gone, but an exact replica has been placed in the secluded alleyway off Heddon Street. This is exactly where *Hunky Dory* sleeve photographer Brian Ward brought Bowie, ill with flu, to shoot the back sleeve for its follow-up. Today, the box smells very strongly of urine. Much of the plastic window space has been covered in graffiti: Ziggy-era song lyrics such as 'Put your ray gun to my head' from 'Moonage Daydream' and 'Breaking up is hard but keeping dark is hateful' from 'Time.' If Bowie were an American high school student, this would be his yearbook page. 'Thanks, David, I hope you in Spain,' someone writes. 'I hope you' *what* exactly seems to be left, possibly forever, to the imagination. This box, or booth, as we Americans call it, as well as the spot just around the corner where Bowie posed for the front sleeve, is hallowed ground, not just for Bowie fans but for rock 'n' roll fans in general. Short of the site where the Beatles' *Abbey Road* cover was shot, it may be the most famous locale in the city's rock history.

David Bowie posed for these iconic photos with little way of really knowing whether his Ziggy Stardust concept was going to succeed. When Bowie first had the notion to fashion together the songs he'd written in the spring and summer of 1971 into a loose narrative about a doomed rock star messiah, a character he would actually embody onstage and before the media, one wonders if, like anyone might, there was a moment where he said to himself, 'Oh, no, I'll just go the safe route and release a proper album. Maybe I will get lucky and have another big chart hit,' or if he could have imagined just how far he would take this new persona – all too far, as it happened; he actually became Ziggy for about a year. Nobody had really done this kind of thing before. Mick Jagger sang 'Jumpin' Jack Flash' in the first person. John Lennon did the same with 'I am the Walrus,' but both those alter egos ended when the recording sessions ended (and anyway, the Walrus was Paul). Alice Cooper had a bit more fidelity to his stage transformation but he didn't really sing about being Alice Cooper very frequently. There was no context. And Peter Gabriel, then of Genesis, could put on a fox head, but when he took it off, most everyone resumed yawning.

The sleeve itself might be a hint. Bowie is still David Bowie, not Ziggy, on the album's cover. He is blond and, despite the flu, looks as dewy-fresh as he does on *Hunky Dory's* cover. Ziggy, the saturnine mutant with the red rooster cut, would grace the covers of the next three albums (*Aladdin Sane, Pin Ups* and *Diamond Dogs*). On Ziggy Bowie wears no theatrical makeup, only a clinging blue jumpsuit, open almost to the navel. On the front sleeve, he carries his guitar and exposes his calf-high boots as he props a foot up on a stack of boxes. He is merely a fragment of Ziggy on this first sleeve. Other people were pieces of Ziggy as well, whether they knew it or not. Meeting Iggy Pop, and to a slightly lesser extent Lou Reed, put him in the mind of fallen rock stars: larger than life personalities gone down unlit detours. American singer Vince Taylor, who started as something of a quasi-Elvis figure with a huge following in France and ended up a demented, Jesus-touched, raving lunatic, was someone who also came to mind. 'The guy was not playing with a full deck at all,' Bowie, who encountered Taylor on the club scene when he was still a struggling musician, has said. 'He used to carry maps of Europe around with him and I remember very distinctly him opening a map out on Charing Cross Road outside the tube station and putting it on the pavement, and kneeling down with a magnifying glass, and I got down there with him, and he was pointing out all the sites where UFOs were going to be landing over the next few months.'

Ziggy's first name is, of course, an alteration of

Iggy. His surname is a tribute to the Legendary Stardust Cowboy, whose record he was given on his first U.S. trip in early 1970. From Lubbock, Texas, Buddy Holly's hometown, the Legendary Stardust Cowboy is best known for his twanging sci-fi single 'I Took a Trip on a Gemini Space Ship,' which was released in '69 (Bowie covers it on 2002's *Heathen*). The 'Ledge' published his own autobiography to accompany the single, full of wiggy self-descriptions like 'My favorite type of girl is a blue-eyed blond. I like blonds because I have blond hair. A blue-eyed blond is the most beautiful thing in the whole universe besides the stars in the night sky. If I had the opportunity, I would kiss every blue eyed blond in the world.' 'Stardust' may also be an homage to the Hoagy Carmichael pop standard, another provocative mix of the fringe and the mainstream.

There was a bit of his memory of playing with crippled and odd-looking rock 'n' roll pioneer Gene Vincent at Tom Ayres's house in the Hollywood Hills in the Ziggy mix as well. All those whom Bowie drew from seemed to have one foot in the grave and another in the future. Bowie knew he could never be like them without permanently damaging his body, his psyche and, more crucially, his hard-won career, but what if he wrote himself a part and acted it out? Then he could be them when he needed to be – during performances – and remain himself, a fabulous rock 'n' roll artiste, committed to his project but safe from any real

302

harm. Like Dr Frankenstein, he severely under-estimated the power of his creation. Strictly as a symbol, Ziggy Stardust could not have enjoyed the same impact in the sixties. He was not a utopian figure, but rather the cracked and not entirely legit messiah that the debauched humankind of the seventies had come to deserve. He's the 'all right, this will do' savior and the perfect antihero for the seventies because he is the embodiment of the dead sixties dream. Ziggy is the space-race anticlimax, Manson and Altamont and Nixon's reelection and the breakup of the Beatles made sexy. Rock 'n' roll ecdysis is a crucial element of his appeal. Ziggy says to all those in pain, 'You have failed as human beings, but it's all right. We will succeed as slinky, jiving space insects. Let all the children boogie!'

To be in England in 1972 was to believe that the end was near. 'There was a sense of not so much apocalypse as entropy in that there'd been the first great miner's strike,' Charles Shaar Murray says, 'the one the miners actually won, which caused serious power outages and the three-day week. There was a period when for several long periods of time, hours, London was without power.' Ziggy was literally born in darkness. Superficially, he would look like no other rock star before or since. Bowie's Bromley Tech friend and ex-bandmate the artist George Underwood started making sketches of Ziggy shortly after the concept was mooted, and Bowie's Sombrero Club muses, costumers Freddi and Daniella, started sketching looks for the antihero as well. In creative sessions fortified with barley wine, cigarettes and hash joints, there under the stained glass in the great living room in Haddon Hall, Ziggy Stardust started to spread his leathery wings. Ideas were thrown out and almost never shot down. It was more like 'dare we?' If someone suggested a pair of lace-up wrestling boots, calf high and red vinyl, they could certainly be found somewhere in London (in this case ordered by boot maker Russell and Bromley) and all that was required was the conviction of Bowie pulling them on and pulling it off. Much like Johnny Rotten walking around the King's Row four years later in his homemade I HATE PINK FLOYD T-shirt, chutzpah and conviction was all one really needed to alter fashion forever.

With the portals opened, any number of influences fell into the cauldron of images, visions, and characters they were mixing together for Ziggy. Kubrick, as he had with 2001: *A Space Odyssey*, figured into Bowie's new vision. A *Clockwork Orange* had opened in London and Bowie was inspired by the androgynous but brutal Malcolm McDowell as Alex. In his February 11, 1972, review of the film, critic Roger Ebert wonders, 'What in hell is Kubrick up to here? Does he really want us to identify with the antisocial tilt of Alex's psychopathic little life? In a world where society is criminal, of course, a good man must live outside the law. But that isn't what Kubrick is saying. He actually seems to be implying something simpler and more frightening: that in a world where society is criminal, the citizen might as well be a criminal, too.' This was basically the debased state of affairs in which Ziggy would breed: suburban drudgery and shockingly violent youth energy. 'It's no world for an old man any longer,' a drunken vagrant moans before Alex and the Droogs stomp his guts. 'You can feel the mean streets of England,' film writer David Thomson observes in his 2008 compendium '*Have You Seen . . . ?*,' 'where young people have grown steadily more callous.' Ziggy had his own Droogs in Ronson, Woody Woodmansey and Irever Bolder, the latter two redubbed Weird and Gilley on a whim. This street gang would be called the Spiders, and they would move like tigers on Vaseline. Ziggy's concerts would, in further tribute to *Clockwork,* open with Beethoven's 'Ode to Joy,' from the film's iconic moog-tinged soundtrack.

The *real* key to Ziggy Stardust was the hair. Suzi Fussey, later Mick Ronson's wife, was a hairstylist who worked in a local salon next to the Three Tuns pub. She did Bowie's mother Peggy Jones's hair every Friday. Mrs Jones, who traveled in from Bromley, never let on that the local cross-dressing kooks who would parade up and down Beckenham High Street were of any relation.

'I remember him and Angie and the baby would walk down the street past the hairdressers,' Suzi continues. 'He had long hair and wore a dress.

She had a butch little crew cut. They'd push their pram through the Beckenham High Street.'

One day Angie walked into her shop alone and asked for a new look. Fussey gave her red, white and blue Bomb Pop stripes. She styled it short and spiky and passed the test. Angie invited Suzi back to Haddon Hall and there Bowie, with his long, blond hair, asked her, 'Do you like the way my hair's been cut?'

Fussey observed, 'It's a bit boring.' Fussey, weary of greasy hippie locks, suggested short hair for Bowie as well. Magazines were produced and pored over. The cut comes from three different models in three separate fashion spreads. Today this cut is infamously dismissed as a shag mullet. In 1972, however, it was fabulously different. Angie claims it was she who suggested, 'Let's dye it red'; however, this has been, like much in Bowie lore, the subject of more debate. What's agreed on is the name of the color, which was called Red Hot Red, and that it fit with the shape of the cut and Bowie's pale complexion perfectly. Defries reportedly stated, succinctly, 'It's very marketable.' In fact, at one point, Defries tried to get all MainMan employees to wear the Ziggy haircut but ended his campaign early when most of the New York-based Warhol kids declined. Still the hair unlocked something in Bowie. The same way Jane Fonda's *Klute* cut transformed her from sixties ingenue to seventies radical around this very same time.

Finally, Ziggy would not be hampered by

conventional mores of sexuality, not with Armageddon time imminent. He would be a poly-sexual messiah, and Bowie's notorious self-outing interview in *Melody Maker*, also in January of 1972, was essentially an invite posted to all poten-tial followers, no matter who they liked to screw.

As the new year began, Bowie sat down with reporter Michael Watts in the offices of Defries and Myers's GEM management company to give an exclusive interview promoting *Hunky Dory* and an upcoming festival appearance in Lancaster.

He was already transforming, in partial Ziggy mode, with red boots and hair. The tone of the piece is flirtatious from the start. Watts, who described Bowie as camp as a row of tents, stresses that in person he was 'looking yummy' in an 'elegant patterned type of combat suit, very tight around the legs with the shirt unbuttoned to reveal a full expanse of white torso.' Watts outs Bowie before Bowie has a chance to out himself. 'He's gay, he says,' the writer informs readers, and then provides evidence of the singer's burgeoning gay cult, who, like the cast of *Pork*, flocked to check out his performance at the Country Club: 'about half the gay population of the city turned up to see him in his massive floppy velvet hat, which he twirled around at the end of each number.'

It's hard to read the piece without the benefit of hindsight, but there is an energy of expectancy here, as if you're reading an early profile of Marlon Brando just before the opening of A *Streetcar*

Named Desire. 'A tape machine is playing his next album, *The Rise and Fall of Ziggy Stardust and the Spiders from Mars*, which is about this fictitious pop group. Everyone just knows that David is going to be a lollapalooza of a superstar throughout the entire world this year, David more than most.'

If Bowie was simply declared a homosexual by the writer rather than declaring, 'I'm gay and always have been, even when I was David Jones,' as he did, the piece might not have had the same impact. And its impact, in relative terms, was seismic; the story was picked up by proper tabloids beyond the cult of the weekly music press. It's not homosexuality but rather unapologetic bisexuality that made the story so irresistible. Watts talks about Bowie's wife and 'baby son.' Similarly, if Bowie had not had such strong material behind him, nobody would have cared. 'Don't dismiss David Bowie as a serious musician just because he likes to put us all on a little,' Watts fortuitously states in the piece.

Bowie the interview subject seems to know that his stellar new material will make him a big star. 'I'm going to be huge, and it's quite frightening in a way,' he tells Watts, and then, to fireproof this destiny, he announces, 'I'm gay and always have been, even when I was David Jones.' Those who loved rock 'n' roll would know the name David Bowie given the quality of the new music, but those who did not would know the name David Bowie as well. Watts notes the 'jollity' about the statement but also the power. 'He knows that in these times it's permissible to act like a male tart, and that to shock and outrage, which pop has always striven to do throughout its history, is a ballsbreaking process. And if he's not an outrage, he is, at the least, an amusement. The expression of his sexual ambivalence establishes a fascinating game: is he, or isn't he? In a period of conflicting sexual identity he shrewdly exploits the confusion surrounding the male and female roles.' Bowie concludes the interview by making two clarifications: the dress he wore on the cover of *The Man Who Sold the World* was not a woman's dress but rather a man's dress, and more generally, 'I'm not outrageous. I'm David Bowie.'

Forty years on, with homosexuality still a political football, there's a lasting power to the device of self-outing. The courage it took is only slightly lessened upon learning that Mick Ronson was encouraged to 'come out' as well and flatly refused. 'It got a bit lonely out there,' Suzi says. 'David was like, "Come on, mate." When the *Melody Maker* came out, Mick's mother was just aghast. "Your son's a faggot." He got a lot of flack for that. Even my mother came in with the paper, threw it down and said, "What's this?" But he was from a council project. He was a northern lad. The music is why Mick stayed. David longed to be one of those avant-garde people and I think he succeeded. But his songs were fabulous.' That same week the London *Evening Standard* picked up on the story and repeated it. This was the sensation that the founder of the Society for the Preservation of Animal Filament was unable to achieve in the sixties, the excitement he'd been dreaming of since childhood.

'As *Melody Maker*'s news editor at the time, I was a party to the decision to stick him on the front page with the headline "Oh You Pretty Thing,"' Chris Charlesworth tells me. 'We were all pretty broad-minded on MM, so the gayness didn't put us off him. I don't recall any adverse reaction from anyone. We covered him fairly intensely because having him on the front page sold papers, just like Morrissey did in the eighties for NME and MM. He gave great interviews and he was a favorite of ours because of this. He was good for headlines, controversial, articulate, intelligent, always interesting, so us and NME and *Sounds* liked him for that. I would say that Bowie, Townshend and Lennon were the three best [British] interview subjects there were for us. It was a pleasure to interview them because you always came away with a strong story.'

'I think he said it very deliberately,' Watts has remarked. 'I brought the subject up. I think he planned at some point to say it to someone. He definitely felt it would be good copy. He was certainly aware of the impact it would make. I think it was or had been true. I think he'd had a relationship with a man at some time in his life, so it wasn't a lie. I don't think he was lying. There may have been something between him and Mick Jagger. I think it was something Defries encouraged. He [Defries] understood the news value of something like that. I was aware of a changed mood toward gay people, not just in rock but in culture as a whole.'

Bowie's actual bisexual proclivities were probably the opposite of his former lover Calvin Mark Lee's – i.e., 95 percent women, 5 percent men – and by the height of his fame, circa 1975, he would be exclusively heterosexual, but that one interview would forever afford him the 'is he or isn't he?', mystique, the kind that helped propel the likes of Michael Stipe, Ellen DeGeneres, Angelina Jolie, and most recently, Lady Gaga and *American Idol* runner-up and avowed Bowie-ist Adam Lambert (who performed a three-song Bowie medley on the show's annual summer tour) from mere stars to pop icons.

Unlike actual gay stars, the fair-weather bisexual Bowie would distance himself from this when the mood hit him. However, his later denials might be as deliberate a means towards the same 'keep 'em guessing/keep 'em interested' marketing strategy as the initial declaration. 'When I brought the subject up four years later, Bowie denied it completely. "Bisexual? Oh, Lord no, positively not,"' Watts said. '"That was just a lie. They gave me that image, so I stuck to it pretty well over the years. I never adopted that stance. It was given to me. I've never done a bisexual action in my life, onstage, on record, or anywhere else. I don't think I even had much of a gay following. A few glitter queens maybe, but nothing much really."'

Yet later that same year, talking to Cameron Crowe for *Playboy*, Bowie said, 'It's true. I am bisexual. But I can't deny I have used that fact very well. I suppose it's the best thing that ever happened to me. It didn't really matter who or what it was with, as long as it was a sexual experience. So it was some very pretty boy in class in some school or other that I took home and neatly fucked on my bed upstairs.'

Is he or isn't he?

'He gave great interviews,' says Mick Rock. 'I think they really helped garner him some serious attention. He knew how to be intelligent and provocative at the same time. He made the front page in *Melody Maker* with 'Oh, I'm bisexual,' and that certainly got people buzzed. Listen, English boys, who knows what they do in bed? There were a lot of straight young men back in those days who would come on as queer as clockwork oranges but watch out for your girlfriends! It's true that a lot of sexual experimentation went on. After all "Glam" ruled the hippest young Englishmen of the period. *Le vice Anglais*, the French would call it, although, lord knows, there have been a panoply of amazing French queers. There was certainly plenty of ambiguity about David. He really worked that. It was the hip thing at that moment in time and coincided with the advent of the gay liberation movement, this I'm bisexual androgynous "I'll fuck anything" kind of thing. Who really knows what anyone else does sexually unless you're in the same room or in more recent times if you've made a home video and it gets into nefarious hands! I really only know about what I got up to, and I ain't telling. Everything else is just fodder for the rumor-mongers.'

'There are rumors that he did it with Lou Reed, but maybe they just did it to get acquainted. I don't know,' Danny Fields says. 'I don't think he was sexually motivated toward males, but it was handy. He saw that gay men were setting the pace for a lot of the culture that was happening then.'

'He was skilled in dealing with a journalist,' says Charles Shaar Murray. 'David and Marc Bolan were sixties people who made it late. They were actually the contemporaries of people who had made it in the sixties. You have to remember that the Who made it when Pete Townshend was nineteen. Bowie's big breakthrough came when he was twenty-five. Both Marc and David had been in the business much longer than the sixties heroes had been when they made it. When the Beatles broke through George Harrison was nineteen. When the Kinks broke through Dave Davies was seventeen. Bolan and Bowie were around for much longer before they broke through. They were that much more grown up and that much more experienced. I think Brian Ferry was near thirty when Roxy made it. Much more mature when they had their first taste of serious success. They'd been consuming media for a long time and on a smaller scale they'd been dealing with media already. Much better idea of what to do and how to present themselves than their sixties forebears; their sixties forebears were making it up as they went along.'

While Angie writes that she assumed Tony Defries would be shocked when he saw the copy run in the January 22 issue of the weekly, there are others who note that the perfect timing and timber of the piece had to be some kind of inside job.

'That was one hundred fucking percent set up,' Shaar Murray says today. 'I can't remember. Mick was probably in on the gag to begin with. It wasn't journalism, it was collaboration, a calculated move and a great one. Beautifully done all 'round. A perfect media event. Let me lay this on you. Get me in a certain mood and I will say that the major artistic project of the whole Ziggy exercise from spring of '72 to summer of '73, the major work of art, was actually the media events. The records and the shows were part of the superstructure. The real masterpiece artwork was the media event.'

The *Melody Maker* interview made David, technically still a one-hit wonder, a media star before the *Ziggy Stardust* album even came out. 'I bought the paper and it looked all right,' he has said. 'But from then on, the way other papers picked up on it and just tore at it like dogs on meat! They made this enormous thing out of it.'

His mother, Peggy, never publicly commented on David's sexuality in her lifetime, and in private, it's likely that she did what she always did when something troubling came up and simply refused to address the issue. It must have been bittersweet for her to observe his skyrocketing success after years of struggle and not be able to fully embrace it. (Bowie would tell Dick Cavett in 1974 that he and his mother were not close but that they had 'an understanding.') John Jones never lived to see his son reach such professional heights, and while Terry followed David's career well up to his megastardom in the early eighties, because of his institutionalization and the growing phalanx of freaks, fans, business partners and bodyguards surrounding David, his access was severely limited, and there is no record of him sharing any commentary on the method and detail by which his younger half brother conquered British pop. One thinks Terry would have appreciated the intellectual subtleties and camp disclaimers a bit more than his mother might have. Ronson's mother up in Hull heard about it and had to be assured by Angie that her son was not being corrupted. Ironically, by the start of 1972, David had become the gay superstar that Ken Pitt always dreamed he would be. Why it didn't happen in '69 or '70, despite Bowie's access to the media and Pitt's insistence that this potential fan base is among the most loyal in history, may come down to Pitt's outdated referencing of Judy Garland as a career model rather than her young hip, activist fans who resisted a police raid at the Stonewall Inn in New York's Greenwich Village the week that she died in June of '69. Bowie was inspired to finally do so after absorbing much edgier elements of modern gay culture, such as the classic 1963 novel *City of Night* by John Rechy. *City of Night* is the sexual flipside to Kerouac's *On the Road,* full of male hustlers, fag hags, drag queens and closet cases. Having grown up on Jack Kerouac and been excited by the Sombrero scene, Bowie found the book irresistible.

'A gay novel,' he has said. 'A stunning piece of writing. I found out later that it was a bible among gay America but I didn't know it at the time. There was something in the book akin to my feelings of loneliness. I thought this is a lifestyle I really have to experience. I really opted to drown in the euphoria of this new experience, which was a real taboo with society. And I must admit I loved that aspect of it.'

'David sensed there was something there,' says Tony Zanetta. 'There was something attractive about being a sexual outlaw. And he definitely absorbed that into his Ziggy Stardust character, because Ziggy Stardust was a very sensual presentation. It was like the ultimate alien, but there was something very beautiful and desirable about Ziggy Stardust. So that all the little alienated kids all over the world, like the fat girls and the gay boys that didn't fit in, were attracted to this kind of alien-ness. And yes, he did use it.'

With Ziggy Stardust, Bowie was no longer a joiner, he was finally a leader, and he was just starting to get an idea of the responsibility therein. Like Bob Dylan before him and Kurt Cobain, Ice Cube and Eminem after him, David wasn't exactly comfortable with it. While genuinely happy that his public announcement may have had a liberating effect on heretofore-closeted people, he knew that he was an artist, not a spokesman.

'I was quite proud that I did it,' Bowie told the great music journalist Robert Palmer in 1983. 'On the other hand, I didn't want to carry a banner for any group of people and I was as worried about that as the aftermath. Being approached by organizations. I didn't want that. I didn't feel like part of a group. I didn't like that aspect of it: this is going to start overshadowing my writing and everything else that I do. But there you go.'

CHAPTER 14

Released by RCA on June 6, 1972, *The Rise and Fall of Ziggy Stardust and the Spiders from Mars* is one of those rare albums that would have still made a legend out of its maker if he'd released absolutely nothing before or since. There are only a handful of such albums in rock. The Sex Pistols' *Never Mind the Bollocks, Here's the Sex Pistols. Colossal Youth* by Young Marble Giants, perhaps. *Grace* by Jeff Buckley, certainly.

If Bowie's entire sixties and very early seventies output had never existed, and he was struck down by a double-decker bus in the spring of '72, we would still be talking about Bowie, and people like me would still be writing books about him. This is the magnitude of *Ziggy*, the album. It opens with a drum beat and the kind of slow, spare, scene-setting that marked teenage disaster epics like 'Leader of the Pack' by the Shangri-Las or 'Dead Man's Curve' by Jan and Dean. 'Pushing through the market square,' Bowie sings, 'So many mothers sighing . . .'

The news has just broken that the Earth only has five years left. Bowie's narrator is a kid, standing

318

possibly on the Bromley High Street, watching the reality sink in and recording it all as he tries not to go numb. The social norm changes, and suddenly every pedestrian, fat, skinny, tall or short, is equalized, or at least equally doomed. There's no time to erect and maintain false barriers with race, sexuality or class. Thematically, it resembles Dylan's 'A Hard Rain's Gonna Fall' or, though it's much darker, Louis Armstrong's 'What a Wonderful World.' By the third verse, however, Bowie addresses the listener directly, which is yet another of the album's innovations, as this seldom happened in pop lyrics. Bowie sees us enjoying a milkshake in an ice cream parlor. We are blissfully unaware of our fate. We don't even know we're being sung about, according to Bowie. The burden of knowledge is all on Ziggy. It's a lot to pack into four minutes and forty-two seconds. The track fades out with Bowie screaming out the title as Ronson, Woodmansey and Bolder join in, transforming the histrionics into a jolly pub chant. A split second allows the listener to catch his or her breath before another drum beat, this one a bit more funky, announces track two.

'Soul Love' follows with its hand-clap rhythm and a sense of pre-apocalypse frustration. 'Inspirations have I none,' Bowie sings. Circumstances demand 'new words' but he can't come up with any, hence the 'la la la' melody that takes it out until the avalanche that is 'Moonage Daydream''s opening chords drops in. 'Starman,' the album's first single (and Bowie's first hit since 'Space Oddity') follows, with Ronson's dramatic string arrangements. Bowie, using the cool patter of a jazz nighthawk, explains, Marvel Comics-style, the creation myth of Ziggy. He would elaborate on this to William S. Burroughs during a *Rolling Stone* interview two years later. 'Ziggy is advised in a dream by the Infinites to write the coming of a Starman, so he writes "Starman," which is the first news of hope that the people have heard. So they latch onto it immediately . . .' Ziggy has been talking about this amazing spaceman who will be coming down to save Earth. He arrives somewhere in Greenwich Village. Bowie describes the 'Infinites' as 'black hole jumpers.' There are several of them. One of them apparently resembles Marlon Brando.

'It Ain't Easy' is something of an intermission and the most straightforward number on the album. Unsurprisingly, it's the only nonoriginal, and it returns us to pre-appocalypse London (the stage of the Marquee, to be precise), with its talk of 'hoochie coochie' women and the satisfactions they bring to a young man. What else to do while waiting for the end of the world? From here, the album gets sexed up even more intensely – gay sex is first, as the slow tempo of 'Five Years' returns with the torchy piano ballad 'Lady Stardust.' A misfit with long black hair and a heavily made-up face, the Lady might be Ziggy before he realized that he was a prophet for the Infinites. There are people who think it's Marc Bolan. Or Freddi Buretti. 'I smiled sadly for a love I could not obey' harkens to Wilde's lover Lord Alfred Douglas's famous line 'I am the love that dare not speak its name,' from his poem 'Two Loves' (which appears in Douglas's volume *The Chameleon*). The theme of transformation from Lady Stardust to Ziggy Stardust is cleverly acknowledged as well.

'Star' picks up the tempo. It's a song about rock 'n' roll ambition, autobiographical, given Bowie's pre-Defries struggles. 'I could do with the money / I'm so wiped out with things as they are.' It's a great example of those Instamatic Bowie numbers that introduce peripheral characters, friends of his that become friends of us as listeners ('All the Young Dudes' is another one of these songs). As listeners, we may feel we too know a 'Bevan' who tried to change the nation, or with regard to 'Dudes,' a 'Lucy' who steals clothes from unlocked cars, for that matter. He clearly picked this song-writing trick up from his hero Lou Reed, who filled every post-John Cale Velvet Underground album with a cache of local characters. 'Hang On to Yourself' invents the Johnny Ramone riff four full years before the punk legends' 1976 debut. The Spiders are all together, moving like tigers on the aforementioned Vaseline. We (the blessed) can only gape as they instruct us what to do if we're gonna 'make it.'

Speaking of riffs, the album's title track rarely gets mentioned anymore for just how great a riff it has, one that's instantly recognizable and primal but complex. It's not just an up or downstroking slash but resonates like one despite its three integrated sections. Bowie uses three different voices to sing the hell out of it. From verse one ('Ziggy played guitar') to verse two ('Ziggy really sang') to the chorus, he seems to the outside observer a composed narrator, a jaded hipster and finally ('So where were the Spiders?') an enraged and regretful participant in the decadence. Straight sex next: 'Suffragette City' predicts the swirling, carnal Ziggy Stardust roadshow to come, full of mellow-thighed groupies and hangers-on who can't afford their tickets to ride. It ends with typical Bromley-bred politeness: 'Wham, bam, thank you, ma'am.' Again, wouldn't mother be proud? 'Rock and Roll Suicide' closes the album. It finds Ziggy (or is it a post-Stooges Iggy or a post-Velvets Lou?) discredited and disenfranchised, wandering the streets of London as doleful brass is played and Bowie, the lone true believer, promises, 'You're not alone!' and that if he'll only turn on with him, they will be 'wonderful!' Bowie recorded strong non-LP material in Trident as well, including B sides 'Sweet Head' and 'Velvet Goldmine,' and the A side 'John, I'm Only Dancing,' but it's with the closing string arrangement of 'Rock and Roll Suicide' that the 1970s officially begin, two years in.

'He's one of the dominant influences of the 1970s in terms of the culture, as the culture was shifting from the sixties into the seventies,'

Professor Paglia tells me. 'He is like the muse of the seventies.'

During rehearsals of the new material that February, Bowie's band of taciturn Northerners even began to relish this new identity as a sexed-up gang of outer-space rebels. 'At first we were very reticent about the outfits and the makeup,' Woody Woodmansey said. 'I think we were tricked into the makeup thing by being told the big theatrical lights we were using would wipe out the features of your face – "You'll look like boiled eggs!" 'Makeup makes you look normal!' Mick hated the outfits; he packed his bags and left. David asked me to go after him and handle it. I spent a good hour or so on Beckenham station with him!'

Ironically Ronson had been bleaching his own hair for some time (in a masculine way, one must suppose). 'A horrible color when I first met him,' Suzi says. She professionally dyed his hair platinum blond to complement Bowie's hot red. 'He was naturally very fair as well, so it worked. They looked very attractive up there together, him and David.' Ronson was small but strapping; there was nothing remotely fey about him, and it's as if his very presence, along with that of Woody and Trevor (who were less pretty and wore any glam accoutrement about as well as Twisted Sister would a decade later), served to remind any potential naysayers that this was a badass rock 'n' roll band, albeit one with a lead singer who wore more makeup than most women.

Eventually Mick embraced the whole pose. 'He got to love dressing up,' Suzi says. 'We'd go to a department store and he'd go right to the mascara counter.'

'Mick was the perfect foil for the Ziggy character. He was very much a salt-of-the-earth type, the blunt northerner with a defiantly masculine personality, so that what you got was the old-fashioned yin and yang thing. As a rock duo, I thought we were every bit as good as Mick and Keith . . . ,' Bowie would say in 1994.

The first proper Ziggy Stardust and the Spiders from Mars tour date took place before sixty people in the back room of the Toby Jug pub in Tolworth, where John Lennon's seafaring father, Alf, had once worked in the kitchen. By the time the tour ended, they would play before fourteen thousand at Earls Court Exhibition Centre but the Ziggy juggernaut could not have had a more humble beginning. Tolworth had been a favorite tour warm-up spot for established bands like Led Zeppelin and Jethro Tull, but nobody had ever attempted to turn the bar into some kind of theatrical production, complete with Beethoven fanfare and choreographed lighting. From there they played colleges in Brighton, Sheffield, Bristol, Portsmouth, Manchester, Oxford and Liverpool, traveling in a van and urinating in the sinks in pub kitchens. While you'd never know it to look at them, the Spiders did play some grimy spots. The audience reaction was mixed. On some nights, they would be carried out of the venue and into the street on a wave of hands, like sports heroes. On others, arms would stay folded.

By the summer, with the first single, 'Starman,' climbing the charts, the Spiders had a high-profile London gig coming at a benefit concert for the save-the-whales fund Friends of the Earth at London's Royal Festival Hall. By then they were skintight and more than ready for the press in attendance. After a set plagued with technical problems by openers Marmalade, the lights dimmed. Bowie walked out holding his Harptone guitar. The band followed.

'Hello, I'm David Bowie, and these are the Spiders from Mars.'

The energy in the three-thousand-seat room was electric as the band kicked into 'Hang On to Yourself,' the set opener. Most of the material drew from *Hunky Dory* and the new *Ziggy Stardust* album, with his previous hit 'Space Oddity' and a cover of 'The Port of Amsterdam' by Jacques Brel rounding it out. At the end of the set, Bowie announced to the crowd that a special guest from America was in attendance. Lou Reed, a little sheepish, walked onstage carrying his guitar. Reed had just landed in London to record his second solo album, which Bowie and Ronson were set to produce. As in America, most in London had no idea who he was. 'I had the feeling that as much as David wanted to pay tribute to Reed, the inclusion of the American into the act was quite unnecessary,' one reviewer noted.

In its July 15, 1972, edition, the *New Musical Express* confirmed what everyone at the Royal Festival Hall knew after leaving that night. David Bowie had arrived in that rarified air that Marc Bolan and Elton John were breathing. After six years, three failed albums and nearly a dozen flop singles, he had finally hit on something that worked. 'Anybody still unconvinced that David Bowie will sweep all before him in the coming months of the year should have witnessed the end of his remarkable concert last Saturday at the Festival Hall. With elegant flash, and just a little help from "surprise" guest Lou Reed, he coaxed the younger section of the audience down to the foot of the stage and nearly caused one girl to fall out of her box as she enthusiastically waved a banner which simply said: "Ziggy."'

Most everyone in the crowd knew it was David Bowie up there, but they also believed that it was Ziggy Stardust, the mark, no doubt, of a successful invention. It was the effortless suspension of belief, something that, by the London debut, was gradually weeding its way into David Bowie's brain, even though at the time he was still very much convinced that he was acting the role of Ziggy Stardust.

'In the past he'd acknowledge me from the stage,' says Ray Stevenson, who was there to take photos of the show. 'He'd wink or say, "This is my best side." At that show, I got nothing off of him. Much later I realized he was in character. He was immersed and determined. Acknowledging me would be trivial and out of context. He was just doing his job.' Three days beforehand, Bowie returned to *Top of the Pops* for the first time in three years to perform his new single 'Starman.'

There are no Alice Cooper snakes and no pyrotechnics other than the dazzling Ziggy assemblage itself. Bowie's performance of 'Starman' is notable in part because of the impact it had on a dozen English teenagers who would, within the decade, form legendary bands of their own (Joy Division, Echo and the Bunnymen, the Smiths, Siouxsie and the Banshees). It's straightforward performance with few theatrics, the kind of spot that every other act, including sturdy rockers Status Quo, who also played that day, offered whenever they taped *Top of the Pops*. Bowie sings live (altering the line 'Some cat was laying down some rock 'n' roll' to give Marc Bolan a shout out: 'Some cat was laying down some get-it-on rock 'n' roll'), but that's not what makes the *Top of the Pops* appearance more of a landmark than their performance of 'Queen Bitch' on *The Old Grey Whistle Test* a half a year previously. It's a triumph of timing: the right song. The right band. The right clothes, and the right hair, of course, and as I indicated above, the right audience in dire need of exactly whatever the heck this was. It wasn't English. It wasn't American. The newness might have come from the unplaceability of it all, but the right kid in front of the right tube knew that whatever and wherever it was, he or she was welcome there.

'It's the concept of hope that the song communicates,' Woodmansey said. 'That "we are not alone" and "they" contact the kids, not the adults, and kind of say get on with it, "let the children boogie." It kind of spearheaded the whole Ziggy Stardust concept both musically and visually, on *Top of the Pops*. It was like reaching the summit of Everest, after seeing so many great bands doing it over the years. I recall waiting to go on, standing in a corridor, and Status Quo were opposite us. We were dressed in our clothes and they had on their trademark denim. [Vocalist/lead guitarist] Francis Rossi looked at me and said, 'Shit, you make us feel old.' The success of "Starman" really opened it all up for us; everything changed. Mick and I would go out shopping for food, clothes, etc, and every shopkeeper would ask what we'd want and then they wouldn't take money for it! We would try really hard to pay them but they wouldn't take it no matter what we did.'

'I think it stands as one of the pivotal moments of modern music, or, if not music, certainly a pivotal moment in show business,' says Gary Numan today. Then a fifteen-year-old, he watched it in his East London living room. 'It must have taken extraordinary courage and/or a monumental amount of self-belief. To say it stood out is an epic understatement. Even as a hard-core T. Rex fan I knew it was special.'

More fantasy bands were formed that night than possibly any other night in modern rock history, as in one three-minute TV appearance, suddenly everything that wasn't Bowie-touched seemed too small and bland. For these kids, this was the equivalent of Bowie first playing that Little Richard 45 on his gramophone back in Bromley. If they were watching with the family (as most English kids didn't have a TV in their own room at the time), all the better. A father dismissing Bowie as a 'pouf' or a mom shouting, 'Oh, turn it off,' made it that much more arresting.

'I was only thirteen but I watched *Top of the Pops* and thought maybe I was Ziggy Stardust all along. I felt and still feel that there was Ziggy Stardust in me,' says Ian McCulloch of Echo and the Bunnymen. 'I used to draw it in the back of exercise books or wherever, and I'd always draw – it'd be roughly Bowie's face but with my lips on it. The Ziggy album was my way out. I used to sing it all the time, but not in front of people, just closed in at home, and I'd wait for everyone to go out or be downstairs, and I'd sing along to Ziggy and try to hold the notes like he did.'

'It was simply being sucked in by that larger-than-life, slightly unreal persona that makes people want to be more than they are. It's something a lot of rock stars have but Bowie, at that time anyway, had it more than anyone,' Gary Numan says.

'Bowie represented a way for me to get out of myself, and also to escape from where I was,' Dave

Gahan of Depeche Mode recalled. '[My home-town] Basildon was a factory, working-class town. Bowie gave me a hope that there was something else. This world that he seemed to be a part of – where was it? I wanted to find it. I just thought he wasn't of this earth. And that was really attractive to me, to live in a different persona.'

'He was my hero,' says Dave Wakeling, then a Birmingham teen and later cofounder and singer in post-punk ska legends the English Beat. 'I wasn't much one for theatrical kind of pop. It can be such crap. I couldn't watch something like "Pinball Wizard."' But Bowie got away with it 'cause he'd actually been in theater productions and added this lovely backdrop of Buddhism and all the things I was interested in. He had his aesthetic down perfectly I thought. I'd practice having conversations with him as a kid. I'd think about all the things I'd ask him. When I finally did meet him years later, I just stood there making noises like I had a mouth full of cotton balls.'

Siouxsie Sioux watched *Top of the Pops* while in the hospital with ulcerative colitis. The performance provided her with three minutes of escape from her bleak and antiseptic surroundings. 'It meant such a lot,' she tells me. 'I was in a room where all kinds of people were coughing their guts up or walking around with blood hanging from a cradle on a support.'

Seeing Bowie seemed just as important as listening to him, if not more so. Once the images started getting out (and they have only just recently stopped), there was nothing that could contain him. The full flowering of the visual Bowie was well timed to his meeting with writer turned photographer Mick Rock in mid-March of 1972. While backstage at Birmingham's Town Hall, Bowie and the Cambridge-educated Rock discussed Syd Barrett. Rock had met the tragic Pink Floyd leader and taken photos of him that were already iconic. He wanted to know about Bowie's involvement with Iggy Pop and Bowie was interested in hearing all about Syd.

'Oh, Mick Rock. Love your name. Is it real?,' Rock says, imitating a twenty-five-year-old David Bowie the first time they met. 'Of course his given name was Jones,' Rock remembers. Mick Rock began taking photos of Bowie almost immediately thereafter and remains, to this day, the photographer most closely associated with the star. 'From the get-go I found him to be a fascinating person. He had a way of being very quite visceral, but also absolutely cerebral. He's a very intellectually inquisitive person for somebody who is so kind of tactile. He synthesized in all these influences: Kabuki theatre, mime, the Living Theatre, 2001: *A Space Odyssey, Clockwork Orange*, the Velvet Underground, and they all went into the character and music of Ziggy Stardust and the timing was perfect.' The photos manage to frame both Bowie and Ziggy, the subject appearing both warmly human and almost impossibly beautiful and superhuman at the same time.

'David and Syd, they did have similarities in the sense that they were both incredibly beautiful and experimental, plus they sang with an English accent which was virtually unprecedented at that time,' Rock says. 'David could switch it on for the camera very easily. More aware of the camera than anybody I had known up to the time and since. He revolutionized the image of rock 'n' roll.'

Rock, Bowie and Angela took in a Joe Littlewood play in London's East End and soon Rock joined the Haddon Hall extended salon. 'I was not an artist before the first time I picked up a camera (and even then it was many years before I seriously considered myself in that light),' Rock says. 'I had a scholarship to Cambridge University to study modern languages and literature. Deranged poets that used chemicals and sex and sleep deprivation to open themselves up to new ways of expressing themselves fascinated me. So starting with Syd and on to Bowie, Iggy, Lou Reed, Freddie Mercury, the people that drew me in, I saw them like Baudelaire or Rimbaud or Byron. Of course you gotta remember how young we all were and how young the alternative culture was. This was a new age and I wanted my piece of it and photography turned out to be my means of access. To me these characters were not just rock 'n' rollers. They were visionary artists.'

Rock spent the rest of the spring and early summer traveling on the tour and documenting the ascent of Ziggy Stardust almost from the beginning, early on capturing another shot that became a part of the pansexual Ziggy myth.

'He'd really hit his stride that summer with the release of the *Ziggy* album. It was at Oxford Town Hall June 12, 1972, when I took the infamous guitar gnawing shot.' Rock is speaking of his famous photo of Bowie, his feet splayed, biting Ronson's guitar. Of course it only suggests fellatio, but that was enough for those with sexually fertile minds, in other words, everyone in the audience and everyone who saw the photo. 'There were a thousand people there, his biggest audience to that date' Rock says. 'He really was just trying to bite Mick's guitar,' Rock says. 'He's not really on his knees. His feet are splayed. He is tenderly gripping Mick Ronson's buttocks, of course.' Ronson had been desperately searching for a guitar move to call his own. Townshend had the windmill; Jimmy Page had the violin-bow solos. Perhaps this was not exactly what he had in mind. After the show, Bowie rushed offstage and asked Mick if he caught the moment on film. Mick went home, stayed up all night and developed it. Defries purchased a page in *NME* and the shot was run as an ad, thanking those who caught the tour.

'It certainly caused some fuss and helped fuel David's controversial image,' Rock says. 'The summer of '72 changed everything not only for David but also for Iggy Pop, Mick Ronson, Lou Reed, and of course in a more modest way at that time, myself. It all spins around David Bowie. And it's all done on a shoestring. Smoke and mirrors. I remember sitting in a cab with David driving through Hyde park that summer going to his new management office, and he told me he hung out with Overend Watts of Mott the Hoople a night or two before,' Mick Rock says. 'They'd just been dropped by their label, Island Records, and they were going to break up. They didn't know what else to do. David thought this was crazy. He thought they were a great band although to be fair to Island Records they had never really taken off or sold many records. And he told me he already had a song for them. We got to his manager's office and David picked up his acoustic guitar and cranked out "All The Young Dudes," which of course was a huge hit and finally put Mott the Hoople on the map and into the annals of rock 'n' roll.'

The members of Mott were not pretty. They were pub rockers, but they had a genuine appeal and a great front man in Ian Hunter, who wore sunglasses everywhere and had a great voice. Ronson would join Hunter's band after leaving the Spiders. Mott was about to break up when he offered them 'All the Young Dudes.' Defries negotiated a deal and signed them from Island to CBS, where the Stooges were newly signed.

'Well, he offered us "Suffragette City" first,' Hunter says today, 'but I knew that wouldn't work because it was okay, but it wasn't that great, and English radio was closed up to us because we had two or three singles out already and our time was up. But then he came back with "Dudes," and very seldom in your life if you're in music do you get to sit behind a hit and know it's a hit. We were sitting in an office on Regent Street and he sat on the floor and played it on acoustic guitar and the first thing was "Can I do this?" and the second was "Why is he giving it to us?"'

'If they were doing okay at the time, I don't think they would have wanted to link up with me, because they were quite macho, one of the early laddish bands,' Bowie told *NME*. 'But things weren't good, and I literally wrote that within an hour or so of reading an article in one of the music rags that their breakup was imminent. I thought they were a fair little band and I thought, "This will be an interesting thing to do, let's see if I can write this song and keep them together." It sounds horribly immodest now but you go through that when you're young. How can I do everything? By Friday? So I wrote this thing and thought, "There, that should sort them out." Maybe got my management to phone up their people.'

Ian Hunter had worked in a factory and knew well that being in a band was better. 'It's a question of alternatives, it's as simple as that,' he says. 'I've been in factories, I know what that is and I don't want to go back there.'

Mott didn't absorb into the Bowie circle as smoothly as the already perverse Iggy Pop or the opportunistic Reed, but they were won over by his drive and talent. 'I think Bowie was more analytical than we were and definitely more ambitious. He was a planner. And he's an extremely bright individual,' Hunter says. 'There was obviously something different with David right from the off. I mean, we were doing all right but David was meteoric at the time. And he still had time to be pretty unselfish. He liked Mott so he therefore gave more to us. If I had been David I wouldn't have given. He helped a few people along the way.'

Mott dutifully put on the glam drag as well. They felt funny about it but realized it was necessary to succeed. 'People were going to grab it and use it,' Hunter says, 'because there were thousands of bands trying to get on. David took it to the extreme, you know; we sort of did it, but it worked. Otherwise you're going back to the factory.'

Rock shot a video for Bowie's new single 'John, I'm Only Dancing' during sound check for Ziggy's sold-out show at the Rainbow in August. Lindsay Kemp and his troupe performed onstage behind Bowie and the Spiders for the full theatrical effect. In essence, the teacher had become the pupil. 'David gave me the music which he'd recorded for *Ziggy Stardust*, and then as we played the songs I outlined my ideas for the production,' Kemp said. Kemp found David in the full flush of fame to be recognizable, however. 'David said to me, "Look, you may not like some of the songs from *Ziggy Stardust* because they're very rock 'n' roll,"'

Kemp tells me. 'But I loved them all, obviously, I loved the gentler, more romantic, say sentimental numbers like "Lady Stardust." That was the opening of the show. But I mean, I staged them all. "Queen Bitch" was me, you know, wearing my Flowers dress actually. And Starman was me as well. And we danced together during those numbers. I just loved that world, but it was also my world. I've always been kind of a rock 'n' roller. Someone once said I was probably the world's most famous silent rock 'n' roll star. Certainly that world of hedonism and bright lights and living for the moment appealed to me. I was terribly thrilled, but I was also absolutely amazed, because it had only been like, you know, a year since he was performing for ten pounds a week.'

Meanwhile, both Iggy Pop and Lou Reed wound their way to London, both struggling a bit with the transition from American, urban toughs to slinky glitter femmes. Iggy was writing lyrics for what would become the Stooges' third album, *Raw Power*, and Reed had moved with his then girl-friend Bettye Crondston into a small furnished apartment in the Wimbledon section of London, far beyond the excitement of Soho.

'Lou was a junkie as far as I could tell,' says Suzi Ronson, who was dispatched to do his hair. 'I went over to Wimbeldon and thought, "What a wreck these people are." I had a similar thing with Iggy a bit later. Went to do the Stooges' hair and they couldn't hold their heads up. And they smelled awful. Never had any experience with drug users. I'm young. No clue. I remember apologizing to Tony. "The haircuts might not be straight, they couldn't hold their heads up.""

Being transplanted to a strange country, surrounded by Bowie's people and strongly advised on what to do and essentially how to 'be himself,' was disorienting for Iggy Pop. Under pressure, he had recently altered the core lineup of the Stooges, transferring Ron Asheton to bass and appointing James Williamson, who was deemed more marketable, to lead guitar. Lou Reed, not a MainMan artist, was just as shaken up but far less malleable. 'My first impression of him was of a man honor-bound to act as fey and inhuman as he could,' Angie writes of Reed at this period. Mick Rock, a huge fan of the Velvet Underground, was fortunately around at this time and provided a warm, bonding energy, acting as Reed's UK emissary.

Early sessions for Reed's album at Trident Studios that summer were tense. It became obvious that the new material was very strong. Perhaps because of the pressure on Bowie as his Ziggy persona ascended, or the fact that Reed was older and nastier and out of his element, the spark and tension sometimes blew up. There was not a surplus of clean communication.

'There's only one person with a viler temper than mine, and that's Bowie,' Reed is quoted as saying. Bowie counters with, 'When he's not being troubled by things around him, Lou's a very generous person, with time and conversation.'

Angie recalls in *Backstage Passes*, 'Though Lou and David managed to create a brilliant mix, they attempted to outdo each other in performing the roles of tortured creative artists.' She describes seeing David curled up in a 'fetal ball' beneath the toilet at one point.

Ronson, solid, good-natured and even, held the project together. 'We are concentrating on the feeling rather than the technical side of the music,' he said at the time. 'He is an interesting person but I never know what he is thinking. However as long as we can reach him musically it's alright.' Ronson helped Reed flesh out his musical ideas and Bowie prompted him to delve into tales of New York City that so fascinated him. From 'I'm So Free,' to 'New York Telephone Conversation,' to of course 'Walk on the Wild Side,' it's one of the essential Big Apple records. Fortunately the edginess and unease of Reed's London stay worked well with the tone of the record. The sneering phrasing, the world-weariness, the lost sighs that bleed, almost reflexively, into 'Perfect Day' and 'Make Up' works on *Transformer*; fatigue and desperation become sexy. It's Reed's most famous album but it's also his best. There have been musically more interesting and lyrically more poetic or wittier songs on other Reed records ('The Power of Positive Drinking' from *Growing Up in Public*, and 'Romeo Had Juliette,' which opens *New York*, come to mind) but *Transformer*, even more than its follow-up, the bona fide concept album *Berlin*, is its own desolate sonic planet. 'Mick was very proud of the *Transformer* album,' says Suzi Ronson today. 'He knew the songs were fabulous and was given a free hand. When you're a musician, that's what you want. You don't think about "When am I going to get paid?"' Ronson was paid under his MainMan contract and has no points on the record, which has sold consistently over the last four decades. Nobody really expected *Transformer* to be a smash anyway, but early in the new year, it became Reed's first recording to chart, cracking the American Top 30, and remained on the charts for most of '73. 'Walk on the Wild Side' was all over the radio.

'When you think about it, it was one of the quote-unquote unlikeliest hits in the world,' Reed once mused to me in an interview. 'As far as my abilities in that direction, you don't notice "son of 'Wild Side'." There hasn't been a sequel. These really simple things are really hard. As far as I'm concerned, there's this thing you managed to grab hold of for a second and then it's gone. You can't do it again 'cause it's not there to do. Very strange process. I don't for a minute understand it. I've given up a long time ago any explanation for anything.'

The cover photo, shot by Mick Rock, shows the former black-clad downtown bohemian Reed fully immersed in glitter rock androgyny, something he would later, somewhat sheepishly, trade back for his downtown tough black leathers.

'The year started out with David Bowie fast gaining recognition as one of Lou Reed's trendy disciples,' *Billboard* wrote; 'the year will end with the tables neatly turned.'

On tour, Bowie got his wish by vicariously introducing fans of 'Wild Side' to the music of the Velvets. Reed's set was full of VU classics. 'I decided maybe some time has passed,' Reed told me in his iconic sneering style. 'Maybe they'll get it this time around.'

With England fully conquered, Bowie began to truly plan out the American invasion. The cult of Bowie was taking root in the major cities but there was nothing about the Ziggy album to warrant the grandiosity with which they were about to tour across the States. In the fall of '72, with both Reed and Pop in tow, David, Angela, Tony Defries and the MainMan entourage hosted a press event at London's posh Dorchester Hotel for American journalists flown in at RCA's expense and select members of the British press. The event was conceived as a preview for the fall tour of America, and journalists from *Playboy* and *Rolling Stone* were put up and treated to cocktails, hors d'oeuvres and quips. The event has passed into Bowie legend, largely because of a photo of Bowie, Iggy and Lou that Mick Rock snapped. Iggy is in the center holding a pack of Lucky Strike cigarettes in his mouth, like a dog holding a chew toy. He appears elated to be there. His posture is loosey-goosey, his hair platinum blond. Reed, in dark aviator glasses, is the exact opposite. His posture is rigid and he is smirking. Bowie looks determined and proud. Defries lurks in the background, grinning at the spectacle of it all. Marc Bolan is represented by proxy on Iggy's T. Rex T-shirt.

It is the modern-rock equivalent of the famous Million-Dollar Quartet shot of Elvis, Johnny Cash, Carl Perkins and Jerry Lee Lewis over a piano in Memphis's Sun Studios. 'It was just a hotel suite,' Charles Shaar Murray says. 'The whole project was staged in the media . . . as much as Ronson was Bowie's chief collaborator on the music, Defries was the main collaborator on the media event: Ziggy Stardust the event.'

The press event was akin to improv theater, with Angie swanning in as if on cue to deliver a bon mot into the ear of a journo, who took up a pen to quickly scribble. Then she'd exit and Cherry Vanilla would appear. The whole thing seemed both painstakingly staged and anarchic at the same time. 'I've wondered about how staged it all was in retrospect,' Shaar Murray says. 'I was twenty years old, not that sophisticated. Before I fell in with the Bowie crew, I only ever met one out gay man in my life. I was ragged, I was naïve, it was a heaven. I was a reasonably smart but provincial young man with, you know, comparatively little sophistication in terms of polymorphous perversity. Very likely to accept a lot of what was staged for my benefit and the benefit of those around me at face value. I won't say I got taken for a ride, because I gleefully signed up for it. I loved it. It was fabulous. It was really exciting and I enjoyed every moment of it. Let's say, you know, they took full advantage of me and I did my best to take full advantage of them.'

The press was treated to a Ziggy show at the Friar's Club in Aylesbury and returned to America raving. Ziggy was coming. 'David had security. One of the first people who had security,' Suzi Ronson says. 'They'd rehearse running David offstage into the car and driving off. Three vans outside, jumping in the car. Speed off. Before anyone even wanted to touch him, they'd do that. Within six months, they really needed to know how. It all got so successful so quickly.'

CHAPTER 15

I t's hard to believe now, with satellite radio and the Internet seriously diminishing the power of AM and FM radio to break new artists, but in the early 1970s a handful of disc jockeys and station managers at free-form terrestrial radio stations like KMET in Los Angeles, WNEW in New York and perhaps the most famous free-form station of the era, WMMS in Cleveland had the ability to turn a cult artist into a worldwide star. Bruce Springsteen, Tom Petty and Rush are just a few of the arena-filling career artists who benefited from early free-form radio support. The *Ziggy Stardust and the Spiders from Mars* album's American buzz was due largely to a handful of devoted jocks who responded to the tough and punchy rock songs full of emotional complexity and progressive ideas. Bowie, who listened to pirate stations throughout the fifties and sixties, knew the power of radio to bewitch a young listener. (In England, he'd already found a strong supporter in disc jockey John Peel, who recorded Bowie and the Spiders at the BBC. Sessions with Peel – who died in 2004 – were collected and released in 2000 on the excellent *Bowie at the Beeb*.)

On Bowie's first trip to America in '71, he'd met the disc jockeys and program directors at stations like KSAN in San Francisco. He and Defries knew that American radio was his way in, and blue-collar Cleveland was isolated as the somewhat improbable beachhead. 'Changes' and 'Life on Mars?' from the previous year's *Hunky Dory* were WMMS staples already. 'Suffragette City' and the title track of *Ziggy Stardust* were in heavy rotation. U.S. tour number one would launch from Ohio.

'In Cleveland we were early,' says Denny Sanders, then a DJ at WMMS. 'So as soon as *Ziggy* was released, man, that audience was ready and they were familiar with Bowie and they were accepting of his style. And it just exploded. It was only natural that it'd be done in Cleveland. They were barely playing it in Boston. Boston is a hip city but it was late when it came to David Bowie. You don't want to play to a half a house in a market where he's barely being played.'

Bowie and Angie sailed to New York City on September 10, 1972, aboard the cruise ship *Queen Elizabeth II*. They arrived one week later and this time, like Oscar Wilde, the press was there to greet him, along with assorted RCA executives; MainMan staff, including road manager Leee Black Childers; and a handful of hipper New York music fans. Between his first American promotional tour and this one, Bowie had developed a fear of air travel. While morbid, it was yet another opportunity, according to Defries, to exploit his grandeur and uniqueness. The Bowies, it had been announced, would 'sail' to the New World in style, creating an air of great anticipation.

While in New York and checked into the Sherry-Netherland hotel off Central Park, Bowie and Ronson auditioned a keyboard player for the American dates. Given the elemental rock that the Spiders had been playing throughout England, it may have seemed superfluous, but according to the MainMan philosophy, superfluity was a virtue. Recommended by a mutual friend, Mike Garson, nearing thirty, had been playing bread gigs in jazz lounges in Greenwich Village.

'I worked a few nights with Elvin Jones, who was John Coltrane's drummer, a year after John died [in 1967],' Garson recalls. 'And the way I got that gig was the piano player fell off the bandstand drunk and they dragged him out onto the streets, and Elvin said, 'Is there anyone who plays piano in the house?' And I walked up and played.'

At the time that he joined the Spiders, Garson was growing tired of playing tiny jazz clubs to three or four tourists and was starting to wonder about his career path. He auditioned for Bowie and Ronson with 'Changes.' 'I played eight bars; it took about twelve seconds, or eight seconds. And as soon as he heard what I played, he said, "You got the gig."'

Given how dominant Garson's playing would be on the next record, 1973's *Aladdin Sane*, it's clear that Bowie was already taking the Spiders' sound somewhere in his head. *Aladdin* would be written along the whistle-stop tour.

'He was looking for another sound,' the pianist would tell me, 'so these mixtures of jazz and classical and rock started coming together. Here I was superimposing that on his music, but it worked with his belief systems, his mind, his philosophy and his aesthetic. I just was playing how I felt. I really didn't know his music.'

With the lineup complete and the tour about to launch, Defries began writing audacious clauses into the venue contracts. The largest grand piano in each city would have to be provided by the promoter at every venue. If it wasn't at least nine feet in diameter, the show would be canceled. While the Bowies traveled to Cleveland via a private Greyhound bus, the Cleveland Music Hall promoters scrambled to meet Defries's demand.

'They couldn't find one that was a certain number of inches,' Childers tells me. 'Tony told me, 'Well, then cancel the show.' I said, 'They can't get a bigger piano. It's not like they won't give it to us, they don't have it.' He said, 'Cancel the show. That's our rules. Cancel the show; they should have had that piano.' And I refused to cancel the show because first of all I wanted there to be a show, but second of all I didn't know what was coming but I knew this show was sold out and

I talked to the DJs and people and I knew they were very enthusiastic. So the sound was great, the audience was up for it, it was packed.'

David Bowie played his first proper American concert date at the 3,500-capacity Cleveland Music Hall on September 22, 1972. With Lindsay Kemp and his dancers left behind in London, Bowie and his Spiders were a leaner, fiercer rock 'n' roll combo. It was a loud, brash, bourbon-and-domestic-beer-chaser-style show, as rough and tumble as the Stones' tour of the same year, with both Garson's piano and Bowie's lyrics and complex sexual allure adding a crucial emotional depth.

On September 27,1972, the MainMan entourage checked back into the Sherry-Netherland to prepare for what was, at the time, Bowie's most important concert yet: a sold-out engagement at Carnegie Hall. The marquee at the venue, possibly the most famous concert hall in the world and host to performances by Tchaikovsky, Judy Garland, Leonard Bernstein, Harry Belafonte and the Beatles, read, simply, FALL IN LOVE WITH DAVID BOWIE. Before a crowd of celebrities (Andy Warhol, socialite Lee Radziwill, actor Tony Perkins, Bob Dylan's manager Albert Grossman), journalists and fans, David presented Ziggy in full, taking the stage to the Walter Carlos version of the 'Ode to Joy' from *A Clockwork Orange* as strobe lights blinded the fabulous and powerful tastemakers in the crowd. From there Bowie played the equally prestigious Kennedy Center in Washington, DC, and traveled on to Boston, Indianapolis, St Louis, Kansas City and Salt Lake City. Throughout the tour, Childers acted as the 'advance man,' getting to town early and making sure things were together.

'In St Louis, the Spiders were booked into an arena that held eleven thousand. I think six hundred people showed up,' Childers says. 'We had really worked St Louis too. So we were real apologetic, everyone who had been working on it. So we were really down in the dumps. Being Midwestern kids, they had taken the seats that were on the numbers of the tickets they had bought. So looking out over the arena of eleven thousand empty seats, there would be people here, and people there, and in the balcony and down in front, and all scattered here and about. So David just came out, stopped the show immediately, and walked to the edge of the stage and said, 'Everybody come on down.' And so they all got up, and they all came down and just took seats there in front of the stage, and there and then he drew out the set list and altered the whole show, and pretty much did a lot of it just sitting on the edge of the stage singing directly to the audience. Stood up for the dramatic bits. Used the lighting, used the facilities, but he made it an intimate show tailored to his audience. And that, I think, made as much difference to St Louis on the next tour being a successful show, because those six hundred people went away feeling special.'

What Bowie lacked in actual record and ticket sales he more than made up for in media appeal. The October 9, 1972, issue of *Newsweek* magazine featured a short profile of Bowie, putting his rooster-cut visage in millions of American homes. Entitled 'The Stardust Kid,' the piece accurately, if a bit ornately, frames Bowie as the perfect star for the seventies: 'This is a time of confusion, a middle ages, an appropriate breeding ground for the dark, satanic majesty of England's David Bowie.' This being America, there was much made of his sexuality. 'He sings songs about homosexuals,' the writer observes, 'but there are just as many straight songs as bent ones.' Bowie has his way with the writer, who is either amused or confused. 'My sexual nature is irrelevant,' he says. 'I'm an actor, I play roles, fragments of myself.'

Defries, who had started to affect the cigar-chomping, fur-coat-wearing style of a rock 'n' roll manager, as opposed to that of a buttoned-down British solicitor, knew that overtaking the United States wasn't about this tour anyway. U.S. tour number one was a theater tour. Bowie and Defries had their eye on a sold-out arena juggernaut and Bowie was instructed to act like a standing-room-only arena rock star until he became one. Promoters were furious at MainMan's threats to cancel shows, but there would be no scaling back of the outrageous demands. This became the company's general philosophy: one has to spend, and often lose, money to make it. Given the unsold seats and five-star accommodations, MainMan was in debt to RCA for well over a million dollars already (about five million when adjusted for inflation). Defries was confident that every full seat would, via word of mouth, turn into three or four dozen more in the very near future.

As the tour rolled on, Garson, the only American, slowly became acclimated to the pandemonium and bonded with Mick Ronson especially, as the guitarist had begun as a pianist and could talk classical and jazz theory. Bolder and Woodmansey discussed spirituality with him. Garson was, at the time, a devout Scientologist. After the shows, when stuck in a less cosmopolitan city, Garson and Bowie, in full Ziggy makeup, would invade the cocktail lounge of whatever Ramada Inn they were lodging in and shock the other guests with impromptu concerts of Sinatra.

'He would sing 'My Funny Valentine' and I would back him up on the piano just for fun in a bar,' Garson says. 'And he sounded like his version of Sinatra. Mouths would drop. I wish I had a video; it would be on YouTube now.'

Attendance picked up significantly as U.S. tour number one hit the West Coast. They had dates in Los Angeles at the Santa Monica Civic Auditorium and in San Francisco at Winterland, where future disco sensation Sylvester (who would record the indelible dance singles 'You Make Me Feel (Mighty Real)' and 'Do Ya Wanna Funk' before becoming one of pop's early AIDS casualties in 1988) provided support. Defries clashed with notoriously tough promoter Bill Graham after insisting that a wall be constructed from the load-in area to the dressing room so that David and his entourage could enter the venue in private. The trek was also yielding major creative dividends, with a whole album nearly complete by the time they reached the Pacific. The notion of seeing America, the whole country and not just the major cities, comes up in those songs and brings Bowie back to his boyhood and the Beat literature that his half brother Terry encouraged him to read.

The forty-six-person U.S. tour number one entourage hit Los Angeles in the third week of October. The city was ready for them. Rodney Bingenheimer had almost singlehandedly turned Hollywood into London West, running his Bowie-inspired E. Club then centered around the Chateau Marmont. The Spiders had no trouble selling out two nights at the 3,500-seat Santa Monica Civic Auditorium. At one point the most famous bootleg in the Bowie unofficial discography, a recording of one of the shows was formally released by Virgin Records in the summer of 2008. Listening to it now, it's hard to imagine just how different Bowie and his band must have seemed to the casual concertgoer, fresh off shelling out for Eagles or Santana tickets. After 'Five Years,' for example, you can actually hear people screaming in psychic elation. It's not just white-noise applause but rather shouts of 'Yeah! Yeah! Yes!' Is it the sound of minds being blown? Surely this is what the city had been waiting for, someone to make their decay seem not only sexy but also . . . meaningful. 'Five Years' meant something. The album stands as a document of just how on fire the Spiders were. Ronson is as solid as a walnut tree, adjusting the speed of his backing vocals (fast on 'Changes,' slow and chantlike on 'Five Years') with killer instinct and throwing the shred in a way that would have seemed downright impolite on a record ('The Width of a Circle'). Garson's piano makes the *Hunky Dory* tracks, like 'Life on Mars?' soar. Bowie himself is breathy and so English he makes asking for a pair of pliers before 'Space Oddity' seem grand. As he screamed, 'You're not alone,' at the end of 'Rock and Roll Suicide,' the show closer, he could not escape the irony of staring out into the crowd to see so many of them dressed like him. '*Santa Monica* '72 is the sound of a cult act pushing hard for breakout success,' Pitchfork observed in its review of the reissue.

Bowie was feted by the famous disc jockey Wolfman Jack at the aftershow party, which drew every freak in the Golden State. RCA paid for the cocktails. The Wolfman had a fully functional disco in his home (much like Steve Martin's during the decadent third act of *The Jerk*), complete with a pro sound system, spinning mirror ball and flashing lights. Bowie stood in the center of it.

Nobody approached him. Bingenheimer and Fowley arrived. As the party went on, joints were lit up, cocktails passed around and the dance floor filled up. Bowie spotted a girl he fancied dancing with Fowley. 'We were dancing away and Bowie comes up to me on the dance floor the way Gene Kelly would slide up to Fred Astaire in one of those old Hollywood musicals,' says Kim Fowley. 'Anyone seeing it would say, "Oh, gay man sliding up to other feminine man to have a giggle." He slides up and says, "Are you in love with this woman or may I take her into the bathroom? Why don't you and her follow me if she's not your girl-friend or wife?" I looked at the girl and said "David would like to have a word with you." Then he said to her, "How do you do, I'm David Bowie. I'd like to discuss life or the universal whatever, my dear." He gave me a wink, a bit of a thank-you wave. A David Niven-style wave. Went to the bath-room, obviously, to have an intimate discussion. I always thought he was so clever pushing that androgynous thing. They went into the bathroom and soon heard, "Oh no." Two drag queens were there, hoping that David Bowie was gay. When they saw their hero going in a bathroom with a woman, they went ballistic. I heard him lock the door and the drag queens took their high heels off, smashing the door, screaming, "Whatever she's doing, we can do better. Let us in, throw the bitch out. We can do a better job on you than she can no matter what's going on in there."'

Bowie was more or less a teetotaler on the tour. There was far too much to do, and the rigors of being onstage and turning in a stellar performance every night required him to be a dead sober workaholic. Sex, of course, was another story: it was good exercise and, in Los Angeles in 1972, the equivalent of a politician glad-handing a potential voter. 'Wham, bam, thank you, ma'am,' indeed. While he would later dismiss it as the most vile locale on the planet, the love between Bowie and Los Angeles was in full flush.

'L.A. was tailor-made for Ziggy Stardust,' Leee Black Childers agrees. 'L.A. is like David. The city changes its personality to suit whoever is in town. So they had all become spacemen for that weekend that we were there. Whereas if it had been a reggae band they would have all been, you know, Rastas. And they all have all the necessary outfits and equipment in their obviously well-appointed homes. Nobody's poor in L.A. And so all the groupies were dressed in glitter and platforms galore. And all the kids were dressed with makeup on and everything. So it looked like the town was totally behind David.'

The Spiders' entourage had checked into the Beverly Hills Hotel, the massive, shell-pink structure off Sunset Boulevard, on the advice of Lisa Robinson. They lived off the fat of RCA, with roadies bringing back tourists from up the street and signing away for surf-and-turf dinners and champagne. There were groupies floating in the swimming pool.

355

Cynthia McCradu was a young friend of Rodney Bingenheimer's who had met Bowie earlier in the year while on a trip to London and spent a day with him in Haddon Hall, until Angie shooed her away. 'David was the most funny, giving, intelligent person,' she says today. '[During that visit] he showed me his garden. I said, "What are you growing?" And he said, "Mostly weeds right now." He was so gentle and funny and intelligent. I'm really happy that I met him before it was all ruined.'

McCradu felt special in sleepy, leafy Beckenham. She'd seen a more artistic and domestic Bowie, perhaps more David Jones than Ziggy Stardust. Only a few months later, in the Hollywood groupie jungle, she was aghast at the behavior she witnessed at the E. Club and the fervor with which Bowie, now in near-total Ziggy mode, dove in. The club itself was a mirror-lined speakeasy type of place. They served beer and wine and food, and had a doorman card people to keep out the underaged, but fake IDs were plentiful.

'I'm with David at a table,' McCradu says, 'talking, and we danced and suddenly this little girl comes in and she pushes me off the chair and says, "I'm gonna be with him now. You've already had your time with him." And I go, "Who the hey are you and what the hey are you doing? Little girl, you need to put your clothes on." That was my introduction to Queenie and Sable and Lori. Little girls twelve, thirteen, fourteen years old.

Quite frankly if I was a mother or father, I would have whipped their hide and made them stay home. [The next time I saw him] David was now fucked-up, into the frenzy of everybody wanting to have sex with him in the limo on the way to the recording studio. On the sidewalk in front of the hotel. In the bathroom. Everywhere he turned, everybody wanted to sex him. And he was enjoying that. That was exciting to him, I believe. I think after a while, these people, they just start sucking the life out of you . . .' As it was at Bromley Tech, David viewed sex as a means to capture and hold attention. He had become an Elvis or a Little Richard at last; his rock 'n' roll made the girls and boys lose control.

'It was a very sexual period,' Mick Rock observes. 'A lot of sex going on but initially less drugs than you might think but certainly a hell of a lot of rutting! David generated a lot of sexual heat. He had a totally futuristic charisma and energy. He did have those amazing facial bones, a very skinny body, and photographed in a unique and sexy way. Everybody was buzzed about David, boys and girls and everything in between!'

'Suddenly David was not to me a man you can talk to anymore,' McCradu says. 'He was consumed by all the *sexualness*.'

Bingenheimer shrewdly made sure that everyone knew that Bowie was associated with the club. 'Oh, he signed a contract with the club to be on the board of directors,' Bingenheimer says. Rodney soon parlayed that association into moving and expanding the E. Club into the more iconic Rodney's English Disco. By the time that opened a few blocks farther east up Sunset Boulevard L.A. had gone glam crazy and Bowie was its king.

Bowie remained in Los Angeles to do some work on Iggy and the Stooges' MainMan debut, *Raw Power*. 'Originally Tony wanted David to produce us,' Pop said, 'but I wanted to produce myself. He still wanted David to remix the tapes, adding some horns or whatever. I didn't want that.' Pop relented, but in 1997 *Raw Power* was rereleased with an alternate, Iggy-approved mix. Fans remain polarized and which *Raw Power* is superior remains the subject of rock-geek round (bar) table debate. Bowie then returned to England in December for a short series of dates, including two benefit shows for his late father's employer, Dr Barnardo's children's charity, at London's Rainbow Theater. Bowie spent the Christmas holidays of 1972 with Zowie and Angie in Haddon Hall. It would be their last in Beckenham, as a tight family unit.

The Bowies must have certainly found it strange, after the whirlwind of sex, spending and speed-traveling through America, to be back in the suburbs. Angie could not retrieve the mail without hearing high-pitched screaming. In certain circles, she was just as iconic as he was, but when he became Ziggy Stardust the experience got bigger and more people were sharing in it. David did not, at that time, flaunt his dalliances, and neither did Angie. They were progressives. Their marriage was open. Angie felt flattered that so many people of both sexes wanted her husband. Increasingly it was not women or men but fame itself that was the third party in their relationship. History is littered with failed 'open marriages,' including those of Sigmund Freud, Charles Darwin, Simone de Beauvoir and Jean-Paul Sartre. Open marriage may be a genuinely progressive notion, but it's clearly easier in theory than practice. If such a union is to work, it requires close and consistent proximity between the two agreeing partners. The couple must grow or evolve together, but even if they do, throw in fame and long periods of estrangement often due to professional commitments, and it ceases to be a liberating union and becomes one that can foster suspicion and jealousy and spite even with the must liberated partners. In their study *Open Marriage*, Nena and George O'Neill, for example, write, 'The central problem in contemporary marriage was relationship. The attempt to solve the problem by moving into group and communal situations did not seem to mitigate the problems we discovered in the interpersonal relationship.' David's steadiest companion post-fame was Ava Cherry, an eighteen-year-old African American beauty from Chicago. Like Bowie, she had a unique and soulful voice (check out the Astronettes' rarity 'I Am Divine'). She also matched his flair for attention-grabbing and would spend the remainder of the glitter era with a platinum blond crew cut. According to Zanetta and Edwards's *Stardust*, the Bowies' laissez-faire attitude toward sex was something she had to grow into. The morning after their first night together, Bowie casually introduced Cherry to his family, stating flatly, 'This is my wife and kid.' While Angie would come to loathe Cherry, at the time she was up for anything, as was their rule. Two years into their relationship, Bowie and Cherry would practice the same openness for better or worse. 'If David kept an affair secret, it meant he had some feeling for the woman,' Zanetta and Edwards write. 'Otherwise he had a friendly discussion with Ava about the one-night stand and gave her an evaluation on his partner's performance.' Eventually Bowie and Ava Cherry's relationship would go the way of his first marriage, making the notion of a lasting open marriage or steady relationship that much more challenging if not utterly dubious. Sometimes progress can break your heart.

Around this time, Angie attempted to re-create herself as an actress named Gyp Jones, an abbreviation of 'gypsy' – clearly a nod to the headier, happier days when she was careening through London with her undies in a bag – and 'Jones,' her husband's given name. 'The initial plan was to work on his career and make him famous and then he and I would work on my career and make me famous and successful too,' she says.

While in L.A. Angie auditioned for the part that

Linda Carter eventually got on the CBS series *Wonder Woman*. By the time the Bowies moved out of their suburban nest in Haddon Hall in early 1973 and found a proper rock star apartment on Oakley Street in the Chelsea section of London, their marriage was unraveling. Zowie was largely cared for, like many children of the very famous, by trusted friends and expensive professional nannies. David would later cite not being around for much of his son's formative years as one of his biggest regrets and took pains to make amends later in the decade.

Angie comforted herself with retail, decorating the place in opulent fashion with antique dressers, Chinese carpets, a grand piano and the best audio-visual equipment available.

With glitter becoming all the rage (and running the gamut from bubblegum heroes sweet to blunt-edged carpetbaggers like Gary Glitter and Mud to the openly gay cabaret of Jobriath and the sublime art-school-educated geniuses in Roxy Music), the business of keeping Bowie and MainMan ahead of the curve was not cheap, and in the Regent Street offices in London and their Park Avenue offices in Manhattan, amid the leather armchairs and framed portraits of Bowie, charges and chits on George Underwood-designed MainMan letterhead flew around like ticker tape. Bills would come in and pile up: travel expenses, promotional expenses, charge accounts, clothing, food, rent, studio time and limousines.

On the surface, MainMan looked like what Defries envisioned it as, a Disney-like, catchall entertainment company. 'He wanted to be a star-maker,' says Cherry Vanilla. 'He wanted to go much bigger than he ever went. He wanted to have a building on Park Avenue with his name on the top of it. He wanted to have an empire. A huge empire. He really wanted to have movie companies. Cecil B. DeMille and Colonel Tom Parker all rolled into one.

'MainMan was a great, great company in its day,' she continues. 'It had a mystique. We all had secretaries. We all lived in New York. It was a glorious, glorious time, but I always knew it couldn't last because at some point something had to kind of implode, and it kind of did.'

'Ah, but what did justify it was the end result, which was people believed that MainMan was this huge, rich entity. It was like Hollywood in the thirties,' Tony Defries biographer Dave Thompson, who has also written several great books on Bowie, counters. 'They weren't just launching a musician, they were launching a *star* – the idea was, we're not gonna have David build from the ground up like everybody else. He's not gonna grind for thirty years like Slade or T. Rex. He is going to *appear* as a star. So the first thing you do is you hire him bodyguards. "Why does he need bodyguards?" people start asking. Then the word goes out: "Well, David's worldview is a little unusual and there's a lot of crazies out there." The headline the next

362

day: "David Bowie Under Attack." If somebody from MainMan can go out with their company credit card and order this huge meal for fifty people, it conveys wealth, it conveys importance, it conveys strength.'

When asked about the expense accounts, Leee Black Childers just chuckles. 'The word that does not apply in that sentence is "accounts." There were a lot of expenses. No one seemed to be keeping track of the accounts, however. There was no cash flow really. There was no cash. And this is fairly well known, that we took limousines because we couldn't afford taxis.'

The lifestyle seems glamorous – it seemed so to me when I read about it – but imagine living like that all the time when you just want to relax and watch TV and eat a hamburger in peace and not have to be outrageous. 'Everyone thought we were living this incredibly easy fabulous lifestyle, when in fact if you think about it, it's really hard, because *nothing* is free,' Cherry Vanilla says. 'If you're eating at Max's for free and drinking champagne at rich people's houses for free, you have to be on, on, on! You can't just be sitting there. You've got to be "Cherry Vanilla." You've got to be constantly telling stories. And every day was exhausting. So when you say the office, again, we were *always* in the office. The world perceived us as doing nothing; we were working our butts off all the time. We never missed a trip; we never missed a chance to forward David's career, thereby forwarding our own fortunes. And hopefully keeping the ball rolling for a while. Tony Defries told us almost daily that we were not going to be successful otherwise, which may have been his way of getting us to work all the harder. He was like the big daddy to us all, you know, even though he was our age. I think he was *younger* than me. We all approached him in that way like Daddy. And he treated us that way purposely. Like instead of giving us a regular salary, we all got a hundred dollars a week and our rent paid. And an expense account at Max's Kansas City and the use of limousines. So we were kept more like children. So was the band, so was Bowie. It was like a control freak thing.'

What really guzzled up the cash was the need to duplicate the success of Bowie. For all of his success with his primary client, Defries could not duplicate it with anyone but Bowie. Lou Reed had Bowie-associated hit records, but he was not a MainMan artist and excluding Mott the Hoople's revival with 'All the Young Dudes,' Defries didn't seem to know how to bottle lightning twice. Dana Gillespie had a failed record; the Stooges' *Raw Power* had been released in early 1973 and sold nothing. There was no tour budget and Iggy was too zonked on heroin to promote it anyway. During one in-studio appearance at a local radio station, he got naked and began playing with himself on the air, providing the listeners with a running commentary.

As with Bowie, all MainMan artists had their

every need taken care of so that they could concentrate on creativity. They were assured that all MainMan artists were equal, but they were also obliged to sell, and with the exception of Bowie, who would not be selling anywhere near a Rolling Stones or an Elton John-like level until 1975 or so, nobody did.

Meanwhile, Bowie, the company's cash cow, returned to London and entered Trident Studios in the third week of January 1973, again with producer Ken Scott, Ronson, Woodmansey, Bolder and now Mike Garson to finish the material he'd written during U.S. tour one. He was under enormous pressure. Without the overhead, Bowie might have deviated further away from Ziggy even sooner than 1974, but he simply could not afford to. *Aladdin Sane*, the resulting album, is seen by some critics as subpar on the heels of something as momentous as the Ziggy album, but it has achieved classic status as well, and clearly the songs, which are topnotch, are all the evidence one needs that the artist was still way ahead of the game. The sleeve features an emaciated, lonely Ziggy with a lightning bolt painted across his face and a teardrop pooling in the left clavicle of his bare chest as if to say, 'I am the only one striking.'

'Watch That Man' opens the record with a crunchy Ronson riff and a post-party inventory: 'Shakey threw a party that lasted all night. Everybody drank a lot of something nice.' He is still the observer of or Kerouacian commentator on others' debauchery,

365

but for the first time on record, he sounds equally jaded or wasted. The track is propelled by the kind of fifties-style doo-wop backing vocals that had become a powerful trend thanks to the debut that year of *The Rocky Horror Show* in London. David, Angie and their entourage took in the show multiple times and, as they'd done with *Pork* two years earlier, were clearly taking notes in the margins of their programs. Like most of *Aladdin Sane*, 'Watch That Man' is given a geographical marker (New York) that reflects the peripatetic year that Bowie had just experienced. The title track is marked quite elegantly with the name of a cruise ship, the HRMS *Ellinis* (which sailed from Britain to Japan, where Bowie would tour later in the year) as well as cryptic birth/death/rebirth dates (1913–1938–197?), said to be the years immediately preceding the two world wars and, according to fan speculation, the imminent World War III. The track itself is not shot through with dread as much as languor. Along with Elton John's 'Goodbye Yellow Brick Road' (also a title track to a 1973 release) it is one of the best 'come-down' tracks ever, another perfect segue from party to post-party to hangover. Garson's playing is broad, almost a bebop/Thelonious Monk parody, but it fits perfectly with the loss of equilibrium implicit in the lyrics. 'Drive-In Saturday' is another door-wop pastiche with campy lyrics ('His name was always Buddy') that, like those of 'Life on Mars?' bring to mind the cinemas of Beckenham and the spark of the London mod scene, now a decade gone

('It's a crash course for the ravers'). London luminaries like it-model Twiggy (who would pose with Bowie on the cover of his next release *Pin Ups*) and Mick Jagger are name-checked (although the geographical mark is an incongruous 'Seattle-Phoenix'). Bowie scats playfully over the fade-out. 'Panic in Detroit' returns us to the apocalypse already in progress. A portrait of Iggy Pop ('He looked a lot like Che Guevara') written while mixing *Raw Power*, it's a Bo Diddley 'bum de bum de bum bum bum'-style beat treated with wailing backing vocals that call to mind Merry Clayton's on the Stones' equally nightmarish 'Gimme Shelter.' 'The Prettiest Star' gets a second life, as does 'Queen Bitch,' in the form of its left-coast counterpart 'Cracked Actor.' Opening with Ronson's feedback, it's another fifties-style, basic rock track with lyrics that are seventies L.A. to their sleazy, catty core. In full Warhol-damaged mode, Bowie embodies an aging star admonishing a piece of junked-up rough trade ('Forget that I'm fifty cause you just got paid' and later, 'Smack baby smack is that all that you feel?'). It's geographically tagged, unsurprisingly, 'Los Angeles.' 'Time,' the album's second single after 'The Jean Genie,' is marked 'New Orleans' and opens with a ghostly Dixie brothel piano before Bowie again invokes Belgian singer/songwriter Jacques Brel (whose 'My Death' he covered on the *Ziggy* tour). It's possibly his weirdest single since 1967's 'The Laughing Gnome,' but unlike that track, it's uncut and highly effective troubled-teen

367

catnip, almost surgically assembled to appeal to kids in smoky bedrooms with Bowie posters on their walls ('You are not a victim / You just scream with boredom,' after all). There's a dramatic pregnant pause, then Ronson's guitars spiral in, screaming like horror movie damsels. Like 'Rock and Roll Suicide,' 'Time' ends with an audience-inclusive sing-along, a string of 'La la la' before Bowie punctuates it in vaguely corny fashion with 'Yes, time!' The passing of time is an age-old theme (check the Stones' 'Time Waits for No One,' the Pretenders' 'Time the Avenger' and every Smiths track ever written) but it's never been tackled with an unabashed, almost giddy theatrical pretension ('Goddamn you're looking old!' Bowie shouts). 'Let's Spend the Night Together' is covered very, very campily, with a revised breakdown toward the end ('They said we were too young / Our kind of love was no fun'), complete with Ronson's 'talking guitar' (five years before Van Halen's debut) and a headphones-friendly shout of 'Do it!' The album closes with its best track, 'Lady Grinning Soul.' Like 'Aladdin Sane,' It's driven by Garson's piano and Bowie's saloon singing at the high, torchy end of his range. Like 'Panic' it's a portrait in lyrics of a dangerously soulful black chick who drives a VW Beetle, plays a mean hand of canasta and will, if you are not careful, 'lay belief on you' and 'be your living end.' with its Spanish acoustic guitar fade-out, it manages to be hypersexual and objectifying but never sleazy. It's in fact as genuinely affectionate a song about getting regally shagged by a hot black groupie as you will ever find. The yin to 'Brown Sugar''s yang?

'*Aladdin Sane*, that's me having a go at trying to redefine Ziggy, and making him what people wanted,' Bowie would tell the NME years later. 'The Ziggy Stardust album told the whole story. There was nothing more to say. And I knew when I was making *Aladdin Sane* that the bottom had just fallen out of the whole idea. That was a tough period and I felt for the first time and the only time like I was working for somebody else. Tony Defries and his MainMan organization had seemingly made me a star and I felt obliged to do something to live up to Tony's expectations. Yeah, *Aladdin Sane* was kind of a sellout.'

As such, it worked brilliantly. Released that April, *Aladdin Sane* was, at the time, the biggest advance hit in UK chart history, debuting at number one in April of 1973 and cracking the U.S. Top 20. 'The Jean Genie,' written in New York and recorded in Nashville and London, was released as the first single. Shortly before the Winterland tour date, Mick Rock had shot a video with Marilyn Monroe lookalike Cyrinda Foxe on the streets of San Francisco. Bowie does his best James Dean in black leather. The short was fed to UK and American music shows in advance of the album's spring release. 'I actually directed four Ziggy videos in total. This short was supplied to music shows in the UK and America, although in truth there were few outlets for 'promo' films as they were then dubbed. It was shot in one day and one night on a shoestring in San Francisco to promote his new single 'Jean Genie.' It was edited in one eight-hour day, and I drove the editor nuts. He said he'd never work with me again. You'll note that it's full of cuts. No special effects. There isn't even a dissolve. We didn't have money for anymore time, but with the advent of MTV in the early eighties, the legendary rock critic Lester Bangs said it was "the moment the modern music video began,"' Rock says of the landmark clip.

U.S. tour number two began in February of 1973. This time, as Defries had strategized, the venues were twice as big (the tour opened on Valentine's Day at Radio City Music Hall and closed a month later with a March date at the Hollywood Palladium). As strategized, or prophesized, Bowie actually needed the bodyguards who were employed for the show this time. Bowie's head security man, Stuey George, kept busy twenty-four/seven filtering out the crazies and facilitating the groupie access.

'I was like the Paris Hilton of my day,' says Lori Mattix today. Mattix, best known as Jimmy Page's seventies girlfriend, was, at the time, the queen of the Sunset Boulevard glitter scene. 'I was young. I was also a teen model. I was very aware of what was going on. At the time I had this girlfriend named Sable [Star]. She was a dedicated groupie. All she wanted to do was fuck rock stars. When

I told her that Bowie's security had called me and that he wanted to take me out to dinner and was going to send a limo for me. She said, "Oh, no, you can't go see David without me. If you fuck David and I don't, I'm gonna kill you."'

According to Mattix they were picked up in Bowie's limo. After the show, Bowie wanted to go to the Rainbow on the Sunset Strip, but once there, they were accosted by a drunken patron. 'Some guy jumped over the table. He screamed, "Fucking faggot." Started attacking him. Yelling all these profanities. This guy swung at David. Leaped over the table . . . the bodyguard stepped in.' Paranoid about the violence that was still hair-trigger in America, they piled into the limo and headed to the hotel. Ironically the mellow soft-rock hit 'Danny's Song' (written by Kenny Loggins and most famously sung by Anne Murray) was playing in the car. 'And Sable leans over,' Mattix says, 'and sings to him, "Even though you ain't got honey, I'm so in love with your money."'

Back at Bowie's room at the Beverly Hilton, they reportedly sat around the white shag carpet smoking a joint with Bowie's security crew, while the star was secreted somewhere in the luxury suite. 'We were in the living room getting high and drinking champagne. Sable was fogging up the windows and writing "I wanna fuck you" on them. At first I said, "Yeah, go, you can have him." 'Cause I was afraid. Forty-five minutes went by.

And then an hour went by. All of a sudden the door opens, David comes walking out. So beautiful. I was mesmerized. He had flawless white porcelain skin. Carrot-red hair. Red kimono. A sight to be seen. My fear was gone.'

Following the American tour, the Bowies sailed alone to Japan on the cruise ship the SS *Oresay*, departing from Los Angeles. The band followed via airplane the day after his arrival. While Bowie was working to conquer America, the *Ziggy Stardust* record was selling steadily on the Japanese charts, and by the time he was able to take up a local promoter's lucrative offer ($6,000 per show for ten shows) to perform there, he had accumulated both a loyal teenage and college-age fan base and the kind of curiosity – and on occasion, scorn – from their parents' generation that he had inspired in England and America at the start of the decade.

A student of Kabuki theater, thanks to the tutelage of Lindsay Kemp, Bowie eagerly consumed the local sights and culture, and the Japanese would come to have a major impact on Ziggy's third stage costuming. Bowie could now afford costumes and commissioned nine new stage costumes from designer Kansai Yamamoto (whose models had inspired the Ziggy haircut the previous year). The new look for *Aladdin Sane* would be drawn from both Noh and Kabuki and feature high-collared satin cloaks designed to be removed with flourishes to reveal a second layer underneath, or sometimes just a pair of briefs.

While the Bowies were taking bullet trains all over Japan, the Stooges were stuck in *Los Angeles*, their career in limbo despite the masterpiece that was *Raw Power*. In lucid moments, they rehearsed for a tour that was not destined to come together.

'The whole world was a bit stoned and upside-down,' Stooges guitarist Ron Asheton told me in an interview shortly before his death in 2009. 'A wild unknown frontier. I enjoyed it but it got scary and very tiresome after a while. All that drug stuff happening and seeing your world crumbling. Toward the end of the first Stooges, I was the only one that was not using, and I'd see pieces of equipment missing – "Hey where's that practice amp? Hey, wait a minute, where's that reverb unit?" And just to see no interest in music. Music only became the means to get some more money to get some more drugs. "Okay, we played the show, where's my money?" And they'd say, "Oh, we played for drugs."'

Hard drugs had sunk in, and they became impossible to manage or promote. Leee Black Childers had the unenviable task of minding them during this period. 'There we were, the top of the Hollywood Hills with nothing happening,' he says. 'We're thousands of miles from the center of activity, which was New York, and nothing was happening but rehearsals, rehearsals, rehearsals. That was horrible. And then, right, all of a sudden after this long period of don't do anything, let yourself go flabby, then they were just suddenly pitched out.'

Word came from London: the Stooges were no longer MainMan artists. It was down to Childers to inform the band. Throughout 1972 and '73 it was made very plain by Defries that the ax could come down on anyone at any time if they didn't pull their weight. It was Defries's way of keeping everyone in line.

'This is the way the company worked with everyone, from roadies to stylists to everyone. And it's part of what also kept it functioning to the point that it did, but it's also part of what made it so exhausting,' Childers says. 'It was made clear to you daily. You were told by either David or Tony Defries daily. One of them would say. 'You know, Tony's not really happy with what you're doing.' And then the next day I'd hear from Tony, 'David doesn't really see what you're here for. He's starting to question why you're on the tour.' I'll admit there were days while staying at the Beverly Hills Hotel, all expenses paid, when I would go into the stairwell where no one could find me and sit in there and cry and shake. Because you're put in this position of 'If it's all taken away from me, then I'm absolutely nowhere.' I had nothing to fall back on. I'm worse than I was to begin with. And every once in a while, and frequently, someone got the chop to keep that feeling always at hand.'

In New York, Zanetta was the firing squad. He'd

take the soon-to-be-ousted victim to a small Midtown café. He'd buy a lavish dinner, and when the check arrived, he'd inform the unfortunate scenester that they were no longer a part of the MainMan organization or the scene. Defries soon cut his losses with Iggy in a similar way, sending word to Leee Black Childers that they were beyond the pale. 'Unfortunately promoters were scared of booking us,' Pop said at the time. 'I kept the group writing and rehearsing, building up enormous studio rental bills because I wanted to play somewhere. If I couldn't play on stage, I'd play in a rehearsal room.'

'It was a tragedy, really, for the business and for rock 'n' roll, that a lot of people who might have been contributing a lot of stuff were put on hold through what could have been very, very, very important creative periods in their lives,' says Childers. 'It was very "Show me some results."' And there were no results. All we were doing was hanging around by a swimming pool. We were all in Siberia. We were all forbidden to show our faces.'

Asheton did not blame MainMan for putting them out. The fact that he claimed to be having an affair with Angie wasn't even a factor. 'Iggy's insatiable appetite for other drugs progressed,' Asheton said. 'We didn't have a lot of product [to promote]. We didn't have a big following. It has nothing to do with David Bowie. It was just about the disintegration of a band.'

After a couple of abortive recording sessions and comeback attempts, Iggy Pop hit the streets. Evicted from his MainMan-funded lodging, he was homeless and strung out. The Ashetons returned to Ann Arbor, and what many consider to be one of the more perfect bands rock 'n' roll has ever known was put on ice for three decades.

By the time the Spiders returned to England for another round of tour dates, they too were fraying as a unit. There was talk of another U.S. tour looming, as well as an extensive Australian trek, but many seats on the last tour had not sold. U.S. tour three was not booked but within the next few weeks, it would be abruptly 'canceled,' as Bowie and Defries were cooking up another PR masterstroke. Ziggy was about to 'retire.'

'The stardom was kind of illusory, everyone was exhausted, and the Spiders had finally realized that they should be getting paid,' Tony Zanetta says. 'I mean the fact that they asked for money. Well, the thing was that all the money was like in a paper bag. I mean it was literally in a brown paper bag. And the money would be doled out as people needed it. In the spirit of those times, when you're young and you're doing something because you have a passion for it. Most of us didn't care about money. It was just fun to be a part of this whole thing. So once money started coming into it, it did become a little bit corrupted. And when those boys asked to be paid, it was taken as treason. Of course they should have been paid but

David took that really as a betrayal. So when he retired, it was a business decision; it was also an opportunity to rest and recoup. I don't think anybody ever intended that he was never gonna work again.'

Bowie did not inform anyone but Ronson, whose silence was secured with the promise of all of MainMan's attentions as a solo artist (whether he wanted to be one or not, and by most accounts, he did not). The rest of the band had reportedly first become indignant once Mike Garson filled their heads with empowering Scientology dogma. Angie claims Garson was only there in the first place to infiltrate Bowie and the Spiders and bring them and the MainMan dollars to the church, something the pianist (who has had no ties with Scientology since 1982) now denies. Regardless of the actual motivations, it was decided that the Spiders would be done after their sold-out July 5 show at the Hammersmith Odeon. Filmmaker D. A. Pennebaker was hired by RCA to shoot the concert at the Hammersmith Odeon and capture Ziggy's curtain call for posterity. It was intended for release as one of the first home video cassettes, a technology that RCA was then developing, but would remain in the vaults until 1983. The story of Ziggy's retirement was also leaked to the press so there would be no second thoughts. The kids were killing the man and Bowie was breaking up the band. He would do it in style, in front of adoring fans, at the height of his popularity and power, with Mick Jagger in the audience and the documentarian who'd shot the iconic Bob Dylan documentary *Don't Look Back* recording it all. Who cares whether it was true or not? Was it ever true to begin with?

'Tony Defries had very grandiose ideas on this next tour that he wanted to do, which we called tour three,' Zanetta recalls. 'It was to be this mega-mega-tour. But the truth of it was, the business didn't warrant a tour like that. David's stardom was kind of illusory, it was more in the press. It didn't translate into real numbers. So the promoters were very hesitant to do the kind of deal and the, you know, really major arena tour that Defries wanted to do. "Retiring" was a business decision.'

'*NME* had already gone to press by the time he made the statement onstage. Already had our front page ready,' Shaar Murray says. 'Bowie knew when the papers went to press. He knew that somebody had to have the story before he made the announcement, otherwise it would be almost a full week before the music press could cover it. Somebody from the MainMan office called me to ask for a contact number for Jeff Beck.' Beck ended up sitting in with the Spiders but does not appear in the Pennebaker film. 'Ronno [Mick Ronson] wanted to invite Jeff to the show. I gave them the number, then it was, "Can you hold on a second, Charles, David would like a word," then David came on the phone and basically said this was going to be the last Spiders show. Cleverly ambiguous. He wanted the *NME* to know in advance. The previous week. I went of course straight in and told the editor. We started working on that front page immediately. Everybody in the office was sworn to secrecy. He told me I was the only person who'd be getting this story. He'd picked the *NME*. If anybody let it slip, if it reached the ears of anybody on any of the other music papers, it would be considered virtually a sacking offense.'

John Hutchinson, from the Buzz, had been sitting in with the Spiders throughout the last American tour and the English tour (along with a flautist and horn players). Before the band went on that night, he was pulled aside by Bowie. 'He came and found me and said, "Hutch, don't start playing 'Rock and Roll Suicide' until I tell you to." Now, I would normally have started that because it was an encore song. I would wait till the applause died down and play the intro on the twelve-string, but he told me not to do that. He told me something was gonna happen. So I figured he was going to say something – "We've had a great tour, thanks very much and good night," you know? So I was kind of waiting to see so he wouldn't catch me by surprise. I wasn't really listening. Trying not to screw up the intro. I better be ready to hit that chord.'

Instead Bowie, out of breath and clearly exhausted, uttered the following words to a crowd that included his new pal Mick Jagger: 'Not only is it the last show of the tour, it's the last show we'll ever do.'

Hutchinson hit into the C chord as the band, thrown a bit, tried to work through to the long end of 'Rock and Roll Suicide' without messing up. 'I heard him say, "It's the last show we'll ever do,"' Hutchinson says. 'And I thought, "*What?*" On the tour? It was only after we came off and I heard Trevor say, "He's fucking sacked us!"'

While the band was sorting out what just happened, Steve Jones, future Sex Pistols guitar player, was stealing their gear out of the back of the venue. 'We knew we wanted a band and there was no way we could afford to buy the gear, so we stole it,' he told Jon Savage in *England's Dreaming*. That very gear might have been used in early Sex Pistols rehearsals. It serves Bowie right. In 'Hang On to Yourself,' Bowie indicated that the beat comes out better on a stolen guitar.

The after-party at the nearby Café Royale was fraught. Bowie was celebratory and relieved. The Spiders were sulky and bewildered. Ziggy would live on long enough to record and release one more album. The following week, Bowie and Ronson almost immediately flew to France to record a collection of cover songs that inspired him called *Pin Ups*. The album was recorded at composer George Sand's studio at the Château d'Hérouville in France. Marc Bolan, who recorded T. Rex's

1972 album *The Slider* there, recommended it to Bowie. Elton John had immortalized it the previous year on his smash *Honky Chateau* album (its success was largely due to the 'Space Oddity'-indebted 'Rocket Man').

In the sunny countryside, Bowie reflected on the last year's ascension. The music of *Pin Ups* seemed to give him closure; he was taking the hits from the sixties, by the Kinks ('Where Have All the Good Times Gone'), the Easybeats ('Friday on My Mind'), Pink Floyd ('See Emily Play'), Them ('Here Comes the Night') and the Who ('I Can't Explain,' 'Anyway, Anyhow, Anywhere'), ones he could not make, and finally making them his own by camping them up Ziggy style. The album's single, a cover of the McCoys' 1965 ballad 'Sorrow,' is easily its most restrained moment. The rest is maximum R & B slipped a 'lude (the tempos are slowed to the point of grinding) and laid out on a Vegas floor show (which is exactly how they would soon be presented).

Later that summer, Bowie returned one last time to Wardour Street to shoot a special promoting *Pin Ups*, called 1980 *Floor Show*. With Aynsley Dunbar, who drummed on the *Pin Ups* album, replacing Woody Woodmansey, and a three-piece backup band called the Astronettes, featuring his new girl-friend the now platinum-haired Ava Cherry who he was intent on turning into 'the next Josephine Baker.' Bowie took over the Marquee's stage, where he'd performed in three failed R & B combos as a teenager. Ziggy Stardust killed the sixties. Before being killed off himself, he would revive them.

Bowie first appears in Yamamoto clothing, debuting a new song, '1984,' its Orwellian themes and funky chicken-scratch guitar showing the direction he was headed musically. As tacky as it is (dancers spell out the title credits), the *Floor Show* should not work, but it's a sexy production; the antithesis of the Kenneth Pitt-produced mid-sixties showcase *Love You Till Tuesday*. '1984' segues into 'Dodo,' and Bowie reappears goatlike. He has no eyebrows, having spontaneously shorn them off during U.S. tour two (reportedly after Mott the Hoople rejected 'Drive-in Saturday' as a single). A Calvin Mark Lee love jewel is affixed to his forehead.

Bowie makes a devil sign as he serenades a Euro-trash blonde and yet another would-be MainMan star, gender-bending Amanda Lear, on 'Sorrow.' 'Space Oddity' feels like an oldie among *Pin Ups*' new-oldies. The high point of 'I Can't Explain' is sure, sultry backing vocalists the Astronettes dancing in slow motion. Marianne Faithfull appears in a nun's habit and duets with Bowie on Sonny and Cher's classic 'I Got You, Babe.' She sounds like Natasha Fatale from the *Rocky and Bullwinkle* cartoons. She returns later for two more numbers, her signature song the Jagger-Richards penned 'As Tears Go By' (also given the Natasha treatment) and a *Cabaret*-indebted wedge of cheese called '20th Century Blues.' The Troggs make an insane appearance as well. Watching a bootleg of 1980 *Floor Show*, one wonders if they were placed on the bill to make Bowie look that much prettier. They resemble cave children. Lead singer Reg Presley appears genuinely demented. After the Troggs, the event's last act, a Spanish flamenco group named Carmen (which Tony Visconti was then producing), somehow makes absolutely perfect sense.

The show was broadcast on U.S. television show *The Midnight Special*, one of the weirder moments in seventies TV (and this is an era that includes *Lidsville*, *Circus of the Stars* and 'Next Stop Nowhere,' aka the Punk Rock Episode of *Quincy*). 'I remember watching it,' says Camille Paglia. 'He had one costume with the two hands coming from behind to grab his breasts. It was the most sexually radical thing you could ever imagine seeing on American television at the time. He was pushing the envelope so far. He was a performance artist even before the phrase 'performance artist' was in circulation.'

And with that, Ziggy was gone. 'Each man kills the thing he loves,' Wilde wrote in his most famous poem, 'Ballad of Reading Gaol.' Ziggy Stardust was killed by all three of the means Wilde itemizes. The 'flattering words' and 'kisses' of others made Bowie see his creation as a great triumph but a potential millstone. Surely the option to do so was there. Bowie might have remained Ziggy Stardust for decades. Ultimately Ziggy is done in with Bowie's own 'sword,' to use Wilde's word, shocking even those close to him, like the Spiders, with its abruptness, as though if there were second thoughts, he might be spared.

The haircut remained for another half year or so. Some things are harder to kill.

I associate certain rockers with certain drugs. When I think of Sid Vicious, I think of heroin more than I think of, say, the bass guitar. I love the Pogues, but when I think of Shane MacGowan, I think of streams of whiskey. I associate certain rockers with certain drugs mostly when I am actually consuming those drugs. There's an old punk rock album by a Los Angeles eccentric named Black Randy (and his band the Metro Squad) entitled Pass the Dust, I Think I'm Bowie *(Randy re-creates the* Hunky Dory *sleeve on the cover). When someone is passing me the disco dust, I don't necessarily think that I am Bowie, but I certainly have thoughts about Bowie. When the Beastie Boys acted like they still did coke, they thought of Bowie. You may recall this lyric from 1989's 'Car Thief' (from* Paul's Boutique, *still their best record): 'You be doing nose candy on the Bowie coke mirror / My girl asked for some but I pretended not to hear her.'*

They actually make *Bowie coke mirrors. I bought one on eBay UK. But since I don't do coke anymore, I gave it to a girlfriend as a gift. She uses it as a compact.*

CHAPTER 16

Although there's no way to measure this in any forensic sense, it's wholly possible that David Bowie did more cocaine in the mid-1970s than anyone else in popular culture: the Eagles, Elton John, the Stones, Rick James, Oliver Stone, Hollywood Henderson or Julie Your Cruise Director.

By 1973, cocaine, long a recreational substance and status symbol with an extensive history of glamour, was so firmly entrenched in the culture that President Nixon declared war on the cocaine cowboys importing it from Colombian killing fields in private planes and disseminating it throughout the cities and suburbs until coke abuse took on the properties of a biological epidemic. Disco swingers wore 'Coke Adds Life' pendants, and 18-karat gold spoons against their hairy chest or perfumed cleavage. Consumption was often done in restaurants and bars with the same elan one would use to sample from the wine list. As late as 1974, many people still weren't convinced it was at all addictive.

'So much publicity has gone out on heroin that

people don't want to get started on it,' Irwin Swank of Chicago's Bureau of Narcotics is quoted as saying in a *Newsweek* cover story on the cocaine craze. 'But you get a good high with coke and you don't get hooked.' Mr Swank, clearly a glass half full kind of Narco.

Bowie certainly got hooked, and like most doing the white line at the time, coke provided more of a psychological balm at first. Bowie likely used massive quantities of gak to completely remove all traces of Ziggy Stardust and cauterize the wounds. Even then, there were detectable particles of Ziggy in his personality and so, Bowie surmised, his entire psyche needed breaking down until there was absolutely nothing left. Each bump he plugged his nose with, fed into the nostril on the end of an antique knife (his prefered method), was rock 'n' roll chemotherapy. As a former mod, Bowie's appreciation for the energy that speedy drugs can afford a busy and enthusiastic artist was already in place. The blow would, as is its way, get the better of him eventually, but for a time, it certainly fuelled a dizzying period of creativity and action. Bowie used coke like a sculptor uses a chisel.

'David was actually very grounded. He was, like, a very solid individual,' Tony Zanetta says. 'He really wasn't a very wild person at all. He was a very disciplined artist. Where he went astray was in his experimentation with coke. It was like one day he had to drink a glass of wine, and the next day he was a terrible cocaine addict. It seemed at first that it was an affectation, that it was part of his stardom personality. But because of the nature of coke, you don't just dabble in it. I think it affected him more than he bargained for.'

Cocaine helped David Bowie exist as a fabulous rock star *offstage*. Sigmund Freud, another celebrated user, wrote of ingesting 'a little cocaine, to untie my tongue,' and this was likely a bonus for David, who was at heart a painfully shy, suburban kid and now was suddenly looked upon as the life of the ongoing glitter party.

Cocaine makes for good ritual as well. Whether you are alone, writing, or at a party, it actually slows things down (speedy as it is) and gives one the illusion of control as it's prepared, mathematically divided and shared. When you no longer recognize your life as it was, the heartbeat-like *chop chop chop* rhythm of lines being cut can be soothing, as ironic as that might seem. There were even medicinal properties. A smoker since his teens, Bowie was emptying two packets of Marlboros a day into his lungs. The cigarettes punctuated every second of his seemingly ceaseless inspiration and facilitated him in getting it all out and down on paper, again via rhythm and ritual. A natural bronchodilator, cocaine is appealing to smokers as it deconstricts the vascular tissue in the lungs, making it easier to chain-smoke and, certainly for a time, sing.

Finally, Bowie was working-class. He spent the

sixties and early seventies watching friends like the much younger Peter Frampton, and later Marc Bolan, as well as peers like Pete Townshend enjoy the spoils of fame while he struggled to pay bills. The preponderance of coke seemed to function as confirmation that he'd made it. It was also an ideal drug for Bowie's highly sexualized new world. 'Until you've got a mouth full of cocaine, you don't know what kissing is. You never get tired! You're on 4th speed all the time, and the engine purrs like a kitten with the stars in its whiskers,' Aleister Crowley wrote. Every wham-bam assignation went off more smoothly with a toot.

Bowie had already recorded two tracks for the follow-up to *Pin Ups* in October 1973 at London's Olympic Studios: '1984,' that sinister Winston Smith-meets-John Shaft wah-wah-pedal orgy, and the B side 'Dodo.' The following month, however, he was no closer to completing a follow-up to *Pin Ups*. With MainMan losing capital by the day, the pressure was on. However, fueled by cocaine, titanic creative ambition and the sense that from now on everything he laid his long fingers on would be golden, Bowie ignored it all and set about planning another elaborate stage show, or perhaps a film or a Broadway show. He also began work on writing and producing an album for Ava Cherry. He produced a version of his 'The Man Who Sold the World' with English pop sweetheart Lulu ('To Sir with Love'), who was looking to move her career and image in a more adult direction. This is another Bowie hallmark: taking an artist at a career crossroads, usually one who has seen better days professionally, and reinventing them as a different pop entity, one boasting the Bowie glow.

'He invited me to his concert. And back at the hotel, he said to me, in very heated language, "I want to make an MF of a record with you."' Lulu said. '"You're a great singer." I didn't think it would happen, but he followed up two days later. He was übercool at the time and I just wanted to be led by him. I loved everything he did. I didn't think "The Man Who Sold the World" was the greatest song for my voice, but it was such a strong song in itself. I had no idea what it was about. In the studio, Bowie kept telling me to smoke more cigarettes, to give my voice a certain quality. My take on it is that he wanted me to sing on something of his and wanted to produce me. He wanted to make me different somehow. It was the package that was great. We were like the odd couple. A lot of people had raised eyebrows.' This must have delighted Bowie. While 'The Man Who Sold the World' was not a chart-topping hit (while Bowie's background vocals can be clearly heard on this faithful version, it's not a duet), it got a lot of attention for both of them, especially after a short film was shot to promote the single. Lulu is featured in a full man's suit and fedora hat. 'It was very Berlin cabaret. "The Man Who Sold the World" saved me from a certain niche in my career.'

Bowie spoke enthusiastically about adapting the Russian underground comic book *Octobriana* for the screen as a vehicle for 1980 *Floor Show* starlet Amanda Lear, but shortly before the holidays, his own theatrical production began to occupy most of his time. Rumors that Bowie was even being tapped to produce Queen's second album began to circulate around this time.

Once he finally did enter the studio early in the new year, he produced and performed much of the new album himself, and when another musician was required, like bassist Herbie Flowers or drummer Aynsley Dunbar, Bowie would dictate how he heard the music in his head, and it was re-created faithfully. Call it cocaine precision, or whatever you like, but for the next three records, right up until his first Eno collaboration in '77, Bowie was the last word in the studio.

'I have to take total control myself. I can't let anybody else do anything, for I find that I can do things better for me,' he admitted to the writer William S. Burroughs during a tête à tête moderated by Chris Copetas that November (it appeared in a February 1974 issue of *Rolling Stone*). 'I don't want to get other people playing with what they think that I'm trying to do.'

In London early in the new year, Burroughs was invited to Bowie's Chelsea home for dinner. Bowie, who'd been an avid reader of Burroughs since his teens, spent much of the interview discussing writing technique and the future of media. Burroughs and his partner the British modernist writer Brion Gyson had famously developed a 'cut and paste' style of writing where words were randomly chosen from a hat or basket and strung together toward the end of achieving an alternate, spontaneous and truthful form of communication – randomness as its own medium, in a sense. Bowie would employ the cut-and-paste technique, as he informed Burroughs, not as a means to write lyrics, but as a means to create the actual story. He would write forty full scenes, put them in a (very large) hat (maybe a chef's hat?) and randomly select the content and order of the production. 'I get bored very quickly and that would give it some new energy,' he said. Bowie also volunteered that he would like to bring an actual black hole onstage. Burroughs, with typical dark wit, warns him that black holes can be very expensive.

Pork director and MainMan artist Tony Ingrassia was flown to London to help develop the theatrical production, a musical adaptation of Orwell's 1984, but the project soon fell through when MainMan failed to secure the permission to adapt the book from Orwell's widow, Sonia Blair. 'I did a fast about-face and recobbled the idea into *Diamond Dogs*: teen punks on rusty skates living on the roofs of the dystopian Hunger City; a post-apocalyptic landscape,' Bowie told the *Daily Mail* in '08.

Bowie decided that he would tell his own paranoid, politicized dystopian story, transposing his creation *Hunger City* for Orwell's London, and a 'real cool cat' named Halloween Jack for Winston Smith. '1984' and the Orwell-quoting 'We Are the Dead' would remain in the production, and Bowie would write the rest of the score around them. Paranoid, dystopian fantasy was all the rage in the Watergate era, just check Woody Allen's Orwellian slapstick *Sleeper*, released in December of '73.

Meanwhile MainMan was in credit free fall. Bills were coming due for limousines, studio time, expense accounts, rent, mostly for projects that tanked. Product from their only reliably successful artist was crucial. They lacked the time to plot a full stage production, so the master plan shifted slightly. Bowie would record an album, and the tour itself would be the production, a brilliant bit of making a virtue of necessity. Why couldn't the rock 'n' roll tour be the stage show, after all? Inspired, Bowie dedicated himself to crafting his own record in a way that he hadn't displayed before. Without Visconti or Ken Scott or Mick Ronson and the Spiders, the music's quality all fell to him and he was determined to meet the challenge. Drummer Dunbar, bassist Herbie Flowers, guitarists Alan Parker and Tony Newman, as well as Garson, the lone holdout from the Spiders purging, convened in December at Olympic Studios, with engineer Keith Harwood (who produced 'All the Young Dudes' for Mott the Hoople and was then fresh from work on Led Zeppelin's *Houses of the Holy*) assisting with the production. Work was quick and disciplined. Everything was laid down smoothly until MainMan failed to pay the Olympic Studios bill and the album work relocated temporarily to Ludolf Studios in Norway.

'We did *Diamond Dogs* very fast indeed,' Flowers said, 'doing basic tracks in three days in the little studio at Olympic. Bowie was writing a lot of the stuff as we were going. I think it was a semi-rescue attempt from his proposed George Orwell musical. The music was weird. I have to say I found it mildly unattractive at the time.'

Diamond Dogs was Bowie's most brutal and hopeless statement since *The Man Who Sold the World*. The warmth of *Hunky Dory* was almost completely gone, save the stomping first single 'Rebel Rebel,' which was rush-released that February (with the two-year-old 'Queen Bitch' hastily slapped on as B side) to provide the company some much needed fiscal plasma.

Diamond Dogs opens with a sucking, electronic hound's bay, played on an electric guitar. Bowie's voice melts over the creepy soundscape, as does a muted version of the Rodgers and Hart standard 'Bewitched, Bothered and Bewildered': 'And in the death / As the last few corpses lay rotting on the slimy thoroughfare . . .' In a sort of proto-*Star Wars* 'crawl,' a monologue (entitled 'Future Legend') tells the story of packs of marauding dogs with 'red mutant eyes' patrolling the wasted streets of Hunger City. The party is over. It's the year of Diamond Dogs. It's also not rock 'n' roll, we are informed as 'Diamond Dogs' begins, it's 'genocide.'

The sound of a concert crowd is heard, then a cowbell and finally a Stax-style groove from the underworld. Bowie's *Diamond Dogs* band was a funkier crew than the Spiders from Mars ever were, and they work it out as Bowie spits non sequiturs in the jaded commentator's voice he'd honed on *Aladdin Sane* ('As they pulled you out of the oxygen tent / You asked for the latest party').

'Sweet Thing' and 'Candidate,' a mini-suite (whose lyrics were among those completely written, according to Bowie, with the Burroughs cut-and-paste technique) broken by an extended saxophone solo, introduces a new Bowie voice to the palette, the crooning coke-lizard basso profundo. Bowie would employ this one on virtually every album that would follow. It's not quite English, vaguely American, slippery with coke nasal drip but certainly no less beguiling than any of his other voices. It will appear later in both 'Rock and Roll with Me' (which actually mentions 'lizards lying in the heat') and 'We Are the Dead' (which contains the cut-and-paste-derived phrase 'defecating ecstasy,' perhaps an argument against the technique?). 'Rebel Rebel' is heralded by a strange, scratchy loop, until that magnificent riff blasts through. It's Bowie's last great glitter anthem, one for the road for the English Disco kids on Sunset (where it was played every ten minutes by the house DJ). It revisits familiar

Bowie territory: a 'hot' young 'tramp' worrying his/her parents with his/her sexy nihilism ('You got a few lines and a handful of 'ludes'). The world is ending, but who cares, 'Rebel' suggests; 'we like dancing and we look divine.' '1984' is slotted in and segues into the equally Orwellian 'Big Brother,' which is one of those songs where the verses and choruses are okay but the bridge is a must-hear: 'I know you think you're awful square / But you've made everyone and you've been everywhere,' Bowie sings. (Did the end of jaded glitter have a better lyrical summation? If so, I can't come up with one.) 'Don't live for last year's capers,' Bowie warns on the track, and it's clear that he has officially ceased to do so himself. *Diamond Dogs* was no fun. But it was Bowie's best-sounding, most complex record to date, and it still pulls you into its romantic and doomed world three and a half decades on.

The recording was completed at Ludolf at the suggestion of the Rolling Stones (who had just finished their own 1974 release *It's Only Rock 'n' Roll* there). Bowie and Jagger's friendship, begun the previous year when Jagger attended Ziggy's retirement show, was still in full bloom, with the elder, more famous icon often sharing advice or recommendations with the younger star . . . that is, until he realized that Bowie would steal all the best ones.

Local artist Guy Peellaert was commissioned to do the cover art for *Diamond Dogs*. His book *Rock*

Dreams (a collaboration with English rock journalist Nik Cohn) sat on every suburban hipster's coffee table. Like a gatefold album, it was glossy and ideal for the de-seeding of weed. In dreamy, color-saturated Edward Hopper-style portraits, Peellaert would depict, say, Elvis and John Lennon chatting in a malt shop. Peellaert had just completed the sleeve for *It's Only Rock 'n' Roll* when Bowie commissioned the cover for *Diamond Dogs*, which would beat the Stones to the shops and mark the end of career tips and raves coming from Jagger's famous lips whenever Bowie was within earshot. The *Diamond Dogs* cover depicted Bowie's head (still with full Ziggy flaming-rooster haircut) atop the body of a reclining greyhound in a carnival freak show setting, with the dog's bollocks on full display. When RCA saw the cover, they balked and insisted that the pooch genitals be airbrushed out.

Diamond Dogs was always conceived to be performed live. On the track 'Candidate,' Bowie sings, 'My set is amazing, it even smells like the street,' so by the time a returning Tony Visconti was brought in to assist with strings and final mixes (this after falling out with the increasingly egomaniacal and now culturally irrelevant Marc Bolan), Bowie set about planning how to present the tracks live.

Toni Basil, the actress and choreographer who had appeared in *Easy Rider* and would go on to create David Byrne's iconic hand gestures for the

Talking Heads' 'Once in a Lifetime' video (and of course have one chart-topping hit of her own with the immortal 'Mickey'), was hired to put together dance numbers for a set list that would include tracks from all of Bowie's RCA albums as well as *The Man Who Sold the World* and the 'Space Oddity' single. Nothing would simply be sung and played this time around. In fact, the *Diamond Dogs* 'event' would be so theatrical that the lighting designer hired, Jules Fisher, was a Tony Award winner. Furthermore, Fisher suggested that Bowie hire an actual theatrical director for the tour.

'I had long been wanting to bring theater and rock 'n' roll closer,' Fisher says today. 'Even at this juncture, I suggested we hire a director. So I introduced him to Michael Bennett, who was a rising star at the time.'

The New York-born Bennett, a dancer and choreographer himself, had worked with Stephen Sondheim on *Company* and would direct the original production of *A Chorus Line* two years later. Bowie and Bennett took in productions of ongoing shows in midtown and hit it off socially, but ultimately Bowie decided not to hire the future legend.

'David thought, "Well, I'll do this myself,"' Fisher says. 'I've created my own persona. I built everything I am. Why do I need another person to do this? I tried to explain that Michael wouldn't make him do something that he didn't want to do, like dance steps. That he'd build the show around what David could already do. But he wasn't interested.'

Defries convinced RCA to bankroll the Diamond Dogs tour by insisting that it would put Bowie in and even beyond the realm of the Rolling Stones. With peerless sound and unprecedented sets and presentation, it was designed to make Bowie. The groundwork had been laid in America with the 'cancellation' of the never-actually-scheduled U.S. tour number three following Ziggy's retirement.

U.S. fans who were convinced that they would never see Bowie again would not only be able to see him; they would be treated to the grandest, deepest, loudest rock spectacle ever mounted. Hunger City would be constructed onstage, an actual urban landscape built up, then torn down and transported to the next city after the final encore. 'He was very clear in his vision for the set,' Fisher says. 'He wanted something that referenced German expressionism. [Robert Weine's 1920 silent film] *The Cabinet of Dr Caligari* and [Fritz Lang's 1927 masterwork] *Metropolis*, were two films that he was fascinated by.' Fisher flew out to London to meet with Bowie, who would watch these films in his high-tech screening room on a Virtual loop. 'We had a very casual tea, which I drank and relaxed. He said, 'This is the world that I want. This is what I'm interested in now and this is what I want to show.' He was dealing with nihilism, the emptiness of the world. I think that fit in with *Metropolis*. The lonely man, the lonely figure in the big world. So a lot of our images onstage fit that.'

Fisher hired New York-based scenic designer Mark Ravitz, who studied under Fisher at NYU and had recently begun working with Kiss (he'd go on to create their famous lit-up logo). 'The three words that were relayed to me were: power, Nuremburg and Fritz Lang's *Metropolis*,' Ravitz tells me. 'I drew up a whole Chinese menu of ideas. Columns A, B and C. Different sketches. Roughs and different looks. He came to New York and I put them all out in front of him and his whole entourage. They'd pick like you'd pick from a menu. 'I like this. I like that.' Nobody said anything to me about a budget. It was pretty much the sky's the limit.'

The set would include a bridge that would rise and fall with the aid of brakes designed by the Porsche motor company. The backdrop would be a series of silk-screened paper skyscrapers, each one dripping blood. At the climax of each show, Bowie would tear them down, as if to lay waste to a dying city and, as was becoming a recurring theme, start again. 'It was creative destruction,' Ravitz suggests. 'Urban decay.'

The set was built in New Jersey and shipped up to Toronto, where tour rehearsals began in the late winter of 1974. There, spectacular new devices like the bridge (which would rise and fall hydraulically, seemingly at Bowie's whim) and a crane that would place Bowie high above the audience during 'Space Oddity' were tested.

'It looked real,' Fisher says. 'You saw a bridge with streetlamps held up by two buildings. And it was actually held up by steel cable and was an elevator and could lower onstage. So this bridge lowered while he was on it, under a streetlamp; he was wearing a trench coat, on a rainy night. Like *Casablanca*. One night in rehearsal, the bridge fell very rapidly while he was on it. It was very scary. It was frightening. It was a tech rehearsal in Toronto, where we put the show together. It went very fast and he jumped off at the bottom and we all ran to him and he was okay. He said he was okay and he didn't break anything. It was a drop of maybe fifteen feet. It wasn't a free fall, but it was high speed. It really crashed to the ground with him on it, very fast and very, very scary for all of us.'

That spring MainMan issued a press release formally announcing the tour. The touring band, Flowers, Garson, drummer Tony Newman, guitarist Earl Slick, and keyboardist Michael Kamen (with backing vocals and dancing from Guy Andrisio and Bowie's childhood friend Geoff MacCormack, who performed as 'Warren Peace'), seemed to further liberate Bowie from his past. Leading this new crew through untested material during rehearsals at the Capitol Theater in Port Chester, New York, that June, he found himself playing with his vocals, singing the material any way he liked.

'When I started rehearsing with the band for this tour, I suddenly realized I was enjoying singing again,' Bowie told *Los Angeles Times* critic Robert Hilbum, then writing for NME. 'I hadn't enjoyed it in a long time. It was just a way to get my songs across. But when I started rehearsing I began enjoying it and I found I actually had a voice. That's really exciting for me. My voice has improved in leaps and bounds. I've been flattered by some of the things the musicians have said about my singing.'

The Diamond Dogs tour opened at Montreal's Forum on June 14. Anticipation was massive. Audiences filed in as weird tape loops and animal noises bleated out of a PA system which was set in the middle of the floor for maximum impact. There was no opening act and a delay of nearly an hour ratched up the suspense.

Finally, the lights dimmed, and the eerie 'Future Legend' blared out of the PA. Then Bowie appeared, seated in the palm of a giant hand, set inside a massive, glittering mirror ball. The lights flared up and hit the mirrors just as the guitarists stroked out the wah-wah riff of '1984.'

'Each song is linked together so that no delays occur during the show, and he doesn't even take a bow at the end,' journalist Chris Charlesworth wrote in his *Melody Maker* review. The band was often hidden behind flats at stage right, and Bowie did not break down the fourth wall and address the audience with any 'Hello, Cleveland'-style salutations.

'I think it was the first time I saw a rock show where the star didn't connect with the audience at all,' Charlesworth says today. 'He behaved as if the audience wasn't there. I don't think they were put off by it. As I recall David's fans accepted it because his fans were more open than most, knowing as they did that David was a rock singer who experimented with different ideas. They expected him to be different and adopt personas like an actor, and that was why they liked him. I think, by and large, David attracted a more intelligent, well-read, cultured fan than, say, Led Zeppelin, or – heaven forbid – out-and-out boogie merchants in blue denim.'

Some of the material over the course of the two-part two-hour concert was familiar ('Rebel Rebel' was quickly followed by 'Moonage Day-dream' from the Ziggy album) but Bowie no longer resembled Ziggy Stardust. His hair was flat and parted. He wore a designer suit and suspenders. For 'Sweet Thing,' he stood on the bridge in a trench coat. His backing singers/dancers would tie him in ropes for 'Diamond Dogs'; for 'Cracked Actor,' he sang into a skull, Hamlet-style, and 'Panic in Detroit' found him singing and shadowboxing in Everlast gloves. Bowie appeared in the crane, over the now dazzled crowd, singing 'Space Oddity,' and during the encore of 'The Jean Genie' and 'Rock and Roll Suicide,' a spotlight was thrown on David and the dancers, creating shadows that extended to the rafters of the arena. Each new number seemed to stand and satisfy on its own but blend perfectly into the production at the same time.

'The audience realized they were witnessing something totally different from a normal rock concert,' Charlesworth wrote. 'The cheers grew louder, but few could imagine the surprises in store . . . To grasp every detail one would have to watch at least three shows . . . He can only be described as an entertainer who looks further ahead than any other in rock, and whose far-reaching imagination has created a combination of contemporary music and theatre that is several years ahead of its time.'

The following concerts in Toronto and Ottowa hockey arenas were equally successful both critically and commerically. Word-of-mouth reached America, where tickets quickly sold out, many at a then unheard of price of ten dollars per person. The first leg of the tour ended in mid-July with two sold-out dates at New York's Madison Square Garden, rock's most prestigious arena. Filling 'MSG' was confirmation that he'd succeeded at everything he'd set out to do with regard to rock 'n' roll, theater and personal reinvention. Coke-stoked ambition had brought something entirely new to the Garden. Combining Broadway staging and Hollywood sets, and a loud, fluid, sexy rock 'n' roll road show, Diamond Dogs the tour is the precursor to every ostentatious and risky outing that played there ever since, as well as each lazy and gilded one. Of all Bowie's innovations, the first leg of his 1974 trek might have altered show business the most. Parliament Funkadelic's Mothership Connection tour (in which a giant spaceship hovers and lands onstage) and Elvis's Vegas period (not to mention every other pop star's Vegas period, from Elton John to Cher to Celine Dion) would not have existed without it. Nor would U2 or Madonna's early-nineties stadium tours or the millennial spectacles that 'N Sync, the Backstreet Boys and Britney Spears undertook (Mark Ravitz worked on the boy band's tours as well). Kanye West's 2008 Glow in the Dark tour, with its talking spaceship, neon piping and elevated pyramid, owes Diamond Dogs tribute. Following such a lasting creative triumph, not to mention a genuine commercial triumph, another artist might have done a victory lap. Typically, Bowie was about to rip it all down again and reinvent Diamond Dogs as a stripped-down soul revue (while casting himself not as the prophet of urban doom but rather as a skinny, slinky white soul boy in Puerto Rican street hustler gear). Hunger City's sky-scrapers and props would be placed in deep storage. There were rumors that the expense was simply too much to keep it going, but most likely Bowie had already moved on to something new. 'After all the effort, I honestly don't know why,' Ravitz says. 'Maybe it was too much to deal with. The trooping around was too much. Or maybe it just didn't fit anymore with the new music that he was hearing.'

★   ★   ★

'If You Only Knew' by Patty Labelle; 'Me and Mrs Jones' by Billy Paul; 'Wake Up Everybody' and 'Bad Luck' by Harold Melvin and the Blue Notes (with Teddy Pendergrass on vocals); 'When Will I See You Again?' by the Three Degrees: this is the wonderful sound of Philadelphia. 'TSOP.' It's elegant strings, a gently vibrating electric piano, velvety drums, a sax nuzzling in to fill a pocket of silence in the arrangement, filling up the mind with images of cognac-warm romance, fur rugs, a crackling Duraflame log, high heels and long, glossy leather coats with elaborate buckles and belts. Even the Philly soul that takes on man's inhumanity toward man (like the O'Jays' 'Back Stabbers') is arranged like a lusty and plush pop suite. This kind of stuff ruled the radio in the first half of the 1970s, and post-Ziggy David Bowie fell in love with these records so much that he started making them. When I was five years old, this same Philly soul nurtured me like Jif peanut butter and Kool-Aid did. With the exception of Chicago, Led Zeppelin, Elton John, Jethro Tull, Carole King and Wings, this is all I can remember listening to as a child, most of it via eight-track tapes played through the side speakers of a white plastic Weltron 2001 ball. Even today when I hear 'Betcha By Golly Wow' by the Stylistics or 'Games People Play' by the Spinners (who started out in the sixties as a Detroit-based Motown act and having had a hit with the Stevie Wonder-cowritten 'It's a Shame' but became a bona fide Philly soul phenomenon in the seventies), I am taken back to the summer of '75, a certain time in American life when gloom, terror, anger *and despair (exemplified by the Nixon resignation, which I watched on television with my babysitter the year before) seemed to be waning and Americans began hoping for a better way again. 'Young Americans,' the Bowie song that shared radio space with much of the abovementioned soul songs on 'black' radio, spoke to this hope. 'Do you remember your President Nixon,' he asks. It's one of Bowie's least detached vocal performances throughout, and listening to it now makes me believe that his hope and love for America, his spiritual country since childhood, was painfully sincere as well. Bowie wonders, 'We live for just these twenty years, Do we have to die for the fifty more?' It's the sound of the seventies finding its better angels. Even today, as we in the twenty-first century search again for those angels, 'Young Americans' has the power to erase some dead, hopeless feelings inside. Like every damn song I've mentioned in this section, it can still make me break down and cry.*

CHAPTER 17

The stripped-down and funked-up Diamond Dogs tour, renamed 'Philly Dogs,' after the soul hit by the Mar-Keys and attendant dance craze, rolled back into the greater Los Angeles area for a full week of sold-out shows at the Universal Amphitheater in early September of 1974. Fans hadn't been warned that this was an entirely new Bowie and were expecting a hard-rocking glitter gator, not a slicked-back soul boy in a blue Pierre Cardin suit. 'They were staying at the Beverly Hills Hotel,' recalls Jeff Gold, then an employee at Rhino Records (not yet a label at the time but the city's hippest record store, located in the Westwood area). 'We went down there and waited outside to get his autograph on some records. There was a very nice black guy out there who would talk to us. He said, 'He's not gonna be out for another three or four hours. Get something to eat and be back then.' We thought this guy was a bodyguard. Later that night, we went to the show at the amphitheater and the guy's singing with Bowie on a disco song called 'Fame.' The 'bodyguard' we were talking to was actually

Luther Vandross. And somehow between the last tour and this new one, Bowie had gone disco?'

During July and August of 1974, Bowie had indeed 'gone disco,' causing many fans of Ziggy Stardust to quite literally do some soul searching. 'Now I see disco as art, great popular art,' Gold says. 'But at the time, Bowie going disco was a horrifying, horrible, reprehensible betrayal by our hero. A betrayal of the highest order.'

Unlike that of Gold – an obvious music fan who would enjoy a long career as an executive at both Rhino and Warner Brothers records – some anti-disco sentiment would occasionally manifest itself as subtle, and sometimes not so subtle, racism, as with the notorious 'Death to Disco' rally-turned-riot in Chicago's Comiskey Park in 1979, and while it seems quaint now with popular music being more or less fully integrated, we should not forget just what a radical thing this must have seemed in 1974 and '75. Bowie would not be the first English pop star to have a crossover hit on 'black' radio – Elton John's 'Bennie and the Jets' was a fluke crossover hit topping both the pop and R & B charts in 1973 – but he would certainly be the first to fully embrace and *pursue* this style of music, with a full album and live presentation indebted to the sound of Philadelphia. Rod Stewart, the Rolling Stones, and of course the Bee Gees would record 'disco' singles within the next two years. It would take the Bowie-indebted Kiss another two after that to go disco. None of them, not even clothes horse Elton, would master the right look to go along with the new sound. Only Bowie did the research. Bowie's new stage wear was an homage to Harlem style. During the break between the Diamond Dogs and Philly Dogs tours, while holed up in the Sherry-Netherland Hotel in Manhattan, Bowie would often venture up to Harlem to study R & B shows and gape at the opulent, post-*Super Fly* fashion statements that the blacks and Puerto Ricans on the sidewalk and in the lobby were making: zoot suits, wide-brim hats, white shoes and fur trim. The next time he stepped onto a concert stage, he would be dressed in Harlem street-hustler garb. His escort during these trips was a guitar virtuoso five years his junior from the Bronx named Carlos Alomar. They'd met while Bowie and Tony Visconti were mixing *Diamond Dogs* in New York and bonded over music. Alomar, then working as a studio musician for RCA, told Bowie, in true warm but uncensored New Yorker style, that he was too skinny and took him up to the Bronx to meet his wife and mother and eat a home-cooked meal. A friendship and creative collaboration that would span the better part of the next two decades was begun. While at the Sherry-Netherland, Alomar was fascinated by a gigantic, black theatrical trunk that never seemed to be unpacked. When he asked what was inside, Bowie proudly opened it to display dozens of vintage records.

'Imagine my surprise when he opened it to show

me his collection of R & B and jazz recordings, from old Delta blues to jazz,' Alomar says. 'He had them all. David was infused with soul music well before his sessions in Philadelphia. It is no secret that the British idolized American black music and studied it religiously. And it was no wonder that given the chance to record at Sigma Sound recording studio, he jumped at the opportunity.' Sigma was founded by Joe Tarsia, the chief engineer at Cameo-Parkway Records, the great Philly-based label responsible for '96 Tears' by ? and the Mysterians and Dee Dee Sharp's 'Mashed Potato Time,' among others. In the late sixties Cameo-Parkway was taken over by Rolling Stones manager the late Allen Klein. Phased out, Tarsia opened up a studio, Reco-Arts, on North Twelfth Street in the Center City district in the summer of '68. He soon noticed that the room had uniquely warm acoustics, likely because the prewar heating system's steam heat had worked its way into the wood. Later, while eating at a nearby Greek diner, Tarsia came up with the name Sigma Sound.

By the early seventies, Sigma had become the favored studio of the producing and songwriting team of Kenny Gamble and Leon Huff (who were inducted into the Rock 'n' Roll Hall of Fame in 2008). Starting with the hit 'Cowboys to Girls' by the Intruders, Gamble and Huff's Philadelphia International Records acts, backed by the MFSB (Mother Father Sister Brother) house band (a sort of East Coast version of Motown's Funk Brothers), launched the career of the O'Jays, Teddy Pendergrass, Lou Rawls and the Spinners. While carrying on his fantasy lifestyle of a bona fide City of Brotherly Love soul man (and allegedly carrying on an affair with one of the Three Degrees) Bowie did not neglect paying real respect to the black music he loved where it counted. For the new album Bowie would put together his own version of a crack Philly soul backing band – Mother Father Sister Bowie, if you will. 'Bowie knew that the easiest way to change your sound was to change your musicians,' Alomar explains to me.

Shy, somewhat effeminate and overweight, Luther Vandross became a key to this new sound. He would, inside of five years, transform into a superstar in his own right, largely due to Bowie's encouragement of his songwriting skills and his one-of-a-kind voice (which he could use to project like a gospel preacher or seduce like the most improbably on-point loverman who ever lived). In late '74, however, Vandross was merely Alomar's old high school classmate, a Diana Ross-worshipping misfit come down to Sigma Sound from New York City to kill an afternoon. Vandross was familiar with 'Space Oddity' and knew who Bowie was but did not even know the correct way to pronounce his name. Bowie was lurking around while Alomar played the version of 'Young Americans' that the band was working up. Vandross instantly responded

411

to the song but felt it needed something and suggested the song's signature backing vocals on the spot. At that very moment Bowie, given to lurking and eavesdropping in such situations, as he had with Tony Visconti upon their first meeting in 1967 at Essex Publishing's offices, walked in. Rather than taking offense, Bowie declared that he loved the idea, and everyone grabbed their instrument, intent on giving this new take a workout. When the jam was over, Bowie enthusiastically picked Vandross's brain for more such ideas and, after some bashful deliberation on Vandross's part, got him to share a song the younger singer had written called 'Funky Music (Is a Part of Me).' This track, more down and dirty than 'Young Americans,' would also be worked up with the Sigma band and appears on the *Young Americans* album retitled 'Fascination.'

'It was the first time that I ever had someone of his stature be encouraging,' Vandross recalled. '[Bowie] was constantly telling me, "You've got to stick with this. You're going to make it. Trust me, you've got what it takes."' Bruce Springsteen, then like Bowie making a transition from cult hero to superstar with *Born to Run*, was another in-studio visitor (he and Bowie discussed UFOs). By the time the tour resumed in late summer, Vandross was both an official backing vocalist and a sometime support act, which made him the unwitting scapegoat for those who were perplexed and even angered by Bowie's new direction. Such fans were legion at first. 'David Bowie was the end-all for me. It was because of him that I wanted to be a stage performer,' says Cherie Currie, then lead singer of teenage proto-punks the Runaways, who was also in the audience at those second-leg opening dates at the Universal Amphitheater. 'But I was disappointed that he was in his zoot suit and didn't have the Bowie haircut out.'

Bowie in this period could still be described as dangerously enthused in a way that brought Terry Burns's Beat-era mania to mind. He simply had no off switch mechanism, by design. Projects were brought up, sketched out and then either abandoned altogether or put on the back burner indefinitely. While on tour, Bowie would turn his hotel suites into mini film sets, using his high-tech video equipment to make short film demos, building sets out of materials he sent out for and constructing elaborately drawn backdrops. David would shoot separate videos of himself later, then have them edited by some tech-savvy MainMan employee at great expense, so that, in the final edit, he would essentially appear to be walking throughout the city as though he was marooned in some nightmarish Sid and Marty Krofft dimension. These videotapes never make it into the many museum retrospectives of Bowie's video work, but there is a pair of documents that clearly demonstrate where Bowie's psyche was at during this period.

Alan Yentob, producer of the 1975 BBC Bowie documentary *Cracked Actor*, had been to the Ziggy

413

retirement concert at the Hammersmith Odeon in 1973 and had remained fascinated by Bowie's pursuit of masks and personas. 'I loved the idea of a guy that was acting out rather than a pop star,' Yentob explains. 'I was intrigued by his art school origins. I called it *Cracked Actor* [named after the *Aladdin Sane* track; it was nearly titled *The Collector*] because I saw that he was trying out different personas. I also thought that he was so much in tune with a generation who was not sure about what they were after either. It could be a culture study too. To that extent I found him rather attractive. I was slightly wary about films about rock 'n' roll stars, but to me it was an interesting canvas. If I could get the access.' Yentob approached Bowie and Defries and was surprised to find them willing to grant him as much access as he required, starting with the Los Angeles tour dates. The only condition was that Yentob and his two cameramen would never know exactly when they would actually get that access.

Cracked Actor took up much of Yentob's professional and personal life for most of the fall of 1974. When he did capture Bowie, it was often at three or four in the morning, when the star, who was neither eating nor sleeping, decided he was ready to communicate. 'During some of those conversations we had, David was speaking partly in riddle,' Yentob says today. 'He was talking about himself partly in the third person.'

Watching it now, as it's available on imported DVD, one can actually imagine Bowie's hair getting thicker as his head shrinks with malnutrition. He weighed around eighty-five pounds (losing a reported two pounds in sweat each night) and subsisted on cocaine, coffee, Marlboros, red and green peppers and whole milk from the carton. 'There's something in them that my system needed,' he later said of the drugs, dairy and veg diet. The film's most famous scenes concern Yentob and his camera man driving through L.A. and the Arizona desert in Bowie's limousine, while the latter is at intervals silent with chilling coke paranoia or rambling mysteriously.

'I was always pursuing the idea of David journeying around America searching for an identity,' Yentob says, 'having dumped Ziggy and the [first incarnation of] the Diamond Dogs tour to become a soul singer. The thread of that narrative was picked up in our conversation. I ask him about him being in America and he talks about feeling like a fly in milk.'

'There's a fly floating around in my milk,' Bowie says during this scene. At first it seems like he's announcing it to nobody in particular, but then it becomes clear that this is his answer to Yentob's question about how he feels being in America. 'He's a foreign body – and he's getting a lot of milk; that's how I feel. A foreign body.'

'I knew what was going on, that he was obviously not eating. He was emaciated. Clearly taking drugs,' Yentob says. 'But I was quite outside it. The relationship was a professional one. Later we became friends.' Yentob would film Bowie at various points in his career, including 1978 and 1997, once he recovered from his cocaine addiction. 'He was much less self-conscious,' he says. 'It was just music and he was a grown-up and he wasn't experimenting with role playing. Basically he'd gotten through that. He'd sort of grown up.'

Cracked Actor stands as proof that at one point, Bowie believed in it all entirely too much; there at 4 AM, with him patiently demonstrating his cut-and-paste lyric-writing method or submitting to a life mask casting backstage, it all seems so grave. Bowie is only twenty-seven but he's already speaking of his life and work with a sense of morbid summation.

'If I've been at all responsible for people finding more characters in themselves than they've ever thought they had, then I'm pleased, because that's something I feel very strongly about, that one isn't totally what one has been conditioned to think one is,' he tells Yentob. 'There are many facets of the personality that many of us have trouble finding and some of us do find. I'm very happy with Ziggy. I think he was a very successful character and I think I played him very well, but I'm glad I'm me now. I'm glad I'm me now.' He delivers the line with a self-deprecating laugh, as if to indicate that he is aware that all is not well, that 'me' is one extremely messed-up cat.

The film also captures just how far beyond his own fans Bowie already is. While 'Oh! You Pretty

Things' plays on the soundtrack, Yentob interviews a bunch of still-glittering fans in the amphitheater as they ramble about space commanders and cadets. 'It's almost like they got the wrong invite,' Yentob says. 'They couldn't quite keep up with him. They were more confused even than he was. Baffled and confused. It's one of my favorite sequences in the film.'

The film was not broadcast in America, but U.S. viewing audiences would get a taste of mad Bowie soon enough with his appearance on Dick Cavett's late-night ABC talk show, shot in New York City and broadcast shortly after the Philly Dogs tour ended, on December 5. Cavett's bone-dry Yalie wit had enjoyed an unlikely chemistry with wild, loose rock star guests like Jimi Hendrix, Janis Joplin and the Rolling Stones. He'd played host to a drugged-up and barely lucid Sly Stone, but nothing compares to Bowie's appearance.

The segment begins with Cavett, dressed in a cream suit and green wide-collared shirt, introducing Bowie with a disclaimer. 'As soon as a critic tries to say what he is, he changes like a chameleon . . .' The camera then cuts to a series of out-of-sequence album cover shots: *Space Oddity*, then *Aladdin Sane*, then *Hunky Dory*, then *Pin Ups*, then *Diamond Dogs*, each one eliciting squeals from the studio audience, clearly full of Bowie fans.

'This is David Bowie,' Cavett informs the home audience. 'This is David Bowie . . . by the same token, this is also David Bowie . . .' A more recent, coked-out soul boy promo shot is shown. 'If all of these are true, can this also be David Bowie? He burst on the scene a few years ago in a dazzling explosion of bizarre costumes, makeup and glitter in an opus called *Ziggy Stardust and the Spiders from Mars*,' Cavett tells the audience. It's clear he's been prepped and is not reading off cards. 'If the audience will hold for just a minute, I'm explaining this for all the square johns at home,' he quips. 'He's the only one I know who has appeared the same year on the best-dressed man's *and* the worst-dressed woman's list . . . Someone's idea of a joke. Rumors and questions have arisen about Dave, such as who is he, what is he, where did he come from? Is he a creature of a foreign power? Is he a creep? Is he dangerous? Is he smart? Dumb? Nice to his parents? Real? A put-on? Crazy? Sane? Man? Woman? Robot? What is this? His fans have seen him do almost everything but sit and talk. Which they will see tonight. It will be a first for them. In this concert there's still another David Bowie. Ladies and gentlemen, David Bowie.'

The band kicks into the '1984' wah-wah pedal-driven riff and Bowie, wearing his Puerto Rican suit with a wallet chain and a short tie with white shoes, his orange hair swept up, slinks out and sings.

After the commercial, Bowie is seated. He wipes the sweat off his skull and taps a walking cane on the floor. Cavett welcomes him like the perfect host he was. Bowie utters a clipped, polite 'Thank you,' but still seems ill at ease. 'You've got a lot of explaining to do,' Cavett then says cheerfully in a mock Cockney accent. Bowie looks genuinely worried. 'You don't have the trappings you've had in the past,' Cavett observes.

Bowie responds with a gigantic snort. It's the loudest snort in the history of broadcast television. 'He was very wired, I would say,' Cavett tells me today. 'That would be my amateur diagnosis. Either that or a severe sinus problem.'

Bowie is clearly thinking too long and too seriously about Cavett's softball questions. He seems at first earnest and then stuck. Slowly Cavett begins to sink along with him, making one valiant attempt after another, to the point of making the audience uncomfortable, to ease his guest. 'I wasn't comfortable but I know how to look like I am,' Cavett says now. 'I feel like if I go lower rather than higher in intensity with somebody who's having trouble talking – or trouble breathing – that it works best and makes it look less like an emergency.' Cavett could have easily turned Bowie's lack of finesse into a punch line, but he does indeed take the high road, and his intellectual curiosity seems genuine, even as Bowie appears to be distracted by his own cane (with which he seems to be drawing something on the floor). 'There was something immediately likeable about him,' Cavett says. 'Although the cane was distracting. I always like it when guests put their canes down and stop fucking around with them.'

Cavett gamely asks him about flying ('It scares me'), his parents (father deceased; he and mother have 'an understanding') and 'black noise,' which Bowie explains is a sound so powerful it can destroy buildings. 'A big one could destroy a city,' he says. Apparently the patent for the city-destroying device is for sale somewhere in France, he adds. Cavett nods politely. 'I was drowning,' he says. 'I had a drowning feeling and I thought, 'Well, I'm going to get through this whether he is or not,' and decided to just cast in any direction.'

Cavett finally asks his guest, 'Do you want to be understood?'

'There's absolutely nothing to understand,' Bowie replies. Bowie returns to his element, strapping on his acoustic guitar and leading the band through 'Young Americans.'

'The reaction to him was all over the map,' Cavett says. 'Some people thought he was just fabulous. Others asked, 'Jesus, was he stoned or snortered or what?' Some were puzzled: 'Did he seem all right to you?' You might say the hipper ones knew exactly what was going on. He intrigued people. Hardly anyone was neutral about it. I think that was the point.'

At the start of 1975, Bowie was hobnobbing with major celebrities like Elizabeth Taylor (whom he'd met at a party circa the amphitheater shows) and John Lennon (with whom he and Alomar had written and recorded 'Fame' circa Lennon's 'Lost Weekend' period of estrangement from Yoko). Compared with what these people had, what he could show for his success was paltry: a town house in London and a rented apartment in lower Manhattan. He began to wonder aloud where the money was going. When Bowie was coming up, his needs were all taken care of, and at the time, he literally had nothing to lose. Now that he was an arena-filling attraction on every TV show booker's short list, things didn't seem to be adding up. Maybe it was drug-induced paranoia or maybe he was finally waking up to his own sense of fiscal responsibility, but Bowie began, to Defries's chagrin, asking lots of questions around this time.

'I do remember one afternoon being in the office when Defries had some contracts for David to sign,' Mick Rock says, 'and he said to one of his secretaries, 'Take these to David and don't worry it won't take long, David will sign anything.' I told David about that many years later and he said "Yeah it's true. I would. I had my eyes on the star prize. Nothing else mattered. Of course later on I realized what I'd done."'

On 'Fame,' written during this period, Bowie sings, 'What you need, you have to borrow,' with the same venom that Jimi Hendrix (another signer of a contested contracts with opportunistic managers, among them former Animals bassist Chas Chandler) sang, 'Businessmen they drink my wine,' on his cover of Dylan's 'All Along the

Watchtower.' There's a segment in Tony Zanetta and Henry Edwards's book *Stardust* that best illustrates this odd, cash-poor rock star purgatory. He'd recently sold out a residency at Radio City Music Hall and debuted his new single on national television . . . and Bowie didn't have enough money to go downtown and buy some records. He had to call his office and have Tony Zanetta loan him some petty cash.

'I have no idea what I've got. I don't know what I'm worth,' he told the MainMan executive. 'I don't know who's paying for everything. Where's the money coming from for all these projects?'

Defries figured that Mick Ronson would be the next big star after Bowie. To promote Ronson's 1974 debut *Slaughter on Tenth Avenue*, the company paid for a huge billboard on the Sunset Strip. Despite his good looks and obvious talent, Ronson lacked front man DNA and the album fizzled. 'It just didn't happen,' says Suzi Ronson. 'It was too soon. People said the record sounded too much like David Bowie without David Bowie. It *was* David Bowie without David Bowie. Mick should have been allowed to be given some time to meet other people. The relationship with Bowie after that was nonexistent. Bowie promised he'd come by the studio. Never did. We never spoke with David, never hung out with him that much afterward. He'd had enough of what we had to give him.'

'Mick was a great second banana for Bowie,'

Charles Shaar Murray says. 'He had everything you needed to be a front man except the temperament. Mick did not have the necessary degree of megalomania. He was comfortable riding shotgun, taking care of the musical details.'

Fame, a muted Broadway musical based on the life of Marilyn Monroe (and directed by *Pork's* Tony Ingrassia) also failed. Wayne County's *Wayne at the Trucks* tanked, Dana Gillespie did not make a mark; each one was a money pit, swallowing up cash that might have put the Bowies on the lifestyle level of his new social circle.

'One of the things David probably objected to was there was no money because it'd all been spent on lifestyle,' former Defries partner Laurence Myers says today. 'This happened very often with artists. They loved driving around in the limos, then they get the bill because their contract says they pay for those things. Then they say, "Well, I haven't got any money." Well, you chose to drive around in limos. You're also often surrounded by a hundred different people every day wanting to party. These people, they either want to become your new manager themselves or they just want to be your friend, so what they do is they say to you, "You're wonderful, you're marvelous, you are brilliant and you are a genius and you are not being served. Why haven't you got this? Why haven't you got that?" Sometimes they're right. Sometimes they're wrong. And then, from the artist's point of view, it's "Jagger's got a bigger house than I do," or "I'm fed up with my old guy telling me what to do and running my life." It's like a marriage. And David was doing loads and loads and loads and loads of cocaine. None of which helps.'

Back in New York, work continued on *Young Americans* through January of 1975 at the Power Plant in midtown Manhattan, with Tony Visconti producing. Bowie had already palled around with Lennon in L.A. Given his near constant coke paranoid state, it's amazing that Bowie pursued Lennon so doggedly. The prospect of becoming matey with an actual Beatle clearly outweighed the risk of drawing FBI attention to himself – as it was suspected and is now well known that the agency had been monitoring Lennon closely for most of the first half of the decade. Bowie decided to record a cover version of the Beatles track 'Across the Universe.' He invited Lennon, then also back in New York City, to come to the studio to play on it. During a jam session, Alomar produced a chicken-scratch guitar lick and an orbital riff that recalled the old R & B hit 'Foot Stompin'' melted down into a slow, molten groove. Lennon and Bowie came up with the lyrics on the spot, with Bowie taking lead and the ex-Beatle providing falsetto backing vocals.

'I got to know David through Mick really, although I've met him once before,' Lennon told Mike Douglas during one of his famous guest spots on that other iconic seventies talk show. 'And the next minute he says, "Hello, John, I'm doing 'Across the Universe,' do you wanna come on down?" So I says, "All right," you know, I live here. I pop down and play rhythm. And then he had this lick. The guitarist had a lick and we sort of wrote this song. It was no big deal. It wasn't sitting down to write a song. We made the lick into a song.' Visconti, also a Beatles obsessive, was not at the sessions. 'I would have jumped on the Concorde at my own expense to be there,' he later said. While he mixed the finished songs from the Sigma sessions in London, Bowie, Alomar and Lennon created a pair of last-minute additions with 'Fame' and 'Across the Universe.'

Involving an ex-Beatle at the eleventh hour could be seen as Bowie building up antibodies or fortifying his stock value for what now seemed like an unstoppable clash with Defries. With the help of his new personal assistant Corinne 'Coco' Schwab, a onetime MainMan secretary, Bowie hired a lawyer, Michael Lippman (who declined to be interviewed for this book). On January 29, 1975, Bowie went to the RCA offices with Lippman to let them know of his professional intentions. Bowie was visibly shaken and paranoid during these meetings. He'd recently taken the master tapes for *Young Americans* and secured them in a bank vault so that Defries could not manipulate them in any way. He'd then sent a copy to RCA to make sure if he broke from MainMan they would be loyal to him and not his imperious manager. Bowie relaxed only after RCA executives assured him in person that they would back him and not Defries whatever transpired. A week later, Defries, like Kenneth Pitt before him, received a memo of severance. According to legend, when the furious Defries asked RCA why they sided with Bowie instead of MainMan, Glancey responded, 'Because you can't sing.' Predictably, Defries sent RCA an injunction to prevent them from releasing the album in America, England and France, freezing all Bowie activity. Laurence Myers, Defries's old partner, who was now doing separate business with RCA, was brought in since both parties trusted him.

'Those meetings between Bowie and Defries was like the Vietnam peace settlement,' Laurence Myers says. 'We had Michael and David in one room, and we had Tony in another room, and the middle room was me and RCA.' A settlement was eventually reached, details of which have been widely reported, though the agreement remains confidential. What is believed by most is that Defries would own a piece of David Bowie's recordings from approximately 1972 up until 1982 (but not, crucially, any of his blockbuster 1983 album *Let's Dance* and beyond). The long-delinquent MainMan accounts would be settled by RCA, who insisted on having their own staff auditors make sure the checks were indeed paid out.

Defries would go on to discover John Mellencamp (renaming him Johnny Cougar). He would resurface in the nineties when Bowie was working out a deal to securitize the RCA material as 'Bowie Bonds.' Neither has publicly spoken about the details of the split, although sources have indicated, off the record, that the bad blood has not gone away some thirty-three years on.

'There are the rumors. And the rumors are very, very powerful,' Dave Thompson, Defries's biographer, says. 'That Tony screwed Bowie all the way down the line, and then when they broke up Bowie screwed him back, and then they've had this sort of acrimonious gimme gimme gimme relationship ever since. David has been content to let people believe what they will, and Tony, I don't think, paid any attention to what was being said. So we've had this incredible game of Chinese whispers for the last thirty years about the nature of their relationship, the nature of their contract, the nature of their parting. And I think we're gonna find that *none* of it is basically true.'

With regard to his personal life, David was increasingly replacing both his longtime MainMan retinue as well as Angie with one of the company's secretaries Corinne Schwab. Schwab, who is still Bowie's assistant, is considered by some the bête noire of the Bowie story, a figure so devoted to him, or supposedly void of her own personality, that she gave over her entire life to facilitate whatever it is David needs.

'There is no Coco. There is only David,' Zanetta writes. 'She's the one who does all the dirty work.

427

She is a very, very sad case. The woman does not have her own life. She's his alter ego, his devil in disguise.'

'Coco was definitely a force to be reckoned with,' Carlos Alomar has said. 'She was definitely branded the biggest bitch in the whole world, which she was. But apparently she loved David very much and she was very dedicated to him so I could never fault her for that. She would forsake her own needs to please David.'

'She's laid down her whole life for him,' Natasha Korniloff has said. 'David has only to utter the words 'I'm hungry' and in the middle of nowhere Coco can cook a meal over a candle and put it in front of him. He can be cold, tired, hungry – but put something warm around him, feed him, and he's happy. He just sits there receiving everything and he doesn't really care where it's coming from.'

This perception is fueled by the fact that in four decades, Schwab has not turned to the media to respond to such portrayals and conduct personal damage control, something even former vice president Dick Cheney eventually took pains to do in an effort to allay long-standing whispers about his dark personal character. In a 1993 cover story on David in the UK men's magazine *Arena*, Schwab granted one rare interview to journalist Tony Parsons, but this reads more like a prepared release than an actual tape-running, all-questions-permitted sit-down. 'His singular vision as an artist also incorporates the ability to transform and to give focus to outside ideas. He moves, progresses, changes and grows with every project,' she says, or 'says.' What is certain is that the fastidious and preternaturally disciplined woman provided some sense of order in Bowie's increasingly unhinged day to day existence in 1975.

The petite Schwab is from a highbrow New York family and was already worldly and fluent in multiple languages. This clearly made Bowie feel comfortable and intellectually matched, but it was likely the consistent efficiency with which she handled his affairs without creating distraction or drawing attention to her own issues that brought her to power. Virtually nobody in Bowie's circle could make similar claims, not his lovers and certainly not his managers or even his band and producers. Even better, Coco had developed a series of tricks and psychological devices to keep the ever-increasing list of personae non grata away, a list Angie Bowie had, by 1975, certainly made. 'After four or five years I had really worn out my welcome with David,' Angie says today. 'He didn't like me anymore.' Angie lives with the fact that it was she who recommended hiring Coco in the first place, impressed by her work ethic when she first showed up as a temp in MainMan's London offices. The Bowies' split had been coming for a long time. In her memoir, Angie heartbreakingly writes of tracking David's postfame activities through the press, as well as sending him messages the same way, by being photographed while out and about. With their child in school or in the care of a more or less permanent nanny, and Ava Cherry and Coco occupying the role of female companions, David and Angela were free to carry their estrangement to its furthest ends. Angie continued to try to make headway as an actress and a writer, and even a singer, only to find herself rejected at every turn. 'As David and I broke up he made sure that I was blacklisted in the entire entertainment business,' she claims. 'I felt betrayed. I felt that I would now never be able to work anywhere doing anything. I just kept thinking about my father and how he would have fought this battle. And I fell down a lot.'

'Angie was probably the most affected because she was really different than all those other rock girls,' says Tony Zanetta. 'David wasn't a star when she met him. She wasn't a groupie like a Bianca Jagger. Angie was very much a part of building the success. And she was kind of left hanging. Because what *is* an Angie Bowie? Her identity has totally been Angie Bowie. It's never been Mary Angela Barnett again. She was wacky, but she was a super-intelligent woman and had lots and lots of potential but got stuck. She could never really bring Angie Bowie to another level.'

David Bowie, meanwhile, was further peeling away the artifice of the Ziggy-era. *Young Americans*, released in March, was the first Bowie album in nearly three years to feature David Bowie and not

'Ziggy' on its sleeve, and looking handsome with a retro matinee-idol haircut and smoldering cigarette to boot. It was rumored that Bowie initially approached Norman Rockwell to paint his portrait for the cover. As a musical experiment the album succeeds because it's at heart a symbiosis and not some parasitic venture – not 'Bowie does black music,' but rather 'Bowie and black music do each other.' Unlike Robert Plant on early Led Zeppelin songs, Bowie never resorts to a stereotypically black voice; he is *always* David Bowie. The title track borrows the piano glissando from the Jackson Five's 'I Want You Back,' and Vandross's vocal arrangements are pure church; but Bowie's lyrics are, as they remain throughout the record, angsty and disquieted, the transmissions of an outsider looking in honestly, never an imposter. Black songwriters often addressed their listeners – as Marvin Gaye does on 'What's Going On' or Curtis Mayfield did on '(Don't Worry) If There's a Hell Below We're All Going to Go' – as sisters and brothers. Bowie never assumes an easy brotherhood, and as a result he comes very close to enjoying one. Black listeners accepted this tribute in the right spirit.

Song by song, *Young Americans* is played so enthusiastically that no by-the-hour house band could re-create such sonic buoyancy. The European as soul *fan* and not soul *man* is the liberating ingredient. 'He would always unblock a musician,' Alomar says, 'and allow him his freedom of expression without

431

losing sight of the musicians' effect on the song. As an example, if you played guitar and you had Jimi Hendrix as the guitarist, would you show him what to play or would you give him a general idea of what the song needed and then adjust his performance to fit the song? Bowie always allowed every musician that freedom. He would play a version of a song on piano, guitar, synth, anything he could use to exact the effect he needed. It was glorious.'

Reviews were largely positive as well. Lester Bangs, who had previously singled out 'Time takes a cigarette,' the opening lyric from 'Rock and Roll Suicide,' as the worst ever penned, immediately saw the album as another in a long line of hipster white guys worshipping black culture and put it in smart context. 'Now, as we all know, white hippies and beatniks before them would never have existed had there not been a whole generational subculture with a gnawing yeaning to be nothing less than the downest baddest niggers they could possibly be. And of course it was only exploding plastic inevitable that the profound and undeniably seductive realm of negritude should ultimately penetrate the kingdom of glitter.' In his raw language, Bangs shrewdly points out that in most gay bars, nobody listened to white English glitter rock anyway. 'Everybody knows that faggots don't like music like David Bowie and the Dolls – that's for teenagers and pathophiles. Faggots like musical comedies and soul music. So, it was only natural that Bowie would catch on sooner or later.

After all he's no dummy.' Bangs adds, 'Bowie has just changed his props: last tour it was boxing gloves, skulls and giant hands, this tour it's black folk.' That, in Lester Bangs's terms, amounts to a rave.

Although it was his biggest hit record to date, Bowie opted not to tour in support of *Young Americans*. He made what would be one of his last public appearances for a full year, looking deathly gaunt but elegant in a white tie and wide-lapel tuxedo, to present a Best R & B Female Performance Grammy Award (he addresses the crowd with 'Ladies and gentlemen and *others*' and rambles in both English and French before announcing the nominees) to Aretha Franklin for her rendition of 'Ain't Nothing Like the Real Thing' in the winter of '75. The Queen of Soul responded with the unintentionally hurtful joke, 'Wow, this is so good, I could kiss David Bowie.' Aretha amended, 'I mean that in a beautiful way,' but it reportedly wounded him deeply.

In April of 1975, with New York 'closing in' on him, as he would tell Cameron Crowe the following year, Bowie made arrangements to leave his unofficial second home behind as well. After drifting from Ava Cherry, he had started dating actress and *Playboy* Playmate Claudia Jennings. Jennings, who was killed in a 1979 auto wreck, is the willowy blonde who appears briefly in *The Man Who Fell to Earth*, naked and making out with Bernie Casey after he emerges from a swimming pool (also naked). She also appeared in the Roger Corman cult film *The Great Texas Dynamite Chase* and continues to be a cult figure among B movie enthusiasts. By year's end, Bowie, more popular than ever, became both a genuine movie star and a death- and sleep-defying Babylonian.

While it's an eternal magnet for rained-on English rock stars, there is something eternally foreboding about Los Angeles. I'm not actually sure what the source of it is. I lived there for five years in the early nineties. I cowrote a book about L.A. punk. Worse, I've walked in L.A. after selling my Toyota for drug money (again, early nineties). It is, with apologies to my many friends who do so, 'dubious' to stay there for any length of time, as David Bowie keenly notes in the Cracked Actor *documentary. Hearing a siren on Sunset Boulevard, he blanches and explains to director Alan Yentob that there is 'an underlying unease; you can feel it on every avenue. It's very calm. It's a superficial calm they've developed to underplay the fact that there's a very high pressure here. It's a very big entertainment realm. How dubious a position it is to stay here for any length of time.'*

Los Angeles makes no sense to me. It is of course a major urban center but it doesn't look cavernous and easily, mathematically navigated like New York or Chicago or even San Francisco. There's no grid logic to it. I tried to read City of Quartz *to figure it out but I just got more confused. Plus, there are skunks and coyotes in the shadowy underbrush. In a city! It's too primal. It's a company town, centered above all on the entertainment industry, but it feels neither productive nor constructive to me. People are dying constantly. They overdose in massive plaster or adobe bungalows and on cold marble floors. Others get their thoraxes shot up with automatic weapons as the sickly smell of jasmine penetrates every surface. Violence hangs in the air like exhaust. You could be buying a paper in a clean convenience store, or a cup of coffee in a Winchell's donuts, and suddenly a burst of gunfire shatters the illusion of safety and suburban calm and homeyness like that scene in* **Boogie Nights** *with Don Cheadle's Buck Swope and the bloody bag of money. L.A. is John Holmes and Eddie Nash and Wonderland Avenue. It's the death of Sal Mineo and Peter Ivers and Jack Nance, who played Henry in* **Eraserhead.** *Wheat germ killers. It's the Black Dahlia and Sharon Tate. Nicole Simpson and Bonnie Lee Bakely and Lana Clarkson sacrificed. The chords of 'Californication' by the Red Hot Chili Peppers,* **Forever Changes** *by Love, Neil Young's* **On the Beach** *and 'Pacific Ocean Blues' by Dennis Wilson, just about everything the Doors ever made, the hazy, burbling death rattle that underpins Sly Stone's 'There's a Riot Goin' On,' 'This Town' by the Go-Go's, 'Welcome to the Jungle' by Guns N' Roses and 'Fuck tha Police' by NWA capture it as do 'Los Angeles, I'm Yours' by the Decemberists and most of Jenny Lewis's recorded output. It's that flute solo in 'California Dreamin.' When I think of L.A. in the nineties, when I knew it, I have tremendous respect* *for the people I know, like Brendan Mullen, Pleasant Gehman and John Roecker, who lived through L.A. in the early seventies, when life was surely much, much cheaper. We lost River Phoenix at the Viper Room, but we had no Manson family or SLA. Joan Didion, as she does, reduces this pervasive sense of unease excellently in her collection of essays* The White Album.

It will perhaps suggest the mood of those years if I tell you that during them I could not visit my mother-in-law without averting my eyes from a framed verse of a 'house blessing' which hung in a hallway of her house in West Hartford, Connecticut.

God bless the corners of this house
And be the lintel blest
And bless the hearth and bless the board
And bless each place of rest—
And bless the crystal windowpane that lets
  the starlight in
And bless each door that opens wide, to
  stranger as to kin

This verse had on me the effect of a physical chill, so insistently did it seem the kind of 'ironic' detail the reporters would seize upon, the morning the bodies were found. In my neighborhood in California we did bless the door that opened wide to stranger as to kin. Paul and Tommy Scott Ferguson

436

were the strangers at Ramon Novarro's door, up on Laurel Canyon. Charles Manson was the stranger at Rosemary and Leno LaBianca's door, over in Los Feliz.

Too much money, too many drugs, too many powerful people and far too many disenfranchised angry spumed poor people around them. When I am in L.A. on assignment, and not at the Chateau Marmont or the Sunset Marquis, where the sheer cost of the room is almost enough to make me feel safe, I double-check that the door is locked. The nights in those hills are so dark. Add to that rampant creepiness enough Bolivian marching powder to stroke out a Himalayan yak, and your awareness of the illusion of calm is heightened to levels that almost guarantee prolonged psychic pain.

'There was something horrible permeating the air in LA in those days,' Bowie told Robert Palmer during their Penthouse interview in 1983. 'The stench of Manson and the Sharon Tate murders.'

In Kenneth Anger's 1975 book Hollywood Babylon, *one I've read more than once, he talks about the evil roots of the industry. 'Yet for the vast public out there H-o-l-l-y-w-o-o-d was a magic three syllables invoking the Weirder World of Make Believe. To the faithful it was more than a dream factory where one young hopeful out of a million got a break. It was Dreamland, Somewhere Else; it was the Home of the Heavenly Bodies, the Glamour Galaxy of Hollywood. The fans worshipped, but the fans also could be fickle, and if their elites proved to have feet of clay, they could be cut down without compassion. Off screen a new Star was always waiting to make an entrance.'*

'There's a form of desperation,' Kim Fowley, a lifelong denizen of L.A., says in typically verbose yet ultimately accurate summation. 'Look where we are. A lot of people south of the border think we stole the land. You have a melting pot not by choice but by circumstances. Then there's the pressure cooker of Hollywood. The rats eating each other in the bottles. If you're totally fake and totally materialistic and selfish, you get an erection when you walk into town – "Goddamn, I belong here. This is where I'm destined to be Billy the Kid, Jesse James. I get to be a motherfucker here and they applaud me as I ravage the countryside."'

CHAPTER 18

Upon his arrival in Los Angeles in the spring of 1975, Bowie crashed at the home of fellow British rock star Glenn Hughes. Hughes was then the bassist in Deep Purple, which had enjoyed several hit singles, including 1968's 'Hush.' Their proto-metal album *Machine Head*, and its titanic single 'Smoke on the Water,' released in 1972, the same year as Bowie's *Ziggy Stardust* album, had made them arena-filling stars thanks to *that riff*. Worldwide engagements kept him on the road much of the year, so Hughes was happy to share his mansion just behind the famed Beverly Hills Hotel in Benedict Canyon. When he left Bowie alone, however, he did not realize the extent of his pal's paranoia.

'My house was four homes from the LaBianca house,' Hughes recalls, referencing one of the city's most notorious crime scenes, where Leno and Rosemary LaBianca were randomly slaughtered by the Manson family just two days after the murder of Sharon Tate and her friends. 'And I guess David found out about that. When I came off tour I found all the knives and all the sharp objects under the bed.' Hughes was, at the time, leading a somewhat debauched lifestyle but soon realized his new best friend was taking such decadence to extremes uncommon even for a rich rock 'n' roller. Unlike Hughes, Bowie was not ingesting blow for the fun of it. He remained awash in neurosis and fears and obsessed with using occult magic to attain success and protect himself from demonic forces. A self-induced cocaine psychosis was, addiction aside, maintained in part because it was a mental instability that he could control, unlike the one that he was convinced was still encoded somewhere in his DNA, waiting to unfold and claim him as it had his aunts and half brother. Regardless of the motives, Bowie's laundry list of pathology could fill reams.

'David had a fear of heights and wouldn't go into an elevator,' Hughes recalls. 'He never used to go above the third floor. Ever. If I got him into an elevator, it was frightening. He was paranoid and so I became paranoid. We partied in private.' Fortunately in Los Angeles, anything can be couriered in. Soon Hughes's home became a sort of bunker, and rock stars like Keith Moon, John Lennon, winding down his notorious dissolute 'Lost Weekend,' and cohort Harry Nilsson, used to catching Bowie out and about, stopped seeing him almost completely.

'If you really want to lose all your friends and all of the relationships that you ever held dear, that's the drug to do it with,' Bowie has said. 'Cocaine severs any link you have with another human being. Maintaining is the problem. You retain a superficial hold on reality so that you can get through the things that you know are absolutely necessary for your survival. But when that starts to break up, which inevitably it does – around late 1975 everything was starting to break up. I would work at songs for hours and hours and days and days and then realize that I had done absolutely nothing. I thought I had been working and working but I had only been rewriting the first four bars or something.'

While planning the follow-up to *Young Americans*, Bowie would sit in the house with a pile of high-quality cocaine atop the glass coffee table, a sketch pad and a stack of books. *Psychic Self-Defense* by Dion Fortune was his favorite. Its author describes the book as a 'safeguard for protecting yourself against paranormal malevolence.' *Psychic Self-Defense*'s instructions ('Sever all connections with suspected originators') seem like a paradigm for the isolated and suspicious mode in which Bowie conducted himself during this period, except, of course, for one of Fortune's key tenets: 'Keep away from drugs.' Using this and more arcane books on witchcraft, white magic and its malevolent counterpart, black magic, as rough guides to his own rapidly fragmenting psyche, Bowie began drawing protective pentagrams on every surface.

'It was very speedy coke,' Hughes says. 'David never slept. Never slept. He was in a coke storm.

We would be up three or four days at a time. I'd leave and come back and continue the same conversation we left off.'

'I'd stay up for weeks. Even people like Keith Richards were floored by it,' Bowie would later recall. 'And there were pieces of me all over the floor.'

Hughes increasingly had no idea what Bowie was talking about. 'Do the dead concern themselves with the affairs of the living? Can I change the channels without using the clicker?' Bowie jokes during his episode of VH1's *Storytellers*, taped in 1999 and released to retail a decade later. Other obsessions included an obscure form of photography called Kirlian, which is supposed to capture the aura as well as the flesh.

'He felt inclined to go on very bizarre tangents about Aleister Crowley or the Nazis or numerals a lot,' Hughes says. 'It'd leave me scratching my head. He was completely wired. Maniacally wired. I could not keep up with him. He was on the edge all the time of paranoia, and also going on about things I had no friggin' idea of what he was talking about. He'd go into a rap on it and I wouldn't know what he was talking about; remember, I was pretty loaded. I was thinking about sex and he was thinking about . . . whatever.'

'My other fascination was with the Nazis and their search for the Holy Grail,' Bowie later clarified. 'There was this theory that they had come to England at some point before the war to

Glastonbury to try to find the Holy Grail. It was this Arthurian need, this search for a mythological link with God. But somewhere along the line it was perverted by what I was reading and what I was drawn to. And it was nobody's fault but my own.'

People down on the streets knew Bowie was up in the Hills. Groupies came and went, along with dealers, hustlers and hangers-on. 'I had certainly collected a motley crew of people who would keep turning up at the house. A lot of dealers. Real scum,' he recalled. Strangers at the door. 'Women coming and going,' Hughes says. 'A lot of sex and debauchery going on. We were going for it. My dealer was always at the house. We never ran out of cocaine.'

'I paid with the worst manic depression of my life,' Bowie has said. 'My psyche went through the roof, it just fractured into pieces. I was hallucinating twenty-four hours a day . . . I felt like I'd fallen into the bowels of the earth.'

Occasionally, David would reach out to people from his past who had recently been excommunicated, former MainMan employees like Tony Zanetta and Cherry Vanilla. According to his old Arts Lab cofounder Mary Finnegan, there are reports that he even rang Chimi Rinpoche, his Buddhism instructor. 'When he was having a very rough time in L.A., he apparently phoned Chimi,' says Finnegan. 'He told Chimi he was in deep trouble and asked would he come out and talk to him. Chimi said no. He said, "If you want to talk to me you come to me; I don't go to you.'"

Angie was in London with their son during this time and received several desperate phone calls, some frightening enough for her to book a flight. 'He sounded like he might just as well have been off in the emptiness of some awful cold black hole, out there in the timeless infinity far beyond the reach of warmth and earthly human feeling,' she writes.

Increasingly, Bowie was convinced that there were witches after his semen. They were intent on using it to make a child to sacrifice to the devil – essentially the plot to Sharon Tate's husband Roman Polanski's 1968 supernatural classic *Rosemary's Baby*. Cherry Vanilla, who no longer worked for Bowie but had recently been discussing plans for him to produce an album that might launch her singing career, recalls one such desperate phone call. 'He had been calling me from California saying he was gonna produce a record for me,' she says. 'But he had this whole thing about these black girls who were trying to get him to impregnate them to make a devil baby. He asked me to get him a white witch to take this curse off of him. He was serious, you know. And I actually knew somebody in New York who claimed she was a white witch. She was the only white witch I ever met. So I put him in touch with her. I don't know what ever happened to her. And I don't know if she removed the curse. I guess she did.'

The witch that Vanilla is referring to was a semi-famous Manhattan-based intellectual named Walli Elmlark. Elmlark taught classes in magic at the New York School of Occult Arts and Sciences, then located on Fourteenth Street, just north of Greenwich Village. She wrote a gossip column in then-popular rock magazine *Circus* and had become friendly with Marc Bolan and the late Jimi Hendrix. She'd even recorded a spoken-word album with King Crimson's Robert Fripp (who would later add his distinctive circular guitar sound to Bowie's 'Heroes') and even published a cosmic paperback full of collages, poetry, personal confessions and observations entitled *Rock Raps of the Seventies*. When she was practicing witchcraft, according to *Rock Raps*, she'd wear a 'floor length clingy high necked long sleeved black jersey, and a floor length chiffon over dress that floats around me like a mysterious mist of motion,' adding, 'Usually I am in pants . . . always black and silver.'

'She was known as The White Witch of New York,' says Timothy Green Beckley, a paranormal book publisher and friend of Elmlark's. 'She had a large clientele which came to her for advice on various subjects in their own personal life. She was into personal power. Candle burning. Whenever she did a spell for somebody she always made sure they protected themselves by surrounding themselves with a white aura of protection. She didn't dabble in Satanism or black magic or gris-gris. She

445

was very positive and always worked with the light and with positive vibrations and always sent people in a good direction. A lot of musicians turned to her for spiritual guidance.'

Elmlark had met Bowie once before at a New York City press conference during the first Ziggy Stardust tour. Summoned to Bowie's residence, she quickly and apparently successfully exorcised the pool. Angie, who was living there at the time, noted that it started to bubble and smoke (but then she also insisted that it was only raining outside David's window while the rest of the L.A. sky was clear). Elmlark wrote a series of spells and incantations out for Bowie, in case the demons return for a dip, and remained on call for Bowie as he continued to wrestle with the forces of darkness. 'He took her word as gospel,' Beckley says. Elmlark departed from this plane of existence in 1991.

What might have actually saved David Bowie from the clatter inside his old head is the same thing that had always been there for him when things grew desperate and dark: his uncommonly strong work ethic and creative discipline. While hopelessly addicted to coke, he managed to act in his first major motion picture and was intent on composing the film's score as well. *The Man Who Fell to Earth*, directed by Nicholas Roeg (who'd already created a pair of seventies classics in *Performance* and *Don't Look Now*), is perhaps not a classic seventies film in the sense of being revolutionary and bold, but it is certainly classically seventies, as it's based on an obscure literary property (a novel by science fiction writer Walter Tevis), it's an indictment of corporate greed (in this case the media giant World Com), has scads of gratuitous nudity and boasts the participation of seventies icons Buck Henry and Candy Clark. It's also, like the blunter end of seventies 'classics,' rife with ham-bone symbolism (footage of sheep being led off to the slaughter). 'Although Roeg and his screenwriter, Paul Mayersberg, pack in layers of tragic political allegory, none of the layers is very strong, or even very clear,' legendary critic Pauline Kael wrote of the film. 'The plot, about big-business machinations, is so un-involving that one watches Bowie traipsing around looking like Katharine Hepburn in her transvestite role in *Sylvia Scarlett* and either tunes out or allows the film, with its perverse pathos, to become a sci-fi framework for a sex-role-confusion fantasy. The wilted stranger can be said to represent everyone who feels misunderstood, everyone who feels sexually immature or 'different,' everyone who has lost his way, and so the film is a gigantic launching pad for anything that viewers want to drift to.' Kael really nails the lasting appeal of the film in that last bit, not to mention the lasting appeal of the David Bowie myth itself.

Performance had starred Mick Jagger as doomed rock star Turner, and Bowie's competitive edge, one he maintained with the Stones singer through much of his career, certainly helped motivate him to keep his head long enough to out-Roeg his rival. Roeg originally thought of Peter O'Toole and the author and director the late Michael Crichton (*Westworld, Jurassic Park*) for the role of Newton, the alien who travels to Earth in an effort to transport water to his wife and family on their dry, dying planet. After seeing the BBC documentary *Cracked Actor*, he was convinced that Bowie was the ideal Newton. Roeg heard rumors about Bowie's drug addiction but did not make it an issue, and for much of the shoot, away from his dealers and hangers-on in the mountains of New Mexico, Bowie was clean and professional.

'I decided to not do anything or say anything [about it],' Roeg says. 'To try to adopt a manner that if anything happened, it would shock me. You can't reason someone out of anything. The one thing you can try to do is make them conceal it more, give them a sense of love. I'm not into the guilt thing or trying to cure anybody of our humanity. Especially in a societal way, everybody has a sense of shame, guilt, secret happiness, accusation or praise. There are certain things I wouldn't want to know about someone anyway, even those nearest and dearest. And I wouldn't want them to know certain things about me. It all goes back to this idea of exposing yourself. You have to live with yourself first.'

Roeg and Bowie drew as much as they could from the actor's real life to bring Newton into focus. His real-life bodyguard Tony Mascia, for example, plays Newton's bodyguard. The limousine in which

Newton cruises through the burnt-orange desert is the same limo from *Cracked Actor*. Each detail fed the kind of 'He's just playing himself' critiques that would later be used to dismiss Madonna in her 1985 debut *Desperately Seeking Susan* and Eminem in his film debut *8 Mile*. This downplays the actual work, which both Candy Clark and Roeg attest to.

'What was really neat about Bowie was that he always wanted to run dialogue and rehearse, which I attribute to him being a musician,' Clark said of the rehearsal period. 'We wanted to get it right and Nic wanted it word for word. So that was our challenge.'

'There were certain people who were concerned about his unconventionality as an actor, wondering if he was being used as some sort of gimmick,' Roeg says.

In the film, Newton crash-lands in a New Mexican lake in a town called Haneyville. He climbs down a mountain with a hood over his head and makes some fast cash at a junk shop. Somehow he has a British passport. He fixes his hair a lot. He meets Buck Henry's Mr Farnsworth and registers nine basic patents, netting him three-hundred million dollars in three years' time. Then he plans to harness the Earth's water and beam it home to his arid (and yet somehow very milky) planet on a blue laser beam.

Hiding out (under the alias Mr Sussex) in a chintzy New Mexican hotel, he meets Clark's Mary-Lou, a boozy housekeeper, after collapsing in an elevator. Mary-Lou carries him to her room and nurses him back to health. Their courtship is played out with equal parts rom-com sweetness and pitch-black wit. 'What do you do for a living?' Mary-Lou asks him. 'Oh, just visiting,' he replies. She is as much a misfit as he is; both of them are now headed nowhere.

As their relationship progresses, Newton tempts fate by revealing his genitalia-free, yellow-eyed, frog-like true self to Mary-Lou. They try to make love regardless but she pisses herself and flees to the kitchen in tears. 'It's that thing about always wanting to know more about your partner, or hear them promise things in a natural way,' Roeg says. 'So all that was already a part of Candy's natural being. Just in her human structure, she'd understand that pleading – for someone to tell her everything about themselves, especially if she's a wife. But I suppose that scene shows that you don't want to delve too deeply into someone. There's a terrible tragedy to that in terms of human relationships and exposing yourself. Rather than 'Who are you?' it's more a question of who someone *isn't*. And Bowie was quite marvelous at that.'

Despite the fact that Roeg and the actress were then an item, the British director filmed sex scenes between Bowie and Clark that are both jarring in length and explicit in nature. 'I think he kinda liked it!' Clark recalled. 'He got a kick out of it. English people can be very kinky.'

Newton's plan goes to hell after a sexed-up college

professor turned World Com executive (played by another great seventies movie touch-stone, Rip Tom) rolls over on him and the government intervenes. Newton is set to board his spaceship and head home. Only the ship is a trap. Newton is prodded and poked in dozens of medical exams but ultimately thrown away. He's left rich, perpetually drunk and beautiful as everyone else around him ages, so it's hard to feel too bad for him. He records an album for his wife, saying with a shrug, 'She'll hear it one day. On the radio.' It's clear he will spend the rest of his life dissolute and sloppy. The last line of the film, after he spills another cocktail, is 'I think maybe Mr Newton has had enough, don't you?' 'I think maybe he has,' Torn agrees. Like the bodyguard and the limo, this conclusion was true to Bowie's actual life as well.

Bowie was sensing he'd indeed had more than enough by the end of filming, but upon returning from New Mexico to L.A. on the Super Chief train, he immediately fell back into his manic habits.

When he was hired to play Newton, Bowie assumed he would be working on the film's soundtrack, only to be told that the soundtrack would be provided by John Phillips, late of the Mamas and the Papas. His assumption, incorrect as it was, placed him back in the mind-set of song-writing, and soon time, and lots of it, was booked at the then brand-new Cherokee Studios in Hollywood. Built on the site of the old MGM Studios, the five-room recording center was conceived by its owners as an alternative studio with top-of-the-line equipment and perfect acoustics but a funky, homey vibe, complete with incense and Christmas lights in the communal lounge area. At the time, most studios still resembled clinics.

'There was no drinking, no smoking allowed at these places. When we opened, we stocked a bar with everything. We wanted it to be a musician's musician's studio,' Bruce Robb, a co-owner of Cherokee Studios, says. 'But if you woke up at four A.M, couldn't sleep, you could say, 'Oh, I know, I'll go to the studio.' It was like having the greatest exclusive club in L.A.'

Both Keith Moon and Ricky Nelson were working on their own albums when Bowie showed up with his producing engineer Harry Maslin shortly after returning from New Mexico, surveyed the scene, listened to his voice reverberate around the room and announced that he would be recording the follow-up to *Young Americans* there. He and Alomar moved their newly assembled band – bassist George Murray and drummers Dennis Davis and Andy Newmark – into the studio's 'big' room and rarely ever left. At one point, Bowie moved a bed in. Recording was 'round the clock. Time did not exist. The big room had no clocks and no windows. 'I'd come in the following day and they were all still working from the night before. I'd leave and they were still working,' Robb says.

If another artist was booked, say, Rod Stewart, who was also recording at Cherokee around this time, they would simply break down their gear, set it up again in a new room and continue pursuing Bowie's latest sound: another inspired hybrid of Philly soul, Detroit funk and the mechanized, 'motorik' industrial sounds of his favorite new German bands Neu! and Kraftwerk, who purported to be robots in the same emotion-checking way that Ziggy Stardust did with his extraterrestrial conceit. 'He was very driven by the feel and the friction,' Robb says. 'The record took on a life of its own after a while. He did this because he had to. You could see the burning desire as the album would go on. Rod used to party a lot. David was fairly serious.'

There were other serendipitous influences. One day Frank Sinatra's people showed up to check the place out. Sinatra was looking to begin recording his post-retirement comeback album (released in 1980 as the triple album *Trilogy*) and had heard about Cherokee. At first the notion of Sinatra's arrival was intimidating.

'They told us, "Don't speak to him unless he speaks to you. Only call him Mr Sinatra,"' Robb says. '"Don't ask him if he needs a mic check. He'll just walk in and do what he pleases when he pleases."' When the great man actually arrived, he was as friendly and sociable as possible, entertaining Bowie, his band and the Cherokee staff with road stories and gossip.

'They became great friends,' Robb says of Bowie and Sinatra, 'hanging out in the lounge. David sang harmony on one of Sinatra's tracks, and Sinatra listened to a version of Bowie's "Wild Is the Wind."' Based on Sinatra's enthusiasm for the track, Bowie was inspired to include what might have seemed an odd choice (a middle-of-the-road ballad sung unironically amid mutant Euro-funk and lyrics about blow and the occult) as the record's closing track.

'David would call up and ask, "Is Frank in yet?"' Robb says. As soon as Sinatra arrived, Bowie would emerge from his studio and greet him. 'David Bowie was David Bowie all the time,' Robb says, nothing that the studio where the album was primarily recorded was protected twenty-four hours a day by an array of candles, symbols and burning incense. 'Some cats have this persona like "This is who I am but outside of that I like to play golf." Sure, he did drugs. And he drank good wine . . . but it kept him in a head space he needed to make the record. It's like an actor losing eighty pounds or gaining a hundred pounds for a role. It destroys them physically but that's what it took. With Bowie, the proof is in the product. It's an incredible work of art.'

True enough, *Station to Station* is another gigantic creative leap forward, as much as *Hunky Dory* was only five years earlier. It's modern enough, with its crisp, precise playing and angsty atmospherics, to be considered the first real New Wave record. It's clear from the title track, ten minutes of gloriously self-conscious coke-crash despair, that Bowie is rewriting the rules. *Station to Station* opens with a chugging train (culled from a sound effects record). There are two full minutes of minimalist piano, a pair of notes any child could play. Next, a deep funk bass, and finally heavy but cleanly strummed angular guitar chords and what sounds like the shake of a rattlesnake's tail (a nod, perhaps, to his recent stay in the New Mexican desert, or perhaps more evidence of coiled coke snakes in his brain). With Bowie's vocals, which don't drop in until about three and a half minutes, the length of most rock songs, his latest incarnation, the Thin White Duke, is introduced. The Duke is a party-crashing Nosferatu, 'throwing darts in lovers' eyes.' It's both thrilling and a colossal bummer ('Once there were mountains on mountains / And once there were sunbirds to soar with / And once I could never be down'). Two years year before Johnny Rotten would scream 'No future' on 'God Save the Queen,' Bowie informs us that it's 'too late' to be faithful, hateful or anything at all; whereas Rotten will scream, Bowie croons his nihilism, too cool or weary and louche to rage at anything or anyone. 'Word on a Wing' is clearly crooned by the Duke as well; it's the same voice, but with dread swapped for introspection ('Don't have to question everything in heaven or hell') and a suite swapped for a warmer melody that's elegant and simple. 'Stay' is urban funk sped up for against-the-wall fucking, as opposed to the horizontal quiet storms of *Young Americans*. That's not to say that romance is dead here. Has Bowie written a more romantic song than 'Golden Years,' the album's hit single (which reached the Top 5 in both England and America)? *Station to Station* is never really credited as such, but in actuality it's an album of love songs, the kind you write when you have no love in your own life, perhaps (or when your girlfriend is swallowed up by the TV set, if 'TVC 15' is considered), but perfect for a coming wave of modern angst in my pants pop.

Before the album hit shops in January of 1976, Bowie debuted 'Golden Years' on the Saturday morning R & B dance show *Soul Train*. As canny promotional appearances go, it's a bit awkward. The dancers, mostly African American, are shaking it, literally oblivious to the sickly white guy with the orange hair standing in their midst. Nobody looks up at him at all, almost as if they've been gently instructed not to. Bowie himself appears as if he's about to fall asleep standing up. He comes to just as it's time to (badly) lip-synch the vocals (even the hand claps are off). Pete Doherty and Amy Winehouse have never looked this wasted. Bowie's cheekbones are caving in like wet cardboard. His yellow shirt and blue suit look two sizes too big. When he sings, 'Doing alright but you gotta get smart,' he points to his brain. They should show it to people in rehab. Three weeks later he appeared on Cher's post-Sonny and Cher variety show to sing a medley. I don't even know what to say about this one, except it goes on for forty-five minutes and encompasses every song that was ever written between 1965 and 1975 except perhaps 'Spiders and Snakes' by Jim Stafford. Intent on making *Station to Station* a hit, he would debut 'Stay' on a third show, the Dinah Shore show with Henry Winkler, before the year was out. In England, Bowie appeared via satellite from 'beautiful downtown Burbank' on the popular talk show *Russell Harty Plus*. Harty, who affected a perpetual air of campy suspicion, had interviewed Bowie in 1973 during the apex of Ziggy Stardust's popularity and takes pains to remind Bowie that he might be out of touch with England's kids and their taste in pop. Bowie, with his yellow-and-orange-streaked hair slicked back, smokes thick Gitanes cigarettes, drinks Tree Top apple juice from a glass and seems equally unimpressed with the entire affair. Watching it now (the entire interview is archived on You Tube), it seems a 'Dueling Brandos' of icy queeniness.

'I'm coming back to England in May to play shows . . . to you, at you,' Bowie informs Harty. 'Look at England. Be there. Be English. As always but English in England.'

'Your accent is not changed, but you've been away for two years,' Harty says. 'Does that mean you've been locked away somewhere?'

'Yes. I don't talk to anybody,' Bowie answers. Given his behavior in Los Angeles, the exchange is played off as a laugh but remains, of course, painfully accurate.

'But do people talk to you?' Harty asks.

'I've heard it rumored.'

Harty wonders what image Bowie plans to use to recapture the public imagination, warning him that a band called the Bay City Rollers might have stolen his fans away.

'The image I may adopt may well be me. I'm sort of inventing me at the moment.'

'You mean 'reinventing me'?' Harty wonders.

'I'm self-invented.'

'From the waist upwards?'

'It's jolly uncomfortable,' Bowie quips, and rolls his mismatched eyes. He could easily be talking about the entire interview.

Like the Diamond Dogs tour, Bowie would play arenas in both America and Europe. He and the band decamped to Jamaica but found themselves without lodging. Bowie's lawyer-turned-manager Michael Lippman was reportedly blamed for this logistical glitch and soon he was an ex-manager as well, marking a long period of Bowie's affairs being run almost exclusively by himself and Schwab. Rehearsals concluded in New York City, and the tour opened, as was Bowie's way, in Canada, at the Pacific Coliseum in Vancouver in early February.

The first thing audiences saw as they took their seats in the arena was Salvador Dalf and Luis Buñuel's sixteen-minute-long surrealist short film

Un Chien Andalou, immortalized by the Pixies' 'Debaser' and famous among film students and art-damaged types for its signature image – an eyeball (actually bovine) being sliced vertically and bleeding jelly. 'Geiger Counter,' from Kraftwerk's latest, *Radio Activity,* was the pre-show sound-track, suggesting Cold War edginess to thousands of stoned rock fans looking for two hours of escapism.

Then a harsh white spotlight and Bowie, his hair again slicked back, walked down the stairs in a black vest, white shirt and black pants, crooning, in a more deadpan register, 'The return of the Thin White Duke, throwing darts in lovers' eyes,' as if he was ruining some mass wedding ceremony by announcing the punch is toxic. Despite the austerity, uncommon to nearly all arena rock spectacles of the day, the White Light tour, as it came to be known, was another commercial and artistic success. Critics praised the minimalism.

'In its own way *Station to Station* was quite styl-ized too,' journalist Chris Charlesworth says. 'Albeit quite different from *Diamond Dogs.* I really liked the white lights effect and the black suit; he looked unbelievably cool with his Gitanes. Just because it was black and white doesn't mean it was a bare minimum. It was another staging idea at a time when staging ideas weren't common in rock. Everybody else was bare minimum with nothing but amps and drums onstage.'

When the tour hit Detroits Olympia Stadium in

March of '76, Madonna was in the audience, certainly taking mental notes about how to keep your fans and critics guessing. A lifelong student and fan, she would induct Bowie into the Rock 'n' Roll Hall of Fame twenty years later in 1996.

Iggy Pop resurfaced again once the White Light tour rolled back into Los Angeles. Since being dropped from MainMan, Iggy had sunk even further. He was arrested for shoplifting, sleeping in a garage, and trying to write songs with James Williamson but mostly in a drug haze.

'Iggy was in such bad odor with the rest of L.A. that most of the dealers refused to let him into their apartments,' Nick Kent writes in his classic anthology *The Dark Stuff*. 'He'd made such a mess of his life during the two years he'd been based in L.A. that everyone had him written off as nothing more than a washed up loser. The word was out on him in all the clubs anyway, and it wasn't just confined to the Sunset Strip and Santa Monica Blvd.' Worse, others who had used Bowie's boost to a more profitable end slagged Iggy Pop off publicly.

'Iggy is very stupid,' Lou Reed said. 'Very sweet but very stupid.'

'I think Iggy's the most overrated star ever,' former Mott the Hoople front man Ian Hunter groaned.

When he began to vomit fluid of unrecognizable origin and indescribable color, and with the police threatening to prosecute him for vagrancy, he finally committed himself to the Neuropsychiatric Institute in L.A. Slowly, he got healthier. While inside, he listened to James Brown's 'Sex Machine' on repeat, boiling up the creative juices. Once Iggy was out of the hospital but broke and too proud (what with drug-demon Iggy at bay), a go-between named Freddie Sessler took it upon himself to call Bowie, who was eager to see his old friend again.

Iggy and David met in David's posh hotel on February 13, 1976. David played Iggy a cassette of a groove he and Alomar had worked up and asked if he might like to record the song and add some lyrics. Iggy was told to pack up a bag and return to the hotel the following morning. David was going to take him on the road. They would try to make another album and help each other become healthy and accountable. 'With Bowie,' Iggy writes in his memoir *I Need More*, 'I didn't feel compelled to go to sleep every time something unpleasant happened.' The slumber, it's implicit, being chemically assisted.

'Bowie lost a brother [to mental illness],' Kim Fowley says. 'Iggy might have been the brother who took the place of the brother that he lost. Sinatra didn't have a brother either. Sinatra's brothers would have been Dean Martin and Sammy Davis Jr.'

Iggy's cultural stock was about to rise as well. When the American leg of the Station to Station tour closed at Madison Square Garden on March 26, Iggy and Bowie went down to a new club

461

called CBGB to see the Ramones. A buzz went through the tiny club. To his surprise the crowd in the tiny, filthy club on the Bowery was thrilled by the notion that Iggy was there. This provided Pop with a much-needed ego boost, given his somewhat downgraded status from influence and major concern to pal and hanger-on with regard to the Bowie universe of the time. The tour was not without its problems though. Bowie and Pop were arrested on marijuana possession charges during a stop in Rochester, resulting in the single most glamorous mug shot in crime history taken during his arraignment and auctioned on eBay in late 2007.

On May 2, Bowie arrived at London's Victoria Station, returning to perform a scheduled six sold-out concerts at Wembley Pool. With fans waiting and cheering (Gary Numan among them) after the show, he got into a Mercedes Landau limousine and then apparently gave the kids a Nazi salute. Caught on film. Six days later the *NME* ran the photo with the caption 'Heil and Farewell,' and Bowie had a bit of explaining to do.

Unfortunately, he was happy to explain. In a *Playboy* interview with Cameron Crowe, Bowie said, 'I believe very strongly in fascism. The only way we can speed up the sort of liberalism that's hanging foul in the air at the moment is to speed up the progress of a right-wing totally dictatorial tyranny and get it over as fast as possible . . . Television is the most successful fascist, needless to say. Rock stars are fascists too. Adolf Hitler was one of the first rock stars . . . I think he was quite as good as Jagger.' Bowie is certainly not a racist, having a live-in lover in African American Ava Cherry, and he would later of course marry Iman, the Somalian supermodel. Nor is he an anti-Semite, considering that he has a lifelong friend in Lou Reed and spent his teenage years worshipping Beats like Allen Ginsberg and heroes like Bob Dylan. 'It was all just talk,' Carlos Alomar has said. 'You have to remember he's a pseudo intellectual. He is what he reads, and at the time, he was reading so much bullshit.' Regardless, accusers and apologists often overlook the important point that the politics of an artist have little to do with the worthiness of his art. Are Walt Disney's films less enchanting given what has been reported about his beliefs? Is Phil Spector's holiday album *A Christmas Gift for You* any less gorgeous once the weather starts turning chilly? The guy who wrote the piano coda for 'Layla' killed his mother. Does that make the song any less balefully romantic? If anything, the location of his perceived '*seig heil*' was unfortunate. Victoria Station to this day stands as a symbol of England's resilience against the Nazi Blitz. The trains run on time. The girders are in place. It's a triumph of British architecture and industry, and any countryman should be proud of it. The timing was poor as well. Alleged anti-immigration comments made by a drunken Eric Clapton that August during a concert in Birmingham would revive the Victoria Station scandal that summer and lead to the formation of the organization Rock Against Racism, which would find support among the burgeoning punk rock community. The Clash played one of its largest public rallies in 1978 and tweaked Bowie in the lyrics to their punk anthem 'Clash City Rockers': 'Come on and show me say the bells of *old* Bowie.' Still, if his perceived political stance placed him firmly in the past, the music he was making, and would continue to make later in the year, would place him miles away from both his peers and the new breed of punks.

'TVC 15,' a follow-up to the 'Golden Years' single, proved an early New Wave hit, and *Station to Station* remained on the charts through the spring, making Bowie a household name (he made the cover of *People* and was even parodied by Cheech and Chong whose 'Earache My Eye' is credited to 'Alice Bowie'). *The Man Who Fell to Earth*, which was not a commercial success, earned Bowie some plaudits as an actor.

When the Station to Station tour ended, Bowie, Pop, Tony Visconti and Carlos Alomar decamped to France to begin recording Iggy's solo debut, named *The Idiot*, both after the Dostoyevsky novel and as a nod to Iggy's behavior. It's as astonishingly inventive, raw, funny and funky as the *Station to Station* record and is as much of a gateway to Bowie's upcoming 'Berlin trilogy' as that record was as well. 'Funtime,' opening with a bleeding electronic hum, a random cough and someone screaming 'Fun!' seems like a mission statement – a bunch of pros, a little buzzed and shaking off their pain with inspired fucking about in the French countryside. 'Last night I was down in the lab,' Iggy drawls, 'talking with Dracula and his crew.' Whether Drac is Bowie or not, the Château d'Hérouville, where Bowie and Mick Ronson made *Pin Ups*, was certainly a lab. You can hear beeps and humming inventions throughout the track.

'Nightclubbing,' like Iggy's later release 'Lust for Life,' was given a second life two decades on in the film adaptation of the Irvine Welsh novel *Trainspotting*. 'Baby' is a demented lullaby where Iggy comforts his child by telling him all about the 'street of chance,' where the chances are always 'slim or none.' Sleep well, kid. The album marks the first appearance of 'China Girl,' later a massive hit for Bowie in 1983. Iggy's rendition is more or less the same melodically, with pretty Chinese bells ringing throughout. It's evidence of his hidden pop (and not Pop) talents. 'Dum Dum Boys' is an elegy for the Stooges, closing the lid on the band's coffin (until their 2007 reunion album *The Weirdness*, anyway) with a roll call: 'What happened to Zeke? / He's dead on a jones / How about Dave? / OD'd on alcohol / Well, what's Rick doing? / Oh, he's living with his mother . . . James . . . he's gone straight.' Well, not exactly, but Pop and Bowie had certainly gone

465

'straighter' than they'd been. Bowie would reinvent Iggy and Iggy would reenergize Bowie. For the next year, Bowie would record two albums of his own and one more of Iggy's, tour the world as Pop's keyboard player and plan another massive arena tour of his own. Both of them, by the almost immovable logic of rock 'n' roll, should have burned way out by '77 as the Stones were doing with Keith Richards losing himself to heroin and facing jail time in Toronto. They not only inspired each other, they inspired the very punks who were taking potshots at their peers, like Rod Stewart and Robert Plant, daily. Of all the British rock titans, only the Who would survive punk in a similar state of grace. Compare Bowie's after-punk fate to that of Mick Ronson, still given to fringe and sequined glam wear, having spent most of '75 playing arenas as part of Bob Dylan's mighty Rolling Thunder Revue tour. His platinum shag was intact as well. 'Punk came in, and when it came in, it came in with a vengeance,' his widow, Suzi Ronson, recalls. 'A total changing of the guard. Went to Wardour Street one night in '76 or '77. Mick was still wearing glitter stuff and high heels. We were standing there getting our drinks. It was scary as hell. Safety pins everywhere and kids taking the piss: 'Look at 'im in 'is glitter gear.' Pushing us a little bit. 'You're not doing so good now, are you?' We ran down the street in our high-heel platforms terrified of these people coming after us. That was our introduction to punk.

David was very smart, you see. He disappeared. Regrouped and absorbed in order to be able to create again.'

'I probably didn't really realize the weight of punk and what it was doing in Britain,' Bowie has said. His lack of canniness did him favors. The fact the *The Idiot* and *Lust for Life* are both excellent didn't hurt either. When the tour hit the Palladium, even the Sex Pistols came out to see Bowie's pal 'the Godfather.'

'Bowie's affiliation with Iggy gave him a punk pass, yes,' says Tony James, another South London suburbanite, the bass player for Generation X. 'It definitely did. Bowie had produced *Raw Power* when we were in New York Dolls-type bands, long before any of us even thought of being a punk band. He was two or three years ahead of everybody else in terms of spotting Iggy. All of the early punk bands loved Iggy and the Stooges. They were one of the few bands that had that raw sound. Bowie has that sort of godfatherish role for having produced that record.'

'The big thing with punk,' says Siouxsie Sioux, 'was that it was the first time that women were actually involved in music. Bowie especially with all that turning around of gender and role playing, we felt attracted to and felt empowered by that. Rod Stewart and Led Zeppelin were too blokey. Too male and very hetero. They just didn't open it up and raise any question marks. Or raise any possibilities for any other way than just straight down the middle.'

467

'I don't know if he was even that aware of punk brewing,' music writer Simon Reynolds says. 'He was in L.A. and then went straight to Europe pretty much, right? Did the massive self-immersion in European high culture as a kind of inoculation against America/rock/decadence. Whether deliberate strategy or accidental, being out of the UK for 1976 was a great move. He was able to come in early the next year and eclipse punk, in many people's eyes, show it up as very traditional and backward looking.'

The Idiot marks a reversal in the Bowie/Pop relationship. In the early seventies, as Bowie was figuring out his identity (or identities), the Stooges proved a powerful influence. Listening to Iggy's solo debut, it's clear that the American maverick is now taking cues from his English pal.

'The last offering I'd heard from Iggy was the *Metallic KO* live album,' journalist Kris Needs wrote in *Zigzag* magazine in '76, 'recorded when he was still the demented daredevil from Detroit, dodging bottles and getting bashed in the face over high speed, pounding riffing from his Stooges.' The live document of the Stooges at their most depraved (circa late 1973/early '74), *Metallic KO* is one of the most beloved live albums of all time, not simply for the music, which is brutal and profane (especially their cover of 'Louie, Louie') but also for the live audio of an almost terminally unhinged Pop taunting the audience and being pelted in return with eggs and garbage.

'Sometimes Iggy sings just like David, especially when he goes down deep. The backings could be straight off *Low*,' Needs continues, adding, 'This is a very strange album, morbid, obscure and unsettling. Like *Low* it's aimed squarely at the cold, mechanical future. An attempt to recycle the 'Search and Destroy' style on record might have sounded posed and hackneyed in the light of the new wave.' Bowie and Pop clearly found various techniques that worked and inspired them both. They'd often sit together in an available room and read each other's notebooks, pulling out the best bits and fiddling with nearby instruments until a song came together (some of 1977's *Lust for Life* was composed on a ukulele). 'I've always been in the habit of watching my instrumentalists and seeing if they get that gleam in their eye,' Iggy has said. 'If they do, I'm off like a shot to get the tape recorder.' While many credit Bowie with restoring such focus and drive to Iggy, others feel he dismantled the more honest and unruly elements that made the first three Stooges albums so thrilling.

'I must admit that while I can see how important the Iggy albums are,' Reynolds says, 'I don't really enjoy them that much, give or take the odd song. I think it's because Iggy is American through and through, and his authentic artistic being is the wildness of the Stooges. It's "Raw Power" and "I Got a Right." When he does the croon it's like he's been forced to wear a tux and a bow tie. It seems more mannered than Bowie's croon, where the mannered-ness seems authentic and to spring from within. But it could just be something where the grain of his voice and its range doesn't suit the croon style like Bowie's higher voice does. Iggy always seems like he's crooning through a belch.'

Crooning through a belch, by the way, was the last thing Joy Division's Ian Curtis ever heard, as *The Idiot* was still spinning on his turntable when he was found hanged in May of 1980.

CHAPTER 19

In January of 1975 Brian Eno, then twenty-seven, was nearly killed by a taxi while walking in the Maida Vale section of London. While recuperating in the hospital, a friend brought him some records to help pass the time. They were mixed in stereo, and when one of the speakers in his room malfunctioned, he could only hear the hum of the muted strings and not the harp that was the intended lead. Eno could not get up so he had to lay there and make do. After a while, he found himself enjoying it. Brian Peter George St John le Baptiste de la Salle Eno was born on May 15, 1948, in the rural town of Woodbridge to a family of eccentrics. A talented but antisocial child, he created internal worlds, drawing and building models. 'I loved it to the point that my mother would ask me why I never went out to play,' he would tell the author Michael Bracewell. 'The feeling I like is the feeling of making a world of some kind, and that's what I still like, the feeling of being inside this world and wondering what it would be like if everything was like that. Creativity is always a very strong desire to make a world of your own, in some way, and that could very often or very likely result in wanting an alternative to the one you're in.'

There was a military base near Suffolk where Eno heard American rock 'n' roll music, developing an affinity for early doo-wop. His working-class father, a postman, took advantage of a government grant to send Eno to art school. Questioning and precocious with a healthy disrespect for authority, he incurred the wrath of his teachers with his inquiries and would be expelled from one school and censured at another before he was through. Like Bowie, Eno was a compulsive scribbler, keeping a series of diaries (some have been published) in small black notebooks.

In 1967, while at art school (his second) in Winchester, Eno bought the first Velvet Underground album. He thinks he may have been the first person in Britain to own it (although the fact that Bowie had a promotional advance copy trumps this claim). Eno is certainly responsible for the most famous quote about it: 'Only a few thousand people bought that record, but all of them formed a band of their own.'

A father when he was barely out of his teens himself, Eno's prospects seemed bleak: genius or postman. He formed a band called the Maxwell Demon (the name of the Eno-Brian Ferry-Marc Bolan pastiche character in *Velvet Goldmine*), named after James Clark Maxwell, the scientist who first separated hot and cold molecules. Rather than a guitar or bass, Eno played an electronics testing device. It would emit noise to signal that hardware was functioning. Eno discovered it after taking a job in a retail outlet. Onstage, he would wear feather boas, makeup and velvet corsets, a sartorial choice he would bring to his next band. As a founding member, Eno helped Roxy Music delineate itself from the glut of post-Bolan glitter rock and become, like Bowie, one of the seventies' true innovators.

'"Re-make/Re-model" uncannily reminds you of all the rock songs you ever heard,' the NME wrote of the debut's opening track. 'Until you listen for Eno's synthesizer.' 'Editions of You,' off the follow-up, 1973's *For Your Pleasure*, stands as evidence that only Stevie Wonder was Eno's rival as far as expanding the scope of a classic pop track with electronic eccentricity and vision. After parting ways with Roxy (who immediately became more of a slick affair with lead singer Bryan Ferry's super-elegance unrivaled and unchecked by the equally personable and naturally questioning Eno), Eno released a pair of solo records that can be considered straightforward, if typically eccentric, pop, but in the wake of *Here Come the Warm Jets* and *Taking Tiger Mountain (By Strategy)*, he was rapidly tiring of the standard procedures of rock 'n' roll studio recording. *Another Green World* (1975), *Discreet Music* (1975) and *Before and After Science* (1977) are direct results of the above-mentioned car accident. *Another Green World* in particular points the way to the sound Eno, Bowie and longtime producer Tony Visconti would perfect on the three Bowie records they would make together between 1976 and 1979. At their best, these records, *Low*, *'Heroes'* and *Lodger*, as well as much of Eno's solo work, are marked by sturdy and masterfully structured songwriting thrown into the sonic playpen and fiddled with by precocious and gifted children. With Eno, Bowie pursued a stripping away of all learned musicianship and a return to primal, childlike innocence. Unlike many wealthy and world-famous artists, they preserved an urge to ask 'Why not?' and retained a boundless enthusiasm for new toys (in this case, prototypes and rejects from the rapidly advancing synthesizer technology). Each album from both Bowie solo and Eno solo is unique. Eno's rhythm section tends toward the jazzy and noodling (see *Another Green World*'s 'Sky Saw'), whereas Bowie prefers a more smashing and dramatic drum sound and a louder, more danceable bass, but for this period, which was crucial not only to Bowie's career, but to the progression of modern pop, or pop as 'art,' the two men shared a cause. When they'd find themselves losing inspiration, Eno had devices to illuminate their path. Among these, perhaps his most famous, were the Oblique Strategies. These were aphoristic suggestions printed on cards and randomly generated and applied. These instructions ('Honor thy error as a hidden intention') were supposed to subliminally inspire the musicians to create spontaneously and more freely. Bowie adored them.

'I'd got tired of writing in the traditional manner that I was writing in while I was in America,' Bowie recalled in 1978 (while in the midst of his Eno period), 'and coming back to Europe I took a look at what I was writing and the environments I was writing about and decided I had to start writing in terms of trying to find a new musical language for myself to write in. I needed somebody to help with that because I was a bit lost and too subjective about it all.'

Bowie, Visconti and Eno even chucked out the traditional approach to recording an album, even more remarkable given the back-to-back commercial success of both *Young Americans* and *Station to Station*. Given the support that RCA threw behind Bowie during the split with Defries, Bowie might have felt obliged to deliver a third big hit and further solidify his status. Instead, he threw out the model and any schedule and decamped to France to see what would happen. Musicians now do this all the time. A band like Radiohead will routinely bunker for two or three years, recording bits and pieces of ideas from rehearsals or jams or experimentation among its individual members. In 1976, this was unheard of. Artists turned in records in time to be released for holidays and summers. 'The three of us agreed to record with no promise that [the new album] would ever be released,' Visconti wrote of the sessions for Bowie's follow-up to *Station to*

Station. 'David had asked me if I didn't mind wasting a month of my life on this experiment; if it didn't go well, hey, we were in a French château for the month of September and the weather was great.'

Life in the Château was, in its way, a return to the Arts Lab for Bowie, a shift back to art by the eternally metronomic art vs. commerce swing. It was highly glamorous hippie-style living. For the most part, RCA left him alone, a decision they would soon come to regret. Bowie was committed to the process, sensing that it was a key to his future, and so he placed himself far from any shortsighted influences for the time being, knowing full well that they would eventually weigh in. The inevitable scolding he knew he would receive only made the experimentation that much more satisfying.

'One of the reasons that a lot of interesting music appeared then was the more subordinate role taken by company accountants,' guitarist Ricky Gardiner, who lived in the Château and played on these sessions, says of the period. 'We made albums we wanted to make; we experimented. To be an artist necessarily involves raising one's head above the parapet to take whatever follows.'

The Château was wired with an elaborate and clunky bank of synthesizers collected by Bowie and Visconti. Eno would saunter into the main room, pick up a small keyboard and begin pressing buttons. Occasionally he'd ask Visconti what these instruments were meant to do. One, the Event Harmonizer, he was told, 'fucks with the fabric of time.' Eno grinned and loudly declared that they must use it as much as possible. Eno brought some loopy prototype instruments of his own, such as a synth housed in a leather briefcase and manipulated by a joystick. Built by an electronics company called EMS, it was deemed unsuitable for the marketplace but fit perfectly with their symphony of rejected instrumentation.

'Then, as now, technology was on the move, so every recording studio had something new to explore,' Gardiner says. 'Perhaps the difference then was that things were being invented which meant we had no reference points. Now, things are being developed, copied and modeled and used to *re-create* rather than to create.'

The psychic scars of his isolation in Los Angeles had not yet healed, but Bowie instinctively threw himself headlong into this recording, and like his experience filming *The Man Who Fell to Earth*, the immersion in an ambitious creative endeavor eventually delivered him into a safer realm. 'He was pretty much living at the edge of his nervous system, very tense,' Eno observed. 'But as often happens, that translated into a sense of complete abandon in the work. One of the things that happens when you're going through traumatic life situations is your work becomes one of the only places where you can escape and take control.'

Once actual songs like 'Sound and Vision,'

'Breaking Glass' and 'Always Crashing in the Same Car' began to take form, it became clear to all not only that an actual album was being constructed, but that this album would, perhaps more than any other, reflect Bowie's mental struggle. The songs that ended up on the album's first side, for example, are uniformly short (three minutes each) and sung by an artist not looking to mask or poeticize his mental anguish, but rather to scream at them with what amounts to a strange pride, or at least the absence of crippling shame or devious encryption. He, like many of the synths they were using, was a reject, dysfunctional, discarded. Vocally, it amounts to a demented soul record, a future sound that, unlike that of Kraftwerk, makes no attempt to hide the fact that it's assembled by human beings with all their frailties and vulnerabilities. The rhythms of *Low* sometimes emulate factory floors and chemical labs. Drums crash like steam shooting from a vent pipe; the bass burbles lightly like a toxic substance in a glass beaker being purified over a Bunsen burner. The guitars come in cold and impossibly mellow and the misfit synthesizers, especially on the more modal second side, float every empty sonic space like a new pollution. It all shakes and bends like it's being played by hand and not machines but feels riveted together, a modern machine.

'They were doing what few other people were trying to do – which was to create an art within the realm of popular music,' classical composer Philip Glass (who released a symphonic version of the album in 1992) has said. 'I listened to it constantly.'

An entire movement of post-punk bands, including Joy Division, Magazine, Gang of Four and Wire, all fed off *Low*'s odd anti-aggression and unapologetic, almost metaphorical use of synthesized music. Many of these bands were comprised of working-class kids with no money, but in emulation of what they thought Bowie behaved like and how he had come to dress post-Ziggy, they fortified their new movement with an air of art and ennui-damaged café decadence. By day, they walked the same streets and lingered in the same pubs that they always had, but when they sang, they were in Berlin or Warsaw or Prague or Paris, or, in the case of Joy Division (who covered the Velvet Underground's 'Sister Ray'), in the back room at Max's Kansas City off Manhattan's Union Square.

Bowie had used synths before. There's the Stylophone on 'Space Oddity' and Walter Carlos's Moog-ed Beethoven that Ziggy and the Spiders took the stage to. Synths can be heard on *Aladdin Sane*, *Pin Ups* and *Diamond Dogs*, but they had never taken a front seat as they did on *Low*, and they were still viewed with a stigma by many rock purists.

'People had used synths,' Thomas Dolby says, 'as some quirky fellow instruments. And there'd

479

been some pure electronic stuff in the charts like 'Popcorn' and *Switched-On Bach*, but nobody had done serious rock, pop music with electronics. Nobody of his popularity certainly. It was an incredibly powerful time, really. I think that was really the sort of incendiary moment when the whole generation of us started looking to electronics, exploring coming up with a new sound.'

'I also think it's *Low*'s inhibition and repression that Joy Division and others responded to,' Simon Reynolds says. 'The fact that the music, while guitar-based and harsh and aggressive, never rocks out. It's imploded aggression. And that's very British, and particularly very northern British. People do bottle it all up. So Iggy going from 'Loose' to a sound that was very much not-loose resonated for your British.'

When Low was completed and delivered to RCA, the label brass, predictably, had a fit. They could not follow up back-to-back hits with this. Bowie insisted that the record was complete and ready for them to release. RCA, so desperate for sellable summer product, opted to issue a best-of instead, *ChangesOneBowie*, in May. This album stands as one of the most satisfying singles collections ever released, proving just how agile Bowie had become with regard to including at least one perfect radio song on each of his post-Ziggy RCA albums. The Mercury single 'Space Oddity,' bought back by Tony Defries before his departure, opens side one. The label used the stopgap period to try to reason with their immovable star, but soon the Christmas shopping window came and went as well. Low finally hit shops intact in mid-January of 1977. Some critics were as baffled and incensed as RCA was. Charles Shaar Murray gave it more of an indictment than a review in the *NME*.

'I had gotten through a nasty eighteen-month amphetamine addiction,' he says today. 'I recognized in *Low* a depiction, possibly a glamorization, of the kind of speed psychosis. Bowie had a much bigger budget than I did. I recognized it as the psychosis of soft white powder. I thought he was glamorizing the state from which I just clawed myself. I put it to him and he admitted, 'Yeah, that's what it was.' I think *Low* is a fantastic record. I never had any misgivings concerning its artistic merit. But I found it an evil record at the time because of my personal situation. It made what I just rid myself of seem cool again. With a major speed thing beginning to happen among punks at that time, this is a great piece of art but it's seriously not helpful socially.' *Low* certainly did much to make mental illness, chemically induced or otherwise, seem a bit more fashionable, but this is more a triumph of confidence than some prurient and conscious decision to spread such antisocial energy as if it were a dance craze. Bowie made coming apart seem elegant, but *Low*, as self-aware as any dawn-of-the-decade, denim-clad-singer-songwriter affair, gave an often overlooked depth to the act of putting one's fractured self back together. Released just a week after his thirtieth birthday, *Low* would mark the beginning of Bowie's 'mature' period. This, when speaking of rock stars, is of course relative, but *Low*, named the greatest album of the seventies by Pitchfork, provides a well-engineered bridge to elder states-manhood. Like Iggy, Bowie had now become a godfather.

The divided Berlin that David Bowie, Iggy Pop, Tony Visconti and Coco Schwab inhabited in early '77 while recording Pop's second solo album Lust for Life *and Bowie's* 'Heroes,' *the only somewhat more commercially minded follow-up to the heroically uncompromising* Low, *isn't the same unified Berlin now available to visitors. Today, chipped pieces of the Wall are mounted on postcards and flogged in gift shops along Potsdamer Platz. In '77, a careless wanderer could still get shot at by guards at Checkpoint Charlie.*

The Berlin of 2009 is a new bohemia full of art kids, galleries, clubs, squatting punks and Gothic hipster bars. It's not different than the Williamsburg section of Brooklyn. There is a common element, however, to unified Berlin and Cold War Berlin. Both the culture-mall city and the broken, divided city full of addicts, criminals and radicals were kinetic. The movement never stops, and for a mind as electrified as David Bowie's it provided an ideal cerebral clock-work. Visit Berlin for three days and you will remain kinetic for three days, mostly via very short rides on the U2. Even drunks, staggering on foot, don't stand still for too long. Every pedestrian seems to be mounted on tracks.

Berlin was and is the perfect city for a person to escape to, as nobody looks up from their pagers or laptop. Every Berliner is so deep in their own head, starring in their own one-person Spalding Gray meets Synecdoche, New York-*style internal monologue, that it's easy to see how it would be appealing for a superstar like Bowie was in '77. It's a private metropolis, each denizen existing inside their own expressionist cinema show as they go out or go home for the night, but really just . . . go.*

CHAPTER 20

The neighborhood along the Haupstrasse, where Bowie and Iggy settled upon arriving in West Berlin, was a cheap, seedy, down-market-hip Turkish neighborhood. Today, it's a semigentrified, somewhat more expensive, seedy hip Turkish neighborhood. Locating the building that Corinne Schwab rented for them is easy. The number is unchanged, and so is the facade with its cream-colored plaster walls, huge marble-arched doorway, and ornate brown metal door. To the right, there's a red bubble gum vending machine with dirty, smudged glass. To the left, the Lotus tattoo parlor. The foyer, with its mosaic tiles, dark mahogany molding, high ceilings and winding, red-carpeted stairway, is also unchanged.

The building is over one hundred years old. It survived two world wars. There are a lot of stories to tell about it. The misadventures of David Bowie and his best friend Iggy Pop are just two of the life stories that unfolded up those stairs. Bowie and Iggy were able to work and enjoy more peace and privacy here than either of them had ever known. Unlike in L.A., the hustlers and dealers were kept away unless they were summoned, and that summoning only happened on the weekends.

Bowie, as he sings on the title track of '*Heroes*,' drank 'all the time,' weaning himself off cocaine as he sat over a pint of German beer in his proletariat garb: tweed cap, simple shoes or sandals, black leather coat and wool trousers. At the top of the week, they would write and record; the remainder of their days were earmarked for recreation, essentially cutting in half their potential drug intake. Massively influenced and excited by the German expressionism that he'd mined for the White Light tour, a life in Berlin, among the people, seemed a logical next step.

'It was the artistic and cultural gateway of Europe in the twenties and virtually anything important that happened in the arts happened there. I wanted to plug into that instead of L.A. and their seedy magic shops,' he has said.

Exit the old building and one will likely spend some time lingering in the bins in front of the Bucherhalle, a cavernous antique bookstore directly left of the flat. This shop must have added to the appeal of the neighborhood for Bowie, a major bibliophile. Standing under the yellow-and-white-striped awning, thumbing through clothbound copies, one can not only forget that one is an English rock star, but possibly that one even speaks English. Bowie had succeeded, once again, in disappearing. 'Hansa [Studios] was more austere,' says Ricky

Gardiner (who plays on *The Idiot* and came up with the immortal bouncing riff for 'The Passenger') of the studio where *Lust for Life* and '*Heroes*' were created. 'It had larger spaces. It had huge curtains for making different spaces. It had stark lighting. It was probably technically better, but does this make for better music? It depends what music you are after. David was interested in Kraftwerk at the time, so I expect that had a bearing on it. It was handy, new premises, new vibe, new inspiration.'

Iggy Pop recruited Hunt and Tony Sales, then just out of their teens. The Sales brothers had played with Todd Rundgren during his short-lived period as leader of the art rock band Runt and backed Iggy and James Williamson on the cult 'demo' album *Kill City*. The sons of legendary children's television show host Soupy Sales, they were barely out of their teens when they arrived in Berlin. The Sales brothers, Hunt on drums and Tony on bass, would round out, with Gardiner and Bowie (on keyboards), Iggy's touring and recording band. The tracks on *Lust for Life* would take *The Idiot* to a new level. The title track, which kicks off with Hunt Sales's open-tuned drumbeat (inspired by session drummer Shelly Manne's round, swinging percussion on the *Man with the Golden Arm* soundtrack and the 'Peter Gunn Theme'), is of course ubiquitous now thanks to its use in the 1996 film *Trainspotting* and, to a more cloying effect, on the Carnival cruise line commercials.

'When I hear it now on television,' Hunt Sales tells me, 'it's just primal. It gets everything going.' Few tracks in pop history – James Brown's 'Funky Drummer' and Led Zeppelin's 'When the Levee Breaks' among them – are iconic in and of themselves. The first line of 'Constructive Summer,' for example, the opening track on indie heroes the Hold Steady's fourth album, *Stay Positive*, is this: 'Me and my friends are like the drums on "Lust for Life."'

Lust for Life is more carnal than *The Idiot*. In a lot of ways, it's the better record, but it certainly finds its narrator panting after underage girls in knee-high leather boots ('Sixteen') as much as it finds him searching his soul (or maybe the panting is part of the soul-searching).

'Sex, booze, drugs,' Hunt Sales says. 'Berlin was open twenty-four hours a day. Bars, clubs. It had a vibe then. You had all these people within the Wall. That's gotta do something to people's psyche. You know what I mean? Being trapped in this place. I think it found its way into the records.'

'Hansa Studios was an interesting place at the time. The Berlin Wall was still up. Berlin was really something you couldn't pin down at all,' John Cale, who recorded with fellow ex-Velvet Underground member Nico in the city around this time, recalled. 'You'd have to drive through East Germany to get there. Being in West Berlin was very different from what it is now: everyone was nuts, living on the edge. It was a real circus over there. When Brian and I did that Nico concert where she insisted on singing 'Deutschland über Alles' [in October 1974 at the Nationalgalerie], they went nuts. All the young people there were living with the Wall. It was a fiery place to be. There was a lot of distrust near the border, but West Berlin was partying twenty-four/seven.'

Inside Hansa there was always the uneasy sense of being monitored, which might have contributed to the defiant emotionalism of the lyrics Bowie began to write (as well as the vocals he would soon deliver). One day, while staring out at the Wall from the studio's fourth-floor window, Bowie spotted Visconti and his mistress, the singer Antonia Maas, sharing a kiss only a few hundred yards in the distance. He imagined the Communist guards, who stood constantly atop the checkpoint looking down on them, clutching their rifles. Bowie knew a bit about what life was like on the east side of the wall. He and Visconti had crossed the borderline as tourists and were familiar with the radically different way of life on the other side, how everything seemed to have frozen a quarter century before them, the cars, the fashions, the queer old Trabant autos.

As he wrote, Bowie imagined two lovers, one on the East Berlin side, another on the West Berlin side, who must meet quickly and fleetingly, a sort of Cold War Romeo and Juliet. Under constant risk of arrest or death, they dream of being free, swimming together like dolphins (anyone who has been to the area on a hot afternoon can attest that the notion of sleek aquatic mammals gliding under cool waves does not come immediately to mind).

Bowie and Eno, the song's cowriter, agreed that the idea, lyrics and melody were among his strongest ever and quickly began parsing out musical options. What makes 'Heroes' arguably David Bowie's finest song, however, was a product of happenstance. Robert Fripp, the former King Crimson guitarist, knew both Bowie and Eno (he appears on *Another Green World*) and was suggested by the latter. In New York at the time, he flew out to Berlin on short notice, went straight to the studio, was played the melody and immediately began improvising the signature circular riff, which articulates the longing, aching lyrics and Bowie's dramatic, Judy Garland-worthy larynx-straining delivery.

'"Heroes" was a searing, wonderful guitar thing,' recalled Adrian Belew, who would play the riff every night on the subsequent world tour. 'He was so hot, he'd rip your head off. Robert was always able to carve out his own little ideas in guitar playing that are instantly recognizable.' Fripp did three full takes once the riff was down, and after rewinding it for playback, Visconti, at the desk, accidentally played all three at once. 'I casually played three guitar takes together and it had a jaw-dropping effect on all of us,' Visconti writes in his autobiography. 'The constant mutation of the three sounds was entirely complementary and we had the intro of 'Heroes' without doing anything more. It's now instantly recognizable as sound in our collective psyche.'

Using a device developed and perfected on many of Iggy's *Lust for Life* tracks (such as 'Success' and 'Turn Blue'), the backing vocals used for 'Heroes,' on which Eno can be clearly detected, repeat and thereby reinforce the lyrics. 'I . . . I can remember,' Bowie shouts; 'I remember,' Eno and the band echo, doing much to gin up the emotions, and deftly complement the swirling drone of the multi-tracked guitars.

Bowie took time out from the *'Heroes'* album sessions to play keyboards on Iggy's tour in support of *Lust for Life*. Amazingly, tour rehearsals actually marked the first time Bowie ever saw Iggy perform live. Tickets sold quickly, largely because of the rumors that Bowie would be singing as well. Fans clamored to see Bowie play in small theaters and large clubs. When the tour opened in Canada in the summer of '77, many were puzzled. Bowie sang background vocals exclusively and remained seated at his piano bench to the side of the stage for the entire set. The concerts were Iggy show-cases. If Bowie's status as band member was the bait, all were confident the newly healthy Iggy would be the hook. If people could see the man perform live, they would be won over. While many new fans were indeed converted, if one looked at the stage from the lighting rig, with a bird's-eye view, it would have been obvious that Bowie was the draw. The general-admission floors were lopsided: thinned out at the center and packed in front of the keyboardist. Bowie didn't encourage any of this attention, barely glancing at the crowds as he played. His regard for Iggy kept his ego in check. He even deigned to fly from gig to gig when the tour bus was too slow, evidence, if any was needed, of his commitment to his friend's career. 'David was a good band member and he played that role very carefully,' says Ricky Gardiner. 'At no time did he make any attempt to upstage Iggy, which, given the circumstances, may have been tempting.'

Blondie was one of the bands Bowie and Iggy heard about while in New York on the '76 White Light tour. They had just released their debut, which was a hit in Australia but had yet to take hold in America, and Bowie and Iggy chose them as the opening act for Iggy's tour. Within two years, they would be New Wave superstars, and the tour with Iggy and Bowie amounted to their training.

'We did two nights at Max's before we left,' says Blondie drummer Clem Burke, 'and after the second night we all got into an RV with one bed and went up to Canada. Woke up and we were in the dressing room. David and Iggy come in: "Hi, it's gonna be a great tour." It was like a dream. It was a big thing for us. It was a dream sequence. To wake up sitting in a dressing room half-asleep in Toronto and having those two walk in . . .'

'What happened was, after our sound check,

both David and Jimmy come running up the stairs to our dressing room to say hello,' keyboardist Jimmy Destri elaborates. 'We were initially told, "Don't bother the star. Don't bother the star." Of course we weren't gonna bother them. We were in our own fantasy world of trying to be little stars ourselves, so we were looking at Bowie trying to pick up clues on how to do that. They came upstairs and then it became obvious why they were so friendly. They both were rakishly misogynistic guys looking at Debbie. Probably why the Ramones didn't get the support slot on that tour. Bowie walked up to Debbie – and this is Debbie's side of the story – and said, "Can I fuck you?" And she turned around to him and said, "*Can* you?"'

Despite the new fans gained on tour, Iggy found it hard to shake the bad luck that had dogged his career. Shortly after the album's release in August, Elvis Presley died and RCA channeled all their industrial efforts into printing up Presley records for mourning fans. That was bad luck for Iggy, because he had made a big effort over a considerable time to get to that point, having a decent tour organized and going down well. 'Sod's law can operate at the most inappropriate time,' Gardiner says.

After the summer Iggy tour, Bowie committed himself to completing and then promoting '*Heroes*' (the quotes were meant to convey irony, according to Bowie) as much as possible. The Bowie that television and concert audiences would see that fall would be a casually attired bloke with short brown hair.

'As his appearance gets straighter the music gets weirder,' Kris Needs observed in *Zigzag* that October, the month the record hit shops. Critics gushed once again (NME named it their record of '77). The album opens with much suspense: two notes repeated like John Williams's *Jaws* theme, and Eno's 'Sky Saw'-like guitar sizzle, until Bowie finally emits a cry of 'Ooooh' and then a barrage of esoteric phrases ('Weaving down the byroad, singing a song / That's my kind of high roll gone wrong') in yet another Bowie-voice, that of an atonal robot wired for maximum angst. Robo-Bowie warns of 'slaughter in the air / Protest on the wind,' and a malevolent ghost in his very own machine ('Someone else inside me / someone could get skinned'). 'Joe the Lion' finds Bowie fascinated by West Coast art radical Chris Burden, the performance artist who was famously crucified on a Volkswagen in a 1974 piece entitled *Transfixed*: 'And he said, "Tell you who you are / If you nail me to my car."' 'Sons of the Silent Age' is 'Heroes' in the abstract. A love song of equal passion ('Baby, I'll never let you go,' Bowie wails), its lyrics are much less direct ('Don't walk they just glide in and out of life / They never die, they just go to sleep one day'). Opening with an Eno-treated, shimmering fanfare complete with ascending sax melody, it's played for maximum drama but its meaning and impact, especially compared with the song that immediately follows it, gets muddled.

The title track is next, and Bowie sings it as if he could only do it once before perishing. Sensing the song was bigger than him and rather one of those songs ('Bridge over Troubled Water,' 'Respect,' 'Sweet Caroline') that the world owns, Bowie recorded versions in both German ('Helden' is available on the *Sound and Vision* box set) and French. 'Blackout' imagines Bowie on the street during the New York City power failure in July of that year, revisiting the coke paranoia that he returned to Europe to avoid: 'Get me off the street,' he pleads, 'get some protection.' Like *Low*'s second side, side two of *'Heroes'* is largely instrumental. 'V-2 Schneider' is a motorik-beat-driven homage to Kraftwerk's Florian Schneider. 'Sense of Doubt' could have functioned as a Fritz Lang score, with its minimalist descending piano riff a sort of cue for some sweaty, bug-eyed, Peter Lorre-esque villain. 'Moss Garden' draws its inspiration from David Lynch's cult classic *Eraserhead* (a Bowie favorite, also released that year, complete with a creepy, urban industrial soundtrack). 'Neuköln' is an homage to the district where Bowie and Iggy rented their flats. In keeping with the neighborhood's bohemian bent, the track features Bowie blowing John Coltrane-style free-form notes on his sax. The album closes with a vocal track, 'Secret Life of Arabia,' a Middle Eastern disco number that hints at the world funk Bowie and Eno would pursue on 1979's *Lodger*.

Bowie, who raved about those spud boys in Devo to anyone who would listen that year and was for a time scheduled to produce their debut *Q: Are We Not Men? A: We Are Devo!* (Eno eventually did the job); was not the only one reinspired by New Wave. Marc Bolan looked to be making a comeback by 1977. Bolan had fallen on hard times since the heyday of T. Rextasy by refusing stubbornly to adapt. Visconti had changed camps and was making monumental new music with Bowie and Eno. Bolan was left recycling his old glitter riffs and hippie poetry. He still had the capacity to write great songs like 'Dandy in the Underworld,' but seemed rudderless when compared to his old friend Bowie.

By the late summer of '77, however, Bolan, still only twenty-nine, had dropped his mid-seventies bloat and booked a comeback tour with hot punk act the Damned as support. Bolan also was offered his own television show for Granada TV (entitled simply *Marc*), in which he would greet the audience, play an oldie or two and welcome another act for a solo spot and then a jam. Bowie, still promoting '*Heroes*,' was booked as a guest in September of '77. Bowie's arrival, however, only underscored how big he was and how humble Marc had become. Bowie traveled to Granada studios in a limo with a full entourage. Security was tightened and the set was closed down. Bowie's reps essentially took it over. Bolan reportedly responded by drinking and sulking. The two jam on an inchoate blues number called 'Standing Next to You,' after which a tipsy Bolan stumbles. 'Marc fell off the stage halfway through the number,' says Tony James, whose Generation X was the other musical guest scheduled that day. Bolan's tumble was symbolic. He would be dead before the show aired the following week. 'It's poignant,' Shaar Murray says. 'What Bowie understood and Bolan didn't was you present a moving target. Bolan was a one-trick pony. Kept trying to do his single one trick even after he got too fat to jump the hurdle.'

Bolan was killed in a car accident a week later. Bowie, along with Elton John and Rod Stewart, attended the funeral and paid his respects before the coffin, on which a swan-shaped bouquet lay. The following month, Bowie promoted and sang 'Heroes' on Bing Crosby's holiday special, *Bing Crosby's Merrie Olde Christmas*, topping a special-guests bill that included Twiggy and Ron Moody (best-known as Fagin in the Oscar-winning musical *Oliver!*). During Bowie's non-solo segment, one of the most famous in the history of holiday TV programming, Bing, seventy-four and frail in his cardigan, putters around before a twinkling tree in an old country estate. There's a ring at the door. It's David Bowie!

'Hello, are you the new butler?' he asks.

'It's been a long time since I've been the new anything,' Bing quips.

'I'm David Bowie, I live down the road. Sir Perceval lets me use his piano when he's not around.'

Crosby asks Bowie what he sings.

'Mostly contemporary stuff,' he answers. 'Do you like modern music?'

'I think it's marvelous, some of it, really fine,' Crosby says unconvincingly.

'You ever listen to any of the older music?'

'Sure, like John Lennon and the other one, Harry Nilsson.'

Crosby seems to warm up when Bowie mentions his six-year-old son. 'You go through any of the traditional things in the Bowie household on Christmastime?' Bowie makes a bad joke about agents sliding down the chimney, and then, mercifully, the shtick ends and they're crooning together. Supposedly this was going to be a straight duet on 'Little Drummer Boy,' but Bowie decided to weave a lesser-known melody, 'Peace on Earth,' into the mix because it suited his register better. Crosby abided. It's become a holiday classic and I will show it to my six-year-old son as soon as he . . . exists. Sadly it would be Crosby's final appearance as well, prompting Bowie to joke, with characteristic black humor, that he was planning to stop going on television.

Personally, Bowie settled near Montreux, Switzerland, a quaint resort town popular with tax-exile rock stars because of its state-of-the-art recording studio and annual jazz festival. He spent his days in preparation for the extensive world

497

tour that would keep him on the road for much of 1978. For the first time since Haddon Hall, he also felt like a hands-on dad to Zowie, who would soon answer permanently to Duncan. 'The tabloids called me Zowie,' Duncan Jones said in a 2009 interview. 'It was my middle name. Then I decided I wanted to be called by my given name when I was fourteen.' Bowie spent every day with the boy, and in the next decade he would accompany his father to movie and video sets and boarding school, fostering his interest in film. He would attend the London Film School and release his debut Moon in the summer of 2009. Bowie even recorded a charming narrative for a version of Prokofiev's *Peter and the Wolf* with music by the London Symphony Orchestra for the boy and even presented him with an early home video copy of *Star Wars*. He also reconnected with his mother, putting the tension he'd publicly referred to on the Dick Cavett show only three years earlier behind him and seemed to gain energy from a sense of family. Bowie's new respect for family was well timed to his son's adolescence, and this availability after an early childhood in which the boy often felt 'alone' surely kept him from becoming another resentful, spoiled child of celebrity like so many of Bowie's peers' offspring did. No less a social realist than Howard Stern opined on the air after seeing a screening of *Moon* and finding it surprisingly intense and engrossing: 'You hear David Bowie's kid and you think he's going to be a fuck up.' Or worse, a crap musician. 'I rebelled against him,' Jones has said. 'By showing no interest in (music).'

Meanwhile, Angie was coming apart. She'd met with Bowie in Berlin during the recording of '*Heroes*' and there it was formally decided they would divorce. 'I was no longer able to share him either with black girls, other artists, drag queens or Corinne Schwab,' she writes. 'The fantasy had slipped from the frame and was hanging askew.' While in Berlin, the Bowies seemed positive and resigned, celebrating their imminent divorce with a night of partying. When discussion turned to the settlement, a darker pall was cast over everything, as it soon became apparent to her that she was not going to be able to pursue what she believed to be her fair share of the Bowies' assets.

'I was looking for a lawyer to help me get rid of David,' she says today. 'I couldn't get a lawyer to even see me. In Switzerland they were like, "Ha ha. Women hadn't even got the vote till 1974 we're not really concerned if you get your half."'

Proceedings turned even darker around New Year's 1978, when Angie arrived in Switzerland expecting to see Duncan. Bowie, upset that she did not call or visit the child over Christmas, had taken him away. Angie, alone and stranded in the mountains, was inconsolable. That night, she ingested a near lethal dosage of sleeping pills and woke up in the local hospital in Vevey. The incident was covered by the worldwide tabloid press. 'I tried to kill myself,' Angie admits, 'but my heart wasn't in it. I'm very competent. If I really wanted to kill myself I think I would have succeeded.'

Divorce proceedings accelerated from there, with Angie's suicide attempt easily empowering Bowie's lawyers to portray her as unstable. By decade's end, Angie was heartbroken and dissolute, living off her small settlement and unable to see Duncan, as Bowie was awarded full custody of the boy. The birth of her second child, daughter Stacia, and the poetry she started putting to music and performing in clubs in the eighties (eventually released as the album *Moon Goddess*) helped her slowly piece herself back together over the years. The release of her autobiography, published in 1993, put her back in the center of public scrutiny, thanks to the intimation she made on both the Joan Rivers and Howard Stern shows that she once caught David and Mick Jagger in bed. She now lives quietly in Tuscon. When Angie speaks of Bowie today, nearly thirty years after the finalization of their divorce in 1980, one can detect a complex mix of emotions in her voice. There's pride, anger and, if not affection, certainly respect. She talks about him like someone she no longer really knows, like an abstract thing rather than a person. Her tone tends toward the analytical so much that at one point, I ask her to tell me about the downtime, what the two of them did when they were alone together and nobody else

500

was around – if they just enjoyed a shared silence; whether there was any kind of affection that was pedestrian or if it was all sex, ambition and convenience. He had written love songs about her, after all: 'The Prettiest Star,' 'Golden Years' and 'Be My Wife,' among them. She alludes to a few shared vacations early in the marriage but very little else. Angie is either keeping such memories to herself, and rightfully so, or the passing decades have diluted them a bit.

The level of Angie's responsibility for David's success is impossible to gauge. She certainly refuses to claim credit for it. 'That's for other people to say. People who are respected among the industry have said that I changed his focus and the way he worked and how he presented himself. He was very talented and when he met me, he was driven. He's from Yorkshire. They know how to make money and he had a very weird family life. Most people who are very successful have suffered. And he didn't really suffer but he suffered because he could never suffer to the extent or have the experiences that Terry had, and Terry went crazy because of it. In his heart he always felt guilty and the self-loathing is what makes him the great artist that he is. It's a common motivator for a lot of great artists. They either get molested when they're children, have a terrible experience – they nearly die falling off a cliff going to see the Grand Canyon – and you think whatever. Something happens that causes them to take life and twist it into what it is they think life should be giving them back for what they suffered.'

Bowie tried to duck the tabloid scrutiny of his marriage, using, as always, an imminent project, in this case, a world tour, as a means to keep himself focused and sane. The '78 tour reunited Bowie with his White Light/Station to Station touring band, expanded to include synth players Roger Powell and Sean Mayes – whose tour diaries were posthumously published as *We Can Be Heroes* – to handle *Low* and '*Heroes*' material. Electric violinist Simon House and lead guitarist Adrian Belew, whom Bowie poached from Frank Zappa, completed the lineup. Zappa, a Bowie hero from the sixties, was apparently not happy to lose Belew.

'David and Frank tried to talk to each other, or rather, David tried to talk to Frank, but Frank wouldn't have anything to do with him,' Belew recalled. 'Frank kept calling him 'Captain Tom.' It was kind of an ugly scene, really. In the end, it worked out pretty well. A few days later, I talked to Frank about it and he gave me his blessing and said, "Go on. I hope it works out for you."'

Despite the blatantly uncommercial material on both of his Eno records, each contained big radio hits ('Sound and Vision' and 'Heroes,' respectively). Coupled with the popularity of the *Changes* compilation and his reputation as a stellar live performer, Bowie was able to take this uncompromised new material back into arenas in America, Europe,

Australia and Japan. The first section of the set list relied heavily on the *Low* and *'Heroes'* material, with 'Be My Wife,' 'Weeping Wall,' 'Speed of Life,' 'Breaking Glass' and 'Blackout' leaving some, as the NME observed in their live review, 'plainly restless.' The middle section of the show was earmarked for hits like 'Fame' and 'TVC 15,' with the Ziggy-era material saved for the climax (even in '78 there were still kids in attendance in full glitter drag). 'Rebel Rebel' was the nightly encore. While the tour was Bowie's first of the seventies to focus on musicianship over theatricality, there seemed to be reminders of the cavalcades of old everywhere.

'When we showed up for the sound check at Madison Square Garden,' Belew recalled, 'the Ringling Brothers and Barnum and Bailey circus was also housed in the bowels of the building, which was a huge labyrinth of a place. I was standing onstage doing my guitar check when I turned around and saw four elephants behind me. I think they had maybe thirty or forty of them, and they'd bring them up four at a time, square them off and let them eat. It was unreal. Later that day, we had a banquet room where there was lots of food laid out, and some of the wives, children and band associates were there. The door burst open and suddenly a chimpanzee in a houndstooth suit and roller skates came whirling around the table, chasing the kids all over the place, followed by his handler in an identical suit, holding a little placard that read "Here's my chimp. He's done a thousand commercials and movies." It set the tone for that particular evening. Talking Heads, Dustin Hoffman, Andy Warhol and other famous faces were in the audience. I'd have to say that was the most memorable and exciting show we'd done.' A '78 tour document was released, in all its sectioned glory, as the double album *Stage*.

As the seventies ended, England's first post-Bowie decade was gearing up. Some of the teenagers who watched Bowie perform 'Starman' on *Top of the Pops* were now pop stars themselves, like Tubeway Army, Joy Division, XTC and Lene Lovich. Bowie's Eno collaborations inspired dozens of British youths – like Depeche Mode from Basildon, the Human League from Sheffield, Blancmange from Harrow and OMD from Liverpool – to acquire inexpensive synthesizers and begin composing avant-garde pop singles. 'Warm Leatherette' by the Normal was the first and among the finest. Even the classic guitar/bass/drums acts of the new wave, like Northampton's Bauhaus, were Bowie-informed. It must have been gratifying and infuriating at once. Bowie was only thirty-two, but already he was being treated like a great star from a bygone era. Worse, many of these acts were vying against him for chart success. Tubeway Army leader Gary Numan's 1979 solo album *The Pleasure Principle* (powered by the chilly dance smash 'Cars') outsold Bowie's release from the same year, *Lodger*. The Associates, a wry, romantic Scottish New Wave band, didn't even bother to write their own Bowie-indebted hit that year but rather gained serious rock-press attention with an accelerated but faithful cover version of Bowie's *own* '79 single 'Boys Keep Swinging.'

CHAPTER 21

Nineteen seventy-nine began with the first true creative flop of Bowie's otherwise flawless decade. The actor David Hemmings, star of the quintessential swinging London film, 1966's *Blow Up*, had befriended Bowie and filmed his sold-out concert at London's Earls Court the previous year for a proposed documentary, which was never released. Hemmings was attempting to make the shift from actor to director and convinced Bowie to appear in his debut, a World War I period piece called *Just a Gigolo*, largely because legendary German film icon Marlene Dietrich had signed on. Dietrich received a reported $250,000 for a few days' work, playing a cynical madam who hires out war-scarred young men to horny European ladies. Dietrich, pushing eighty and apparently too frail to act while standing, recites inane dialogue like 'Dancing, music, champagne. The best way to forget until you find something that you want to remember,' from her seat. Bowie seems like he's suppressing his gag reflex. 'I'm the head of a regiment of sorts,' Dietrich muses. 'The gigolos! All you need is a battlefield.' The film, which also stars Kim Novak (attempting a Eurotrash accent), and all involved were pilloried by critics upon its release in February. Bowie good-naturedly referred to it as 'All my thirty-two Elvis movies rolled into one.'

Perhaps reckoning with his first misstep put Bowie on the defensive when it came to his younger musical rivals. 'I've seen a few of Gary Numan's videos,' he quipped to an interviewer that year. 'To be honest, I never meant for cloning to be a part of the eighties. He's not only copied me, he's clever and he's got all my influences in too. I guess it's best of luck to him.'

Numan and Bowie were actually booked to perform on the UK talk show *The Kenny Everett Video Show* in late '79, but Bowie refused to be in the studio at the same time. The younger performer, a lifelong fan, was crushed. 'If I'd met him before *Kenny Everett* I'd have stood awestruck, overwhelmed and probably dribbling like a simpleton,' he says today. 'If I'd met him in the weeks after *Everett* I'd have called him a small-minded cunt and gone about my business. He had no reason to be afraid at all. No matter what we achieved, whether we became more successful or not, nothing could be taken away from his amazing career. If he'd handled it differently I would have remained his biggest champion. He was legendary even then and I was just part of the latest wave of new upstarts. I think the majority of the new electronic people worshipped the ground he walked on, so it came as a huge shock to me to see that he obviously felt threatened in some way. I couldn't believe that he would A, have me thrown out of the building and B, have me taken off the program. That he could see me as a threat seemed ridiculous when, to me, he was close to God and I was a spotty nothing. It mattered nothing to me that I was selling more records. He was the man. What he did, although no big deal to me anymore, changed the way I felt about him forever. He suddenly became very, very human, no longer larger than life. As I've grown older and seen my own career ebb and flow I understand far more how he must have felt, even though I've never had the same fears or felt the need to try and harm someone else's career.'

Lodger is strong enough an effort to stand alongside any of the great New Wave releases of 1979, from the Cars' *Candy-O*, to the Police's *Regatta de Blanc*, to Blondie's *Eat to the Beat*, to Public Image Limited's *Metal Box*. While included in the 'Berlin trilogy' of *Low* and '*Heroes,' Lodger* was not recorded at Hansa but rather at Mountain Studios in Montreux, near Bowie's home, shortly after the close of his 1978 world tour. Work was completed in New York City in the new year. The same major players – Eno, Visconti and Alomar, and the Dennis Davis and George Murray rhythm section – appear, as does Belew. The popular opinion among critics upon its release was that the record was the least of the three, but in time, its reputation has improved and world-beat tracks like 'African Night Flight' and 'Yassassin' can now clearly be heard as influences on Talking Heads' much more highly regarded 1980 album *Remain in Light* (also produced with Eno), the David Byme/Eno experiment in sonic collage *My Life in the Bush of Ghosts* and Paul Simon's 1986 masterpiece *Graceland*. While hardly happy-go-lucky (the single 'DJ' begins with the priceless verse 'I'm home, lost my job, and incurably ill') it lacks the shocking newness of *Low* or the emotional immediacy of *'Heroes.'*

'Lodger is a nice enough pop record,' Jon Savage wrote in his NME review, 'beautifully played, produced and crafted, and slightly faceless. Is Bowie that interesting?' He dismisses it as 'avant AOR.'

'Before *Lodger*, the music was darker and probably less experimental,' said Belew. '*Lodger* was more of a world record – urban and eastern at the same time. It seemed he was spreading his wings in that direction, incorporating world music styles. It really inspired me to open up my guitar playing. David was great at stretching you out. It was perfect preparation for working with Talking Heads, where they knew what they wanted but needed a sprinkling of fairy dust on it.'

Lodger's promotional *videos*, however, were as innovative as anything Bowie had ever done before. Bowie and director David Mallet created original clips for each of the album's three singles, 'Boys Keep Swinging,' 'DJ' and 'Look Back in Anger.' Two years before the launch of MTV, the artists who bothered to make videos at all shot mostly performance clips against white backdrops. Bowie spent both time and money and brought real invention to the form before it became commonplace.

'They're authentically strange,' director David Mallet says of the early clips (Mallet would shoot videos for singles from the next three Bowie albums). 'The age of video became the first time anybody had any freedom in the British cinema. Hammer horror [films], I guess, in the fifties and sixties, maybe, but what music videos brought to Britain and Europe was really the equivalent to the French avant-garde. It was the first time UK filmmakers were able to spend money and do what they wanted.'

Bowie's commitment to leading this movement is in evidence with the 'DJ' clip, in which he traipses into a busy London street at night unannounced while Mallet films him. Pedestrians slowly realize who he is and run up to kiss and touch him while he lip-synchs. Dangerous, sure. But Bowie knew it would make a great shot. 'That was real, that was as completely real as you can get,' says Mallet. 'Wasn't even anybody notified that it was going to happen. On my mother's life that was real.'

Bowie was spotted at one of the Human League's London concerts that April and popped up at a

Nashville stop on their first American tour, studying them from the crowd. He found the League, who projected slides on themselves while performing, to be a bit more inventive than most of the other Bowie-indebted New Wavers. 'They sound like 1980,' he commented. It was Bowie's video clips, however, not the Human League's or Gary Numan's, that *looked* like 1980 and beyond.

Sensing an opportunity to distinguish Bowie from the already expanding glut of New Wave acts (even Tom Petty and the Heartbreakers were referred to as such in '77), RCA marketing executives came up with an effective slogan to promote '*Heroes*' in early '78: 'There's New Wave, There's Old Wave and There's David Bowie.' It immediately placed him in a class by himself, while acknowledging the new breed but reminding them that he's been around and survived.

Booked to make his return to late-night American television to promote *Lodger* on the January 5, 1980, episode of *Saturday Night Live*, Bowie wisely focused his attention on another thrilling video presentation. The performance stands as one of the best and strangest moments in the late-night variety show's three-and-a-half-decade run. To Bowie's left, a small man, dressed all in black, stood and stared straight ahead. To Bowie's right a taller man, dressed all in red, with dyed red hair, did the same. As an eerie synth chord gurgled, the two men picked Bowie up and carried him to the microphone, upstage.

Bowie is wearing a large bow tie, the size of two slices of New York pizza placed end to end. It's pinned to a PVC breastplate in the shape of a tuxedo shirt. His black coat is covered in glittering plastic sequins. His sleeves are long and loose. His trousers are striped. His high cheekbones are covered in a pink Kabuki blush. To this day, most bands come on *SNL* and simply play their hit single. Bowie was playing 'The Man Who Sold the World,' the title track to an album that was at the time nearly a decade old. When the number was over, the side men carried Bowie back to his original mark. He stood rigid as they placed him down, and Blondie moonlighter Jimmy Destri's keyboard emitted a series of sci-fi burps and hums. A collective reaction of 'What the hell was that?' could be detected as the crowd, stunned, applauded. Bowie's black-clad backup singers didn't allow themselves any satisfied smiles as the performance concluded. One, Klaus Nomi, then in his mid-twenties, was a solo performer and already a fast-rising star on the New York New Wave club scene. He was born Klaus Sperber (Nomi is an anagram of *Omni*, as in the defunct science magazine) in the small mountain town of Immenstadt in Germany. Sperber moved to Manhattan in the mid-1970s. While working as a pastry chef, he refined his act. Shy and gentle offstage, he spoke with a thick German accent. Onstage, he was completely without peer, and by the late seventies, he and his backing band were selling out trendy discos like Xenon and established hipster venues like Max's Kansas City with their highly theatrical mix of sixties pop (a great version of Lou Christie's falsetto classic 'Lightning' Strikes' appears on his self-titled debut) and opera. Nomi was not classically trained, but he had an uncanny multioctave range that managed, when required anyway, to skirt camp for genuine beauty. Nomi was slight and balding but worked that into his otherworldly appearance as well. The pointy black hair on either side of his skull was waxed into sharp triangles. A phallic clump of it, rounded at the end, protruded from the top of his elfin skull like a single antenna. Nomi's stare was blank but his expression was wry. His lips were painted black and bee stung. His cheeks were deathly white. Klaus Nomi looked like Felix the Cat's demented German cousin. On any other stage, he could have been (and often was) a sensation. But there, to Bowie's right, he was merely part of the act. The other singer, dressed in red, was Joey Arias, also in his mid-twenties and a performer and New Wave disco figure who sang background vocals in Nomi's act. Arias was Hispanic and handsome. Like Nomi, and virtually everybody who figured into the Manhattan New Wave scene that held the city enthralled in the post-disco late seventies, he was a transplant from somewhere else.

New York City in 1979 was nothing like the family-friendly squeegee-free shopping mall city it is in 2009. Three years previous, President Ford had famously told its bankrupt civic leaders to 'drop dead.' Times Square was full of porno. The Lower East Side was a haven for shooting galleries. Mugging, rape and murder were rampant.

'The thing that made that whole New Wave scene possible was the fact that the city was falling down,' says Destri. 'All these bands could perform around each other and afford to live in a central venue. Every time the economy goes south, art grows. If you were an actuary or an accountant you'd consider those years horrid, but if you were an artist, you'd consider them magic. New York was peeling. It was piss stained. It was falling down but at the same time, it was vibrant.'

Painters, rockers, experimental theater troupes and drag queens poured into these neighborhoods. No matter how oppressive it was, for many of them, it was better than the unhappy home life they'd fled. And with a modicum of street smarts and a few dollars for the cheap rents, they could establish a genuine scene.

'You could live on practically nothing, which meant you didn't need to get a "real" job, which left one time to be endlessly creative,' says actress/singer/performer Ann Magnuson, who moved to the East Village from West Virginia in 1978 and hosted several of the New Wave revues at venues like the Mudd Club and Irving Plaza.

'Making art or music or performance or just turning your everyday life into a spectacle. Bowie had turned into something godlike to certain kids who loved the weird, the edgy, the arty and the glam. By that point he had become deified.'

It makes perfect sense that he'd be drawn to Manhattan at the end of the decade. The sounds of both New Wave and the more caustic 'No Wave' movement (the ranks of which included Teenage Jesus and the Jerks, D.N.A., Mars and other bands collected on the 1978 *No New York* compilation, also produced by Eno) and the bass-heavy cut-and-paste styles of early hip-hop acts like the Funky Four Plus One and Grandmaster Flash and the Furious Five would provide sonic inspiration, appealing to his eternal art school sensibility. Destri, the Blondie keyboardist, and therefore a downtown Manhattan New Wave god, would be his nocturnal tour guide.

'He had a driver named Tony and we'd go out to nightclubs. It was a seedy underbelly of fun,' he says. The pair and their respective entourages would hit the uptown disco Hurrah and repair to the secret back room, which housed a coke salon. But it was downtown, in a year-old converted Tribeca loft called the Mudd Club (a nod to Dr Samuel Mudd, the physician who treated Lincoln's assassin, John Wilkes Booth), where Bowie actually dug the new breed in '79, many of them stone Bowie disciples. 'All the people who graduated from CBGB's would take over the

Mudd Club. That was just the period when it was hopping. I was David's ambassador to these little bands,' Destri says. 'He was really, really interested in New Wave.'

'The Nomi thing was happening really strongly at that moment that we first met Bowie,' Joey Arias says today. 'We were at the Mudd Club one night, and we were upstairs on the top floor and everyone was getting fucked up and drinking and laughing, very after-hours. We were about to leave when someone said, 'There's David Bowie sitting there.' We just froze.'

'David saw them and said, "Oh, I gotta have these guys,"' Destri, then at Bowie's table, recalls. 'He treated his life like it was a gallery.' Arias and Nomi were summoned to the table and soon the latter was put in the odd position of being aggressively flattered by his seductive hero. 'David was saying to Klaus, 'Oh my God, I can't believe I'm meeting *you*!' To Klaus!' Arias recalls. 'Klaus had met Bowie years ago in Berlin at a train station when Bowie was on a European tour. And Klaus actually carried David Bowie's bags from their train. And he had a photograph that showed David at the height of the Ziggy Stardust period. And there's Klaus with long hair like a hippie, with a beard, carrying the bags for Bowie.'

Nomi and Bowie would exchange phone numbers at the Mudd Club and meet a second time a few days later at a Soho loft. During the second, more formal meeting, they watched footage of surrealist films and planned what was going to be a huge New Year's Eve concert, choreographed by Bowie's choreographer Tony Basil. Time constraints forced them to postpone the show, however, and soon they were refocusing their collaborative energies for something truly special to mark Bowie's booking on *Saturday Night Live*. Although the show had been on for five seasons and had hosted artists as big as the Rolling Stones as well as Bowie-influenced acts like Blondie, he had never appeared there. For his *SNL* debut, at the close of a decade that seemed to see one Bowie-led culture-changing event after another, Bowie had one last wow up his sleeve.

Nomi happily ceded the spotlight to his idol, knowing, like so many do, that to brush up against David Bowie's aura even for a short time leaves some residue of it lingering for all time. Even today, when people speak of Nomi, the first thing many mention is *Saturday Night Live* (it's one of the focal points of the great 2004 documentary *The Nomi Song*).

When Arias and Nomi reported to rehearsal at a midtown studio owned by Bowie's record label, RCA, a few days later, they were shocked to see their hero unshaven and rumpled. 'We expected David to be very, like, alien looking. Very totalitarian, very Big Brother. But he was very casual during rehearsals. His hair was really scruffy looking, and you almost didn't recognize him because he just kind of blended in with everybody.

I couldn't believe it. I just laughed. It was all so natural. I asked, "Where's David?" And they said, "You're right next to him." Oops.'

Bowie had specific ideas about the visual composition of the piece. He'd base it on a red, black and white color scheme – the same striking combination that rock stars from Marilyn Manson, to the White Stripes, to My Chemical Romance and Green Day have used in the years since. The Nazi flag. The Coke bottle. Red, black and white was the scheme of icons both concentrated evil and the wholesomely universal. 'David's ideas were really strong and specific,' Arias says. 'He knew that he wanted me to have the red hair and Klaus to have the black hair.'

Bowie ran through the vocals for the three tracks he would be performing. Singing there in his rumpled shirt and five o'clock shadow, it was still Bowie. He could turn it on just by opening his mouth. 'David started singing, like, all of the material. It was, like, literally a concert for Klaus and I. We were, like, gagging a little bit, it was like we were being serenaded by Bowie. We played it cool, though.'

Both men were starting to get famous on their own. Arias was affiliated with the Italian fashion retail outlet Fiorucci. He worked in the midtown store and modeled for various high-and low-end designers. Nomi's act was hot and label interest was already there. This was a different level: a national television spot . . . with David Bowie. Inside, they were barely retaining their composure.

'I knew Laraine Newman, who was an original [*Saturday Night Live*] cast member,' Arias says. 'We knew each other from the Groundlings improv group in L.A. [where many SNL cast members begin]. So I used to go to *Saturday Night Live* every weekend and sit there with her and watch them rehearse and watch the show. And I remember asking Laraine, at one point, "If David Bowie ever comes to this show, please, please, I gotta be here. I'll do anything but I've gotta see this man in person."'

Bowie's performance on SNL even shocked his band. While they were not shocked to see a rumpled version of their leader during the week of rehearsal that led up to the live spot, he had not clued any of the musicians in on what he would be wearing – or doing – on Saturday night. 'For "The Man Who Sold the World,"' Destri says, 'I was totally unprepared for the plastic suit. All that week we're rehearsing in jeans and sweat-shirts . . . come show day he wouldn't tell anyone what he was wearing. The whole band was shocked. We were totally thrown. We still knew our chord changes and our little bits. Then for the next song, he's wearing a dress, with his hair parted. He looks like Katherine Hepburn.'

'TVC 15,' the piano-driven boogie woogie off 1976's *Station to Station,* would be the second number revived, and Bowie had changed costumes. He now wore a full-length dress that appeared to be gunmetal blue. 'It was a Chinese air hostess uniform,' Arias recalls. The collar was tightly buttoned. He wore what looked like thick pantyhose and matching shoes. A cold, utilitarian number, not feminine but certainly a dress. He kept his hands in the pockets as he sang the vocal melody line. Behind him, Nomi stood frozen while Arias casually read the newspaper. Bowie grabbed the microphone and the camera zoomed in on his face. By the end of the song, Nomi had dragged a hot-pink stuffed poodle across the stage on a leash. A television screen was embedded in the dog's jaws, and it flashed the performance as they performed it.

'Boys Keep Swinging' was the third and final number performed on the episode and heralded another costume change. Bowie had replaced his Chinese airline hostess dress – in fact, he'd replaced his entire body – with a puppet's torso. The head of David Bowie sang the song. A marionette's torso and limbs danced under his giant Bowie head as though on strings.

'They pulled the mic over to a green screen and he puts a little puppet under his head,' Destri says. 'He pulls the strings with the puppet and all you see is the puppet with David's head going, and we're off to the side just being the band, like, "Okay, let's watch the head for our cues"!'

'It was all very Dada,' Arias says. 'He was into this whole German expressionistic thing and very surreal. But it was fun; we just sat there having a good time. David was on the screen and we were standing there doing it and we could see him on the monitor and we were just doing this bit.'

More slow, stunned applause followed. People all over the world were discussing the performance in the hours and days immediately afterward. 'It seemed like Manhattan was at a standstill that night,' Arias says. 'You can ask people in New York what were they doing that day; everybody will say "I was home watching *Saturday Night*, watching Joey and Klaus with David Bowie."'

'We were all thrilled to see Joey and Klaus on SNL with him,' Magnuson says. 'Being "annointed by Bowie" was something every teenager obsessed with glam rock in the early seventies dreamed of.' Nomi and Arias wondered when it was all over if they were indeed part of Bowie's performing company. Would there be more pieces like this? At the afterparty, at One Fifth Avenue in Greenwich Village, the two camps mingled and there was talk of developing this act. Bowie seemed enthusiastic about the prospect. But ultimately, he'd forge ahead into the new wave alone, having primed himself for the early eighties right there in front of millions, using Arias and Nomi as his New York City mechanisms. 'I think that's his genius,' Arias says today. 'He works with people and then he gets touched and all of a sudden it triggers something in him and he moves on.'

It would be almost fifteen years before Bowie appeared solo on SNL again (with *Tin Machine* in 1991, doing an excellent cover of Roxy Music's

'If There Is Something'), primarily because his debut appearance was so hard to top. Klaus Nomi passed away only four years later, becoming one of the first icons of the New York New Wave scene to die of AIDS. Arias saw Bowie a few times after that, but only very briefly. A quick hello backstage at an Iggy Pop show, a warm moment at a fashion show.

'That night, Bowie opened the gate to the eighties,' says Destri. 'He sniffed out the new wave and fashioned an eighties thing.'

CHAPTER 22

Although he would end the decade no more a musical leader than he'd been in the sixties, for a while, about four years, Bowie's eighties reign was glorious. He began the decade by instructing his angry kid brothers, the primarily English punks, on how to reinvent themselves, essentially functioning as the Rosetta stone for post-punk and New Wave. Would Johnny Rotten have been able to survive the flameout of the Sex Pistols had it not been for Bowie destroying Ziggy Stardust and saying, with all the conviction required, 'I am a soul singer now. This is the new me'? Lydon has that very conviction when he appears, with Keith Levine, on Tom Snyder's late-night *Tomorrow Show* in 1980 to promote his post-Pistols band Public Image Limited. Bowie's notion of a self-invented rock star, 'not me but an idea from me,' which both Ziggy and the Thin White Duke were, allowed someone equally savvy like Lydon to call his new group, well, not a 'group' at all, but a corporation.

'We ain't no band,' Lydon tells the perplexed and hostile Snyder while bumming a cigarette.

'We're a company simple. Nothing to do with rock and roll doo-dah.'

'Okay,' Snyder replies, wishing, perhaps, he was anywhere else.

'Companies can mess about with musical instruments. There's no limits,' Lydon says, later adding, 'History does not matter. Your program is called *Tomorrow*.'

But Lydon knew his history well. Post-Bowie, the reinvention of a band's entire identity now had a precedent. One can still detect the Pistols in Public Image Limited's 1978 debut single 'Public Image,' with its slashing guitar and caterwauled vocals, but not so in '79's second PIL album *Metal Box*, issued in its vinyl version in a tin canister and available today on CD as *Second Edition*. Gone are the Ramones and *Nuggets*-indebted guitars. When they come in, via stone-faced Keith Levene, on tracks like 'Death Disco' and 'Albatross,' they seem instead lifted from eccentric Jamaican producer Lee 'Scratch' Perry's Black Ark Studio sessions. Jah Wobble's bass is dubby and doomy, and Lydon's vocals, often buried in the mix, now seem genuinely and not ironically disturbed. It's as close to *Low* as a major artist had come.

Then there were the New Romantics. Once a sexually, racially and intellectually integrated movement, punk had, on both sides of the Atlantic, become a haven for violent and often racist young men by 1980. Even enlightened alternatives, sister movements to the more emotionally revealing post-punk, such as the Coventry-based 2 Tone movement, led by the Specials, the Selecter, Madness and the Beat, attracted skinheads and National Front members to the clubs. First-wave UK punks who sensed that rock steady was not a good fit for them kept an eye open for something else, and their answer, too, was David Bowie.

'I think Bowie's influence on that generation of British pop kids was immense,' Jon Savage says. New Romantic restored Wildean wit, sensitivity and flamboyance to the pop aesthetic, with ruffles, velvet, elaborate jewelry, costume and quips becoming the norm. Ziggy-style theatricality was also favored, as was, of course, a smart sexual ambiguity. In early 1980, as Bowie finished work on his new studio album, *Scary Monsters*, at the Power Station in midtown Manhattan, London nightlife was becoming as Bowie-mad as it had been nearly a full decade earlier, at the apex of glitter rock. It was a full-on Bowie revival, the first of its kind, really, as the artist's output did not really lend itself to nostalgia. But for the transitioning punks, the hits of '72, '73 and '74, the 'Starman's and 'Jean Genie's and 'Rebel Rebel's, were the perfect tonic for the troops.

Steve Strange, one of the leading lights of the New Romantic scene thanks to his tenure in the electropop band Visage and his cofounding of the popular 'Bowie Nights' at London club Billy's and, later, the larger Blitz, grew up in Wales.

During the Ziggy era, he was not only a superfan but a self-created Bowie doppelgänger, courting trouble from his teachers and local bullies.

'I was so into the music I wanted to copy him,' Strange says today. 'I copied his hairstyle, which got me banned from school. I was a straight-A student until around this time.' After school in 1976, Strange took up an offer from then-Sex Pistols bassist Glen Matlock to come down to London and stay at his apartment. He decided this was his way out. 'After school you were either going to be very athletic and take up rugby and become a rugby player or you'd have to do what your father and your grandfather did before and go down the mines,' Strange recalls. In London he fell in with the Pistols-following 'Bromley Contingent,' which included Siouxsie Sioux, Generation X's Tony James and Billy Idol, and future Pistols bassist and junkie death icon Sid Vicious, among others. Strange worked for Pistols manager Malcolm McLaren, selling and modeling clothes at Seditionaries, the shop he'd opened with Vivienne Westwood. He also made paste-up posters for Pistols gigs and roadied on the Anarchy tour. A record collector, by punk's flame-out, he'd amassed an impressive collection of hard-to-find 'new' music, browsing in local bins along each tour stop. A local scenester named Rusty Egan, also bored with punk, had been doing the same, and one night while sitting around the stereo in a friend's flat, they determined that the 'new' music sounded excellent when mixed in with the glitter 'oldies.' 'We'd play Nina Hagen, Bauhaus, early Eno, Kraftwerk. We thought, "What if we had a club and between this new futuristic music we would mix in favorite Bowie tracks and glam-period?"' Strange had been ensconced in the punk scene long enough to know that just about every punk, from the Clash's Mick Jones (a great Mott the Hoople fan) to the cantankerous Lydon (a massive Alice Cooper fan) could not resist a good glitter-age number.

They booked a 'Bowie Night' at a local bar on Dean Street in Soho. The venue used to be a social club known as the Gargoyle, where Noel Coward sipped cocktails with Tallulah Bankhead, but it had gone seedy. This was Billy's bar. 'The working girls would come into the club and they mixed in with all these freaks,' Strange says. 'They'd come in just for a shot to keep warm on a cold night.' They'd pass out flyers and soon the club became so popular that Strange would have to work the door, where he got a reputation for imperiousness. He'd often hold a mirror up to a particularly tacky or obnoxious would-be partier and ask, 'Would you let you in?'

'I'd become known as a real bastard on the door,' he says. Strange's rope policy was Wildean in its embrace of well-contemplated hedonism and invention, not just crass bids for attention or acceptance. 'Basically the philosophy on the flyer was "Let your creativity flow." Don't disappear into

527

a pastiche wallpaper. But I was not talking about being ludicrous. One guy turned up in a bloody wetsuit. I said, "No no no." Most probably he thought this was real creativity and I thought, "What a fucking arse-hole." We moved from Billy's after about three months and decided it must be time to move to a bigger venue.'

The Blitz Club was a wine bar decorated with images of the Nazi Blitzkrieg, and each Tuesday, it would be filled to capacity with Bowie nuts, with another hundred of them patiently waiting in line outside, determined to breach Steve Strange's phalanx of 'tude, to which even rock 'n' roll legends were not immune. Often they'd have live bands, and future legends like Depeche Mode played some of their earliest gigs there. Visiting performers like Divine, Nona Hendryx of Labelle and David Byrne made it past Strange and his mirror. When a drunken Mick Jagger and his entourage were turned away, however, it made the red-top tabloids the following day, and by the subsequent Tuesday, the Blitz was even more impenetrable. One celebrity guest, however, could still reduce the impossibly fierce and fire-code-wary Strange to the likes of a cloying Olive Garden hostess. A few weeks after the Jagger debacle, which was picked up by the tabloids, Bowie turned up unannounced and requested entry.

'This black limousine circled for about an hour, a limo with blacked-out windows,' Strange says. 'I'd seen it in an hour go around at least three

528

times, and in this hour the queue had gotten bigger and bigger, then a lady came up and said, "I need a private word."' This was, of course, Coco Schwab. 'She was a bit abrupt and a bit rude. She said to me, "I have David Bowie in the back of the limo and we'd like it if he could be entertained. David really liked what he's read about you and the club." I was like, fucking hell, David Bowie has finally come!'

Bowie was there on a mission. As Strange visited him in a makeshift private section to the side of the dance floor, Bowie, as he had at the Mudd Club with Klaus Nomi, made his proposal. 'He said, "This club is what London's been missing for a long time. I just love what you're doing. I would like you to pick and style four people for the music video to my new song 'Ashes to Ashes.'" I couldn't believe it.' It was well after midnight and Strange was instructed to be at the Hilton Hotel by six AM with his extras and costumes ready to go. 'Since it was the Hilton, I figured we'd be flown to some exotic location to do this video. Little did we know he sort of shut off Southend beach.'

'The beach was my idea,' the 'Ashes to Ashes' clip's codirector David Mallet says today of the famous location for what remains one of music video's most genuinely odd and innovative high points. 'It was in Hastings in Sussex, a location I'd known since I was a little boy. One of the very rare places you can get right down to the water and there's a cliff towering over you.'

While on location on that blustery morning, Bowie spied an abandoned bulldozer on the beach and its owners were located and the machinery quickly employed. The bulldozer follows Bowie, in Pierrot clown costume, as he leads Strange and his mates, dressed in black ecclesiastical robes, along the shoreline. 'My robe kept catching in the bulldozer,' Strange recalls. 'That's why I kept doing that move where I pull my arm down. So I wouldn't be crushed. Bowie liked the move and used it later in his video for "Fashion"!'

The song, the first single off *Scary Monsters*, was a bit of a Bowie revival itself. While musically it's synth driven and New Wave-ish, lyrically it reintroduces Major Tom, the hero of 'Space Oddity.' 'Do you remember a guy that's been / In such an early song?' Bowie sings, in a clear, earnest falsetto. He could easily be singing to Steve Strange's generation.

They, of course, not only remembered but still lived for Major Tom. *The Face* magazine, founded by Nick Logan in the spring of 1980, fast became the monthly of record as far as fashion, art and style went for London's youth culture. For the editorial staff and readers, many of them grown-up Ziggy kids as well, Bowie was not only untouchable but a template for all the profile subjects and models included in this new culture bible, from Duran Duran to Boy George to Echo and the Bunnymen. Even its stylists and photographers were all Bowie-mad early on. 'There would not be a *Face* without

Bowie,' says Jon Savage. 'And *The Face* was essential. Avant-grade. I mean, I don't know what the phrase is now . . . What is the phrase now when marketers want to get the kind of future thinkers and the elite group? It was those kind of people. Trendsetters would buy it.'

That Bowie was still actually breaking new ground justified all this adoration and made looking back at the early seventies, for the time being, anyway, less of a slippery slope than it would soon become. The video for 'Ashes to Ashes' was completed over the course of three days. When it debuted on television, with MTV still a year shy of launching, the clip was like nothing anyone had ever seen, and the single became Bowie's first UK number one since 'Fame' a half decade earlier. The *Scary Monsters* album was well received too. Released in late summer of 1980, it opens and closes with 'It's No Game' (Parts 1 and 2). A sucking sound, like an airplane's windows being unlocked midflight, is heard. An agitated woman (singer Michi Hirota, who can be seen on the sleeve of Sparks' landmark *Kimono My House* album) begins a series of non sequiturs in Japanese ('. . . he's literally tearing out his intestines . . .') and Bowie screams about being insulted by fascists. It's improbably thrilling where in lesser hands it would be some pretentious trash.

There are those who consider *Scary Monsters* Bowie's last perfect album. There is certainly an energy that *Scary Monsters* possesses that many of his worthy 'good' records (1995's *Outside*, 2002's *Heathen*) cannot claim. More accurately, it may be Bowie's last 'young' record. That's to say his last perfectly confident statement, the final time that David Bowie's search for the 'new' in our world of sound feels pure, as opposed to betraying itself, somewhere in its sequenced tracks, as a means to merely revive himself. 'There is an opportunity to draw a tidy line there,' Charles Shaar Murray says.

There are tracks on *Scary Monsters* that vie with his best seventies work. 'Up the Hill Backwards,' one of the album's four singles, has an acoustic Bo Diddley beat and decidedly un-Diddley-like lyrics about tabloid culture (Bowie's divorce from Angie was finalized the year of the album's release). The title track finds Bowie singing in his Michael Caine Cockney voice for the first time since the late seventies. 'Fashion' has a great dissonant guitar, courtesy of Fripp, and a bass line that wouldn't be out of place on a post-punk effort by Gang of Four or the Slits.

Scary Monsters was another American Top 20 hit record, but Bowie was not through keeping critics who might have been prone to relegate him to the past on their toes and remained, as Charles Shaar Murray had pointed out, a 'moving target.' How else does one explain the sudden decision to take over the role of John Merrick in the touring company of the Victorian gothic tragedy *The Elephant Man* and open it on Broadway? Bowie was, after all, one of rock's more classically handsome stars. Much discussion commenced over how on earth he could convincingly inhabit a horribly deformed sideshow freak, which was likely the point. The other key factor had to have been the pure challenge of it all.

'No one with a history of back trouble should attempt the part of Merrick as contorted. Anyone playing the part of Merrick should be advised to consult a physician about the problems of sustaining any unnatural or twisted position,' a warning in the print version of Bernard Pomerance's play reads. Bowie was a student of movement since the days of Lindsay Kemp's traveling show *Pierrot in Turquoise*. He might have connected with the Merrick character on an empathetic and emotional level as well. He too had been an attraction, a performer many people immediately dismissed as freaky (recall Aretha Franklin's Grammy acceptance speech). Merrick was erudite, sensitive and quick witted, as intellectually sharp as he was physically frightening and fascinating. This juxtaposition appealed to Bowie as well. Bowie's tormented memories of MainMan and Tony Defries might have had a hand in his unpredictable choice to take on the stage play. Merrick was managed by 'Ross,' a vulgar individual who had no real respect for his client's intellect and chewed on and on about 'tuppences' he received from gawkers, also oblivious to the real man underneath all the grotesque folds and boils.

While recording *Scary Monsters* in New York City,

Bowie'd met with the play's director Jack Hofsiss to discuss the part. As with his first major film role in *The Man Who Fell to Earth*, Bowie would have to prove himself to investors and the established crew. And as ever, Bowie did so with strict professionalism and commitment. According to Hofsiss he impressed the director with his new take on the character. He would play Merrick as a streetwise Cockney with a wry delivery, not the slurping hamminess some less intuitive artist might have gone to.

'His perceptions were right on the money,' Hofsiss has said. Bowie and Corinne Schwab flew to London to view the body cast of the actual John Merrick at the London Hospital archives and his hood and coat sketches and models he'd built. 'David asked pertinent questions . . . he wanted to know how Merrick walked, how he spoke,' P. G. Nunn, the hospital official, has said. 'I told him he could not have run because he had no hips. And there was a great distortion of the mouth because the tongue was thick and pushed to one side.'

As with his role as mere keyboardist on the 1977 Lust for Life tour, David found it easy to become a working part of a larger production, keeping his ego in check and collaborating with cast and crew toward a greater end during the arduous rehearsal period. After playing in Denver and Chicago, *The Elephant Man* was the most talked-about show of Broadway's fall season, thanks to good word of mouth for Bowie's performance, which found him disappearing into Merrick as deftly as he had disappeared into the Turkish section of West Berlin after his L.A. psychosis. While the Bowie name on the program ensured a sold-out run, Bowie the artist could find anonymity in this role and, as he had with *Low*, deliver something wholly inventive. View what little footage is available from the Broadway run and it's uncanny. Moments after his startling appearance, one quickly loses track of 'David Bowie,' international superstar, onstage. He acts mostly with his eyes and body and uses his gift for mimicry to affect Merrick's impaired speech. 'I completely forgot that I was watching Bowie,' says then rival Gary Numan, who took in a performance while on tour in New York. 'He became this grotesque figure and I gave him a genuine heartfelt standing ovation at the end of it.'

Reviewing his performance in the *New York Times*, John Corry wrote, 'When it was announced that David Bowie would play the title role in *The Elephant Man*, it was not unnatural to think he had been cast simply for the use of his name. Fortunately, he is a good deal more than that, and as John Merrick, the Elephant Man, he is splendid.'

Fans clamored to catch a view of Bowie as he walked the short trip from his hotel to the theater every day. Security became an issue. Hofsiss has stated, 'David had to isolate himself to come down from the performance and avoid the crowds outside the stage door. A lot of theaters on Forty-fifth and Forty-sixth streets had connecting passageways, so David could exit the theater several ways.'

Another fan had come to see the show as well. Mark David Chapman, in New York with an evil mission to assassinate John Lennon on December 8, caught Bowie in the show just days before. 'The day after John was shot, I offered to restage the show so that David could leave the stage periodically when he wasn't needed to keep his time onstage to a minimum,' Hofsiss has said. 'He absolutely refused. We increased the security at the theater, but he made no demands.'

If anything, Bowie must have felt grateful to have a few hours of distraction each night. The murder of Lennon, as it did to any fan of rock 'n' roll music, shook him to his core. Lennon had been a sort of substitute Terry figure, the older brother he could genuinely look up to and admire. Marc Bolan, whom he'd lost in '77, had also played that role early on; while technically younger, he'd been the alpha personality to the shy and searching David Jones. The horrible suddenness and violence forced Bowie to reevaluate. After completing his run in *The Elephant Man*, Bowie flew back to Switzerland and spent the next three years out of the public eye, raising his son and resuming the semihabitual low profile that had always enabled him to cook up projects that meant something to him and eventually to his fans.

A second best-of, *Changes TwoBowie*, marked the end of his contract with RCA. Anything Bowie recorded for another year and a half he would have to share with Tony Defries, per their severance agreement, so he found other ways to record and create.

Bowie was in Switzerland in July of 1981 when he got word that Queen was in town recording *Hot Space*, the follow-up to their worldwide smash *The Game*, in Montreux. Bowie dropped in. A jam session and John Deacon's bass line led to 'Under Pressure.' The entire song was written, recorded and mixed in one day. Its legacy was once in question, thanks to Vanilla Ice's sampling of it for his 'Ice Ice Baby,' but the song has in the intervening years seen its dignity restored. Roller-disco-friendly bass line aside, it's one of the more complex singles in either Bowie or Queen's discography, a suite of sorts, complete with scatting, finger snaps, 'Young Americans' – style faslsetto and 'Heroes'-worthy emoting. Bowie and Queen's Freddie Mercury might have been tempted to engage in a camp-off (as Bowie would do with Mick Jagger mid-decade on their much less enduring duet, 'Dancing in the Streets'), but both men, especially Mercury, are uncharacteristically restrained. Next he collaborated with Euro-disco king Giorgio Moroder on the song 'Cat People (Putting Out Fire)' (with gasoline, no less), the theme from Paul Schrader's kinky remake of *Cat People* starring Nastassja Kinski and Malcolm McDowell. It was recently revived by Quentin Tarantino for a New Wave inspired set piece in his World War II epic *Inglourious Basterds*. French actress Mélanie Laurent stands in a blood-red cocktail dress as she applies makeup and prepares to meet her fate. It looks like a Berlin music video.

Bowie continued to act as well. There was talk of him playing Abraham Lincoln in avant-garde theater person Robert Wilson's opera *The Civil War*. He played the title character in the BBC production of Bertolt Brecht's *Baal*, with stained teeth, filthy clothes and fingerless gloves. 'Bowie is dressed down, and looks sufficiently debilitated, but one fault of the production is that we don't get a really convincing impression of either his bodily deterioration or his supposed intellectual brilliance,' the *NME* griped in its review. 'But the point is more Baal's unceremonious way with spectators, the violence he inflicts upon the social habits of upper and lower classes alike; he is a free-traveling germ, and the only tension in Brecht's narrative is over the question of Baal's ruthless misanthropy – *can* he discard *everyone*.'

In 1982, Bowie appeared as Catherine Deneuve's mysteriously aging vampire lover in Tony Scott's horror film *The Hunger*. That year Bauhaus, yet another Bowie-mad act from Steve Strange's generation, cracked the British Top 20 with a cover version of 'Ziggy Stardust.' Bauhaus was not post-punk or New Romantic, but rather the alpha band of a subgenre of both: Goth rock. They appear in the killer opening sequence of *The Hunger* performing the genre's most iconic song, 'Bela Lugosi's Dead.' Siouxsie Sioux had also transitioned out of punk and post-punk into a more Gothic realm, as had the Cure. In America, bands like L.A.'s Christian Death adopted the slim, elegant-Nosferatu pose of Bowie's Thin White Duke, as well as the more strangled end of his druggy croon, and made it a touchstone of the movement.

'Again, almost without exception, the Goth performers were glam fans who briefly got caught up in punk and then reverted to type,' Simon Reynolds says. 'Bauhaus were totally about that. Their cover of 'Ziggy Stardust,' it's almost like karaoke. It shows the circularity of glam, where fans grow up to be idols, having learned the art of posing from their idols.'

The Hunger is a cult hit among Bowie's Goth fans today, but it was not the acting triumph that *The Elephant Man* was. There are moments of great, MTV-informed style (lots of gauzy light, neon and doves) and impressive makeup effects (Bowie ages seventy-five years), and who can fault a lesbian sex scene between Susan Sarandon and Deneuve? But by the third act it plunges into the standard blood-and-gore horror film it had initially been, according to director Tony Scott. 'The original script was like a B horror movie,' Scott says of the film today. 'My focus was to make it esoteric, and, um . . . strange and sexy. I was fighting what was on the page. We were one step away from giving them teeth. You know, vampire teeth. And I fought that to the death. I got criticized. I got slammed. It's a Goth rock touchstone, yeah, but at the time, people hated it. It took me four more years to get another movie.' (That movie, by the way, was *Top Gun*.)

Viewing these smaller pursuits, from *The Elephant Man* to his Queen and Moroder recordings, to *Baal* and *The Hunger*, one could wonder, especially with a pop chart now ruled by Bowie clones and drones, whether he was done trying to compete on a larger scale and becoming a more selective and less commercially ambitious artiste, à la Brian Eno. One would certainly be dead wrong. The Bowie that was to emerge from semi-exile and resume recording and touring would be yet another reinvention. He would again successfully remove all competition, old (the Stones) and new (Duran Duran and Spandau Ballet), from his path. The eighties, however, with their greedy lust for everything big, loud and tacky, would inform Bowie and not vice versa. The culture of the decade would inflate him to a stardom even bigger and more unwieldy than Ziggy had been. The new Bowie – let's call him 'Straight Bowie' – would no longer be able to handle it. Straight Bowie would never be truly, authentically, crucially and comfortingly freaky again.

'I said, "End up in a suit,"' Kim Fowley says, recalling a conversation he had with Bowie in 1972 when Bowie asked, jokingly, 'How should I end up?' 'After all of the masquerades. All the masks and the costumes, at the very end of it, end up in a suit,' Fowley answered. 'Like Sinatra. He had a sixty-year career. The guys who have long careers always ended up in a suit. When I saw the suit in the 'Let's Dance' video, years later, that guy actually listened and observed everything. Maybe he was gonna end up in a suit anyway, but he certainly ended up in a suit. You can only be Liberace so long.'

CHAPTER 23

The force with which MTV took over the culture between 1981 and 1984 and changed the way we process entertainment (essentially in rapidly edited bits) has been well documented, but MTV also changed rock stars themselves, officially transforming them from marketable images to genuine corporate brands. What is David Bowie of the early eighties but a logo or mascot for his own corporation as well as MTV's? His yellow hair, Cyndi Lauper's bright red hair, Ric Ocasek of the Cars' inky helmet head, Tina Turner's frosty wig, Mark Knopfler's stupid headband – they all became icons of the age, selling their own product and the lifestyle and ethos of the 'MTV generation.' 'Too much is never enough' was the slogan, recited by Bowie, and Lauper, Billy Idol, and the Police, in one of the channel's promo bumpers from this era. Not since the post-Beatles sixties had Bowie invested so heavily in such a preprogrammed zeitgeist, and while the rewards were considerable in terms of record and concert ticket sales, the participant in such synergy ran the risk of becoming indistinguishable from the other brands and icons that flashed across the sixteen-inch screens in millions and millions of homes. What is a David Bowie if he is indistinguishable anyway? No different than Huey Lewis or Pat Benatar or Men at Work?

'Bowie seemed like the veteran of the business,' says original MTV VJ Alan Hunter (who appears as a dancer in the video for 'Fashion'). 'I was worried about his direction at the time. I would pine for these artists from the seventies that I loved. People like Bowie and Yes. Are they going to have to take that Kajagoogoo approach to continued success?'

What does the early-eighties David Bowie stand for? In a word: positivity. This is why the Straight Bowie of *Let's Dance* was such an easy sell to the masses. Gone was any trace of the nihilism and decadence of the early seventies. *Let's Dance* put forth as feel-good an ethos as the Cars' 'Shake It Up' or Prince's 'Let's Go Crazy.' That the motivation for this existential hedonism was Cold War-era mutually assured nuclear destruction – was only a formality. Choosing worry-free happiness or, as Wham's T-shirts read, 'life,' was self-empowerment. Around this time, Bowie sat down for an interview with his *Hunger* costar Susan Sarandon and explained, 'When you're young and you're determined to crack the big dream of "I have a big statement and the world needs to hear my statement," there's something a bit irresponsible about your

attitude to the future. A nonrecognition that the future exists. I think it's important for youth to have that. My son keeps me remembering that there is a tomorrow. That never really occurred to me before. "Tomorrow? This is it. This is now. This is what's important. Everything's impermanent, therefore I will just live for the second."'
'Do you worry about the world he is inheriting?' Sarandon asks. 'Yes, naturally one has to start taking very positive stands on things. It's much easier to be nihilistic.' This was the very man who wrote, in the single '1984,' a decade earlier: 'You'll be shooting up on anything, tomorrow's never there,' and sang those lyrics with a perverse air of encouragement, as though he tacitly approved.

Bowie was for the most part free from the drug addiction that nearly cost him his health and sanity in the mid and late seventies. He was a single parent with a son on the edge of his teens whom he adored. To try to fake the angst that fueled his late-seventies work (as well as 1980's *Scary Monsters*) would be hard in the new age. He was thirty-five years old, rich and beloved by millions. He spent his days skiing the Alps and his nights with his loving son in a gorgeous house. It seemed a good time to explore this positivity rather than cast around for a superficial edge.

'In the history of the arts one is a rebel when one is young. The high romance dies. Wordsworth was a radical revolutionary in his youth but oh, over time the artist always matures, becomes automatically more conservative,' says Camille Paglia. 'Anyone who is still a rebel in middle age or in old age is a fraud! Rebellion is a youthful mode. How can you continue to be a rebel when you're a millionaire? People who demand that a maturing artist remain a rebel are stuck in adolescent crisis. They want to mummify the pose of rebellion in a major artist of Bowie's rank. I completely and totally reject that. Bowie, my goodness, broke through so many boundaries. Then he would have been a lesser artist than he is if he had continued like that. Major artists evolve. You can't have the audience tyrannizing the artist. "No, no, stay the same."'

'It's hard to say "Hey, you can be a nice guy without being a wimp." It's hard to make people believe you don't have to be a tooth-gnashing, vampiric drug creature of the night to say something important,' Bowie said in '83. 'That same attitude, that same image, has been coming from one particular area of rock for the last fifteen years but it hasn't done anything except produce casualties.' As he prepared to reenter the pop arena, he had the notion that if one could transform the great futurescapes of 1974's Hunger City setting for *Diamond Dogs* and template for its groundbreaking tour or the Los Angeles of *Blade Runner* (released in '82 and directed by *The Hunger* director Tony Scott's brother Ridley) into something uplifting, it would be quite impossible to resist: a disorienting spectacle of preconceived good feeling.

'I wanted to put the stage environment into a place one couldn't actually pin down,' Bowie told an interviewer that year. 'With high-tech columns against a fifties Singapore look. I'd seen *Blade Runner* and was intrigued the way Ridley Scott did that. There was a huge element of Chinatown in his twenty-first-century city.' *Blade Runner* offers a double-edged metaphor for his new career path as well. 'A new life awaits you in the Off-World Colonies,' a creepy, emotionless voice intones at the start of that film, as the camera pans across the rainy, corrupted, neon Hellscape that is Los Angeles, 2019, patrolled by hovercrafts and lousy with Replicants. 'A chance to begin again in a golden land of opportunity and adventure.' Ironically, the soundtrack, by Vangelis, owes much to side two of Bowie's *Low*, that hallmark of gloriously negative angst rock.

Nile Rodgers, who'd signed on to produce *Let's Dance* after meeting Bowie in a New York City nightclub, was expecting to produce a catchy but typically suspicious and unsettled David Bowie record (as all of his albums of the seventies as well as *Scary Monsters* had been, with the exception of *Young Americans*). 'I was expecting *Scary Monsters* 2,' Rodgers has said. Bowie shocked him by confessing, 'I just want to make a good groove record.' Rodgers, with a then unbroken string of number one records with both his own band, Chic ('Good Times'), as well as Diana Ross ('Upside Down') and Sister Sledge ('We Are Family'), was the go-to man for such an affair. He and his partners, bassist Bernard Edwards and drummer Tony Thompson, knew R & B, obviously, but they were also fans of the old and new waves of rock 'n' roll. In 1982, four full years before hip-hop integrated rock, only a handful of artists in America – Rodgers, Michael Jackson, Blondie and Prince among them – were chipping away at that wall that Aerosmith's Steven Tyler would smash through with a mic stand in the video for their Run-DMC duet 'Walk This Way.' All of them had enjoyed crossover success except Rodgers. Jackson had drafted Eddie Van Halen to loan his signature guitar sound to 'Beat It,' creating a crossover smash in the process. Blondie topped the charts with 'Rapture.' Prince and his racially mixed band relied on angular New Wave riffs and angsty, staccato synth grooves as much as they did roller-disco funk or sexy slow jams. It had angered Rodgers, a onetime member of the Black Panthers, that Chic's music was only played on pop and R & B radio despite its New Wave sensibility and futuristic production. The Clash's dance hit 'The Magnificent Seven' was in heavy rotation on New York City R & B and disco bastions like WBLS and WKTU. There seemed to be a double standard at work, and for Rodgers, whose stepfather was white (his teenage mother had had an affair with a conga player), it was especially vexing.

Raised in Greenwich Village, Rodgers began playing guitar at sixteen. By his early twenties, he was making a living with a series of high-profile gigs, including with the house band at Harlem's Apollo Theater and on the classic PBS children's program *Sesame Street* (where future Bowie collaborator Luther Vandross and Fonzi Thornton also worked for a time). By twenty-seven, Rodgers was an international star, but one who could not get played on MTV or white radio as an artist or a producer. He had crafted Debbie Harry's 1982 solo debut *KooKoo* but it had failed to achieve the kind of success Blondie had enjoyed.

'Working with [Rodgers] was an eye opener,' Bowie told *Penthouse* the following year, 'because he pointed out to me a lot of things I hadn't really noticed about America, about the changes that have taken place for him and how difficult it is now for him to get music played on white radio or white television and boy – he's talking white radio, white television. When I started watching the cable music channel MTV, I found the racism extraordinarily blatant,' Bowie added.

'Bowie was the most outspoken critic of the Michael Jackson issue,' says Alan Hunter of the channel's refusal to play Michael Jackson and other R & B pop artists pre-*Thriller*. 'He slammed [late VJ] J. J. Jackson [an African American]. He was being interviewed and out of nowhere he said, 'Why don't you play any black people?' J. J. sputtered for an answer in defense of MTV.'

Rodgers, then only thirty, was a huge Bowie fan, having toured England in the Ziggy-mad year of '73. He felt out of place in his outfit at the time, a straight R & B combo called New York City. 'I was very embarrassed doing those old soul standards,' he told *The Face* in 1984. 'I just didn't fit. Sometimes blacks can be straighter than whites, older middle-class blacks. I'd come in with brocade jackets, patched jeans, and silver purses dangling from my shoulder. I was doing lots of acid. I saw myself as a rock superstar.' Chic, according to legend, was inspired to add female singers Norma Jean Wright and Luci Martin to the band's then unsuccessful lineup by noticing the models on the covers of Roxy Music sleeves.

Since the mid-seventies, Rodgers had envied the career path of his old acquaintance Carlos Alomar. 'My whole life I've been following Alomar,' he said. 'All the things I wanted to do, he got there first. He had the Apollo job, the Bowie job . . .' When the Bowie collaboration began, the Chic leader figured he would finally have a chance to demonstrate that he could make a real New Wave record for a mostly white audience. As they worked through the winter, recording the demos Bowie had written in Switzerland during his extended hiatus (as well as Iggy Pop's 'China Girl'), it became clear that it was now both David Bowie and Nile Rodgers's turn to cross over with something that not only combined the best of both genres but, like *Station to Station*, created something new entirely, a sort of future-funk blues that felt both modern and classic at the same time. The sound that Rodgers and Bowie hit upon in the winter of '82, holed up in the Power Station, would also be used to create Rodgers-produced soulful New Wave hits for Madonna ('Like a Virgin,' 'Material Girl'), Duran Duran ('The Reflex,' 'Wild Boys,' 'Notorious'), INXS ('Original Sin'), the Thompson Twins ('Lay Your Hands on Me'), the B-52s ('Roam') and even Mick Jagger (*She's the Boss*) by the end of the decade.

David Bowie the free agent was a hot property but the star opted to sign with EMI on the strength of Queen's recommendation. Finally free of Tony Defries in a contractual sense, eight years after leaving MainMan, with his divorce final and enough artistic credibility and cultural cachet to bank for life, he was no longer hampered by the past. Like Roxy Music's *Avalon*, a major hit for the veteran art rockers in 1982 (also granting them a fresh, young MTV audience), Bowie's new material would be unapologetically romantic and defiantly pleasing to listen to. In fact, that would *be* its edge.

In the years since *Let's Dance's* worldwide release in the spring of 1983, it has been unfairly maligned by Bowie purists as his sellout record, but it's every bit as high concept as his canonized seventies efforts. Unlike some of its more diluted, less successful follow-up efforts, like 1984's *Tonight* and '87's *Never Let Me Down*, *Let's Dance* was, in its way, as revolutionary as *Ziggy Stardust, Station to Station* or *Low*.

'This record is pure celebration,' Charles Shaar Murray raved in his NME review of *Let's Dance*'s title track, 'a tribute to love and life that is as uncontrived as anything he's ever done in his entire career . . . With this album, Bowie seems to have transcended the need to write endlessly about the dramas of being David Bowie and about all his personal agonies. This album just goes straight to the heart of it: it is warm, strong, inspiring and useful. You should be ashamed to say you do not love it.'

Side one opens with a chukka-chukka rhythm at once funky and strange, followed by a soothing electronic riff and Bowie announcing, 'I know when to go out, I know when to stay in. And get things done.' 'Modern Love' is the sound of someone who's been away, reflecting some ('It's not really work / It's just the power to charm'). The new times terrify him some, but he's going to use the fear and stay positive. 'China Girl' differs from Iggy's '76 version primarily thanks to Bowie singing the melody and a soulful 'little China girl' before the verse (which is more or less identical to Iggy's). The arrangement of the Chinese bells is altered slightly for maximum pop impact as well, but who can blame him? How else does one take lyrics like 'I stumble into town, just like a sacred cow / Visions of swastikas in my head' into the British and American Top 10? And just putting the song on *Let's Dance* enabled Iggy to survive the eighties and probably the early nineties too (up until his fluke Kate Pierson duet hit 'Candy' anyway). Completing the front-loading of the album (three hit singles in a row) is the title track, easily the most unconventional number one hit single of the modern era. With wood-block percussion, short bleating horns and Tony Thompson's titanic drums driving the track for nearly eight minutes, Bowie pours out his most romantic and insistent vocal performance since 'Heroes.' He starts out cool and flirty ('Put on your red shoes and dance the blues') and finishes all sweaty ('If you should fall into my arms, tremble like a flower'). I interviewed the singer/songwriter M. Ward in the summer of 2009 and took a moment to ask him about his striking cover of 'Let's Dance,' which breaks the hit down to its basics and reimagines it like a Nina Simone torch song. 'I always wanted to do a stripped down version of a dance song,' he says. 'The beautiful thing about 'Let's Dance,' I found are the lyrics. The production is great but it tends to hide the fact that the lyrics are so good. It's a song I remember from my childhood, but I didn't really realize what Bowie was saying in that song until I recorded it.' 'Let's Dance' also introduces the concept of 'Serious Moonlight,' the title of the world tour. Bowie told an interviewer around this time that the term 'serious moonlight,' a refrain throughout the song and the moniker of the *Let's Dance* world tour, is essentially meaningless.

'It was an Americanism that I liked. Serious

this . . . serious that . . .' Lyrically, however, the magic comes from trying to picture said moonlight. Is it blue? Yellow? Low hanging and full or an intriguing sliver peering through some windblown clouds? Or maybe it's a half moon, like the tour set's model or the mylar balloons dropped on the crowd in the 'Modern Love' video? The other hallmark of 'Let's Dance,' of course, is the appearance of guitar god Stevie Ray Vaughan, contributing just one blues note midway through and taking the song out with his distinctive, fat but tough, weirdly melancholy style. Vaughn, then just twenty-eight, was a Dallas-born hotshot whose band Double Trouble had just started to come up from the bar circuits thanks to high-profile appearances at jazz and blues festivals like Switzerland's Montreux (where Bowie first saw him in '82). By the time 'Let's Dance' topped the charts, he had released his own hit record *Texas Flood* and opted out of playing on the Serious Moonlight tour (there were rumours that he'd fallen out with Bowie after Double Trouble were booked and then dropped as the opening act for the entire tour). Nobody has sounded quite like him since his death in a helicopter crash in August 1990, and each time another guitarist (whether it's Earl Slick, who did the tour in '83, or Peter Frampton, who toured with Bowie in '87) plays the song, they can do nothing but humbly imitate the man. Most people stop listening to *Let's Dance* here, but the album still has much to offer. 'Without

You' is a classy midtempo ballad that strongly resembles early-eighties Roxy Music. 'Criminal World' has a pop reggae groove that acts like Sade and UB40 would do much with as the decade wore on. 'Cat People (Putting Out Fire),' Bowie's 1982 collaboration with Giorgio Moroder, reappears as well. 'Shake It,' with its falsetto delivery and female backing vocals, is something like a godparent to U2's 1993 hit 'Lemon.'

Straight Bowie appears stripped to the waist and shadowboxing on the album's sleeve. He is tan, rested, with a little meat on his bones (he actually looks like he might be able to take you in that fight). The real achievement is the hair, however, his most radical tonsorial statement since the Red Hot Red Ziggy rooster cut a decade earlier.

'I thought the Serious Moonlight preppy look was a terrific contrast to the sort of spaced-out pale scrawny look,' says David Mallet, who shot the trio of videos for the album's three smash singles. 'It was so different and unexpected. And he looked great.' 'To me the *Let's Dance* persona was the last massive and significant change to his image,' Simon Reynolds says. 'He went from being cocaine-ravaged thin, with this totally gaunt, pallid face, to this new healthy look – blond hair, tanned looking, very exuberant.' Presenting himself to a live audience, Bowie would choose a peachy yellow/orange zoot suit. As a student of painting he must have known that the color of the fabric, like the color of his new hair, called sunshine and positive energy to mind. There were few rock stars of Bowie's caliber touring the world in 1983. The Rolling Stones had made their stadium run in '81. The Who had played their 'farewell tour' in '82. Rod Stewart, Billy Joel, AC/DC and Def Leppard were playing arenas, but none of them promised the theatrical experience that a Bowie concert did, and advance ticket sales were beyond brisk. Only the Police's tour in support of *Synchronicity* came close. The Serious Moonlight tour kicked off in Brussels on May 18 and then traveled to Germany on May 20, followed by dates across England. American audiences were given a preview when David Bowie headlined the third and final day of the second annual (and last) US Festival in southern California (along with Stevie Nicks, the Pretenders and U2). Bowie, Van Halen and, most controversially, opening-night headliners the Clash were all rumored to be paid seven-figure fees by the festival's sponsor, Apple Computers.

Serious Moonlight hit American sports arenas in July before traveling to the Pacific rim in late '83 (over two million people would purchase tickets by the end of the run). Bowie's big band (Slick; Alomar; Thompson; bassist Carmine Rojas, replacing George Murray; sax men Lenny Pickett, Stan Harrison and Steve Elson; keyboardist Dave Lebolt and backing vocalists the Simms brothers) all dressed in retro hepcat zoot suits and wide-brimmed hats in uplifting shades of green and peach. The set list drew from Bowie's entire career, opening most nights with a bluesy 'The Jean Genie' (Mick Ronson sat in with the band during a tour stop in Canada) and spacing the *Let's Dance* material and other hits like 'Heroes' and 'Rebel Rebel' throughout lesser-known material like *Low's* 'What in the World' or the Velvets' 'White Light/White Heat.' 'Modern Love' closed the show most nights. This would be Bowie's first tour to employ massive monitors on either side of the stage, which the visually savvy star knew instinctively how to work for the nosebleed seats of stadiums. Thanks to rave word-of-mouth from the European dates, anticipation for the American leg and the chart success of 'China Girl' on the heels of 'Let's Dance,' Bowie became one of the rare rock stars to grace the cover of *Time* magazine. 'Yes, Michael Jackson may have sold more records, and yes, the Police can sell out Shea Stadium. But Bowie, in many ways, can meet them and match them both, and offer something else too. A Bowie concert, shorn of excessive theatrics, is a raved up tutorial in rock 'n' roll survival. A history lesson with a horn section. This show is about the fall and rise of David Bowie,' writer Jay Cocks observed. Serious Moonlight was a blockbuster in part because it marked the first real generation shift in ticket buyers, from baby boomers to teenage future Generation Xers.

Serious Moonlight was, like the '78 tour, unencumbered by darkness, but Bowie's taste in film roles had not mainstreamed along with his music.

Prior to the release of *Let's Dance*, Bowie filmed a small part in a homoerotic film called *Merry Christmas Mr Lawrence*. Bowie played a yellow-haired British army officer who becomes the object of the painfully unrequited love of a Japanese officer, played by Ryuichi Sakamoto, then a Japanese pop star in Yellow Magic Orchestra (themselves a synth-pop act highly influenced by the Berlin trilogy). Sakamoto was in the crowd when Bowie took the Ziggy stage show to Japan and remained a devotee for a decade. The film, directed by Nagisa Oshima, the Japanese maverick who helmed *In the Realm of the Senses*, was filmed in the Pacific islands. Bowie shared an intense, blue-lit love scene with Sakamoto, who snatches a lock of his hair before leaving him to die, buried up to his neck in the hot sand.

'He's buried and he's dying and he understands the love between enemies.' Sakamoto tells me, discribing the scene today, 'He is generating some special vibrations and I really felt that. It was a Christlike death . . . When I cut his hair when he's buried, that moment in life really felt that spirit. I'd heard of that kind of love going on in the army. A man's world.'

It was a brave film for its time, and Bowie confused many of his long-time gay fans by giving an interview to *Rolling Stone's* Kurt Loder early in the year where he dismissed his liberating early-seventies revolution as 'youthful experimentation.' If there was one real contention that came with the massive success of the new Straight Bowie, this was it. With homosexual men just starting to die of 'the gay cancer,' some felt this was an act of betrayal. Now that he was a mainstream pop star on the cover of *Time*, he was turning his back on the very community that supported him all along.

'That's about the time he was being very coy about not really being bisexual . . . that appealed to me because I was hoping that my sexuality, that I would outgrow it too,' says performer Justin Bond, a Bowie fan since the mid-seventies. 'A couple of years later though, I was really turned off by him. I didn't like him at all. Because of that bullshit. "Experimentation." By then I was a politicized queer radical and I was like, "Fuck him and fuck that." I didn't feel betrayed, I just felt like he was a product. But then he lost his touch, didn't he? For many people it was a betrayal. You can't take that back. 'Oh, no, I really am cool. I really am on your side.' At a time when Reagan was in office and AIDS was rearing its head he decided he was going to cash in on his white, male privilege and put a distance between him and his stigmatized fans, and by doing that, he basically said, 'Okay, I am the dick that you love hating. I am Rod Stewart.' And that's what he's like now.' Professor Paglia offers a counter-theory. 'Throughout the eighties, because of AIDS, a lot of punitive stuff was coming from gay activists. It was a period of censoriousness. If so and so does not fulfill the agenda for the socially approved message du jour then they're a traitor.

I hated that about gay activism. I follow the Oscar Wilde theory here, that the artist has no obligation to any social cause. The artist has an obligation only to art. This business of reading artists the riot act is what the Nazis did and what the Stalinists did. You're asking art to serve a propagandistic purpose. Art is not a branch of sociology. It's not a branch of social improvement. Not a branch of the health sciences. Bowie, in my view, had no obligation to say "I'm gay." His obligation is only to his imagination. It's the extreme view but I think, quite frankly, it's the authentically gay view. The other view is from people who have driven a wedge between gay culture and the arts. It's the same attitude Gloria Steinern has about Picasso. Picasso was a bad man and therefore a bad artist?'

I remember seeing the 'Let's Dance' video world premiere on MTV. I would spend full days laying on the cool, white-tiled floor in my grandparents' house, which was situated on the eighteenth hole of the Woodlands Country Club in Fort Lauderdale. Between 1981 and 1988, I watched MTV seven hours a day. I wanted my MTV. It showed me how to live, or at least how to look. I bought a pair of army pants with ties at the ankles and lots of pockets for the storage of ammunition (I put Jolly Ranchers in them) after seeing Joe Strummer in the 'Rock the Casbah' video. Pants weren't much of a commitment, of course. You could take them off and put on another pair, maybe some Guess or Girbaud jeans. Bowie's new videos made me commit. I had not been motivated by Billy Idol, Dale Bozzio, Nick Rhodes, Terri Nunn or any of the other great blondes of the day to dye my own hair, but when I saw Bowie tapping his toe while strumming his guitar against the wall in that sweaty café, something clicked over in my brain and I found myself standing for the first time in hours. I got a ride to the Eckerd drugstore in my grandfather's car and endured the full blast of the air conditioner and the Mantovani cassettes, which made the molecules slow and the ride feel three times as long. I found the ladies' hair products aisle and bought a bottle of something called Sun-In, because the poster in the display featured a woman whose hair resembled Bowie's as he danced the blues. When we got back, I emptied an entire bottle, soaking my rabbity brown hair. I pulled off my shirt and walked out to the golf course and found the lemon tree that sometimes kept long drives from braining us as we lay out on the chaise lounge, and I baked my head. Every fifteen minutes or so, I'd walk inside and see if I was starting to change. Frustrated by the delay, I bit into the lemons, puncturing them with my teeth, and squeezed them onto my head like it was a fillet of sole. The lemon juice stung my eyes and dried on my cheeks as I reclined and let the chemical reaction take place. I was convinced that by the time I opened my eyes, I would have hair the hue of a baby chick's ass. Just like David Bowie's. Instead, my hair looked brown . . . with blotches of sickly orange scattered across my injured and blistering skull. 'Maybe you have to wash it?' I reasoned to myself as I inspected myself in the laundry room mirror. Something about the chlorine in the water must certainly function as some kind of activator. But the heat of the shower spray and, later, the hair dryer only seemed to set the Cheez Doodle-dust orange. Defeated, I padded back into the kitchen, grabbed a Cel-Ray soda and turned on the TV. Nina Blackwood was announcing a video by the Tubes. I looked more like her than I did before, which was no relief. Her hair was terrible. MTV played 'Let's Dance' constantly in the summer of '83, as they would 'Modern Love' and 'China Girl' later in the year. Each time, I was reminded of the fact that I was not and could not be David Bowie. By the time he released his next album, Tonight, *Bowie's hair was brown, and so was mine. I had already decided that I wanted to be Morrissey and Michael Stipe and Paul Westerberg instead, but who knows what would have happened if I'd achieved that bright, beautiful yellow the first time? Maybe indie rock only exists because of the thousands of kids who realized that they could never, ever look like David Bowie.*

CHAPTER 24

Nineteen eighty-four, the year that Bowie had sung about so worriedly a decade earlier on *Diamond Dogs*, wasn't exactly the end of free society, but it was certainly a bad year for the artist. Bowie's heretofore perfect creative choices slowly veered toward either the apathetic or the desperate over the next four years, up until about '88 (when most agree, he made a valiant effort to recover his mojo).

There's probably no better metaphor for the decline in the quality of David Bowie's recorded work in the mid-eighties than the life, work and death of pop artist Patrick Nagel. Nagel, an L.A.-based commercial and fine artist, would sieze on a photo image, usually of slyly grinning female fashion model, and blow out all realistic facial detail with a saturated and usually fairly gaudy color scheme. The end result would call to mind Warhol's silk-screened portraits without any of the New York-bred street wisdom and wit, but rather a feel-good, West Coast, sun, sex and fitness aesthetic (probably why Nagel rip-offs still grace the walls of strip clubs all around the world). His most famous works include a portrait of *Dynasty* star Joan Collins and the sleeve for Duran Duran's second album, *Rio*, which broke through the same year as *Let's Dance*. 'Health' was the rage in '84. Within a year John Travolta and a lyrca-clad Jamie Lee Curtis would appear on the cover in promotion of the film *Perfect*, in which Travolta's cynical reporter uncovers what most everybody already knew about these fitness clubs: they're social networks, places to party and pick up sex partners who are already sweaty. But like being a drug-crazed miscreant, being a health nut requires some commitment. If your passion isn't really there, participating in either world, dark or light, can prove fatal, as it was in Nagel's case. On February 4, 1984, Nagel died of a heart attack after participating in a celebrity 'Aerobothon' to benefit the American Heart Association. According to the *Los Angeles Times*, the artist was 'out of shape from too many martinis and frozen Snickers.'

In Bowie's case the only thing that died from his new, golden image was his stature. This was the period where some fans got off the bus, griping, 'He stopped being good once he stopped doing blow.' I can remember hearing this as it pertained to Bowie in my own school cafeteria. Bowie was truly healthy. He had stopped doing drugs. He wasn't even drinking, a device he'd used to wean himself off coke in the late seventies. There is nothing wrong, of course, with such physical fitness for Bowie the person, but for Bowie the artist, who still chain-smoked cigarettes and loved good, strong coffee and English breakfasts, embracing the Nagel-propelled, neon-lit, ocean-breeze-blown 'fitness' trend was a means to an end, and it would bite him back. Bowie was, after all, still intoxicated, only in the wake of the Serious Moonlight world tour and platinum sales of *Let's Dance*, it was unprecedented mainstream appeal that made him weave off course. Unsure where to navigate now that there was virtually no trace of the fringe about him, Bowie opted to pursue material success again; the pendulum swung toward commerce, but this time around it got stuck there, rusted, perhaps, by a shower of cash and acclaim.

This is not to judge Bowie or take him to task for an uninspired release or two. He was probably sincerely exhausted, having toured all points east and west and turned in high-energy performances at each venue. A longer spell of rest and salubrious recovery time and he might not have been so easily pressured by those who suggested that he rush out the follow-up to *Let's Dance*. Bowie was, after all, new to EMI, and it's natural to want to maintain a certain stock standard. And so *Tonight*, released in September of '84, arrived less than nine months after he ended the Serious Moonlight tour in Japan. The album contained just two new Bowie originals, both of which are its high points, the infectious fluff of a lead single 'Blue Jean' (another Top 10 hit in England and America) and the moody, jazzy 'Loving the Alien.' 'This Is Not

America,' another bit of dark jazz in collaboration with guitarist Pat Metheny, does not appear on the album but was also released that year on the soundtrack to the Timothy Hutton/Sean Penn spy thriller *The Falcon and the Snowman*. Also very strong, it suggests what the sound of a follow-up to *Let's Dance* might have been if the art/commerce balance had some time to restore itself and Bowie decided to spend more time on a follow-up record. The remainder was comprised of ill-advised covers. Does anyone really need to futz with the Beach Boys' 'God Only Knows'? Other tracks were written in the late seventies with Iggy Pop and Carlos Alomar and already recorded by Iggy, including 'Neighborhood Threat' and the title track. An all-star team of eighties producers, engineers and studio men welded it all together, including Hugh Padgham, a veteran of Phil Collins's solo albums, and Derek Bramble, a veteran of the excellent but monumentally slick disco act Heatwave.

Coming off the juggernaut of *Let's Dance*, *Tonight* sold strongly until most people realized that it was not very good. The same year saw debut full-lengths from Lloyd Cole and the Commotions (*Rattlesnakes*) and the Smiths' self-titled release. These bands appealed to the smart college kids who used to live and die for Bowie. New releases from R.E.M. (*Reckoning*) and Prince (*Purple Rain*) more than delivered and often improved on triumphs of the previous year. And let's not even get into Run-DMC's debut album, which was the warning shot that hip-hop was no longer going to be about shouting out one's zodiac sign or giving one for the treble and two for the bass. The field was a fast one, and Bowie was winded and weighted with subpar material. 'It was rushed,' Bowie admitted years later. 'There wasn't much of my writing on it, 'cause I can't write on tour and I hadn't assembled anything to put out. I didn't have any concept behind it. It was just a collection of songs.'

'The album contains an awful lot of classy filler,' Charles Shaar Murray says. 'There's no center. I think that "Loving the Alien," for example, is a really flawed attempt by Bowie to create a genuine Bowie epic.' Worse, Bowie tried to hang opulent, leaden and often overlong music videos on the whole lazy affair. As this was the era of Paul McCartney's *Give My Regards to Broad Street*, Mick Jagger's *Running out of Luck* (co-starring Rae Dawn Chong!) and Dylan's *Hearts of Fire*, when all sixties megastars decided it was time to 'act,' Bowie, easily the most gifted of the lot, appeared in a twenty-two-minute music video entitled *Jazzin' for Blue Jean*, directed by Julien Temple. Temple, a quintessential 'big eighties' director who, oddly, can create low-key, captivating documentaries like *The Filth and the Fury* and *The Future Is Unwritten* (on the late Joe Strummer), would also bring Bowie into a similarly distended big-screen musical version of *Absolute Beginners*,

566

also starring Patsy Kensit, not yet the chic queen of Britpop but rather the chipmunk-cheeked lead singer of the band Eighth Wonder. I'm not sure if *Jazzin' for Blue Jean* intends to seriously address Bowie's family history of schizophrenia (I'm thinking, er, not), but David is cast in dual roles: the superego (a nebbish named Vic who stalks girls in pubs and has difficulty maneuvering his hair dryer) and id (Screamin' Lord Byron, a campy rock star who enters the video on a stretcher, an oxygen mask over his face as if he's just walked out of a 'Diamond Dogs' lyric). A nod, of course, to Romantic poet Lord Byron and proto-shock rocker Screaming Lord Sutch, he sort of qualifies as a new Bowie 'character' and certainly has his own dance (hold your arms, point your palms at your face, let your wrists go slack, shake them both to the beat). It's fun watching Bowie, notorious for his entourages, try to blag his way past the black doorman with lines like 'Great Jesse Jackson speech,' but the only real payoff comes when 'Mr Screamin'' takes the stage to sing the hit.

Much better is the cameo that Bowie shot for John Landis's 1984 release *Into the Night*, in which Jeff Goldblum plays Ed Okin, an insomniac who somehow gets tangled up in a bloody jewel-smuggling fray involving Michelle Pfeiffer in a red 'Beat It' – video jacket. As this is a Landis movie, Bowie is not the only cameo and ends up wrestling to the death with another rock legend,

Carl Perkins, in a gore-spattered luxury hotel room. As a fifties rock enthusiast, Bowie must have felt a real teenage thrill getting his on-screen ass throttled by a bona fide rockabilly super-cat. His short, funny turn as Colin Morris, of her Majesty's secret service, makes one wonder why he was never cast as a Bond villain in all these years.

There were tragedies of the nonprofessional variety as well in '84. David's half brother, Terry, then forty-seven, was in serious decline after years spent in and out of mental health facilities. He'd met his wife, Olga, as a fellow patient at the Cane Hill asylum, but life outside the facility was never easy, and after several years of conflicts, often fueled by Terry's penchant for self-medication with alcohol, she had recently filed for divorce. Terry fell into deep depression after the breakup of his marriage and was readmitted to Cane Hill, where he reportedly attempted to kill himself by jumping out a second-story window. David visited Terry in the hospital infrequently, but when he did he'd bring gifts, like a cassette recorder, cigarettes and some of his favorite books. On January 16, 1985, one week after David's thirty-eighth birthday, Terry checked himself out of the hospital and walked down to the train tracks in the Littlehampton section of London. He calmly placed his neck on the cold steel tracks and waited for the train to come. All suicide is by definition selfish, but suicide by train is especially so, as it makes a victim of not only the deceased but also the train conductor. It is essentially the act of someone consumed by self-hatred (given the violence it wreaks on the body following the prolonged suspense and dread of first laying oneself across the tracks) and a kind of anger that can no longer be contained inside and is therefore inflicted upon an innocent. Unfortunately, in a country like England, where there are strict gun-control laws, it's also a popular method of ensuring death (only 10 percent of all attempted train suicides survive). Millions of Bowie fans and tabloid readers were shaken by Terry Burns's demise, and some went as far as publicly blaming David Bowie for being a negligent brother, while Terry, ill since David's childhood, clearly needed the kind of constant professional care that nobody would have been able to provide.

Of all people, it's Angie who provided an explanation for David's absence. 'David really loved him,' Angie says. 'I think there is also the regret or the guilt that taking the time and trouble, private care as opposed to the national health care, could have cured him. I think David knew exactly what had to be done and I don't think he felt he had the time or that he could take the time off from working as hard as he worked at his career to be able to support it. So in the end, Terry was just packed off to a national health mental institute and that didn't solve anything. Sometimes people just throw their hands up.'

Bowie did not attend Terry's funeral, opting to

send a basket of pink and yellow roses and chrysanthermums instead. The card was inscribed with a brief message: 'You've seen more things than we could imagine but all these moments will be lost, like tears washed away by the rain. God bless you – David.'

'When all the stories in the press appeared about David not attending Terry's funeral, I don't think it was a case of David didn't want to go.' Angie later said. 'I don't think he didn't want to do something about it. He just looked at the problem and realized the magnitude of it. It was so enormous that to have got involved he really would have been working on a voluntary basis taking care of someone who had already been abused by the system from an age when David was too young to have been able to do anything about it.'

Bowie did not tour in support of *Tonight* but, invited by organizer Bob Geldof, he did perform alongside dozens of New Wave favorites and his superstar peers the following July at the London end of the twin Live Aid concerts at Wembley Stadium in London and RFK Stadium in Washington, DC. The international broadcast of the event, on MTV, featured the world premiere of the music video for a hastily recorded duet of Martha and the Vandellas' Motown classic 'Dancing in the Street' with his old (probably platonic) friend Mick Jagger. Like the chart-topping single of the previous December, 'Do They Know It's Christmas' (on which Bowie did not sing but provided a recorded message of good-will for the extended twelve-inch version), 'Dancing in the Streets' would benefit Ethiopian hunger relief. Morally, it's impossible to impeach the single, but musically, it accomplishes something nearly impossible: it somehow ruins a Teflon Motown classic. Van Halen's 1982 version (and even Shalamar's 'Dancing in the *Sheets*') is far superior. But again, it's for charity, and the old friends certainly sound like they're having fun in the studio.

The video, again helmed by David Mallet and shot the same day as the session on the London dockyards, is the camp-off that Bowie had refrained from having with Freddie Mercury four years earlier, full of eye rolls, mugging and Bowie and Jagger trying to out-boogie each other. 'It's a literal video,' says Mallet. 'They're literally dancing in the streets. It's got its strange bits though. It's basically what you can do in five or six hours. I think they brought a suit for each other to wear but that was it. We literally made it up as we went along. I think it captured the chemistry between the two people.'

For his live spot at Wembley, Bowie had to throw a band together. He turned to Thomas Dolby, the professorial, somewhat Eno-like electronic pop star who was then scoring big MTV hits with 'Hyperactive!' and of course 'She Blinded Me with Science.' 'He kept changing his mind about what he wanted to do,' Dolby says. 'He started

571

off wanting to promote his current single, which at the time was 'Loving the Alien,' and then as he got more focused on the event, he realized it was not about promoting your single, you needed to transcend all that and just do a classic performance that would make everybody smile.'

A quarter-century on, there has yet to be a rock 'n' roll concert event that captured the global consciousness in the same way that Live Aid did, especially in England. For days, it was the common topic of discussion, uniting all classes and races. 'There was a very strong sense of occasion about it, yeah. Like nothing I've experienced since,' Dolby says. 'It's a little bit hard in the States to understand this. Britain is a very small island and we generally have a maximum of six topics at a time. Not like us, where there's multifarious info and culture. On the tip of everyone's tongues here you can strike up a convo with any stranger in the grocery shop. Flopping was not an option.' The pressure to pull off a memorable performance was enormous even for veterans like Bowie, Elton John, Queen, the then estranged Mick Jagger and Keith Richards, the Beach Boys, Bob Dylan, Black Sabbath, Led Zeppelin, the Who and Paul McCartney, especially when performing directly after energized younger acts like Simple Minds, Madonna and U2.

Bowie and Dolby flew into the venue in a helicopter while Queen was performing their now-legendary set before the sold-out crowd. Dolby could see them on the Jumbotron as the helicopter descended. Bowie could only grit his teeth. 'I'd seen things like the *Cracked Actor* documentary,' Dolby says. 'That's what I was expecting before I met him, and in fact all through rehearsal he was the ultimate English gentleman, gracious and demure, tan and healthy, polite to everybody, complimentary. He was anything but the cracked actor. But he was not too fond of flying, as you know, and the only way to get him to Wembley for the performance was in a helicopter, and I think it was his first-ever helicopter flight. Meeting up with him there, he was visibly quaking, wearing this big homburg hat pulled down over his eyes, and he was chain-smoking and very abrupt with the pilot. He became the cracked actor for the ten minutes that it took to get us into Wembley. Got out of the helicopter and into this motorcade weaving through the backstreets of Wembley and was absolutely loving it and I was terrified. Screeched to a halt inside Wembley Stadium, two hundred photographers inside, 'Oh, I love this bit.' A few minutes later we were onstage.' While some of his peers, including Zeppelin and Dylan (backed by Keith Richards and Ron Wood), failed to live up to their legends, it was widely noted that Bowie's set, along with now-legendary performances from Queen in London and U2 in Philadelphia, were among the monumental festival's high points.

Bowie remained in London following Live Aid

to complete work on his second major film role in a decade. Like *The Man Who Fell to Earth*, *Labyrinth* was of the science fiction/fantasy genre. The difference between the two could not have exemplified the difference between art Bowie and commerce Bowie any better. Whereas Nicholas Roeg's film is sexual, cynical, paranoid and misanthropic, *Labyrinth*, written by Terry Jones of *Monty Python*, executive produced by George Lucas and directed by Jim Henson, is a sub-Spielberg, cloying and condescending Muppet-fuck. It costars cherubic future Oscar winner Jennifer Connelly as a young girl who wishes her annoying infant brother would be taken away by goblins. 'Goblin king, goblin king, wherever you are, take this child away from me,' she pleads. When the boy actually *is* goblin abducted, Connelly must venture into the maze of hedges to rescue him from Jareth, the goblin king, played gamely by Bowie. The offended, militant queens who blanched at his 'just kidding, folks' comments in *Rolling Stone* circa *Let's Dance* were quite possibly appeased by the fact that Jareth could not look or sound gayer. 'Sara, go back to your room. Play with your toys and your costumes,' he sasses as the crystal he holds turns into a snake. There's also a vaguely creepy sexual tension between Bowie and Connelly during their dance sequence. 'I think he's got a lot of real chemistry with her,' a fellow rock critic once told me, and I tend to agree. Of all Bowie's costars, from Candy Clark to Catherine

Deneuve, Michelle Pfeiffer and later Rosanna Arquette (in the astoundingly bad *The Linguini Incident*), it may be the fourteen-year-old Connelly whom he generates the most intensity with. 'I was just this side of getting it,' Connelly said of the shoot. 'Getting who David Bowie was. He was really sweet. I liked him very much.'

The script is full of Zen koans like 'The way forward is the way back.' And yet for all its vulgarity, its easy to see why *Labyrinth* remains a cult hit on video and a favorite among the kids of Bowie's boomer and Generation X fans. It's just scary enough to amuse older children, and their mothers and fathers (or fathers and fathers and mothers and mothers) can revel in the high camp. 'I'd be forced to suspend you headfirst in the bog of eternal stench,' Bowie says, threatening Connelly's dwarfish Muppet pal Hoggle; the bog gives off a delicious stench indeed, and the execrable soundtrack was clearly recorded there. 'Chilly Down,' in which Bowie semi-raps, is not exactly 'The Rainbow Connection.' 'Underground,' the film's ostensible main theme song, returns Bowie to his soul-singer mode without any of the passion that he knew in '75. The sensational pipes of Chaka Khan, who provides backup vocals, as she did on every single song released in 1986, are wasted. Upon its release in the summer of '86 *Labyrinth* failed to connect, raking in just twelve million dollars theatrically. 'It was a flop at the box office because it's not a particularly good film,' says John Scalzi, film critic and author of *The Rough Guide to Sci-Fi Movies*. 'I think it's pretty clear that Bowie wasn't brought in to hide himself in the role of the goblin king, he was brought in so that the goblin king could *be* like David Bowie. They didn't hire him to be an actor, they hired him to be a star.'

A brief reunion with Iggy Pop on their third collaboration, *Blah Blah Blah*, resulted in some strong songs – and a minor hit with Iggy's cover of the old Johnny O'Keefe rockabilly hit 'Real Wild Child' – but Iggy's real creative foil on that record was Steve Jones, the former Sex Pistols guitarist.

David Bowie turned forty on January 8, 1987. In an interview with Charlie Rose in 1998, the year after he turned fifty, Bowie explains that the big four-inch was much more troubling. By fifty, he'd released two more very strong albums, 1995's *Outside* and 1997's *Earthling*; fallen in love with Web-based technology and new finance; and seemed to have regained his creative footing and interests. At forty, he'd lost nearly all of it. The artist who prided himself on being hands-on, controlling (he'd occasionally hum guitar solos to his revolving ax men) and perpetually inspired began showing up to photo shoots and allowing himself to be draped in whatever horrible, shoulder-padded and garishly patterned frocks the stylists deemed worthy. Photos of Bowie during this period certainly show him in a lot of animal print. In the video for 'Day-In Day-Out,' the first single off *Never Let Me Down*, his 1987 follow-up to *Tonight* and the *Labyrinth* soundtrack, Bowie is skating. There's a good little bit of metaphor. Like *Tonight* and *Labyrinth, Never Let Me Down* is not a terrible album, it's just another slothful one, the third strike in a row. The hum and the groove of 'Day-In Day-Out' starts out promising, but midway through, the canned quality of the backing vocals (which ruin 'New York's in Love' as well) grows wearying, and people like Hall and Oates and even Robbie ('C'est la Vie') Nevil or Go West were doing the high-tech blue-eyed soul thing much better circa '86 and '87. Iggy and Steve Jones (with Bowie) do the Sunset Strip trash-guitar rock thing better on *Blah Blah Blah* than Bowie does here as well (''87 and Cry'). 'Time Will Crawl,' with its nightmare lyrics about nuclear meltdown (inspired by the Chernobyl power plant disaster in April of 1986), is one of the few genuine high points where Bowie sounds like he actually gives a toss for what's coming out of his mouth and how. The only thing that keeps it from joining the Bowie best-of is the tinny production, something Bowie publicly regrets. He told the *Daily Mail* in June of '08 (where the track was included in a CD of his all-time favorites), 'There are a host of songs that I've recorded over the years that for one reason or another I've often wanted to re-record some time in the future. This track from *Never Let Me Down* is one of those.' Electronic percussion clangs and towers of cheap synth echo all over 'Beat of Your Drum,' as if Bowie was watching *Miami Vice* with Swiss subtitles as he composed the thing. 'I like the smell of your flesh. I'd like to beat on your drum,' Bowie sings. This passes for lust from a man who once wrote, 'This mellow thighed chick just put my spine out of place'?

Physically Bowie looked remarkably unchanged. A journalist observed at the time, 'Incipient crow's feet is virtually the only sign of his age.' He wore forty well from the skin out. Inside, he seemed like his rapidly aging character from *The Hunger*, trying to convince those who encountered him, 'I'm a young man! I'm a young man.' Midway through the record we are told all about the glass spider, the namesake for the monster tour that Bowie would launch in the summer of 1987. Over a dour string arrangement, Bowie – or is it Jareth the goblin king? – takes the spotlight for his 'Stonehenge' moment. 'Up until one century ago there lived in the Zi Duang province of eastern country a glass-like spider . . . Having devoured its prey it would drape the skeletons over its web . . . its web was also unique in that it had many layers like the floors of a building . . .' The tale goes on for nearly six minutes with unintentional hilarity ('The baby spiders would get scared and search frantically for their mother') that makes a Bowie-ist long for the days of rats the size of cats and ten thousand people-oids.

Peter Frampton, Bowie's old friend from Bromley Tech, was surprised to receive a call one day while he was out on tour with Stevie Nicks. Bowie had heard Frampton's latest album *Premonition* and was impressed. 'There were long periods where we didn't acknowledge each other, 'cause we're in different spheres of the world, but every like five years we'd make contact,' Bowie said at the time. 'The last time I saw him was when I doing *The Elephant Man* and he was living in New York. I always thought it'd be good to work with him 'cause I was so impressed with him as a guitarist at school.'

Frampton, unlike Bowie, was no longer the superstar that he was in the seventies and saw the job as both an opportunity to play megastages again as well as a chance to reconnect with his old friend. He didn't bargain for being eaten by the Glass Spider production, with its troupe of dancers (choreographed again by Toni Basil) illustrating each song, countless lighting cues and two full decades' worth of Bowie songs to learn on short notice, each one with its own distinctive guitar sound (from the Fripp drone of 'Heroes' to the Stevie Ray wail of 'Let's Dance').

'Obviously going from being the head honcho on my own tour to David's tour, which was this huge production, was interesting,' he says today. 'I loved it for the most part but sometimes the dancers would keep stepping on my pedal. Once I was in the middle of 'Let's Dance' trying to do my best Stevie and one of the dancers turned me off . . . Another night during a very quiet number one of them turned my fuzz box on. It totally blew the vibe. The dancers were not my favorite things. I'll never perform with dancers again. I'll have them green screened.' Big eighties greed bled its way into the venue sizing as well and exposed Bowie's reach as a bit short. 'Toni had never directed a stadium show in her life,' says Mark Ravitz, who again designed the set. 'I don't recall a full rehearsal of the show top to bottom, so it never had a total cohesiveness about it, despite all the complexity of the dances. When Frampton wanted to do something as an individual Bowie came down on that. Bowie would get upset at me if I told him he could do it. There were a lot of egos. A lot of it just wasn't as whole as some of the other tours had been.'

'I want a performance to upset people to a certain extent, to keep people interested so that they say, "Hey, you can do that stuff – I'm not quite sure what it meant but it was really exciting,"' Bowie told the *New York Times*, with typical prescience, shortly before the tour played Giants Stadium in East Rutherford, New Jersey. He would perform twenty-seven songs from every phase of his career, over two full hours, under the eight steel legs of a sixty-foot-high, sixty-four-foot-wide crystal-bodied spider, lit from within like a Lite-Brite toy. The arachnid was built by Mark Ravitz, designer of the Diamond Dogs and Serious Moonlight tours. For the encore (*Aladdin Sane*'s 'Time') he would emerge from the spider's head, high above the crowd.

'I got up on it myself,' Ravitz says. 'Anything I design, if I can do it, they can do it. So one day I got up in the head of the spider. Sixty feet in the air. There's a three-foot square you're standing on, steel pipe welded to it, strapped with weight lifter straps. Foot pedal to make the wings open up. You gotta shit a brick when you're up there . . .'

Bowie had gotten a pass with *Tonight*, which didn't have to carry a megatour on its brittle back, but the naysayers were in the long grass for him this time around, likely because of the sheer scale of the production, which required two full sets, as it took four days to break each one down. It might have been the hair as well, or the cherry-red suit, borrowed from Huey Lewis's wardrobe for the 'I Want a New Drug' video. Unlike during the Diamond Dogs tour, however, he was no longer all-powerful and could not scrap the giant spider and reinvent himself midtrek. He didn't even have anything to reinvent himself into. He had erected a ridiculous white elephant in the form of a transparent bug and was doomed to stick it out until the end. If anything happy can be derived from this period, it's that the stinging reviews seemed to snap Bowie out of his torpor. According to legend, consumed with the contempt of a man cured of a gambling or cheating vice, he reportedly had the spider burned in a field somewhere in New Zealand post-tour. It took nearly twenty years for him to see it in a greater context. In '87 it was incriminating evidence. 'I have one of the prototypes of the spider body,' Ravitz says. 'Bowie called me up years ago saying that the other one was in splinters. Now he wanted to save it for his archives.'

Carlos Alomar was another victim of the Glass Spider's jaws. After a dozen years and a half dozen culture-changing albums together, the New Yorker was given the heave-ho. 'I knew David wanted to do a different kind of music. But I always thought that if I gave it back to him it would end up going back to the Spiders from Mars,' Alomar has said. 'That's exactly what happened.' Lost and aging fast, he went about looking for something, anything really, in which he could bury himself again. Few besides Alomar were expecting a band, and even fewer figured it was a good idea.

Bowie caused the first (of many) art school fights that I would find myself in. Most of them were over girls or who could pack the most power into a vulgar couplet, but this fight was over whether David Bowie used some kind of lamb's blood or glands or chromosomes to stay eternally young. I insisted that he would never. A junior painting major, one of those rich kids who dressed like a homeless person with designer combat boots splattered with paint, an ironic afro and a cocky rather than needy patina, insisted that not only was this true but it was also keeping him from dying of AIDS. 'He doesn't matter anymore, he's just another AIDS casualty.' Bowie didn't have AIDS. Maybe the kid was being 'punk rock' or thought he was by making outrageously offensive and iconoclastic statements, but his remark seemed too tasteless and baseless to let slide, so I simply had to drink a bottle of Strawberry Hill Boone's Farm for courage, then find him, confront him and punch him in the eye George Underwood style. This is how I remember it anyway. That kid was a rich asshole, but I see it as a completely punk rock thing to say. Bowie was an idol, and it almost behooved the current generation, especially the insecure artists therein, to take potshots, especially when your idol stops being, well, any good. And in 1988, before Tin Machine and goatees and atonal guitars were able to apply their damage control to Bowie's career, he'd finally become fair game. He'd played Pontius Pilate that year in Martin Scorsese's The Last Temptation of Christ, *and after* Never Let Me Down *there were those who now saw him as a comparably sinister figure. His acting in that film, by the way, is solid. 'So you're the king of the Jews?' he asks Willem Dafoe's Jesus, and manages to keep a straight face while doing so. The hair, however appropriate (a Roman emperor's 'caesar' cut), is terrible.*

This would not be the last time I would defend the David Bowie of the late eighties, by the way. As a rock writer in my late thirties, I participated in a 'best and worst gigs of all time' feature package for a British music magazine that will remain unnamed. The topic of Glass Spider as one of the worst-ever concerts came up and I was approached about writing it up . . . and I refused. 'Why?' my editor asked. 'I thought he was really good.' 'Marc, he was a cunt.' This in the British sense of the word, of course, meaning, I suppose, 'rich feckless asshole.' When I was in that audience at Giants Stadium, and I looked up to see the spider, I was thrilled, and that memory sticks with me. But I also realize now (with a little editorial prompting) that I was easy to get, already someone who would buy the shitty album and the overblown concert tickets and the T-shirts with the horribly cluttered and uncommitted design. It didn't occur to me then that Bowie was making assumptions about my loyalty, and it didn't occur to him at the time that we, his audience, would ever let him down.

CHAPTER 25

B owie was behind the times in 1988. In four years, the indie rock and hip-hop that had gotten under way while Bowie was rebranding himself had started producing masterpieces as culture altering as his own best seventies work, fully realized and fearlessly executed albums that felt like works of modern art – *Daydream Nation* by Sonic Youth, *Surfer Rosa* by the Pixies, *Straight Outta Compton* by NWA, *It Takes a Nation of Millions to Hold Us Back* by Public Enemy and *Follow the Leader* by Eric B. and Rakim among them. Even heavy metal, long dismissed as puerile or bubblegum, now sounded essential, with Slayer's *Reign in Blood* and Metallica's *Master of Puppets* (both released the same year as Bowie's *Labyrinth* folly) addressing serious topics like the Holocaust and drug addiction, respectively. Guns N' Roses' *Appetite for Destruction* had combined punk's rush with a love for smart, theatrical seventies rock like Queen, Elton John *and* Bowie. Bowie briefly dated Slash's mother when she was a costume designer on *The Man Who Fell to Earth*, but he could no longer hope to keep up with the now grown-up guitarist as he had with those Bowie-influenced bands of the late seventies. Punk, post-punk, New Wave and New Romantic never made Bowie feel like an old fogie, but as he celebrated his forty-first birthday in January of '88, he had to be wondering whether or not his creative fitness was something he could ever recapture. Musically, Bowie knew that he did much of his best work when paired with a strong collaborator, whether it was Visconti or Ronson or Eno. Erdal Kizilcay, a Turkish musical prodigy who'd worked on the demos for *Let's Dance* in 1982 and remained a sort of all-purpose asset in the intervening years (playing bass on Iggy Pop's *Blah Blah Blah* as well as the *Never Let Me Down* record and tour) assumed this role in the late eighties.

Kizilcay was raised in an Istanbul orphanage but found a way out through music, largely inspired by his love for the Beatles. 'David once said that my knowledge starts with the Beatles and ends with the Beatles,' he recalls today. In terms of preference this may be semiaccurate (he is also a jazz aficionado), but in terms of ability, Kizilcay was a prodigy. A conservatory student, he could play guitar, drums, bass, keyboards and any number of exotic woodwinds, strings or horns. Asked to contribute to the soundtrack of an animated British antiwar film, *When the Wind Blows*, in late '86, Bowie turned to Kizilcay and ended up recording vocals over one of his finished demos. Kizilcay had relocated to Bern but ended up making the forty-five-minute trip to Bowie's chalet in the small lakeside town of Lausanne to eat dinner, drink wine and talk music. 'We used to see each other twice a week,' he tells me, 'to work on songs together. Sometimes he'd come to my place and my wife would cook for him. During one of these sessions, David heard the demo. One day he called and said, "I loved that demo. Can we turn it into a big classical explosion?"' They added trumpet, trombone, more guitar and bass, as well as one of Bowie's most committed vocals of his eighties oeuvre, helping both the film and the soundtrack become a huge hit in England. 'It became something very powerful,' Kizilcay says. A good start back to creative solvency for certain.

If Kizilcay primed Bowie for the give-and-take that yielded quality results, Tin Machine found him in full-on embrace of the device. The party line on Tin Machine varies. Some see Bowie's short-lived band ('88 to '92, roughly) as the sonic and sartorial equivalent of your dad or uncle feeling his age and getting an earring or a too-fast Italian car. However, two decades on from their self-titled debut, this is a totally unfair dismissal, and the notion that Bowie gave himself an authentic jump start by enlisting three other dudes and ginning up the old droog spirit of '72 may actually be the one that holds. I don't want to be one of those rock writers who exult in the contrary just because it's pleasingly perverse, but I tend to agree with theory number two. If I wanted to be perversely contrary, I would certainly try to convince you that *Tonight* and *Never Let Me Down* are underrated. There are entire websites devoted to such second opinions, and one of them does readdress the *Tonight* album.

Tin Machine was guitarist Reeves Gabrels and Hunt and Tony Sales from the *Lust For Life* sessions in Berlin in '77 and its subsequent tour. Gabrels, then thirty-two and a veteran of semi-successful East Coast bands like Rubber Rodeo, was married to Bowie's Glass Spider tour publicist and traveled with the extravaganza with all-access credentials. He and Bowie would hang out backstage, watching television, smoking cigarettes and talking about everything except rock 'n' roll. At night, Gabrels, a huge Bowie fan since the early seventies, would watch the dancers and the theatrics from the floor and wonder what was motivating his hero (if anything). 'I said to myself, "I would love the opportunity to just collaborate with him and bring this back to something that wasn't about having a dance troupe,"' he tells me. 'But it was just a pipe dream, so I didn't bring it up. Instead, we'd watch *Fantasy Island* with the sound off and make up our own story line.'

When the tour ended, Gabrels's wife, Sarah, slipped Bowie her husband's demo cassette, containing short snippets of his solo and band work and showcasing his unique sound, which was improvisational and multinote but simultaneously hard and bluesy. When Bowie called a year later, Gabrels, a graduate of the prestigious Berklee College of Music in Boston, figured he was being pranked by one of his musician friends or old classmates. 'I said, "All right, who the fuck is this?" and David, trying to convince me that he was really himself, said, "Remember we made up a plotline of *Fantasy Island*?" Which was something only he would know.'

Gabrels flew to Switzerland in the early spring of 1988 and spent several days in the studio with Bowie just talking about their favorite records and playing around with guitars. 'He told me that he was confused by the success he had in the eighties and didn't know who his audience was anymore,' Gabrels recalls. 'Suddenly people were mentioning his name in the same breath as Phil Collins. And you know, everything became pastels. Everything looked like you walked off the set of *Miami Vice*. *Let's Dance* was a legitimate artistic thing and the following two albums were the dog chasing his tail. So with Tin Machine what you got was him finally screaming, "Fuck!"'

Gabrels, and later the Sales brothers, figured they'd simply be helping Bowie complete his follow-up to *Never Let Me Down* and were taken aback when he informed them that his next vehicle (appropriately dubbed Tin Machine, after an automobile or an airplane or hovercraft – anything that transports from a less desirable locale to a new one)

589

would be a full-on band project. He would simply be David Bowie, lead singer of Tin Machine.

This was clearly another branding decision, à la *Let's Dance*, but at least it was, after a half decade of meandering as stylists and producers made suggestions, one that was self-devised. Bowie clearly had a vision for the kind of noise he wanted to make and didn't feel like his audience would be ready for it if it were sold to them as a David Bowie album.

'I argued with David that I didn't think it was a good idea to make it a band,' Gabrels says. 'But he needed to make something that would fall on the barbed wire of expectation. Fall on it and absorb the shock so that if all else failed he could run up the back of it. If the band didn't make it through the barbed wire at least he'd have the opportunity to run up its back and jump over.'

As work began on the Tin Machine record in Mountain Studios with producer Tim Palmer, it became clear to all involved that a band was a band, no matter who is singing lead. An authentic gang-of-four dynamic began to take shape. 'He wanted to get back to that sweaty vibe,' says Hunt Sales today. 'Four guys in a basement.' Forget that the basement was an expensive studio in a gorgeous lakeside town in Switzerland. This was, again, art and commerce, Bowie's eternal pendulum rhythm. 'One for them, one for me.' Only it had been 'Three for them, none for me' since *Let's Dance*.

'Heaven's in Here,' the lead of the album's four-teen tracks, serves to formally announce the return of a star to newly sharp focus. It's a hard, unadorned retro blues that calls to mind the early Rolling Stones, while Hunt Sales's live, kit-abusing drums are nothing if not the antithesis of all that awful, canned eighties percussion. On the title track, a chugging rocker with a Sun Studios rockabilly beat, Bowie shouts, 'C'mon and get a good idea / C'mon and get it soon.' 'Crack City' sees the return of the steely rock 'n' roll drawl that had been mothballed since the days of the Ziggy rooster cut. Hearing Bowie spit out lyrics like 'They're just a bunch of assholes / With buttholes for their brains,' one can imagine them being written over a particularly surly breakfast. This was not Bowie's only foray into stinging social commentary. Tin Machine reminds me of 'Repetition,' a brutal track on *Lodger* about domestic violence and economic oppression. Best of all is 'Under the God,' with Gabrels's ferocious riffing and Bowie's disgusted antiracist rants about skinheads in boiler suits looking for minorities to annihilate. If there was any doubt left over about his fascist leanings given his mother's history and his insane ranting to Cameron Crowe in '76, this track served to put it to bed for good. Even the ballad ('Amazing') is as serviceable as anything Aerosmith produced during the same period. And what is it about John Lennon's 'Working Class Hero' (given a reggae-ish workout here) that is so irresistible to a world-beating artist post-stadium tour? (Green Day recorded it in 2007 after conquering the planet with *American Idiot*.)

Some weren't buying the new austerity, of course. According to some, this was filet mignon chopped up to resemble dog food, faux sloppy art rock made by a wealthy professional musician and his more or less virtuoso pals. 'When I first saw Tin Machine, I thought, "Okay, they're well-dressed men playing this angular sharp-edged indie rock sound,"' says Thurston Moore of Sonic Youth. 'The thing that I didn't buy into – this isn't happening because you guys *play* too well. And what is really interesting about truly underground music is that the musicality is really sort of primal and raw and new. Tin Machine can't reference this kind of music because they're too good as players. It's okay to a degree but it was putting on the airs that it was an indie rock band and it was hardly that. I felt a little affronted by it.'

Gabrels himself observed, 'Chops was a liability,' what with their combined playing experience totaling about seventy-five years. The dark suits in which they appeared on the cover of the album could not have helped them avoid this problem, as it tended to make them look like a gang of clean-cut bankers. Even more polarizing was the goatee that Bowie grew for the first time in his career: a neatly trimmed mustache and beard that threw many older fans almost more than the startlingly bleak and unadorned new sound. Bowie with facial hair?

592

In the continued interest of giving the Tinners a measure of respect they have been denied for nigh on two full decades, it should be noted that Tin Machine took the Sunset Boulevard leather and fringe and hair-spray and glitter out of rock 'n' roll a full two years before Nirvana broke as well. In 1989 and 1990 most rock stars took the stage in spandex and fringed leather. Tin Machine, in the mirror at least, was a by-product of three little stars and one very big star fed up with the rock 'n' roll scene.

Released in May of 1989, the album was a chart hit in England and the single, 'Under the God,' was embraced by modern and hard rock radio in America. Critics were divided, however. While Q praised the band for sounding 'hysterical and full of life,' others found them a distasteful fraternity, especially since much of Bowie's appeal hinged on his sensitivity to both his male and female sides. 'I didn't understand Tin Machine, I have to say. It had an ugly macho side to it,' says writer Jon Savage of the music.

'For me that band was absolutely necessary,' Bowie said in 2003. 'It accomplished what it was supposed to do, which was bring me back to my absolute roots and set me back on the right course of what I do best.' Tin Machine embarked on a tour that found Bowie playing large clubs and theaters for the first time since the early seventies (their live set can be heard on the 1991 release *Oy Wey, Baby*). In between *Tin Machine* and *Tin*

Machine II, however, Bowie had to put together a career-retrospective tour he'd agreed to do which seemed, in light of his recent creative rebirth, something of a chore.

In late '89 indie label Rykodisc, which had done a similar thing with Frank Zappa's back catalog, made an offer to rerelease Bowie's now classic RCA albums on newly remastered and repackaged CDs. Bowie saw this as a good business opportunity but insisted that the only way he would agree to it would be if each album included bonuses and rarities. This was long before that became common practice. He shot a video clip with Gus Van Sant (then fresh off his breakthrough film *Drugstore Cowboy*) for a remixed version of 'Fame' as a promotional endeavor as well. Produced by Arthur Baker (of New Order fame), the best thing you can say about 'Fame '90' is that it's much better than the Police's 'Don't Stand So Close to Me '86' but far inferior to George Michael's 'Freedom '90.'

A four-disc box set, named *Sound and Vision* after the 1977 single off *Low*, was also planned, containing even more rarities, including a pair of Bruce Springsteen and Chuck Berry songs ('It's Hard to Be a Saint in the City' and 'Round and Round'). In yet another example of his renewed commitment to innovation, even while filling the coffers, Bowie decided to make the set list selection for the promotional Sound and Vision tour an interactive event. A phone line was set up and fans could call in and vote. The songs with the most votes would be performed on the tour. But there was one glitch. Egged on by a prankish NME editorial staff, many of the callers were voting for Bowie's '67 novelty single. 'The Laughing Gnome' to be played alongside serious fare like 'Station to Station' and smashes like 'China Girl' and 'Modern Love.' Bowie took this with appropriate good humour but disqualified the votes, noting that it was not a sincere request.

Adrian Belew, from the '78 touring lineup, was recruited, as were Erdal Kizilcay, drummer Michael Hodges, keyboardist Rick Fox and yet another dance troupe, La La La Human Steps. As with the White Light tour following the spectacle of 1974's Diamond Dogs outing, Bowie's post-Glass Spider trek was a study in understatement. Even La La La Human Steps was corralled and less intrusive. Bowie hid much of the band in darkness, opting to sing much of the material by large, static monitors (often showing videos of his classic hits), and his stage costume was nothing more elaborate than a white shirt and black trousers. For all its class and commercial success (another sold-out run), Sound and Vision, on the heels of Tin Machine, seemed like more of a professional obligation than something truly new and exciting. This was, critics agreed, good Bowie again, but it was hardly liberated Bowie.

'One thing I can tell you is he wasn't very happy on that tour,' Kizilcay says. 'Something wasn't working. It was a weird atmosphere. Backstage he would get angry with us and say, 'If nothing happens you should move onstage, do something special.' I think he doesn't like looking back.'

Tellingly, almost immediately after the tour closed, Bowie set about working on *Tin Machine II* and seemed happy to move forward once again. Another tragedy, however, would force him to dig back into the catalog one last time. In November of 1991, Bowie's friend and duet partner Freddie Mercury died of an AIDS-related illness at just forty-five years old. Bowie accepted an invitation to appear at a massive tribute concert at London's Wembley Stadium on April 20, 1992. He took the stage wearing a lime-green suit, his blond hair slicked back. Clutching a gleaming saxophone, he seemed more than willing to reference the past. The fact that Tony Defries, his former manager, was in the audience watching the show didn't even seem to put any damper on Bowie's vigor. Everyone seemed to be willing to put ego aside to celebrate Mercury's memory.

'At the end of the sixties,' he told the crowd, 'we were left with a legacy of quite wonderful bands . . . we all used to play the same dance halls and theaters, play the same clubs, try not to wear the same clothes, slept with a lot of the same people. One of the major rockingest bands of that time was called Mott the Hoople.' Ian Hunter emerged with his trademark dark glasses, then another figure from Bowie's past. 'I'd like to introduce you to the guitar player from the Spiders from Mars, Mick Ronson.'

Ronson, looking slightly drawn, with his own blond hair still thick and long in defiant seventies style, launched into the familiar opening riff of that decade's most enduring youth anthem 'All the Young Dudes.' It would be Bowie's first time onstage with his old guitar foil since *The 1980 Floor Show* at the Marquee Club in late 1973. With Joe Elliott and Phil Collen joining Bowie on background vocals, the track seemed more triumph than elegy to the bygone glitter age. Next, Annie Lennox, wearing face paint from the Michael Stipe school of application (part Keane painting, part Lone Ranger) and a Gothic prom dress, filled in for the absent Mercury on 'Under Pressure.' Finally, with Ronson nailing Robert Fripp's esoteric guitar part, they launched into 'Heroes' with Queen's Brian May, Roger Taylor and John Deacon behind him.

The concert featured George Michael, Elton John, Guns N' Roses, Metallica and even Spinal Tap, but Bowie's set was one of the best and certainly one of the strangest. As 'Heroes' ended, Bowie threw the band by falling to the floor and reciting the Lord's Prayer.

'I felt as if I had been transported by the situation,' he would say later. 'I was scared as I was doing it. A couple of my pals were sitting near Spinal Tap, and they were speechless with disbelief . . .' It wasn't exactly a Spinal Tap moment, more like a

Blues Brothers moment, with Bowie doing Belushi in the church as the white light hits him.

'This tribute is for our great friend Freddie Mercury,' Bowie announced. 'I would also like us to remember our friends, your friends and my friends, who have died recently or in the distant past. And friends who are still living, and in your case possibly members of your family, that have been toppled by this relentless disease. I'd particularly like to extend my wishes to Fred Drake. I know you're watching and I'd like to offer something in a very simple fashion but it's the most direct way that I can think of doing it.' He then dropped to his knees and recited the invocation. The 'amen' was met with a huge cheer. He left the stage shouting, 'God bless you. God bless you,' as the surviving members of Queen stared at each other, stunned. 'I remember thinking it would have been nice if he'd warned me about that,' May later said.

Someone as sexually active as Bowie must have had a there-but-for-the grace-of-God attitude throughout the AIDS crisis. Peers from the seventies like Elton John used their money and power to help combat the disease in part as a sort of extended gesture of gratitude that they had been spared Mercury's fate despite similar debauchery. Through the early and mid-nineties, with hard drugs and partying about to return to the zeitgeist with smacked-out grunge and the 'Charlie'-fueled Britpop movement in the cultural queue, Bowie, one of rock 'n' roll's most heroic pansexual substance abusers, would enter a middle age marked by marriage, sobriety and fatherhood, as a human, even approachable space invader.

CHAPTER 26

For much of the late eighties, Bowie was in something of a steady relationship with a younger woman named Melissa Hurley. Hurley, born in New England in 1966, the year David Jones became David Bowie, was a dancer with a slim, elegant build and thick brown hair. They'd met during rehearsals for the Glass Spider tour, as she was in the Peter Frampton-vexing dance troupe. While the relationship with Hurley lasted longer than both his time with Ava Cherry and the happy years of Bowie's marriage to Angie (roughly 1970-1973), the difference in age and, in light of Bowie's remarkable life, experience proved the relationship's undoing. Bowie described it as 'one of those older men, younger girl situations where I had the joy of taking her around the world and showing her things. But it became obvious to me that it just wasn't going to work out as a relationship and for that she would thank me one of these days.' Then Bowie met Iman, the supermodel whose regally high forehead, smoky voice and impossibly long legs were already as iconic in her field as Bowie's mismatched pupils and flair for shape-shifting were in his own. Bowie and Iman were set up on a blind date by a hairdresser and mutual friend at the start of the nineties, who correctly assumed that she had a better chance of holding her own.

If you didn't know anything about Iman (and I knew virtually nothing about her before starting this project except that she was in Michael Jackson's 'Do You Remember the Time' video) or were up late one night channel-surfing and happened to see her selling Iman Global Chic products (glossy faux-reptile handbags with 'fashion planners' described by her cohost as a 'patent croc explosion'), you might incorrectly assume that she was, like most models are perceived to be, a somewhat humorless beanpole with a foreign accent whom people like Halston and Calvin Klein drape material over. But those who have spent time with her insist to me that she is funny, even bawdy at times, and completely accessible as opposed to accessorized. Given her upbringing in the Republic of Somalia, the ancient African country with a history of strife and political upheaval (it's currently known as a source of tanker-plundering pirates), she is both a political and humanitarian activist, and not just in that fashion-y 'real crocodile accessories are cruel' way. Her improbable career path makes Bowie's rise from lower-middle-class mod to global superstar seem like a relative cakewalk. Born Iman Abdulmajid in 1955, by the late sixties she was set to be married to a wealthy older man but fled the arranged marriage. Her father was a diplomat and the family was forced to leave their home in Mogadishu when the government was overthrown by a military coup d'etat in 1969. They lived modestly in exile in Saudi Arabia and Kenya, where Iman studied political science, reading about both the Kennedys and the Black Panthers, gazing admiringly at the visiting Peace Corps officers and fantasizing about America. In Kenya, she was discovered by famous fashion photographer Peter Beard, who spotted her in her casual wear (not herding cattle in the middle of the jungle as was later reported) and requested to take her picture. Iman only agreed to pose for Beard if he'd pay for her fall tuition at the university. He agreed. Like Bowie, she was instinctively adept at the spin of media manipulation, and when Beard returned to the States and spread the word about his 'native' discovery who spoke no English, she played along for a time. Signed to the Wilhelmina modeling agency, her in-your-face ethnicity was embraced by designers and challenged audiences and critics in Europe and America to hold her back.

Both a party girl and careerist, by the late eighties, Iman was divorced from Seattle Supersonics basketball legend Spencer Haywood. She had a fully grown daughter, Zulekha; a personal fortune from modeling; a thriving cosmetics line geared toward black women; and a series of models, from Naomi Campbell to Veronica Webb and Tyra Banks, who held her up as a trailblazer and barrier smasher within their industry. Although ten years Bowie's junior, Iman had few wild oats left to sow when they were first fixed up in October of 1990. They'd met over the years, but it seemed like both were finally ready to experiment with the kind of domesticity that ambition and fate had kept them from when they were in their respective twenties in the early seventies and eighties.

'I saw her about three or four times at different social functions,' Bowie told *Hello* magazine in 1992. 'Once was in the theatre when we leaned over several people and shook hands. I then saw her briefly at a gig in Los Angeles, and so on. Both of us had just, in the last few months, ended previous relationships. For my part, I felt that was it, for me – I didn't want, need or desire any more permanent relationships.' Iman herself was wary and reportedly played hard-to-get at first. Still, the timing was right and the chemistry was real. Courtship became a sort of art project in itself. Every month, on the fourteenth (the day they met in October) they'd have mini 'anniversaries,' and friends of the pair commented that they were acting like lovestruck teenagers. While David proposed marriage to Angela over the telephone, he popped the question to Iman only a few months after that first date during a romantic boat ride around the Seine, choreographed for maximum romanticism. There under a drizzling rain in the Parisian moonlight, he asked her to marry him.

The wedding of these two world-famous fire-brands would actually be quite traditional, down to the month, June of 1992. In an effort to avoid a media blitz, the press were thrown a curveball when it was leaked that the ceremony would take place on the island of Mustique. It actually took place in Florence at the St James Episcopal Church. Seventy or so guests, including Brian Eno, Eric Idle of Monty Python, Bono and Yoko Ono, were put up at the local Villa Massa hotel, a four-hundred-year-old mansion on the banks of the Arno River. David's mother, Peggy, now in her seventies, flew over from London to represent the groom's family, along with David's son, Duncan, then twenty-one. Iman's father, mother and two brothers represented the bride. Her maid of honor was her best friend, fashion model Bethann Hardison. In another bow to tradition, the bride and the groom did not see each other before the ceremony. An atmosphere of intimacy was achieved inside, but outside the church, as word slowly got around, a crowd of about a thousand locals surrounded the building, and after the brief ceremony (which featured original music written by Bowie for the event), they required a police escort to drive them back to the hotel, where the reception, with dinner, disco dancing and a fireworks display on the water, was to begin. Despite the lavish wedding, by many accounts, Iman had a quieting and calming effect on Bowie's affairs. She was not considered as theatrical as Angie or as polarizing as Coco Schwab and relied on her independent star power and charisma to get things done within this new Bowie circle (in which Schwab remained but was perhaps no longer the go-to consultant, what with a spouse well-versed in the entertainment business immediately at Bowie's side). Bowie and Iman instantly became a power couple, magnifying their mutual celebrity stock. He gave her a sense of art-wise rock 'n' roll edge and she introduced him to the high-fashion world where he was already a touchstone but perhaps not a traveler. Both wore these new coats well.

'Road life was a lot more fun,' Tin Machine's Reeves Gabrels says of the band's 1992 tour in support of their sophomore album (which contains a killer version of 'If There Is Something,' from Roxy Music's debut). 'Iman was a nice leveler. David got to read a lot and make up his mind about a lot of things on his own, as opposed to having a personal assistant read it. Iman protected him from the influence of those around him who would rather do other things because it suited their schedule. It had been a very Byzantine world [before that].'

Tin Machine released a live album culled from their club tour in support of *Tin Machine II*. In 1990, U2 entered Berlin's Hansa Studios where Bowie had recorded '*Heroes*' a decade and a half earlier, albeit during a much different political climate. Eno, well into his relationship with the band, again engineered a Bowie-style total image and sonic makeover. The resulting masterwork *Achtung Baby* was released in 1991. It was both a massive commercial success and remains their creative high point. With typical snark, the kind Gary Numan fell victim to a decade earlier, Bowie christened Tin Machine's live effort *Oy Vey, Baby*. Like Numan, U2 was hugely reverential, but the fact that both these artists were raking in the cash by modifying the Bowie model must have been a little galling. Bowie was not yet the wealthy man he'd become in the late nineties. He was merely another rich British rock star living in Rolling Stones-style virtual tax exile. *Let's Dance* was coming on a decade old, and that had really been his last substantial hit record. The Serious Moonlight and Glass Spider tours were block-busters, but the latter had a tremendous overhead and its critical drubbing had lowered his stock. Tin Machine was certainly not going to bring home the roast. Bowie lived in Switzerland and at times kept residences in Los Angeles and Manhattan but soon decided to find a permanent residence with Iman in New York. Any new husband, whether he's David Bowie or not, wants to help feather a nest. A marriage – like having a child or caring for an aging and ill parent or watching a child become an adult, as now college-aged Duncan had – shakes one's sense of gravity, and the natural response is to pay a bit more mind to money in the mattress.

'There was always a lot of pressure to make money,' Gabrels says. 'These money guys didn't get what David was doing at all, but they were really good at making money and David liked money. It was also time to change after three Tin Machine records.' Gabrels's assessment of Bowie's advisers at the time may indeed be sound, but it's hard to fault any business manager for thinking that a quick conduit to another massive hit would be something as simple as reuniting Bowie with Nile Rodgers, producer of his biggest-selling album to date, *Let's Dance*. Surely there is an element of logic to this, and Bowie's new label, Savage Records, was happy to pony up a large advance at the prospect of another *Let's Dance*. Hollywood has basically run on the theory for a century, and whether it's Hepburn and Tracy or DiCaprio and Winslet, they will continue to do so, forgetting each time that you can't re-create a zeitgeist. *Let's Dance* was a moment in culture a decade and a half in the making, not merely a hit record. After virtually building modern British pop and videogenic theatricality, it was Bowie's time to be honored by the masses. There's also the crucial matter of, well . . . good material. You can put Allen and Keaton up on a screen, but without the inspiration you have *Manhattan Murder Mystery* rather than *Annie Hall*. Like *Let's Dance*, *Black Tie White Noise*, Bowie's next studio effort and a reunion with Nile Rodgers as producer, sounded great. Unlike *Let's Dance*, the songwriting was just okay, and the special guests (like light-weight R & B heartthrob Al B. Sure!) felt like relevance gambits as opposed to exciting showcases for unknown megatalents like Stevie Ray Vaughn had been. Ironically, Duran Duran would fall victim to the same thing fifteen years later, counterbalancing middle age with Justin Timberlake and superproducer Timbaland on their *Red Carpet Massacre* album. In a *Record Collector* interview from the period, Bowie is actually asked the following question: 'In the past, you've sung with people like Mick Jagger, Freddie Mercury, Tina Turner and John Lennon. How did you enjoy working with *Al B.*?'

'We used to laugh about Nile Rodgers and then it's funny he goes back and works with him,' Hunt Sales says. 'Nile Rodgers did a great fucking job at a time and a place with *Let's Dance*. I won't dispute that. Nile Rodgers is a very talented guy. His idea to work with him was to recapture what they had, but that's bullshit. You can never go home again.'

If nothing else, *Black Tie White Noise* is historic in that it also reunited Bowie with Mick Ronson, if not his greatest guitar foil, what with rivals in Alomar and Gabrels, certainly the sentimental favorite. Ronson had, in 1992, reminded those who may have forgotten in the intervening years since *Transformer* just how bang-up a producer he could be by working with Morrissey on *Your Arsenal*, widely considered the high point of the ex-Smiths

608

front man's solo work. This achievement was not lost on Bowie, who covers Morrissey's towering 'I Know It's Gonna Happen Someday' on *Black Tie*. He also knew that Ronson had been diagnosed with terminal liver cancer and only had a few months to live. 'Mick was not a drug user,' his widow, Suzi, says. 'He hated pot. I think the illness might have been a product of his drinking. He was a very serious drinker. I think he drank a bottle of spirits a day. I never realized how serious it was. When word got out that he was [gravely ill] it was "Let's get the last record out of Mick before he dies." "Come down and play on my album." They all knew he was on his way out.' Suzi Ronson stresses that Morrissey, an avowed fan of Ronson's work with Bowie and Reed, merely wanted to make a stonking, glitter-informed guitar record, but her take on Bowie's motivations is a bit more suspicious. 'We were going down there for a nice little quiet session [with David] and then when we got there there were cameras. Mick wasn't feeling very good that day. He was really ill during those sessions.' From one perspective it may be seen as exploitative, but such terrible news causes a jumble of emotions and memories, and Bowie, who did return the favor by contributing vocals to Ronson's cover of Dylan's 'Like a Rolling Stone,' was surely sentimental. This version appears on Ronson's final solo album.

Ever the northern pragmatist, Ronson decided that the best way to cope with the new was to keep working and began recording a new solo effort, entitled, with typically English gallows wit, *Heaven and Hull*. 'The T. J. Martell Foundation gave him a record deal when he knew he only had three months to live,' Suzi says. 'It gave him something to think about apart from dying of cancer. Go to the studio and lose himself in his music.' He died just days after the release of Bowie's new album. He was only forty-seven years old. While promoting *Black Tie White Noise* Bowie did remember Ronson on national television, telling talk show host Arsenio Hall, somewhat sheepishly, 'The band the Spiders from Mars – that was the whole situation that sort of got me the kind of fame I had in the seventies. The lead guitarist for that band was Mick Ronson, and unfortunately, tragically he succumbed to cancer three or four days ago, and in his passing, I want to say that of all the early seventies guitar players Mick was probably one of the most influential and profound, and I miss him a lot.' Hall, as was his practice, nodded obsequiously.

As with all of Bowie's lesser work, there are flashes of brilliance on *Black Tie*. 'The Wedding' is a rare instance of Bowie's unguarded emotion and euphoria over his marriage to Iman, and with its Arabic flourishes, it neatly unifies their respective backgrounds, Western pop and Somalia. 'Jump They Say,' the lead single, with lyrics that, like those of 'All the Madmen,' continued to address Terry Burn's sad legacy, was, by contrast,

610

authentically dark (if you discount the Mark Romanek-directed music video, which is pure fashion). Although it topped the British charts, it was not the *Let's Dance*-style commercial come-back the money men had handicapped it to be. Worse, the album was completely upstaged by the release of Angie's memoir *Backstage Passes* and her intimation on the Joan Rivers and Howard Stern shows (Iggy Pop, of all people, was the other guest on Stern's show and refused to remain in the studio with her) that she'd caught David in bed with Mick Jagger. And yet none of this seemed to matter. Bowie's back catalog music simply refused to give up the ghost and join other 'oldies' from the seventies in the classic rock pasture. A third wave of rediscovery, following post-punk and New Wave, came as those indie rockers who realized they could never look like Bowie started selling millions of records – which did much to bolster their 'Hey, maybe I could be Bowie after all' confidence. Dinosaur Jr. did a faithful cover of 'Quicksand' off *Hunky Dory*, turning his fans on to an album that they might have never found. Most famously, in the winter of 1994, completely unsolicited, Nirvana's Kurt Cobain reminded anyone who needed reminding in the wake of another disappointing Bowie album that Bowie was foremost a songwriting genius. During the band's taping of the MTV series *Unplugged* in New York City, surrounded by orchids and candles, Cobain sang 'The Man Who Sold the

World.' He read the lyrics from a piece of paper on a stand but that didn't diminish the feeling that this was some kind of valediction. Dressed in a pale green cardigan, surrounded by his band with cello accompaniment, Cobain demonstrated the versatility of the then twenty-five-year-old song. Bowie praised it as a good 'straightforward' version and after Cobain's death, he added it to his live set list.

'I was at a Bowie concert in 1995,' says Moby today of Bowie's tour the following year alongside Nine Inch Nails. 'The only older songs he played were 'Scary Monsters' and 'The Man Who Sold the World.' He was playing 'The Man Who Sold the World' and the kid next to me said to his friend, 'Wow, this is cool. He's playing a Nirvana song.' It was all I could do not to throttle him.'

Perhaps Bowie's finest album of the 1990s is his most obscure. Bowie's soundtrack to the 1993 BBC miniseries *The Buddha of Suburbia*, based on the novel by Hanif Kureishi, barely even appears in the film (which is mostly driven by pop songs, including vintage Bowie). The book, the sexually charged account of a young Indian man from Bromley caught between the old world and the new who moves to London, discovers punk, grapples with racism and turns to theater to discover his own identity touched Bowie. 'It made him laugh,' Kureishi says. 'Reminded him of his own youth.' Kureishi and Bowie became friendly during the making of the film adaptation, with the icon taking pains to make the author, a superfan, feel at ease.

Bowie and Erdal Kizilcay watched the film (which stars Naveen Andrews, later the star of the hit TV series *Lost*, as Kureishi's alter ego Karim) over and over again in his Swiss recording studio while writing the music. 'He would talk to me about Brixton,' Kizilcay says. 'How his mother worked in a movie theater. I would tell him about Istanbul. We really understood each other. *The Buddha of Suburbia* comes from that and from his connection with Hanif.'

The album track 'Ian Fish, UK Heir' is an anagram of 'Hanif Kureishi.' 'It's very awkward for everybody with Bowie, and he's very aware of that,' Kureishi says. 'He makes sure that you're okay. He knows it's really freaky. "Ah, it's David Bowie." He's just thinking this is an interesting writer he wants to talk to. So he calms you down. He's always in that position with the rest of the world.'

It was Bowie's first full soundtrack, as his work with producer Paul Buckmaster for *The Man Who Fell to Earth* was abandoned after John Phillips got the job. The discipline of having to conform to an already completed film project seemed to help Bowie focus. Despite its status as the interpretation of Kureishi's fictionalized childhood, it's Bowie's most directly autobiographical work since *Hunky Dory*. Bromley is all over it. 'Living in lies by the railway line . . . Screaming along in south London,' he sings. While the film was critically acclaimed and the soundtrack drew his best reviews in a decade, it remained the great, lost late-era Bowie record until it was reissued on CD in 2008. 'He was amazed how little the BBC paid,' Kureishi says. 'Nobody ever paid him so little in his whole life. He was really shocked.' If he felt like a struggling artist after his paltry BBC wage (and the failure of *Black Tie)*, 1995's *Outside* placed the artist back into the willful fringe. In fact, a decade and a half on, it remains possibly the ultimate artfuck record of all time, born out of a jam session in Mountain Studios in the early fall of 1994, shortly after the completion of the *Buddha* soundtrack album, that included Bowie, Kizilcay, drummer Sterling Campbell, a returning Mike Garson, Carlos Alomar and Brian Eno. 'We were just checking levels to separate the instruments and we started to jam,' Gabrels says. 'Suddenly Brian was holding up a sign that said "Just Continue," and he started in with his electronic noises. Suddenly everyone starts to look at each other like 'Hey, there's something happening here,' and we decided to finish an album like that. David was painting the whole time that we were playing. He had an easel set up in the studio. As we went on, Bowie did all the segues that tell the story throughout the album in real time as we jammed. All the different voices. Baby Grace, Algeria Touchshreik, Leon Blank, Nathan Adler . . .' The unusual approach to recording was nothing new to anyone familiar with Eno, but the more classically trained Kizilcay was initially thrown. 'He cannot even play four bars,' he tells me. 'I must say this. He's too clever. An interesting guy but I don't know how he became so famous. He cannot play two harmonies together. No idea how to play the keyboard.'

Experiments like running Martha and the Vandellas' version of 'Dancing in the Streets' (as opposed to Bowie's own duet with Jagger) through the headphones and instructing the band to jam along with it, then playing back the results with the original song dropped out of the mix perplexed Kizilcay. 'He'd spent time writing us letters. Everyone got a different letter,' he says. 'I was in Arabia and I was going to marry the sheik's daughter, so I was to play funky Arabic disco?'

When word got around that Eno, who'd spent much of the eighties and early nineties working with U2 (in addition to producing the Manchester band James' immortal 'Laid' and creating the start-up tone for Microsoft's Windows program) had reunited with Bowie, the anticipation was high that they'd come up with another masterpiece on par with their 'Berlin trilogy.' *Outside,* in my opinion, is as good a record as *Low, 'Heroes'* or *Lodger.* Rather than being ahead of its time or behind its time, it's simply Bowie's most of-its-time work since his late-sixties hippie folk material. Bowie was fascinated by the apparent fin de siècle disintegration of culture, the speeding up of information and the primitivism exemplified by the body piercing, tattooing and body manipulation of the Lollapalooza nation; the performance art of Los Angeles-based artist Ron Athey, an HIV-positive firebrand who shoved spikes into his forehead, leaving pools of contagious blood on gallery floors; and the industrial rock of bands like Nine Inch Nails' Trent Reznor, once a shy Ohioan Bowie obsessive, then a fishnet-clad drug addict who recorded his masterpiece *The Downward Spiral* in the house where the Manson family butchered Sharon Tate and her friends. 'I would put on *Pretty Hate Machine* on the Tin Machine tour to clear everyone out of the back of the bus,' Gabrels laughs. 'And then sometime in '94 David came to me and said, 'Oh, Reeves, you gotta hear this record!' It was *The Downward Spiral.*' Once the music was recorded, Bowie began to put together the album's narrative (sorry, its 'non-linear gothic drama hyper circles' as the promotional material described it). Basically, it's the end of the millennium and society has become so jaded that something called Art Crime or Art Murder has become the next big thing (wasn't it the next big thing in 1974 when Divine declared as much in *Female Trouble?*). Nathan Adler, a kind of Philip Marlowe meets Harrison Ford's Deckard in *Blade Runner*, is some kind of culturally plugged-in detective pursuing a missing child (Baby Grace) who is feared to be a victim of the phenomenon.

For all its highfalutin backstory, *Outside* succeeds largely because the music itself is so exciting. Like *The Buddha* (and unlike *Black Tie*), nothing here feels like a sketch (which is truly impressive given its spontaneous origins).

'Leon Takes Us Outside' is a preamble much like *Diamond Dogs*'s 'Future Legend,' setting the mood. 'It's happening now,' Bowie sings with new confidence on the title track, a middle-aged legend exciting himself. 'The Heart's Filthy Lesson,' the lead single, is NIN-style funk with Garson's distinctive piano running through the track (Reznor, who remixed the song into a minor alt-rock hit, would collect on the favor by pinching Garson for his equally ambitious double album *The Fragile* in 1999). 'A Small Plot of Land' is a flat spread of electronic jazz, segueing into 'Hallo Spaceboy,' Bowie's most convincing rocker in two decades (since 'Rebel Rebel'). Its lyrics hearken back to the halcyon days of glitter as well ('Do you like girls or boys?'). 'The Voyeur of Utter Destruction' asks the question, what if the outro of 'The Bewlay Brothers' was expanded into a four-and-a-half-minute song? On 'We Prick You,' Bowie demands, 'Tell the truth,' as if willing himself completely out of his late-thirties torpor and into the new, abrasive realm of industrial rock 'n' roll (one, of course, fully indebted to him already).

An offer was made for a Bowie/Nine Inch Nails package tour, one Reznor was initially somewhat reluctant to accept. 'There were similar sensibilities in their creation of art,' says Mike Garson, who would work with Reznor on *The Fragile*. 'Trent, being young, obviously he grew up on David and he was a hero to him. But they became peers at that point.'

'I was afraid to meet him because he is my hero,' Reznor says. 'If I had to say there's one person I've wished I could be, for a multitude of reasons it would have been him. I was kind of afraid to really be around him and meet him, because almost everybody that you end up meeting like that, they can't live up to the superhero that you've created in your mind. And he didn't in an odd way.' Reznor at the time was living out the nihilistic lyrics of *The Downward Spiral*, addicted to drugs and alcohol and so full of doubt and self-loathing that the acclaim and fan worship could only seem perverse. Bowie recognized his former self in his new collaborator and tried to offer some big-brotherly guidance.

'I saw a guy that was at peace with himself and seemed happy, and still was making music that I thought was good but wasn't about to die every night,' Reznor says of Bowie. 'I remember a couple of nights of him putting his arm around me like I'm his brother, giving me some advice. I think later we talked and he said, "I saw a lot of myself in where you were at the time," which is bad things about to happen. He had been there himself. And I knew he'd been through a lot of bad shit. And somehow I was in the midst of this bad shit with a lot more bad shit to come, and it made me feel like, all right, someone can come out the other end and still be cool. I was jealous when I saw him, because I was like, "Fuck, man, my life feels like it's spinning out of control, and it's not spinning upward.'"

Like Cobain, Reznor saw Bowie as a sort of older brother figure, a survivor who used his pain to make beautiful art but realized that he did not have to linger in a stale and nihilistic energy field, that age and wisdom were possible, as well as a better navigation system through the obstacles of extreme psychic pain and megafame. Cobain never got there. Happily, Reznor seems to have found his way.

Bowie rehearsed with his new band, anchored by new drummer Zachary Alford and bassist Gail Anne Dorsey, whose extreme-looking crew cut perfectly fit with this gleefully assaulting new aesthetic. 'Aside from her magnificent voice, she played only the fattest, most tasteful bass lines,' says Alford of Dorsey. 'She is a knight in shining armor. That's why we call her "Dame" Dorsey. She has a sense of style and poise. She's just breathtaking. A powerhouse. She adds a smoothness to the music that just glues the whole thing together.' Gabrels and keyboardist Peter Schwartz rounded out the lineup for the rehearsals in New York, and the tour opened in mid-September on the East Coast. NIN, despite being the bigger act at the time, opened, with a characteristically riotous set.

'There was no intermission at all,' then NIN drummer Chris Vrenna says. 'We designed a four-song band segue that would slowly introduce Bowie and his band as NIN and Trent exited. The first song of this segue was 'Scary Monsters.' Bowie came out and performed with NIN. Then we did 'Reptile' from *The Downward Spiral*, where Trent and Bowie shared the vocals. Then our back-drop curtain went up and Bowie's entire band and the entire NIN band performed 'Hallo Spaceboy' off Bowie's record. Lastly, the NIN band all left the stage and Trent and Bowie sang 'Hurt' with his band. Trent would wave good-bye afterward and then Bowie's show continued on from there. It was fairly complicated to pull off, with both bands on moving risers and changing backdrops and scenery throughout the whole segue.'

It was conceived as a seamless shift, and it was, when Bowie's arrival didn't trigger a mass exodus from the venue. It didn't help that Bowie's set only featured a handful of older hits. The bulk of the material was from *Outside*, and no amount of rubber T-shirts or black eyeliner was going to make a depressed fifteen-year-old kid sit through that. Bowie, to his credit, fully acknowledged this and seemed to relish the challenge of having to win them over. What living legend ever gets the oppor-tunity to do that, after all?

'I slip onstage after a set by the most aggressive band ever to conquer the Top 40,' Bowie said at the time. 'I do not do hits, I perform lots of songs from an album that hasn't been released, and the older songs I perform are probably obscure even to my oldest fans. I use no theatrics, no videos and often no costumes. It's a dirty job but I think I'm just the man for it.'

'We had to front-load our set with harder music, industrial music, like "Hallo Spaceboy,"' Gabrels said. 'We had to blow that song early just to come off the peak of Nine Inch Nails 'cause they had built their set to a climax.'

'Oh, it was definitely harder to win over their audience,' Bowie's drummer Zachary Alford says today, 'but I think that is what made it seem real for David. He felt empty just playing the hits again for the umpteenth time. It was like painting by numbers for him. Having to get out there and put your neck on the chopping block, not knowing what the audience would do at the end of the song, that was exciting for him, not to mention for us! I mean, it really made us play our hearts out and probably gave him some of the feeling of the early days. And the material was amazing. There were critics who kept throwing the term "difficult" around. I mean, come on. You gonna tell me *Low* is not difficult? *Lodger* is not difficult? These guys were just idiots who wanted to hear the Sound and Vision tour all over again and David wasn't having it.'

When the Outside tour hit Europe in November, Morrissey was booked as the support act. Like Bowie, the former Smiths singer had his own die-hard fans who would have been perfectly happy to see a full-length set by their own hero, not an abbreviated support set. What began as an honor on the part of the opener soon turned into a war of egos. Morrissey was a major David Bowie fan, just like Reznor had been, but he was not ready to do anything akin to performing a segue number (possibly singing 'I Know It's Gonna Happen Someday' and a shared Bowie or T. Rex song). Morrissey's refusal to alter his set or cede some independence to the older star created an air of tension from the start.

'He got on the bus after sound check and told the bus driver to take him to London,' Gabrels says. 'He left his band there looking all worried ten minutes before they were supposed to go on. He left the tour manager and everybody. He just did a runner. I'd thought it was going great. Maybe he wasn't getting the level of adoration that he required. Not as many flowers as he expected.' Unaccustomed to being treated like support, Morrissey was apparently further irritated by the closet-sized dressing rooms and took to baiting the crowd at earlier performances with 'Don't worry, David will be on soon.' He would later explain, 'I left because Bowie put me under a lot of pressure, and I found it too exhausting. You have to worship at the temple of Bowie when you become involved.'

During a break in the tour, eighties art star turned film director Julian Schnabel was in New York, finishing a biopic on eighties art star turned cautionary tale Jean-Michel Basquiat. When he conceived of the film, a movie 'about an artist by artists,' as he told Charlie Rose, Schnabel reached out to his famous friends and acquaintances to cast it. Making seemingly an odd choice, Schnabel asked Bowie if he would be interested in playing Andy Warhol, Basquiat's mentor. 'He's a very known person,' Schnabel said. 'I need a pop icon to play a pop icon.' Bowie's Warhol is not an impression so much as an abstracted interpretation. He doesn't try to mask his English accent but still manages to affect Warhol's speech with tone and rhythm. He wears the black turtlenecks associated with the art star but reminds us, with his garish leather coat, that this is the eighties Warhol. Crispin Glover in *The Doors* and most recently Guy Pearce in *Factory Girl* have brought the world-shaking sixties Warhol to life on-screen, but only Bowie, using perhaps his own memories of eighties inertia, tapped into the searching, fatigued energy of sixties and seventies icons in the go-go era. 'I don't even know what's good anymore,' he whines to Jeffrey Wright's Jean-Michel as they collaborate on a massive mural. Take away the 'gee' and grimaces and the fey hand-on-hip posture, and it could easily be Bowie talking about his own career at the same point. The film stars many people who actually knew Warhol, including Dennis Hopper, who was amused if not a little freaked out by Bowie's costuming. 'David was wearing Andy's wig,' Hopper says. As he had with his role in *The Elephant Man*, Bowie did the research. 'He was a great actor. Great to work with.'

He was granted access to other items belonging to the deceased artist that were stored in the Warhol Museum in Pittsburgh. 'This little handbag that he took into hospital with him, a very sad little bag with all these contents: a check torn in half, an address and a phone number and this putty-colored pancake that he obviously used to touch himself up with before he went in public anywhere, loads of herb pills too,' Bowie told Charlie Rose.

When Schnabel didn't need Bowie on set, he'd walk into Soho in full costume just to test how people would react, relishing the double shock this would certainly elicit when they discovered that it was not a dead artist but rather a live rock legend looking a scream.

Bowie will always be an innovator because of his pure love for the shape, the feel and the power of a raw idea. He doesn't always come up with the nut of a great notion himself, and certainly as he became more rich and famous, he turned into something of a curator and a champion of other people's visions. Sometimes, in following each idea through to its realization, he will fail, but he remains a great cultural innovator because he sees these failures as part of the whole process. If one out of five hundred endeavors changes the world, who's to say that it wasn't worth it? A half dozen times easily, over five decades, Bowie's faith in the sheer beauty of some thought changed the world.

In the fall of 1996, a thirty-four-year-old Wharton-educated Wall Street trader and investment banker named David Pullman had an idea: why couldn't someone invest in securitized intellectual property? Anything that accrues royalties has value. Why can't you issue a bond against the future earnings of a book or a film or a song, as you would a painting or a classic car? 'John Steinbeck is ideal,' says Pullman. 'Every seventh-grader in America is reading it.'

At the time, Bowie's business managers were looking into their options as far as generating money off of Bowie's back catalog. Bowie owned his master tapes and his publishing and had the option of buying out Tony Defries's share of the generated royalties, provided he could get a large infusion of cash. 'The business manager was trying to sell David's catalog,' says Pullman today. 'He mentioned it to me. "You're on Wall Street. What can you do for this?" They realized David wasn't going to sell his catalog. His songs were his babies. So they said, "Can you help him?" I asked them what they were earning. They were earning millions of dollars a year. A significant number. Sounded good to me. I asked him if the numbers were audited. They said yes. Are they audited by a big six accounting firm? And he said yes. I asked him if he had three years' worth of history. He had five years' worth of history. To which I said, 'I can securitize that.' He said, "What's securitization?"'

Pullman explained that he could offer future royalties from Bowie's back catalog and a fixed interest rate to an investment firm, generating Bowie a considerable advance. There would be no personal risk to Bowie or his family, and with the right stimulation via licensing, there was much money to be made. 'He'd written a lot of iconic songs ideal for commercial film and TV,' says Pullman. '"Heroes," "Golden Years," "Young Americans." Not a lot of catalogs have those type of songs.' There was no indication at the time that every cell phone would have a popular song ringtone or that CDs would ever be replaced as a medium for listening to music. Bowie got it. 'They went to David with the idea and David's reaction was "Well, why haven't you started already?"' says Pullman. 'He picks things up very quickly. Very creative, innovative. He likes new. But not stupid new.'

Structuring the deal was done in super-secret fashion. 'Akin to making a movie,' Pullman says. 'The idea of producing something from so many different disciplines involved things like estate issues. Taxes. Divorce issues. Child-support issues. Wills, trusts. Bankruptcy issues. We had to consolidate all those disciplines of law into one deal. They said it was impossible. From beginning to end, we closed and funded it by January 1997. Delivered it fait accompli, beginning to end, and the whole world was shocked. It was the cover of the *Wall Street Journal*.'

All the bonds had been bought preannouncement

by the Prudential Insurance company, but that did not stop private investors from clamoring for a piece of Bowie in the ensuing media frenzy. 'After the story broke, real investors were like, it's hot. Big players. Pension funds.' Echoing the MainMan strategy of the seventies, the fact that the bonds were not available only made people want them more. Bowie threw every interview to Pullman, his silence only adding to the mystique as the plan rocked the business world.

Pullman dealt with both Bowie and Defries separately because of the still lingering resentment between the two parties. 'He's stuck with him,' Pullman says. 'It's like a marriage. The flipside is Tony is very savvy. I didn't realize he's an attorney, not just a manager. Tony didn't have anything to say about David. They helped each other early on. Tony taught him some of the things he learned along the way about owning things. People don't pick it up right away. Didn't do things the right way to begin with; as he learned he corrected everything.'

Many investors are still holding Bowie Bonds a dozen or so years on, and Pullman, who trade-marked 'Bowie Bonds' and 'Pullman Bonds,' has done similar deals for the catalogs of James Brown, songwriters Holland-Dozier-Holland of Motown fame, and the Isley Brothers, among others. 'You can never listen to music the same way again,' he says. 'You hop into a cab and you hear a song on the radio and you're thinking, 'They're generating royalties.' A lot of people think music is for free. Nobody thought of this. Then they said it would never work. Never pay off. David is someone who grasped it instantly.'

In 2005, a full decade after their touring fiasco, Morrissey still fuming perhaps from the Outside tour debacle, told British *GQ*, '[He is] not the person he was. He is no longer David Bowie at all. Now he gives people what he thinks will make them happy, and they're yawning their heads off. And by doing that, he is not relevant. He was only relevant by accident.' By this time, however, relevance was no longer the point. Trying to hold whatever percentage of Trent Reznor's audience he could manage night after night seemed to be David Bowie's final bid for reaching a younger audience. He never stuck his neck out there to that end in the same way again, as the Rolling Stones and U2 continue to do, always in pursuit of a hit single or an acknowledgment of pop supremacy and competition-worthiness. Bowie would bury himself once again in his fifties, as he had in Thomas Jerome Newton and Berlin in his thirties and Tin Machine in his fifties, but this time he'd retreat inside the World Wide Web, a new technology that he would turn into a sort of command center before anyone else. The Web helped Bowie the Buddhist sustain a sort of postambition state of bliss, where he could remain constantly amused, entertained and engaged. If anything, pop stardom was limiting. From the close of the Outside tour, he pursued whims and entertained offers such as Bowie Bonds with his grace, taste and an organic bravery fully returned, and was rewarded as he had been post-Berlin, with the respect of yet another full decade's worth of younger artists (from Moby and Goldie all the way up to TV on the Radio and the Arcade Fire). His pop stock would never again be vulnerable to the kind of fluctuation too common to rock 'n' roll stars. Freak Bowie had become Straight Bowie and was now Post-Ambition Bowie, turned on, more so than ever before, as he surfed and clicked and edited (he'd joined the staff of *Modern Painters* magazine around this time as well, writing about or querying Balthus, Jeff Koons and Schnabel, among others). He had more to say but nothing to prove.

CHAPTER 27

Like the mod movement following the first wave of late-fifties rock 'n' roll, early and mid-nineties 'Britpop' was a bold reclamation of sharp Englishness after a prolonged era of Americanization. Bands like Manchester's Happy Mondays and Stone Roses released brilliant, danceable rock albums at the end of the eighties, but by the first few years of the following decade, both bands had blown themselves out with the pressures of fast fame and, in the case of the Mondays, enough E, crack and smack to stun a charging herd of megafauna. The Smiths and Echo and the Bunnymen had split. DJ culture and acid house beats ruled the clubs, and what young rock bands existed were so uncharismatic and passive when onstage (despite some genuine inventiveness, especially with regard to My Bloody Valentine) that they were lumped into a subgenre semi-affectionately known as 'shoegaze.' The grunge rock bands of the American northwest – Nirvana, Pearl Jam, Soundgarden, Alice in Chains – were given cover stories in English music weeklies like *NME* and *Melody Maker*. So pervasive was the thick, brooding, whining grunge idiom that British rock acts like London-formed Bush achieved platinum sales by aping it expertly. Bush released a half dozen fine singles (especially the power ballad 'Glycerine') but they were about as English as Stone Temple Pilots. This was a low for British culture, one not seen since the pre-Beatles sixties.

Suede, a quartet who had been going for about four years with varying lineups (at one point including Justine Frischmann, who would go on to form the excellent British power-pop act Elastica), finally made it big in 1993. Their self-titled debut claimed the prestigious Mercury Music Prize, topping the English Charts and selling faster than any record since the days of T. Rextasy. They sounded nothing like Pearl Jam and probably didn't so much as sleep in flannel even on cold, rainy London nights. Fronted by slinky-hipped, floppy-haired androgyne Brett Anderson and classically sullen guitar hero Bernard Butler, they were Wildean in their celebration of intelligent pleasure, but their music and lyrics were pure Bowie: fearlessly sexual, with often homoerotic lyrics that were emotional but tough. The guitars were Mick Ronson-muscular with a nod to the shimmery best of the new shoegazers. As with the Spiders from Mars, the riffs on songs like 'The Drowners,' 'Animal Nitrate' and 'Metal Mickey' were loud, fast and chunky enough to inspire the punters to look the other way at lyrics like 'We kiss in his room to a popular tune.' The British weeklies went ape for Suede, as if they'd all been locked in a sinking sub and someone had just found a hidden scuba tank. The ardor with which the debut was met betrayed a certain measure of shame too, as the British press seemed to realize, en masse, that they'd ceded the pages of their holy music weeklies to a bunch of greasy-haired junkie complaint-rockers. In April of 1993 Anderson appeared on the cover of *Select*, a great and late music monthly in the mold of *Uncut, Mojo* and *Q*, with his midriff bare, the Union Jack as a backdrop and the unequivocal headline YANKS GO HOME! The now iconic cover put an entire youth movement on alert.

By the end of Bowie's tour with Nine Inch Nails in 1995, Blur, Oasis, Pulp, Supergrass and the aforementioned Elastica were hugely influential and fashionable. Bowie, who lived in America at the time, held a good deal of affection for all of them and was treated largely with respect by them. However, his personal tastes seemed to lean toward the more electronic, dance floor-friendly strain of Britpop, groups like Massive Attack, Tricky, Portishead, Underworld, the Prodigy, and a metal-toothed, barechested turntablist named Goldie. He was also impressed that Britpop, like swinging London of the sixties, had its own artists (Damien Hirst, profiled for *Modern Painters* by Bowie), models (Kate Moss), designers (Alexander McQueen), writers (Will Self, Irvine Welsh) and filmmakers (Danny Boyle, whose *Trainspotting*, an adaptation of Welsh's junkie novel, was the movement's quintessential flick). Although recorded in Manhattan, Bowie's next album, *Earthling*, would be Britpop to the core and it would feature his most 'English' singing since his Anthony Newley-besotted youth.

'That's the reason for the Union Jack on his coat on the cover of *Earthling*,' Gabrels says. 'He was aligning himself with that. We'd been away on tour but when we went through London, I was thrilled to finally get to see the kind of England that I had only read about. Hanging out with artists like Hirst and McQueen.' McQueen designed the long Union Jack coat, which Bowie would wear during the sleeve photo shoot and in concert. 'David's wardrobe mistress distressed it,' Gabrels says. 'It showed up brand-new. I remember them spilling tea on it to stain it. Loosening the threads with razor blades. Putting it on and rolling down this hill in it.'

And yet, as the 'London' he'd helped invent raged with smashed pint glasses and paparazzi lenses fueled by mega-piles of 'Charlie,' Bowie enjoyed a quiet, functional domesticity across the Atlantic. After breakfast with Iman, Bowie would leave their new loft at the north end of Soho and walk the few blocks to Looking Glass Studios, composer Philip Glass's recording space, to begin tinkering with a new studio album with Gabrels, Dorsey, Zachary Alford and producer Mark Plati, a master of the new digital recording technology that excited him. Bowie had discovered the British club music known as jungle (or 'drum and bass') and could not get enough of the rapid-fire rhythms (embraced more often than not by squirrelly white college kids clutching glow sticks) and liquid washes of sound, entire epics that could be made quickly and on the very laptop he would carry around with him in his bag.

'Those were heady times,' Plati says today. 'You felt like you were in the middle of a major change as far as how music was being captured and then manipulated. We were excited about the technology as far as the ability to move things about in a freer manner than we had been accustomed to. It was early on as far as making records inside of computers, and we used that to a great degree on *Earthling*.'

Most consider *Earthling* Bowie's 'drum and bass' album in the same way they view Joni Mitchell's *Hejira* to be her 'jazz fusion' record or *Trans* as Neil Young's 'New Wave' album or Morrissey's *Kill Uncle* as his 'rockabilly' album. It's simply another case of a veteran artist pursuing a sound with which he or she has fallen in love. 'David was the first person to play me jungle and drum and bass in about 1992,' says Gabrels. The genre's hallmarks (rapid-fire bass, hailstorm percussion, flashes of distorted guitar, sampling, sudden dramatic pauses) dominate *Earthling*'s tracks, like 'Little Wonder,' 'Battle for Britain (The Letter),'

'Telling Lies' and 'Dead Man Walking.' All of these were farmed out to club DJs and producers to be remixed.

A Trent Reznor remix of the album's first single, the typically prescient 'I'm Afraid of Americans,' gave Bowie his first major radio hit of the nineties. It was well deserved. 'Americans,' a funny, crunching indictment of his gun-and-gas-guzzler-happy adopted home, may have been Bowie's finest single since 'Loving the Alien' a decade earlier. Musically essentially an attempt, largely successful, to create a Pixies-style loud/quiet/loud anthem, lyrically it uses absurdist, vulgar wit, à la early Dylan, to speak larger truths ('Johnny looks up at the stars . . . Johnny wants pussy and cars') before concluding with ironic jingoism, 'God is an American.' With Kurt Cobain dead, grunge over and England dictating American culture, the timing of the track helps deepen the irony in no small fashion.

The video features a malevolent Reznor (ostensibly 'Johnny') pursuing a terrified and goateed Bowie through the streets of New York City. Directed by the then hip team Dom and Nic, it got Bowie back in heavy rotation on MTV for the first time in a decade as well. Despite strong sales (relative to the nineties) and generally good reviews, there were critics, and many fans, who did not take to the new technology. 'To this day I occasionally see *Earthling* derided in the press as David's "jungle" record or "drum and bass experiment,"'

Plati says. 'People are entitled to their opinions, but I do disagree. It's a Bowie record. The drum and bass sound just went through the Bowie filter, like any other Bowie album. When he coopted soul in the seventies, he didn't get that sort of grief – he was rightfully called an innovator,' Plati continues, unaware, of course, that there were thousands of fans who were aghast that Bowie had 'gone disco.' Bowie, on the other hand, knew perfectly well that he would get a similar level of flak from some. Post-ambition, however, he didn't care.

The melodies on *Earthling* are so strong, one simply gets the sense now, over a decade after the sonic craze for jungle peaked, that they don't need the digital adornment. It would be interesting to hear them revisited acoustically today. 'The songs are better than the treatment,' agrees Moby, who knows a thing or two about techno. 'It *feels* like 1997. He wanted to make a contemporary electronic record.'

With *Earthling* being readied for release later in the month, Bowie was nearing another milestone. On January 8, 1997, he would be turning fifty. He decided not to duck the event but to harness its poignancy and deliver a celebration concert at Madison Square Garden, where John F. Kennedy had his forty-fifth birthday and was famously sere-naded by Marilyn Monroe. Billed as 'A Very Special Birthday Celebration,' the event would feature Bowie and his band, along with walk-on guests like Foo Fighters (on 'Hallo Spaceboy'),

Brian Molko of Placebo, Robert Smith of the Cure (on 'Quicksand'), Frank Black (on 'Fashion'), Sonic Youth (on 'I'm Afraid of Americans'), Lou Reed (on 'I'm Waiting for the Man' and a great version of 'Dirty Blvd.' off the *New York* record) and Billy Corgan of Smashing Pumpkins joining Bowie for 'All the Young Dudes' (you know it's a nineties thing when Corgan headlines over Reed as final guest).

With large computer screens embedded in the stage (showing inverted, grimacing faces) and Bowie's odd new look (pale orange brush cut, goatee, brocade coat, mess o' eyeliner), footage of the event is charmingly dated today, but at the time, the atmosphere constituted a love fest, with the host in genuinely good humor. Not much morbid reflection here. 'Good evening, we're your rock band for tonight,' Bowie announced as he took the stage. 'You're going to get party vibes.'

'We just sort of sat down and he blasted the track to us,' says Thurston Moore of how each selected performer was broken in preshow. The band went to Bowie's studio to hear tracks from the then unreleased *Earthling* record. 'And it was this big drum and bass thing with, like, him singing. And I remember thinking how the whole drum and bass underground had kind of been a little played out and I was a little wary of it. Listening to David sing like David sings on top of this drum and bass . . . [it was] extremely energized and proficient, but I felt scared it was gonna be this genre music that gets dated really quickly. He told me, "I think I've really found my ultimate musical bed . . . in jungle!"' Rehearsals took place in an empty sports arena in Hartford, Connecticut. 'They were pre-creating the show,' Moore says. 'Who the fuck rents out a fucking arena? People with his kind of revenue . . . they have airplanes . . . they rent out arenas.'

Bowie's band and Sonic Youth jammed on 'I'm Afraid of Americans,' and live, without the digital brushstrokes, the strength of the track (one of Bowie's best late-era singles, especially after an NIN remix) began to come through. 'It would have been really cool if we were all on the same volume but I realized his band was the predominant thing you were hearing,' Moore says. 'We were flavoring it . . . and I thought, "I don't really want to flavor the song. I want to be the kind of thing that threatens it in a way."' This was a Bowie tribute, however, and nobody dared try to upstage him. If anything guest vocalists like Black and Smith, modern rock icons themselves, seemed a bit intimidated. This was, after all, the guy they listened to as teenagers. Thrown together in the midst of finishing a new album, there were a million things that could have fallen through, but the concert was a great success, and the atmosphere backstage was universally upbeat (complete with a towering, white frosted cake).

'The mood was up, positive, but intense,' says Plati. 'A lot of work had to be done in a very short time. I'd never really been on that side of such an intense live production – I'd been in the studio for the past decade, where you can take your time to some degree. Work started on it when we were mixing *Earthling*, so we basically never stopped. The logistics of it all – so many musical guests, filming and recording – were just staggering to me. 'Hallo Spaceboy' had three drummers! Still, once the ducks were all in a row, the concert was so, so great. Wonderful atmosphere. It went off without a technical hitch. All the guests were so happy to have been a part of it.' To be asked by the man himself, a childhood hero in the case of Robert Smith, Billy Corgan, Placebo's Molko and Frank Black, surely stood as a high point in one's career and personal life. It was the kind of seal of approval that Bowie would soon distribute to yet another new wave of bands (the Strokes, the Killers, TV on the Radio, the aforementioned Arcade Fire), like the queen handing out medals in velvet boxes. These later bands were influenced by bands influenced by bands influenced by David Bowie.

The after-party was held in Julian Schnabel's Greenwich Village apartment, with a beaming Bowie greeting and thanking the performers and being completely in his element as the center of all attention. Shortly after his fiftieth birthday, Bowie embarked on a tour of large theaters, intent on building an interest in his new sound from more modest-sized venues up. If he arrived at the drum and bass party a bit late (and with the enthusiasm of a fan rather than a maverick), it should be pointed out that he was dead right about the technology, as well as the rapidly developing delivery system for music and information. It's almost impossible to imagine just how radical David Bowie's website was when it was first launched in the late summer of 1998. There had been Bowie-devoted websites up and running. Teenage Wildlife, for one, launched as early as 1994. But Bowienet, which was launched on September 1, 1998, would be the first time an artist of Bowie's stature welcomed fans into his virtual home. *Earthling's* 'Telling Lies' would be the first digitally downloadable song offered by a major artist.

Bowie had been using a personal computer and a scanner since 1993, loading his hard drive with software designed for rapid lyric writing or electronically painting or altering his drawings once they'd been uploaded. Bowieart.com was an outlet to share these works as well as the work of painters and artists who inspired him. Bowienet at david-bowie.com would be a more all-purpose site. In '93, the 'Jump They Say' single was one of the first released as a CD-ROM that enabled fans to remix the track themselves on their desktop. The possibilities of personal computing had already been exciting him for a half decade by the time he launched his landmark website. 'He wasn't computer savvy at first,' Gabrels says. 'Andy, my guitar tech, would have to turn it on for him. He very quickly became extremely savvy, however; but before that he was already using the jargon or the vernacular of the day to describe something that he really hadn't experienced without a guide. It's one of his many charms.'

It's not really surprising that Bowie, at that point, was an Internet obsessive who had difficulty dragging himself away from the keyboard. Celebrities and, often, politicians suffer from a stifling cocoon syndrome, with vital information run through a filter by various minders and flacks. The Internet allowed Bowie to reconnect directly with the street, only this street was a superhighway without limits. Those who receive e-mails from Bowie today (his primary form of communication, by most accounts) more often than not find themselves clicking on links to YouTube clips that have knocked him out. EBay is of course another site that perfectly suits his tendency to collect and affection for the obscure.

The tour bus and the hotels on the Earthling trek were, for the first time, dialed in. The outing took the phone-in poll of the Sound and Vision tour in 1990 to its logical next step.

'On tour, we keep updated daily on what our audience think of the show, new songs, different running orders or whatever,' Bowie told the London *Times*. 'We get a good understanding of what people are expecting from us.

Bowie also sensed the social networking potential of the Internet a decade before Friendster,

MySpace and Facebook and was the first major artist to really cultivate a sense of community online. He did away with his icy homo superior persona almost gleefully. This, remember, used to be someone nobody could watch eat, according to Tony Zanetta's account in *Stardust*. Now, for a small fee, we could chat with him; view his paintings, personal archives of photos and writings; and even share an e-mail address suffix! Now, of course, you can read the daily thoughts and whims of every one of your heroes, whether they are interesting or not. In 1998, you still had to imagine what was going on inside all those pointy skulls.

'The idea of fans communicating directly with their favorite artist was nurtured by Bowienet,' says Nancy Miller, an editor at *Wired* magazine, 'offering fans live chats with Bowie and a sense of intimacy [via the Internet] that hadn't been seen before. Bowienet was a proto-MySpace, in a way. I don't think it's overstating it to say that.'

'I welcome all you web travelers to the first community-driven internet site that focuses on music, film, literature, painting and more . . . the purpose of Bowienet is interactivity and community,' Bowie promises in his greeting to visitors. 'Everybody has a voice.'

'Here was the landscape: At that time, there was basically eBay, a fledgling Craigslist, Google had just launched,' Miller says. 'AOL was your ISP [for many] and Yahoo was your search engine. Most acts, like the Spice Girls, used their websites as basically billboards on a smaller screen: they'd advertise their tours, products, movies. If you were a pop star, you had a website, but if you were an "artist" you did not. Artists don't shill their stuff online! No! You were supposed to be a shoulder-shrugging, guitar-picking Luddite with two turntables and a vinyl press. I do think it's fair to say that music sites like Pitchfork exist – or at least the cool music blog model exists – because of Bowienet. The idea of a singular, serious, legit indie music site with great influence where you can get music news, videos, downloads of genuinely cool music? That's definitely germane. I don't think Bowie got the attention he deserved for his influence there, necessarily. In the new-media world, yes, but not necessarily in broader pop culture. Bowie was coming up with ideas to save the music industry ten years ago, while Edgar Bronfman and other major-label execs were doing the twist. If they'd clicked on his website a decade ago, maybe the music industry wouldn't be so screwed.'

In 2007 at the eleventh annual Webby Awards, which honor excellence in Internet innovations, Bowie was granted a lifetime achievement award. Bowie attended the ceremony and made fun of the award show's traditional rule of limiting recipients' speeches to five words. He took to the podium and quipped into the mic, 'I only get five words?'

And then he was off again.

★　　★　　★

I never interviewed David Bowie for Spin *magazine, where I was on staff between the winter of 1997, when I was twenty-eight, and the spring of 2006. My behavior at that magazine and my identity as a music writer was mostly derived from my Bowie-ist nature. I wore sunglasses wherever I went, inside and outside. They were ridiculous aviator-style frames with red lenses. I dangled a lit cigarette from my lips, inside and outside as well, before and after the New York City smoking ban. My look was not modeled on Bowie; as I said before, I'd determined the futility of that back in 1983. It was modeled on Nick Kent, or footage I'd seen of Nick Kent, with his scrawny frame and leather jacket and drawled, vaguely campy speech. Bowie looked at Syd Barrett and Lou Reed, and later Iggy Pop, and said to himself, 'This is the kind of rocker I want to be,' and picked bits for himself from each, fashioning them into something new. I did the same with those who profiled rockers. Not that I left the rockers themselves out of my amalgam. I wore the sunglasses and the leather jacket and smoked my ciggie with total conviction, as Bowie did with his tunic 'man's dress,' on Beckenham High Street or his Red Hot Red rooster cut, hoping that people would notice and it would become something of a delivery system for an ability or an expression that was much more sincere and serious. I also never worried whether the real me, a shy Long Island kid who often had to do a shot of whiskey before I could talk to anyone, much less a rock star, would become subsumed in this invention.*

One of my first print bylines at Spin was what they call a 'sidebar,' a dipshit addendum to someone else's feature, and it was timed to the release of Velvet Goldmine, Todd Haynes's 1998 Bowie-inspired hyper-sexual love letter to the glitter-rock aesthetic. I was to trace all the points in David Bowie's career so that the reader would, I suppose, know what the writer of the Haynes feature was talking about when he cited certain milestones and could then compare them to their treatment in the film. Pre-Google this was more difficult than it would seem but hardly a challenge.

As Bowie spent the sixties trying to figure out a working formula, I spent much of the nineties in Los Angeles, taking meetings on studio lots and trying to sell screenplays and eventually falling on my sword, which was actually more of a hypo needle; in one fit of self-destructive verve, I actually pitched an unwritten script, off the cuff, about a cat that shit money. Sober and finally employed somewhere, I felt like I was playing catch-up.

One day I left my sunglasses and cigarette behind at my desk (which was more like a shared pod with three or four other ambitious new hires) and returned from lunch to find them missing. I checked in the art department offices, and there I found a series of Polaroids taped to the glass door of the art director's office. Each shot was a portrait of a Spin employee wearing my shades and dangling one of my cigarettes from their mouth, affecting the pose that I was sure nobody had noticed yet but was absolutely committed to: the cartoon-decadent Nick Kent facsimile. These were senior staff. The editor in chief, among them. I was horrified, embarrassed too, but mostly thrilled, and in the days that followed, I really amped up that guy, 'Bad Marc,' as he came to be called. The exploits and marketability of 'Bad Marc' finally got the real me ahead. A few issues after that Velvet Goldmine *sidebar ran, I was writing cover stories for* Spin. *They also got the diffident and well-meaning me into a lot of trouble. Bad Marc took drugs, so good Marc did too. Bad Marc picked fights and treated women like shit. Good Marc had to commit. This was 1999, now, the year of* Fight Club. *Dangerous dichotomies. Slippery slopes. But it all went back to Bowie. Ziggy Stardust was the original Tyler Durden.*

CHAPTER 28

'I love *Velvet Goldmine*,' says the film's director, Todd Haynes, just over a decade after its original release. 'I'm so proud of it. It was the first film of mine that met with much more of a mixed reaction when it first came out, especially in the English press, but it was a film I always meant as a gift to young people, as a kind of tripped-out druggy movie, an experience film. Those kind of films don't get made anymore – like *Performance* – weird, trippy, complicated and beautiful. That meant so much to me growing up. A place where your imagination and creativity can be nurtured by a film. What's so cool is the movie became that for a mass of young people. And it's still a film that young teenagers, particularly girls, come up to me and tell me how much it changed their lives. And it became a huge Web obsession and a flash fiction inspirer. They gave out prizes for the best triple-X story, best double-X story, and best softcore story all involving the *Velvet Goldmine* characters. I also love that it inspired kids and exposed them to all this great music.'

Velvet Goldmine takes poetic license with Bowie's

rise and fall but remains more or less a linear biopic fueled by extensive research, done largely by Haynes, a lifelong Bowiephile. It is an important and seldom-acknowledged touchstone in the larger Bowie story, as it marks the first time that the myth and minutiae of the Bowie universe were placed in context in the same way the Frank Sinatra, Elvis Presley and Beatles myths had been treated before it. Many, however, view the film as a noble if ultimately unsuccessful experiment. For all its accurate costumes (designer Sandy Powell received a much deserved Oscar nomination), spectacle, sustained sense of camp, Wilde-via-Warhol acid wit and committed cast, there are those who feel that *Velvet* buckles under the weight of its own fan-boy gushing. Something as culture-shifting as glitter rock needn't be examined or re-created with such a gimlet eye.

'It's important for any hard-core follower of Bowie to remind them that the whole film is very self-consciously meant to be seen through the eyes of the fan – the Christian Bale character – with all the additional embroidery and dreaming that goes on in the eyes of the fans,' Haynes says. 'Also, the language of glam rock was a heightened language. This is grandeur and elegance, rich, lush high camp that distorts reality and pushes it into something else, and I wanted the film to be a product of that – didn't make sense for me to do a hard-core documentary-style version of the glam rock story. Something much more theatrical and winged.'

That the plotline, or subplotline, was borrowed from *Citizen Kane* did little to defend Haynes against those who wished to take him down a peg for his ambitions. Bale plays Arthur Stuart, a journalist and former superfan of Brian Slade, the film's Bowie figure (played by Jonathan Rhys Myers), who creates and then destroys (literally, via an assassin's bullet) an alter ego named Maxwell Demon (the Ziggy figure). On the anniversary of the stunt, Bale is assigned to retrace the history of Slade's rise and fall and answer all the questions left unresolved by interviewing figures from his past, including Toni Collette's Angie figure, Mandy Slade, and Ewan MacGregor's Curt Wild, purported to be a mash-up of both Lou Reed and Iggy Pop, but given McGregor's costume (nicked directly from the Mick Rock-shot *Raw Power* sleeve), lithe body and re-creation of the Stooges' 'TV Eye,' it's, visually at least, more uncut Iggy than Lou. The relationship between Slade and Wild, however, may be more Bowie/Reed at its core. 'The infatuation between the two of them,' Haynes says, 'draws more directly from the Lou Reed and Bowie lore, which they very well may have been performing for the public – performed a romance, whether it was consummated or not. That became the sort of fantasy romance in my film.'

Haynes translates the Bowie history to suit a somewhat overwrought detective story, having his young journalist reveal an allegorical right-wing conspiracy that links Slade to a toothy, blond, heterosexual Reaganite pop star named Tommy Stone, a cartoon blow-up of Bowie's Serious Moonlight–era persona. The Oscar-nominated director (for another stylistic homage, the Douglas Sirk-indebted 2002 film *Far from Heaven*), who first gained attention with his 1987 Karen Carpenter biopic *Superstar*, told with stop-motion animated Barbie dolls and never released (thanks to an injunction by Carpenter's brother and bandmate Richard), was well-intentioned and certainly charming in his self-deprecation when queried about the film's meta conceits. 'I always wanted to do the film this way,' he insists. That the film's mood offers almost none of the effervescence of the best of glitter rock might have something to do with its troubled production. Haynes admitted that the shoot (in London in the spring of '97) was fraught with budgetary woes. He told *Outsmart* magazine, '[I thought,] "This should be fun. This should be the funnest thing I've ever done, damn it." But it was so demanding and so ambitious. Then we lost our financing right before we started and had to find alternate money, and it made the budget go down a million dollars, and the budget was already so bare-bones. That lost million sort of did us in.' The acting, however, by mostly British and Australian stars, is uniformly excellent (especially Myers, then just nineteen, and Toni Collette as Mandy Slade, who helps her husband achieve the fame he so desperately

650

desires only to be pushed to the side and fall into a heartbroken and dissolute state).

Had Bowie himself been involved, as Bob Dylan was in Haynes's far superior 2008 film *I'm Not There*, the end results might have coalesced a bit more gracefully. While the soundtrack is excellent (original versions of and faithful takes on Roxy Music, Brian Eno, Iggy and the Stooges and T. Rex hits from the era), you simply cannot tell the Bowie story (and again in Haynes's defense, he never really claims to) or even the story of glitter without Bowie's music. It wasn't for lack of trying. 'I had so much ammunition and support,' Haynes says. 'From [the film's producer] Michael Stipe's involvement, literally calling Bowie at home, to Harvey Weinstein writing him a letter.'

Haynes's friend and Sonic Youth bassist Kim Gordon explained the concept of the film to Bowie one night over dinner at Julian Schnabel's in late 1996 (Haynes had directed the video for the Sonic Youth single 'Disappearer'). 'Kim tried to get him to concede to have his music licensed for the movie and he said he didn't feel he was ready to do that,' Gordon's husband, Thurston Moore, recalls. 'He didn't want to discourage Todd Haynes's vision but he wanted to keep his music until there was a real Bowie film.'

'My feeling about it was that it was based fairly substantially on Ziggy Stardust,' Bowie said at the time, 'and as I intend to do my own version of that, I'd rather not work with a competitive film.'

'"Lady Stardust" was going to be a song Brian Slade sings when he has his long hair,' Haynes says. 'During the whole dreamy scene of seduction between Christian Bale and Ewan McGregor, I wanted to use the quiet part of "Sweet Thing" from *Diamond Dogs*. We used "Baby's on Fire" [by Eno] where we were going to use "Moonage Daydream." The original script started out with seven Bowie songs in it. Finally, we just made a campaign to get "All the Young Dudes." That would be the anthem that would end the film. But we had to use [Roxy's] "2HB" instead.'

Bowie's music has been used to great effect before and since in ambitious films helmed by auteurs like Uli Edel (the 1981 junkie drama *Christiane F.*), Wes Anderson (the 2004 hipster comedy *The Life Aquatic with Steve Zissou*, in which vintage Bowie songs are sung in Portuguese by Brazilian musician and cast member Seu Jorge) and Gus Van Sant (2008's *Milk*'s brilliant use of *Hunky Dory's* 'Queen Bitch'). Its absence in the Haynes film is, for some, a fatal blow. This is not, after all, the Eno/Ferry story. Perhaps if the film had been a bit more happy-go-lucky, it would have sold itself a bit more easily to skeptics. Instead it seems to try to will Eno, Cockney Rebel and T. Rex songs into Bowie songs. 'A lot of people also had problems with the Bowie character singing a Roxy Music song that was not even written at that time,' says Moore, tweaking the purists. 'But really, so what?' Some critics praised the film, most did

652

not, and except for its sustained cult following on video and the Web, *Velvet Goldmine* was a commercial flop. Bowie, ultimately the only real arbiter who mattered given the subject, offered his own review. Essentially, he'd enjoyed the sex scenes between Bale and McGregor, and Toni Collette and multiple partners in a hazy orgy scene. 'But I thought the rest of it was garbage.' Haynes is naturally 'disappointed' by this. 'The thing that always made me sad about Bowie's reaction to my film – and I understand everyone is protecting their own public depiction – but I just feel like I took everything he created with a great sense of freedom of invention. I took it to task and basically accepted it as a delicious fiction of his own making.'

Perhaps the ultimate verdict on *Velvet Goldmine* goes to Bob Dylan, who was impressed enough by Haynes's body of work to allow total access to his own equally vast myth and Earth-changing music. 'I thought Dylan would be the hardest of all, thought I'd truly lost my marbles even presuming. My career sort of began with some adversarial reaction – the Carpenters being my first denial, then Bowie,' says Haynes. 'I thought, "Oh my god, now I'm taking on the meanest guy of all," but instead he said, "Sure, use whatever you want, you've got life rights and music rights. Pick any song from the canon."' Asked if he applied any of the mistakes he may have made on *Goldmine* to *I'm Not There*, Haynes replies, 'I think I just repeated all my mistakes and stand by them in both films.'

653

In 2001, *Hedwig and the Angry Inch*, a sister film of sorts to *Velvet Goldmine* (they also share a producer) was released. Based on John Cameron Mitchell and Stephen Trask's hit off-Broadway play, the film also traffics heavily in Bowie myth and iconography from the Berlin Wall to the Calvin Mark Lee-style third eye on the forehead of Michael Pitt's rock ingénue Tommy Gnosis. When Mitchell's Hedwig subjects Pitt's Gnosis to a 'six-month curriculum of rock history,' he/she actually points to the famous Mick Rock shot of Bowie, Iggy and Lou Reed at the Dorchester Hotel press conference in 1972 during the montage.

As far as his less canonical music and iconography was concerned, he spent much of the late nineties sketching. He composed tracks for the soundtrack for the French-based video game Omikron before joining Gabrels in Bermuda to work on material for the follow-up to *Earthling*. Unbeknownst to Gabrels, Bowie was about to do a tonal about-face, withdrawing from the agit-art rock of *Outside* and the drum and bass of *Earthling* to produce a series of new material that amounted to his most introspective since the late sixties. Bowie had put forth the notion in the press of revisiting Ziggy Stardust as a musical around this time as well. Like many in the grip of pre-millennium tension, he seemed to be sensing his mortality, and the slow, searching mood of the new songs, like 'Survive,' and 'Thursday's Child' (inspired by the autobiography of the late cabaret singer Eartha Kitt), lend this theory some validity.

'*Hours* . . . was sort of the anti-*Earthling*,' says Plati, who was brought in after the Bermuda sessions, as well as a short session in London, to aid in the production back at Looking Glass in Soho. 'No beats, no technology, just naked songs. I try not to interpret lyrics other than to find my own meaning in them – which I think is the point. "Survive" hit me in particular because I was going through my own rough patch at the time, so I connected with it.'

Hours . . . is a good record to put on the morning after you did something regrettable. It will likely put your transgressions in perspective and allow you to catch a breath or two before calling your rabbi, priest or Zen master. It's easy listening for uneasy people. 'Survive,' the album's best track, is even more explicitly haunted by regret. 'I should have kept you,' Bowie worries, 'I should have tried.' His voice is reminiscent of the old Dream recordings, perhaps deliberately so ('Who said time is on my side?' he laments at one point). Musically, it's an affecting melody, strummed on a guitar that, after *Earthling*, sounds refreshingly solid and wooden. Another track like 'If I'm Dreaming My Life' feels a bit more sketchy and seems musically indecisive but thematically, it's in perfect pitch with the ongoing elegant bummer that is the record as a whole. The actual rockers fare better here.

655

Again confident enough to throw his arms around cyber culture without worrying that the gimmick would hold sway over the music (justifiably so, as much of *Hours . . .* is as strong as its three predecessors), Bowie and online music site Bug Music launched a contest that offered fans a chance to write lyrics to one of his and Gabrels's musical compositions (posted on Bowienet with just a hummed melody). Bowie and Gabrels would record the winning song live on the Web. Of the reported eighty thousand submissions, Bowie chose the submission of Alex Grant, an Ohio student with a New Wave haircut. In May of 1999, Grant was flown to New York City to watch Bowie sing his words – and to be watched. While it seems quaint now, at the time, this was truly inventive and drew heavy traffic to the simulcast (run on *Rolling Stone* magazine's site). During the webcast, Bowie seems respectful, reading the lyrics off a stand and loaning them more conviction then words like 'Grown inside a plastic box. Micro thoughts and safety locks / Hearts become outdated clocks / Ticking in your mind' really deserve.

'"What's Really Happening?" was really cool to do – it was a new way to reach out to his fans,' Plati says. 'Sure, it was an experiment – what wasn't? Remember, there was no blueprint for any of those sorts of things. We were doing webchats around the same time – they felt incredibly cutting-edge!'

'The Pretty Things Are Going to Hell' ('they've worn it out but they've worn it well') is an elegy for the specter of glitter, which still clearly haunts Bowie in his weaker moments: 'You're still breathing but you don't know why / Life's a bitch and sometimes you die.' Well, always you die, and that notion seemed to be sinking in, one that was possibly not, what with the potential Y2K glitch looming, the most sellable fin de siècle product. The cover sleeve to *Hours . . .* based on the *Pietà* by Michelangelo, the statue of the body of Christ displayed in St Peter's in the Vatican, literally features Bowie hanging on to himself, cradling his own visage in his arms as if to telegraph to his fans that a bit of comfort would be quite nice right about now. Few responded to the collection. *Hours . . .* marked the first Bowie studio album to fail to crack the American Top 40 in over a quarter of a century (intent on giving it a post-millennial fair shake, Bowie reissued it in 2004 on his own ISO label as a double disc). Bowie played 'The Pretty Things' on *Saturday Night Live* in the early fall of '99, at the Net Aid benefit concert in October of 1999 and in an episode of VH1's *Storytellers*, and committed to a series of intimate club shows in Paris, Dublin, Italy, Denmark and New York City, marking the first time fans could see him in a relatively intimate venue in three decades.

Shortly after the record hit shops, Gabrels announced that he was leaving the fold after a decade as Bowie's guitarist (a run that rivaled Carlos Alomar's and lasted three times as long as Mick Ronson's). The *Storytellers* taping would mark his last time playing alongside Bowie. Page Hamilton of early-nineties grunge-metal rockers Helmet was drafted as a replacement for the live dates. Earl Slick and Mike Garson, both seventies all-stars, returned, and Plati was given the role of official musical director of the shows. Always one to make a virtue of a possible free fall, Bowie used the occasion to pull up more-obscure songs like 'Quicksand' from *Hunky Dory* and 'Stay' from *Station to Station*. These were true fan shows and seemed the first instance of Bowie realizing he could literally play anywhere he wanted, without having to mount a high-concept stage show for each album. 'Reeves's workload got heavier and heavier,' Zachary Alford says, 'and I think that wore him down a bit.' Gabrels cites various reasons for his choice. It was partly due to a desire to take the business out of the music business and just play again, partly a sense that he'd been there and done it over the course of eleven years and partly because of friction between himself and Schwab.

'She is not a very happy person,' he says. 'I felt like for a long time, I just got tired of doing what was necessary to maintain my own safety against whatever sort of crap she might pull. The band would come off-stage and if she wanted to see a movie that was playing on HBO she would tell David that the crowd wasn't into it so she could get back in time. He's like anybody: you can bum him out, you can grind him down.'

Post-Gabrels, Bowie did exactly what he did post-Alomar at the end of the eighties, shortly before the Sound and Vision tour and the repurposing of himself as a 'band member' with Tin Machine: he started looking to his past for inspiration, or at least some kind of graceful stopgap. That fall it was announced, appropriately enough, that Bowie would headline the first Glastonbury festival of the twenty-first century, some thirty years after he played the inaugural event in support of *The Man Who Sold the World*. As the sun set over the rolling fields, Bowie took the stage, bowed calmly and walked to the mic to sing 'Wild Is the Wind' as the crowd let forth an enormous cheer. He introduced 'Changes' by letting the crowd know he'd just written it the first time he'd played there. The following day, Bowie and the band returned to London to do a recording for the BBC Radio Theatre to be packaged alongside sessions from the early seventies. Between the club dates in the fall and Glastonbury in the summer, Bowie and Plati planned to record an album of revisited material from Bowie's mid-to-late-1960s output. With a working title of *Toy* and a track list that reportedly included. 'I Dig Everything,' 'Can't Help Thinking About Me' and 'Let Me Sleep Beside You,' the album was conceived as a sort of *Pin Ups* without the hits.

The birth of Bowie and Iman's daughter, Alexandria Zahra (Arabic for 'inner light'), on August 15, 2000, put the sessions on hold, and by the time the album was ready for release, Bowie's relationship with his label Virgin had become tense (they were reportedly eager for an album of new material, not a semi-novelty covers album, in order to generate excitement for the back catalog, recently released for digital download).

Bowie began negotiating with different labels, eventually signing a lucrative deal with Sony; the *Toy* material was broken up and either redistributed to B sides or retitled for inclusion on his next project, *Heathen*, which would find him reunited with a key figure from the era in which they were recorded. In the years since producing *Scary Monsters* in 1980, Visconti had kept busy with projects for artists as diverse as the Boomtown Rats and Debbie Gibson. He was recovering from a divorce (from John Lennon's former girlfriend May Pang, who also dated Bowie and appears in the 'Fashion' video) after eleven years of marriage. The reconnection with Bowie marked a sort of acceleration in his producing activity (he'd follow it in rapid succession with albums by the Dandy Warhols and Manic Street Preachers as well as Morrissey's 2006 release *Ringleader of the Tormentors*).

Having a young child in the house again certainly turned Bowie's mind to his past. He has a history of calling people out of the blue after they figured they'd probably never hear from him again. John Hutchinson, Keith Christmas, Mike Garson and now Tony Visconti had all been contacted this way. Visconti's falling-out with Bowie reportedly had to do with his declining to mix the sound for the massive Serious Moonlight tour. They'd reconciled but were no longer as close as they'd been through the sixties and seventies, despite the fact that both men were living in lower Manhattan. A date for coffee led to plans to make their first album together in twenty-two years.

Bowie and Visconti began working on the *Heathen* album in Manhattan but relocated to Allaire Studios, situated on a two-hundred-foot-high top in the Catskill Mountains in upstate New York, on the recommendation of a mutual friend. Bowie had been somewhat blocked in the city and had a spiritual convergence of sorts as soon as he set foot in the building and began. 'Walking though the door everything that my album should be about was galvanized for me into one focal point,' he said at the time. 'It was an 'on the road to Damascus' type of experience, you know; it was almost like my feet were lifted off the ground.' There among the deer and the eagles soaring over-head, Bowie and Visconti created the record, one of Bowie's best, with a renewed sense of purpose. From Picasso to Warren Beatty to David Letterman, you can see once perhaps less-than-accountable alpha males of the arts and letters melting when a little baby comes into their life. 'Overnight our lives have been enriched beyond belief,' Bowie, a father again at age fifty-five, told UK magazine *Hello*. As they raised the little girl, in perhaps the *greatest* testament to his devotion to his new daughter, Bowie gave up smoking. A heavy smoker since the early sixties, Bowie began seeing a hypnotist in effort to stop in the mid-nineties. He'd taken to eating Australian tea tree sticks by the dozen. Cigarettes and coffee were his last remaining vices. With regard to the Marlboros, nothing worked until he became a father again, and even then, it was a struggle.

'I remember him coming offstage during that last tour of his and going backstage to see him,' says Mick Rock. 'He'd officially stopped smoking. Maybe his wife had gotten on his ass, starting to get a bit worried about him. I think his father had died in his fifties. He'd stopped buying cigarettes. After the show, he was looking for a roadie to catch cigs off, looking around to make sure Iman wasn't around.'

Before entering the studio with Visconti, Bowie found time to steal a scene in Ben Stiller's fashion-industry send-up *Zoolander* among an egregiously long list of would-be thieves that included Winona Ryder, Billy Zane, Paris Hilton and Lenny Kravitz. When Stiller's titular male model clashes with Owen Wilson's Hansel ('Who you trying to get crazy with, *ese*? Don't you know I'm loco?'), a 'walk-off' is suggested. Ten minutes later, the rivals meet in an abandoned warehouse and audiences are treated to 'the real world of male modeling.

The one they don't show you in magazines or on the E channel.' As bad techno plays, Stiller and Wilson limber up. 'All right, who's going to call this sucker?' Wilson asks. 'If nobody has any objections, I believe I might be of service,' a familiar voice offscreen offers. And with the cue of 'Let's Dance' on the soundtrack, Bowie nearly makes off with the 'best scene-stealer' honors (and would completely own it if Will Ferrell had not been in the cast).

Bowie and Visconti were upstate on the morning of September 11, 2001. Bowie, an early riser, happened to be at his upstate residence, watching the lone working television, when the first plane flew into the tower. Both Bowie and Visconti were eventually able to reach their loved ones and confirm that they were safe but were then faced with the awkward situation of being stuck up in the mountains while the city recovered. They made a halfhearted attempt to continue recording, but by sundown, they found themselves out on the studio porch watching orange smoke billow up into the sky to the south. They could see Ground Zero burning for the next week. *Heathen*, released the following June, was an across-the-board success, Bowie's biggest critical and commercial hit since the early eighties, breaking the U.S. Top 15 in its debut week and the Top 5 in England. It garnered the most plaudits of any album since *Let's Dance*.

'Bowie seems to have finally realized that he's just been trying too damn hard,' Pitchfork observed in its review. 'Where 2000's *Hours* was a brooding, wrist-slitting account of Bowie's laments about growing old and irrelevant, *Heathen* is the sound of acceptance. He's relaxed, even serene, and the songs clearly reflect this with a nonchalant charm reminiscent of the Bowie of old.'

The album opens with 'Sunday,' which plainly evokes September 11. 'Nothing remains,' he sings. 'Look for cars or signs of life.' A faithfully jagged and tough version of the Pixies' indie classic 'Cactus' from 1988's *Surfer Rosa* follows, with Visconti approximating Steve Albini's startling drum sound and 'you are in the room' ambience. Because *Heathen* is such a New York record ('Slip Away,' a sort of middle-aged 'Life on Mars?' mentions local children's show host Uncle Floyd and his puppet friend Oogie, the Yankees and Coney Island), it's hard to continue to avoid reading into lyrics that in places seem to chillingly foreshadow the city's darkest day as one listens. 'Watching all the world and war torn / How I wonder where you are,' Bowie sings on 'Slip Away' (written for the *Toy* sessions a year before).

On 'A Better Future,' perhaps his most classic pop song of the new millennium, he pleads, 'Please don't tear this world asunder . . . Please make sure we get tomorrow.' It's a terrible thing to say, but these odd bits of tragic prescience actually make the album even more powerful.

As Pitchfork observed, tracks like 'Afraid' take the intense self-scrutiny of *Hours* . . . to more solid ground. 'I wish I was smarter . . . I wish I was taller,' Bowie whines (over one of his better late period riffs) before arriving at actual conclusions: 'I believe in Beatles' – a wry nod to John Lennon's 'God' – 'I believe my little soul has grown.'

Covers of Neil Young's 'I've Been Waiting for You' and the Legendary Stardust Cowboy's 'I Took a Trip on a Gemini Spaceship' are delivered with fan-boy glee and affectionate irony respectively. ('I shot my space gun,' Bowie sings on the latter. 'And boy, I really felt blue.')

When Paul McCartney and others began organizing a 9/11 tribute concert the following month, Bowie was one of the first to sign on and quickly put a band together. 'As New Yorkers, we'd been violated . . . and David is nothing if not a New Yorker at this point,' says Plati, who led the band that night. It's Bowie who opens the entire concert, sitting on the Garden floor playing an odd instrument known as an Omnichord, a hand-held synthesizer that plays preset rhythms and basic chord changes. The melody was not, as a result, instantly familiar until he began to sing. Then it slowly became recognizable as not a Bowie song, but rather Simon & Garfunkel's 1968 classic 'America,' a tribute to the place that had been Bowie's spiritual home since his half brother first gave him a copy of *On the Road* in the late 1950s.

'David's opening of the show – solo, on Omnichord, performing Paul Simon's "America" – was moving, haunting, eerie, to say the least. It was a surreal atmosphere anyway, and that really drove it home. You could hear a pin drop in the Garden. Though once we launched into "Heroes," the roof came off the place,' says Plati. 'From my vantage point the audience on the floor was mostly firefighters and cops, and they loved every second of it – by the time the Who came onstage, they were totally gone.'

Shortly after helping a city deal with its grief publicly, Bowie was forced to deal with his own privately. His mother, Peggy Jones, died in April of 2002 at the age of eighty-eight. Having long since reconciled with her son, she lived in comfort at the St Alban's nursing home outside of London. Work, as it had always been, amounted to the only truly effective way of processing pain and loss. Bowie had not toured since *Earthling*, five years earlier, and an offer to headline the second annual Area tour (Area 2) organized by his neighbor Moby seemed under the circumstances a good idea. The two had struck up a friendship after Moby remixed *Earthling*'s 'Dead Man Walking' (as he would later do with *Reality*'s 'Bring Me the Disco King').

In the months following 9/11 New York seemed to awaken from its cultural torpor and, with regard to rock and art anyway, become a great culture center again. 'New York, I think, is his cauldron,' says Moby. 'So many of his heroes came from here. New York, for all its problems, is still the world center for so many things. Look at his choices of where to live. Geneva. Berlin. If he lived in London his life would be miserable. He'd be tossed into a blender and pureed all the time. L.A., he lived there making *Station to Station*. New York makes perfect sense and there's the historical context.'

Bowie's love affair with the city was further expressed in the fall of 2002 when it was announced that he would perform concerts at venues of varying sizes in each of the five boroughs, following the route of the annual New York City marathon. The October 11 opening show would take place on Staten Island at the music hall at Snug Harbor; from there his arena-ready band would play the intimate St Anne's Warehouse the following day. Four days later, they'd booked the Queens College Golden Center, Jimmy's Bronx Café and a closing night on October 20 at the Beacon Theater on the Upper West Side of Manhattan. 'I could get home from all the gigs on roller skates,' he quipped upon announcing the tour.

It was around this time that lots of Bowie spottings began to take place. 'Bowie was at the show last night!' 'I just saw Bowie.' 'I shared a cab with Bowie.' Ironically, as the city was under implicit siege (on constant orange alert), David Bowie walked around with no protection to speak of. He'd become, as he had in Berlin in the late seventies, very much a man of the people, grabbing coffee in the morning, unbothered, at Café Gitane by his apartment.

'If he wanted off the street, he could do that too,' says Moby. 'It's a bourgeois city. If he wants to have a five-hundred-dollar dinner he can do that. I'd see him walking on Prince Street on the way to dinner and we'd just run into each other. It made him feel more comfortable knowing he had a friendly face a block away. I think he really enjoys it. Every door is open. He and Iman, on their own, they're both iconic superstars. Together they are closer to royalty. They are our royalty.'

Bands like the Strokes, the Yeah Yeah Yeahs, Secret Machines, Interpol and the Liars made a living downtown and went to exciting shows. Bowie started going out again and drawing inspiration from the new rock. He'd be spotted at many of the early club shows of the abovementioned bands and used his influence among Bowienet subscribers to talk many of them up. A visit from Bowie backstage became tantamount to being in the court of the king of New York. It meant your band had arrived. As with New Romantic and Britpop, Bowie drew energy from the scene, and his next album, in the words of Tony Visconti, promised a 'tight New York sound.'

CHAPTER 29

It is hard to listen to *Reality*, recorded in New York in 2003, without considering that it is Bowie's last album at the time of this writing, and if he releases another, it will remain his last musical statement for over a half decade. That's a 'reality.' One listens to swan-song albums a bit differently, whether it's *Let It Be, In Through the Out Door, Closer, Strangeways, Here We Come* or *Unplugged in New York*. As potential swan songs go, *Reality* is worthy. I think it's even better than *Heathen*, bolstered as it was by the confidence-building reception of that project. The songs seem fuller, and with the addition of *Station to Station* – era guitarist Earl Slick to the fold, it's much more of a guitar record. 'New Killer Star' addresses, as tristate luminaries Sonic Youth's *Murray Street* or Bruce Springsteen's *The Rising* did before it, 9/11. Bowie sings of the 'great white scar over Battery Park' in his vaguely sinister Thin White Duke voice (the one that always brings maximum drama). 'Never Get Old,' pushed by a great Gail Anne Dorsey bass line, manages to be both sentimental and existential (not to mention freakin' hysterical).

'There's never gonna be enough money,' a deranged-sounding Bowie screams, 'There's never gonna be enough drugs . . . never gonna be enough sex.' Equally out-there is his rearranged take on the Modern Lovers' immortal 'Pablo Picasso' (already covered indelibly by Burning Sensations on the *Repo Man* soundtrack). Bowie adds the adjective 'juicy' to the type of avocado the girls would turn the color of when the great Spaniard drove down the street in his El Dorado. 'The Loneliest Guy' is Bowie's smokiest torch song since 'Lady Grinning Soul' in '73. As Garson plinks an after-hours melody Bowie croons in a sexless falsetto, 'I'm the luckiest guy / Not the loneliest guy.' 'Days' (not the Kinks song of the same name) is something of a prayer. 'Hold me tight,' Bowie sings over a spare acoustic, 'All I've done, I've done for me /I gave nothing in return, and there's little left of me.'

A faithful version of 'Try Some, Buy Some' by the recently deceased George Harrison is included, as is a revisiting of 'Rebel Rebel,' his most pure and lasting rocker. Rock 'n' roll seems to be tacitly acknowledged on *Reality* as one of the youthful things that grow more and more true as one gets old, not a simple pleasure, but its pleasures a simple truth. Like Joe Strummer, Bono, and Springsteen every time he reunites with his E Street Band after two or three solo albums, Bowie was starting to realize that the rock medium he'd 'tarted up' in his youth was still there to give him dignity and, more crucially, fun in his old age. It meant something. Why else reunite with Visconti? Why play tiny venues in the Bronx when he could still fill arenas? Family mattered, certainly. Bowie, a doting father, spent time with his daughter, taking care to be there in her early years, knowing he was not around when his son was developing.

Bowie's rediscovery of rock 'n' roll purity was reflected in the tour he was planning in support of the album, which was released in mid-September to more strong reviews and sales, hitting the British Top 3 and the American Top 30.

'I always thought if you take the spectacle away, people would just love him to come onstage with blue jeans and a T-shirt and sing his own songs,' Erdal Kizilcay told me when we were discussing the florid and garish Glass Spider tour. 'Even on Sound and Vision, there were bands playing before us without having this light show. Bryan Adams played before us once, and he had great sound. He was really amazing. He sang like a god. I'm ashamed after. People would prefer David to just be near them and sing "Space Oddity" and "Blue Jean" than be the movie guy playing Mickey Mouse.'

The Reality tour, launched that fall, would prove to be the antithesis of 'the movie guy playing Mickey Mouse.' Bowie, looking healthy and fifteen years younger than he actually was, and wearing a black T-shirt and sneakers, would fill arenas by offering nothing much more than a killer rock 'n' roll show played by a top-notch band. The fact that the tour would never complete its scheduled run and may stand as his last ever is beyond disappointing.

Encouraged by brisk box office and some of the best live reviews of his entire career, the run was extended well into 2004 and Bowie was booked to headline various summer festivals in Europe. Then, on May 6, at the James L. Knight Center in Miami, a lighting technician fell from a rig shortly before Bowie and the band were to take the stage. The concert was canceled. At a concert in Oslo on June 18, he was struck in the eye by a fan who felt like it was a good idea to launch a lollipop stick at his face. He briefly stopped the concert, informed the projectile lobber, quite correctly, that she was a 'fucking wanker' and then the show went on. Whether or not these events were harbingers is something for writers like me to say, so I will say: these events were probably harbingers.

In the May 1983 issue of *The Face*, Bowie addressed rumors that he had suffered a secret (and ostensibly coke-induced) heart attack. 'No, never,' he says. 'That was delightful but untrue. It was very romantic but I've got a very sound heart.' Twenty years or so onward, twenty years of stress, creativity and performance, and twenty years of smoking, would catch up with David Bowie in June of 2004. 'I knew for years that he was having some chest pains but he swore me to secrecy, and I should have told Iman,' Gabrels would tell me. 'Because Iman, that's the only person he was afraid of.' Mick Rock, who'd shot a series of portraits of Bowie in middle age, also recalls some unspoken health concerns. 'I remember him coming offstage in Oslo on his last world tour and Coco taking me backstage to say hi and the first thing on his mind was a cigarette,' says Mick Rock. 'He'd officially stopped smoking. He'd started to get a little worried about his health, and maybe he was getting pressure from his wife. I think his father had died in his fifties. He'd stopped buying cigarettes, but, after the show, he was looking for a roadie to cadge a ciggie off. He was looking around to make sure no one noticed and told on him! It was kind of sweet, really. This huge star in a very human moment. Of course it turned out that just about everyone knew what was going on.'

Bowie had a few minor physical setbacks over the course of the tour. In November a show in France was scrapped due to laryngitis. The following month, Bowie performed several European dates while suffering through the flu. But by the spring he seemed in great health. The attack came on suddenly. While onstage in Prague on June 23, Bowie walked off-stage, complaining of a sharp pain in his shoulders. A tour doctor examined him and determined it was a trapped nerve. The following show, two days later at the Hurricane

Festival in Germany, was not canceled. Reports went out later that day that Bowie had collapsed backstage and was being treated for a shoulder injury at a nearby hospital. For a full week and a half, this is what the newswire services reported; however, rumors began to circulate that the event was much more serious.

On July 8, Bowie's publicist Mitch Schneider announced that the singer was home in New York City recovering from emergency surgery to repair an 'acutely blocked artery' to his heart. The angioplasty had been a success, according to reports, and Bowie's prognosis was good, but the condition that required it and the surgery that repaired it were certainly life threatening. 'The heart surgery wasn't routine,' a friend told one of the English tabloids, which had seized on the story. 'It was a lot more serious than anyone's letting on.'

Days later, Bowie released his own statement: 'I'm so pissed off because the last 10 months of this tour have been so fucking fantastic,' he said. 'Can't wait to be fully recovered and get back to work again. I tell you what, though, I won't be writing a song about this one.'

'I saw him about three times on that tour, and he did a brilliant show. He was as terrific as I'd ever seen him, and I'd seen many of his concerts over thirty years,' says Mick Rock. 'And I remember Lou Reed once saying, 'David doesn't seem to do any exercise, but I never hear of him getting sick.' Many people in the music business during those manic and innovative and experimental years had gotten seriously sick and not a few died, but of course in the end David did get himself in a weakened state and had to take time out from the frenzy of it all.'

In 1995, Bowie complained to Moon Zappa during an interview for hyper-stylized, Moon Zappa-employing and now defunct (although I am not suggesting these are related) music magazine *Ray Gun*, 'I think it's so totally unfair that we've got to die, and I've lived a lot of my life kind of thinking that.'

Short of assuring people that he was on the mend, Bowie, Iman and their family closed ranks after the episode. 'He was really private about it,' says neighbor Moby. They began to spend more and more time at their property upstate. Bowie grew a beard and began restructuring his diet and exercise routine. Any semblance of the rock 'n' roll lifestyle was chucked out. Three decades after announcing his false retirement from the stage of the Hammersmith Odeon, it seemed like the real David Bowie was done. David Jones's circulatory system had demanded an actual and substantial hiatus. Bowie being Bowie, however, he could not sit still very long.

With no album or tour, Bowie seemed to be in a position to pick and choose where he would pop up next, as though he was functioning as his own curator. He filmed a cameo as genius inventor Nikola Tesla opposite Christian Bale and Michael

675

Caine in Christopher Nolan's *The Prestige*, a surprise box-office hit. This, as with much of his post-*Labyrinth* film work, like *Twin Peaks: Fire Walk with Me*, *The Linguini Incident*, *Everybody Loves Sunshine* and *Mr Rice's Secret*, was a mere blip on the culture radar. A pair of cameos in 2007 that actually had more impact, given their circulation on the Web, gained more attention than most Bowie albums since the early eighties had. Both relied on his eternally underappreciated sense of humor. Bowie had long been a huge fan of the British version of *The Office* and eagerly accepted an offer to appear opposite *Office* creator Ricky Gervais in an episode from season two of the comedian's HBO series *Extras*. Gervais, who plays a sitcom actor, encounters Bowie in the VIP section of a cocktail party and complains about the 'riffraff everywhere.' When Bowie, with expert timing and an enviable poker face, confesses that he's unfamiliar with Gervais's sitcom, the latter launches into a tirade designed to align himself with someone of Bowie's artistic integrity. 'The BBC have interfered,' he gripes. 'Lowest-common-denominator catchphrases and wigs. It's difficult, isn't it? To keep your integrity when you're going for that first –' Bowie cuts him off and takes to the piano, struck by the muse . . .

'Little fat man who sold his soul. Little fat man who sold his dream. Chubby little loser – No . . . not "chubby little loser." "Pathetic little fat man." Nobody's bloody laughing. The clown that no one laughs at. They all just wish he'd die. He's so depressed at being hated, fatty takes his own life. "Fatty"? "Fatso"? Yeah, let's go with "Fatso." He blows his bloated face off.'

Purported to be a window into Bowie's song-writing process, it's actually the sharpest bit of self-deprecating humor quite possibly ever once it's known that the lyrics were actually written by Gervais and not Bowie ('Little Fat Man's' haunting melody, however, is all Bowie's). The clip was a viral sensation before it ever ran on the cable network.

'I sent the lyrics to him and he put the music to it. When I phoned him up, I went, "Hi. It's Ricky." He went, "Umm, sorry. I was just eating a banana,"' Gervais says. 'For some reason, just the idea of Bowie eating a banana is weird, because still in my head he's got platform shoes on and orange hair and he's got the Spiders from Mars sitting around and he answers the phone and he's got the *Aladdin Sane* stripe and it's still 1974. And he answers the phone, "'Allo. Oh, sorry, I was just eating a banana." And so I told him for the song that we'd like something quite retro, like "Life on Mars?" And he says, with his dry sense of humor, "Oh, yeah. I'll just knock out a 'Life on Mars?' for you, shall I?" And he came and it was great. And he knew what he was doing because he gave us David Bowie. He gave us the version of David Bowie from the horse's mouth and it was great. It was brilliant. It was slightly different than the other guest spots. We didn't deconstruct Bowie or make a fool of him. And it was also the most surreal moment we ever had. It's an original song that David Bowie sings that's meant to be ad-libbed in this strange club.'

Gervais was one of the headliners of the Bowie-curated High Line Festival, a purported annual event in the spirit of the UK's Meltdown festival in which one artist curates a multimedia bill centered around New York City's then unopened elevated rail line turned park. Bowie had experience with such a role, having curated the Meltdown in 2002 – headlining with a full performance of *Low* and *Heathen* over some of his favorite younger acts like Peaches, FischerSpooner and Yeah Yeah Yeahs. Bowie invited the French electronic duo Air, the beat-era poet Ken Nordine, the Polyphonic Spree, Deerhoof, Daniel Johnston, and the Arcade Fire, and selected a series of Latin and Spanish films.

'It's quite another stamp of approval, you know, "Bowie likes you. He really likes you,"' Gervais says of being asked to perform, echoing the sentiments of every baby band who ever welcomed him to sample from their backstage crudités. Initially it was announced that Bowie would perform as well, but short of introducing Gervais (in full formal wear) at the latter's Theater at Madison Square Garden show, Bowie opted to let the selected artists represent themselves. There is no plan, at the time of writing this, by the way, for a second High Line festival, so who knows if the experiment worked at all?

In the fall of 2007, Bowie dove a bit more whole-heartedly into his next nonmusical project. Bolstered by his then seven-year-old daughter's love for the program, he accepted an offer to loan his voice to a character on the massively popular Nickelodeon cartoon *SpongeBob SquarePants*. Bowie's turn as the Lord Royal Highness of Atlantis drew a record nine million viewers to his Bikini Bottom antics, rivaling the *Sopranos* finale for most-watched cable program of the year. In the episode, a mini movie, SpongeBob comes into possession of a magic pendant that unlocks the secret of the lost continent of Atlantis (where Bowie's Lord Royal Highness keeps the peace). Atlanteans, like Bowie, are, we learn, 'eons ahead of their time' and have developed a machine that turns ordinary household items like hair combs into ice cream. All the while, Bowie uses a dead-on parody of monarchic English ('pee-yound' rather than 'pound' notes).

'We'd done the episode and they were suggesting some celebrity casting for that role and they had all these names that were just sort of run-of-the-mill, John Cleese – nothing against him but it just didn't seem fresh or original,' explains Paul Tibbitt, *SpongeBob*'s producer and show runner. 'So my first thought was, 'If there was a British person that I would want to meet and work with, who would it be?' And of course it's David Bowie.

679

I'm a huge fan. I've been a fan all my life. My parents were Bowie fans. He's been a big part of my life. So it was very selfish of me to suggest him. So I put the name out and everyone was like, 'Oh, that will never happen. He'll never do it.' And I thought it didn't hurt to ask. Luckily he was happy to do it and he was a fan of the show because he watches it with his kid.'

His Lord Royal Highness was originally going to be rendered as a giant brain, but as he was sketched out, he began to take on a more classic Bowie look, complete with one dilated pupil. 'The little touch of the eyes came from our colorist, Teale Wang, who is a huge Bowie fan too. She just thought, "Wow, it'll be real subtle." He didn't really want to draw too much attention to it.' The voice, an almost unrecognizable upper-crust lilt, was all Bowie's idea. 'He showed up and he'd been trying out all of these different voices and he was really excited about it,' Tibbitt explains. 'He said, 'Well, I've got these ideas.' And he performed them for me. The one that we used was the one I liked the best. It was very surreal. He had like three different voices that he'd been trying. He had one he based on Prince Charles. They were all really cartoony. They were all really silly. To have him standing there doing voices for me was so bizarre and surreal and amazing for me as a fan. I was just flattered and surprised that he'd even taken time to think about it. You could tell he was really excited to do it, to have that experience with his kid.'

There were other cultural touchstones that were fully Bowie inspired that he had nothing to do with, such as the BBC's *Life on Mars* television program and its spin-off *Ashes to Ashes*, both of which featured a protagonist trapped between two planes of existence (in 1973 and '83, respectively) adapting to the sudden change as he strains to restore himself to right. A good Bowie metaphor, and with regard to both shows, an excellent sound-track array: Elton John for *Life*, Ultravox and Visage treasures for *Ashes*. Visage's Steve Strange even plays himself in a cameo in the eighties-set show. In July of 2007, New Zealand hipster comedy duo Flight of the Conchords paid tribute to Bowie with dead-on style parodies (that's what Weird Al calls them, anyway) in an episode of their hit HBO show. The episode, entitled 'Bowie,' features Jemaine (the one with the glasses and no beard) as Ziggy, '1980 David Bowie from the music video "Ashes to Ashes"' and *Labryinth*-era Bowie, appearing to a depressed Bret (the one with the beard and no glasses), who is having height-related body issues.

'It's not Jemaine, it's 1972 David Bowie from the Ziggy Stardust tour . . . it's all part of your freaky dream. Am I freaking you out, Bret? . . . People used to give me crap about being thin all the time but I just broke through their false barrier . . . The media monkeys and their junkie junkies will invite you to their plastic pantomime; throw their invites away.' Bowie encourages Bret to wear an eye patch for 'a look,' and the Conchords return the favor with 'Bowie,' as good an homage as Peter Schilling's 'Major Tom' and far less annoying than Liam Lynch's smug 'Fake David Bowie Song.' 'Do they smoke grass out in space, Bowie, or do they smoke Astroturf?' goes one lyric.

Once a cult figure and then America's favorite strange object of fascination, a sexual spaceman who made Bing Crosby wonder about his holiday rituals, David Bowie, in his sixties, became even more mainstream then he had been in the eighties when the Target superstore announced in 2007 it would be carrying a line of clothing by rocker turned fashion designer Keanan Duffty entitled simply 'Bowie.' According to the designer, it makes sense that Bowie's outsider sensibility would ultimately find a home in middle-American outlets, among the vast parking lots and shopping carts. Art and commerce, rocking its eternal wave.

'It's safe to say that I'm a committed Bowie nut. So for me, the chance to design a Bowie-inspired fashion collection was too good to be true. The opportunity was the ultimate in synergy,' says Duffty. 'We finally met in December 2006, when I proposed designing a collection inspired by David's style for Target stores in America. Bowie has not been associated with a fashion collection under his own name before. So I proposed this idea to David and he was intrigued. After seeing some of my initial design ideas, he gave it his blessing. During our first meeting David suggested calling the collection KDDB, before rather amusingly pointing out that this sounded a little too close to the KGB. We decided on 'Bowie by Keanan Duffty' – David wanted to be clear that his aesthetic was the inspiration for the line.'

Duffty had no worries about whether or not Bowie's more avantgarde sensibility would sit well under the industrial track lighting or whether the synergy might have any effect on Bowie's cred. 'More than any other rock star, Bowie is associated with bringing left-field ideas to pop culture and inspiring trends in fashion. I am absolutely sure that the collection is helping people, fans and nonfans alike, to get in touch with their inner Bowie. Although I didn't reinterpret Bowie's *Labyrinth* costumes or sequined jumpsuits though – I don't think that would have worked in Texas!'

Still, for all this visibility, there was still a void. The anticipation for a return to his first business order, that of singer-songwriter and performer, was so high that when word got around that Bowie would be singing backing vocals on the debut album from actress Scarlett Johansson (a Tom Waits tribute entitled *Anywhere I Lay My Head*, produced by TV on the Radio's Dave Sitek and heavily indebted to 4AD Records artists like the Cocteau Twins and This Mortal Coil), Bowie had to issue a statement downplaying his contribution as just 'oohs and aahs.'

'I'd seen him right before we left to take the drive down to New Orleans to record the album,' Johansson told me. 'We were talking about Dave Sitek and how great he was. And on my way out I was like, "If you're ever in town . . . ," in the middle of nowhere Louisiana. And then Dave and I always talked about our mutual love for Bowie and how inspirational he's been in every part of my life. Pubescence, adolescence. Later, I was working in Spain on this film at the time and Dave called me and said, "Guess who's in the studio?" I said, "Goddamn it." It was incredible. He came to the studio completely prepared with the lyric sheets. Had all his notes on it. Knew what he wanted to add. He uses his voice as an instrument, fills out the song as much as the horn section would or anything else. Without it it sounds completely unfinished. You didn't realize how unfinished it was until he lays down the vocals. It's more than him having a second career as a backup vocalist. His voice is such an instrument and it's only gotten better. Fresher. It's awesome.'

At the time of this writing, Bowie has reportedly been spending his time with his family at his estate in upstate New York. He doesn't even get to Manhattan as much as he used to by most accounts. When he appears, it's usually to walk a red carpet for a charity event or a real occasion like the premiere of his son's film *Moon* at the 2009 Sundance Film Festival in Park City, Utah.

That film stars indie mainstay Sam Rockwell and covers familiar Bowie-ist territory: an astronaut experiencing extreme loneliness during a space mission with nothing but the voice of his onboard computer, Gerty 3000 (Kevin Spacey), to comfort him. 'It started in utero,' Duncan Jones told *Rolling Stone*, explaining his penchant for existential sci-fi. The film's pacing is certainly a throwback to the auteur era of the late sixties and seventies (including Kubrick's *2001: A Space Odyssey* and Roeg's *The Man Who Fell to Earth*). Jones executes this with real confidence whereas other first-time filmmakers, especially in the Web-age, might be tempted to chuck out mood and tone for the sake of rapid-fire imagery designed to cheaply hold the attention of a Web surfer. The machinations of corporate greed and bursts of Hal Ashby-esque madcap humor (Rockwell vexing his clone by dancing to 'Walking on Sunshine' by Katrina and the Waves) also ground it in the past (for the better). That Jones waited until he was already pushing forty when he decided to make his debut seems in hindsight a wise choice. The film will surely have a life beyond being the footnote in the larger Bowie biography. The screening that I attended at the Landmark Sunshine Cinemas on the Lower East Side of Manhattan was populated with sci-fi nerds, not rock 'n' roll Bowie-ists.

If I had to make an educated guess about his new material, I would say that it might sound a lot like the kind of romantic folk that Scott Walker, one of his musical heroes, is famous for (perhaps a bit like Iggy Pop's underrated late-period *Avenue B* album). Bowie made yet another talking head appearance in the 2006 documentary on Walker entitled *Scott Walker: 30 Century Man* which he also produced. This is a respectful way, I guess, of saying that his days of 'Suffragette City'-style rocking are likely over now. And yet Bowie certainly looked like a rocker singing 'Arnold Layne' with David Gilmour at a 2007 concert tribute to another hero, the late Syd Barrett, so I have already contradicted myself and joined the unusually long-running guessing game full-on. A David Bowie album remains 'TBA' on Pauseandplay.com, metacritic.com and most other upcoming-release bulletin sites.

And as I mentioned before, there were reports of him headlining the Coachella Music and Arts festival this year, and there will likely be next year. If he is in fact retired, then *Reality* is a fine album to close on, but he remains such a part of the rhythm of so many lives that imagining a world where David Bowie does not observe and process the same things we all see every day, whether it's politics, sex, culture, or even bad TV and goofball YouTube clips, just feels, somehow, a lot more lonely. 'How many David Bowie albums do you need?' I recall the writer Jon Savage asking me when discussing the absence of new Bowie music. 'Put it this way: if he was done, then I'd say good on him, and enjoy yourself.' All right then. Good on him. And enjoy yourself. But how about an EP?

I am sitting at a small table under a hanging rack of fashion magazines inside Café Gitane, where Moby told me Bowie comes for his French roast. Or was it Italian roast? This is where the guy gets his morning coffee. He comes in around six in the morning, before any of the tourists or locals would arrive. He sits, I'm told, by the window and stares out at the church across Mott Street. I am not here to meet him. It's long after six anyway. I'm here to be imbued by his spirit I guess. I'm here so that I might be reinspired as if first hearing Kraftwerk or the Velvets. I'm here for maintenance. This is church on Sunday shit.

The warm environment, with its basket of tomatoes; bright yellow cash register, the color of a Tonka dump truck; and portrait of Jimi Hendrix behind the busy counter must have reminded him some of the Giaconda in that other Soho. I stare at the menu and wonder what he orders. Coffee, served with a little cube of dark chocolate, perhaps? Baked eggs with basil and cream? No, probably granola, now that he is heart healthy.

I am now the same age Bowie was when he planned the Glass Spider tour and have survived similar follies. The pretty waitresses with their vaguely French air and pale green aprons flit about among the flow of equally good-looking patrons. Perhaps he leaves here and walks up Prince Street to browse in the aisles of the McNally Jackson bookshop.

One day, maybe he'll find this book in their music section downstairs, flip through it and say out loud, 'No, no no. You got it all wrong.' I think maybe we all have ultimately. There is no getting Bowie right, really. It's like getting religion right. People have been trying for a long time to get God right, even longer to get right with God. Maybe the key is to just treat the idea of Bowie the man – sick, sometimes scared, a little slower on his feet, possibly never to tour or record again – with as much reverence as Bowie the god. To view all that he has achieved simply as a great human achievement.

People who know that I've been working on this book still e-mail me when they see him: 'Saw David Bowie and Iman on 7th Avenue!' 'He stared at your uncle for ten minutes in a cafe in Woodstock!' As if I'm supposed to throw on my coat and head over there. Their excitement always annoys me a little bit. I've seen him too; but again, he was just a guy trying to hail a cab. Those who are invested just like me, who believe, who are Bowie-ists, want to not just see but also feel and believe in him, but this is hard some-times as he withdraws from the public (hear this David Jones, I wrote a book for you).

Later, at the end of another long night at the bar, I let myself into the apartment, sleepless. I stand on the balcony, smoke cigarettes and looked down into the empty yard with the overgrown weeds, cigarette butts (none of them mine) and pink flamingos in the dirt.

Tired of the news, I flip around the channels looking for a movie and see that The Grapes of Wrath, *John Ford's 1940 adaptation of the Steinbeck novel, starring Henry Fonda as Tom Joad, is beginning in eight minutes. I head downstairs, fix myself a vodka tonic and walk back up to the bedroom to watch it. The movie sucks me in. Banks are failing out in California and people have started talking about a coming depression. Familiar. All the drawn faces and glassy eyes of those wiped out by the Great Depression in the 1930s, filmed in shadowy black and white, make me start to well up. All their loved ones, everything that comforted them, have been taken. Even priests like John Carradine's Casy have abandoned the Lord. They are ghosts too, roaming the dust bowl, looking for meaning.*

'There ain't nothing to look out for and there ain't nobody coming back,' one of them says. 'They're gone. I'm just a graveyard ghost . . . that's all in the world I am.'

Henry Fonda in his simple tweed cap: his head is cool. He's just looking for work. Work is meaning. He and the Joad family finally locate a migrant worker camp that seems to treat the hard-luck Joads and their fellow travelers with dignity. There are dances and fair prices and there's no harassment. The family remains but Tom can't rest as long as there's injustice out there. Before leaving the camp to go fight for the common man, he utters his famous speech: 'I'll be all around in the dark. I'll be everywhere. Wherever you can look, wherever there's a fight, so hungry people can eat, I'll be there. Wherever there's a cop beatin' up a guy, I'll be there. I'll be in the way guys yell when they're mad. I'll be in the way kids laugh when they're hungry and they know supper's ready, and when people are eatin' the stuff they raise and livin' in the houses they build, I'll be there, too.'

I suddenly get a feeling of calm and find myself turning off the TV and laying my head on the pillow. My lids feel heavier than they've ever been. I realize that it doesn't matter if I spoke to Bowie on the corner that day, or if I was cueing up his new studio album or standing backstage as he prepared to perform out in Indio, California, or if I ever really understood him after all of the years that I spent working on this book you are now reading. I will have time, and if you feel like you haven't gotten him either after reading all of these pages, first of all, I apologize, and second of all, take heart. You will have more time as well. As he buries himself in what may be his final incubatory state – this one not a movie role or a Turkish neighborhood in Berlin or the series of tubes that is the World Wide Web, but rather reclusivity itself – it's all right to miss him. But realize, thanks to his accomplishments and bravery and often blind foolishness, and of course, his music, there is nothing really missing now and there never will be.

Whenever someone quotes from a heady book they haven't read in full, he'll be there.

Whenever a cokehead closes the blinds at sunup because the conversation with his wired friends is too interesting to conclude, he'll be there.

He'll be in the way we swallow hard, grit our teeth and step out onto the street after a new haircut.

When bands from England and Iceland and Chicago and Atlanta are taking from their heroes and offering up some new music, he will be there.

When that band's next album sounds nothing like this new music, he will be there.

He is like Tom Joad, only prettier.

BIBLIOGRAPHY

Books

Anger, Kenneth. *Hollywood Babylon*. New York: Random House/Bell, 1981.

Bangs, Lester. *Psychotic Reactions and Carburetor Dung*. Ed. by Greil Marcus. New York: Vintage, 1988.

Bockris, Victor. *Transformer: The Lou Reed Story*. New York: Simon and Schuster, 1994.

Bowie, Angela with Patrick Carr. *Back-stage Passes*. New York: Cooper Square Press, 2001.

Bowie, Angela. *Bisexuality*. London: Pocket Essentials, 2002.

Bowie, Angela. *Free Spirit*. London: Mushroom Books, 1981.

Bracewell, Michael. *Re-make/Re-model: Art, Pop, Fashion and the Making of Roxy Music, 1953–1972*. London: Faber and Faber, 2007.

Buckley, David. *David Bowie: The Complete Guide to His Music*. London: Omnibus, 2004.

Buckley, David. *Strange Fascination: David Bowie – The Definitive Story*. London: Virgin Books, 1999.

Buell, Bebe, with Victor Bockris. *Rebel Heart: An American Rock 'n' Roll Journey*. New York: St Martin's Griffon, 2001.

Cann, Kevin. *David Bowie: A Chronology*. New York: Simon & Schuster, 1984.

Carr, Roy, and Charles Shaar Murray. *Bowie: An Illustrated Record*. London: Eel Pie Publishing, 1981.

Charlesworth, Chris. *David Bowie: Profile*. London: Proteus Books, 1981.

Claire, Vivian. David Bowie: *The King of Glitter Rock*. New York: Flash Books, 1977.

Crisp, Quentin. *How to Have a Lifestyle*. New York: Alyson Books, 1979.

Dalton, David. *James Dean: The Mutant King*. New York: A Capella, 1974.

Daly, Marsha. *Peter Frampton*. New York: Grosset and Dunlap, 1978.

de Beauvoir, Simone. *She Came to Stay*. New York: W. W. Norton and Company, 1954.

Didion, Joan. *The White Album*. New York: Farrar, Straus and Giroux, 1990.

Edwards, Henry, and Tony Zanetta. *Stardust: The David Bowie Story*. New York: Bantam, 1986.

Ellmann, Richard. *Oscar Wilde*. New York: Vintage, 1987.

Elmlark, Wally, and Timothy Green Beckley. *Rock Raps of the Seventies*. New York: Drake Publishers, 1972.

Eno, Brian. A *Year with Swollen Appendices: The Diary of Brian Eno*. London: Faber and Faber, 1996.

Escoffier, Jeffrey, ed. *Sexual Revolution*. New York: Thunder's Mouth Press, 2003.

Fortune, Dion. *Psychic Self-Defense*. New York: Samuel Weiser Press, 2001.

Foxe-Tyler, Cyrinda, with Danny Fields. *Dream On: Livin' on the Edge with Steven Tyler and Aerosmith*. New York: Dove Books, 1997.

Frith, Simon. *Music for Pleasure: Essays in the Sociology of Pop*. New York: Routledge, 1988.

George, Boy, with Spencer Bright. *Take It Like a Man: The Autobiography of Boy George*. New York: HarperCollins, 1995.

Gillman, Peter, and Leni Gillman. *Alias David Bowie*. New York: Henry Holt and Co., 1987.

Hopkins, Jerry. *Bowie*. London: Elm Tree Books, 1985.

Iman. *I Am Iman*. London: Booth Cliborn, 2001.

Isherwood, Christopher. *The Berlin Stories*. New York: New Directions, 1954.

Jackson, John A. *A House on Fire: The Rise and Fall of Philadelphia Soul*. Oxford, UK: Oxford University Press, 2004.

Juby, Kerry, ed. *In Other Words . . . David Bowie*. London: Omnibus Books, 1986.

Kent, Nick. *The Dark Stuff: Selected Writings on Rock Music, 1972–1995*. New York: Da Capo, 1994.

Kureishi, Hanif. *The Buddha of Suburbia*. New York: Penguin, 1991.

Levy, Shawn. *Ready, Steady, Go: The Smashing Rise and Giddy Fall of Swinging London*. New York: Doubleday, 2002.

MacInnes, Colin. *Absolute Beginners*. London: Allison and Busby, 2001.

Mayes, Sean. *We Can Be Heroes: Life on Tour with David Bowie*. London: Independent Music Press, 1999.

McNeil, Legs, and Gillian McCain. *Please Kill Me*. New York: Grove Press, 1996.

Meyers, Paul. *It Ain't Easy: Long John Baldry and the Birth of British Blues*. Vancouver: Greystone Books, 2007.

Miles, Barry. *David Bowie Black Book: An Illustrated Biography*. London: Omnibus Books, 1984.

Morgan, Ted. *Literary Outlaw: The Life and Times of William S. Burroughs*. New York: Henry Holt and Co., 1988.

Numan, Gary, with Steve Malins. *Praying to the Aliens*. London: Andre Deutsch, 1997.

Oldham, Andrew Loog. *Stoned*. New York: Vintage, 2001.

Osborne, John. *Look Back in Anger*. New York: Bantam, 1957.

Paglia, Camille. *Sexual Personae*. New York: Vintage Books, 1991.

Pang, May. *Loving John*. New York: Warner Books, 1983.

Pegg, Nicholas. *The Complete David Bowie*. London: Reynolds and Hearn Ltd., 2004.

Pitt, Kenneth. *Bowie: The Pitt Report*. London: Omnibus Press Ltd., 1983.

Pomerance, Bernard. *The Elephant Man*. New York: Grove Press, 1979.

Reynolds, Simon. *Rip It Up and Start Again: Post-punk*, 1978–1984. New York: Penguin, 2005.

Rimmer, Dave. *Like Punk Never Happened: Culture Club and the New Pop*: London: Faber and Faber, 1986.

Rock, Mick, and David Bowie. *Glam! An Eyewitness Account*. London: Vision On Publishing, 2006.

Rock, Mick, and David Bowie. *Moonage Daydream: The Life and Times of Ziggy Stardust*. New York: Universe Publishing, 2002.

Sanford, Christopher. *Loving the Alien*. New York: Da Capo, 1996.

Santos-Kayda, Myriam. *David Bowie Live in New York*. Foreword by David Bowie. New York: Powerhouse Books, 2003.

Savage, Jon. *England's Dreaming: Anarchy, Sex Pistols, Punk Rock and Beyond*. New York: St Martin's Press, 1992.

Savage, Jon. *Teenage: The Creation of Youth Culture*. New York: Viking, 2007.

Seabrook, Thomas Jerome. *Bowie in Berlin: New Career in a New Town*. London: Jawbone Press, 2008.

Seymour, Craig. *Luther: The Life and Longing of Luther Vandross*. New York: Harper, 2004.

Sontag, Susan. *Against Interpretation: and Other Essays*. New York: Picador, 2001.

Stevenson, Nick. *David Bowie: Fame, Sound and Vision*. New York: Polity Press, 2006.

Strange, Steve. *Blitzed: The Autobiography of Steve Strange*. London: Orion, 2002.

Streatfeild, Dominic. *Cocaine: An Unauthorized Biography*. New York: Picador Books, 2001.

Stringfellow, Tony. *The Wizard's Gown – Rewoven: Beneath the Glitter of Marc Bolan*. London: Breeze Hayward Publishing, 2007.

Tamm, Eric. *Brian Eno: His Music and the Vertical Color of Sound*. New York: Da Capo, 2005.

Thompson, Dave. *David Bowie: Moonage Daydream*. New York: Plexus, 1994.

Thompson, Dave. *Hallo Spaceboy: The Rebirth of David Bowie*. New York: ECW Press, 2004.

Thomson, David. *'Have You Seen . . . ?'* New York: Knopf, 2008.

Thorne, Tony. *Fads, Fashions and Cults: Acid House to Zoot Suit*: London: Bloomsbury, 1994.

Tremlett, George. *David Bowie: Living on the Brink*. New York: Carol and Graff, 1997.

Tremlett, George. *The David Bowie Story*. London: Futura, 1974.

Vachon, Christine, and Austin Bunn. *A Killer Life: How an Independent Film Producer Survives Deals and Disasters in Hollywood and Beyond*. New York: Simon and Schuster, 2007.

Visconti, Tony. *Bowie, Bolan and the Brooklyn Boy*. New York: HarperCollins, 2007.

Walker, Jonathan. *Aden Insurgency: The Savage War in South Arabia, 1962–1967*. London: Spellmount Staplehurst, 2005.

Weird and Gilly. *Mick Ronson: The Spider with the Platinum Hair*. London: Independent Music Press, 2003.

Wilcken, Hugo. *David Bowie's Low.* 33 (1/3) Series, vol. 26. London/New York: Continuum International, 2005.

Periodicals

Bromley Kentish Times, November 11, 1960
Melody Maker, February 26, 1966
Disc and Music Echo, July 10, 1969
Jackie, May 10, 1970
Rolling Stone, April 1, 1971
Melody Maker, January 22, 1972
Words and Music, July 1972
New York Times, October 1, 1972
Newsweek, October 9, 1972
Beetle, October 17, 1972
NME, February 24, 1973
Melody Maker, October 6, 1973
Rolling Stone, February 28, 1974
Crawdaddy, September 1974
Playboy, September 1976
NME, March 12, 1977
Zigzag, April 1977
Melody Maker, October 29, 1977
NME, November 26, 1977
Melody Maker, April 21, 1979
Trouser Press, October 1979
Rolling Stone, November 13, 1980
The Face, May 1983
Rolling Stone, May 12, 1983
Time, July 18, 1983

Observer, October 23, 1983
Penthouse, November 1983
New York Times February 10, 1984
The Face, October 1984
Melody Maker, March 22, 1986
NME, October 11, 1986
Spin, November 1986
Rolling Stone, April 23, 1987
Musician, August 1987
New York Times, August 1987
Q, June 1989
Movieline, April 1992
Q, May 1993
Arena, Spring/Summer 1993
Time Out London, August 23–30, 1995
Ray Gun, October 1995
Esquire (UK), October 1995
Mojo, October 1997
Modern Painters, Spring 1998
Independent on Sunday, May 10, 1998
NME, December 2, 2000
Mojo, May 2001
Uncut, August 2001
Mojo, July 2002
Uncut, March 2003
Q, October 2003
GQ (UK), October 2005
Uncut, December 2005
Mojo Classic, January 2007
Mojo, April 2007
Q, April 2007

Q, November 2007
Uncut, June 2008
Daily Mail, June 28, 2008
New York Times, June 7, 2009
Entertainment Weekly, June 19, 2009
Rolling Stone, June 11, 2009
Nylon Guys, June/July 2009

Websites

bowiewonderworld.com
teenagewildlife.com
davidbowie.com (Bowienet)
mywebsite.bigpond.com/roger.griffin/ goldenyears/
   index.html (Bowie Golden Years)
rocksbackpages.com

KT 08/15
BC 11/15
KE 01/16
BV 05·16
BB 6/16